Applying to Graduate Programs in the U.S./UK

A Practical Guide

Florent Gusdorf

LES ÉDITIONS
DE L'ÉCOLE POLYTECHNIQUE

91128 Palaiseau Cedex

To all my students,
past and present,
without whom this book
would never have seen the light of day

Foreword

Florent Gusdorf

Applying to a university in the U.S. or the UK is a challenge for those wishing to study abroad. It requires students to write a statement of purpose (SOP), also called personal statement (PS), statement of objectives (SOO) or statement of interest in addition to the personal history statement (PHS) or diversity statement. It is an exercise in self-reflection and style for which students are unprepared or ill-prepared because it meets specific criteria, both in terms of content and form. This practical guide – how to write application letters – intends to provide answers to questions that students ask themselves as well as provide advice and information likely to steer them in a process fraught with pitfalls.

This guide is meant for university and *Grandes écoles* students who plan to study for a Master's or PhD (or postgraduate) program, whether in the fields of science, engineering, economics, business or political science. Written entirely in English, it places the applicant at the heart of the process by offering the right mindset, tools, vocabulary and approach to self-analysis.

The book is based on first-hand experience gained by helping several hundred applicants over more than 20 years. It is the end-result of a three-fold need: to transmit an experience, to make up for the absence of such a guide in France, and to offer examples drawn from practice. It is in no way a guarantee of admission: no rules are set in stone, there is no magic admission algorithm, and each candidate has a personality of their own whose application it is a reflection of. In addition, each school has a different approach to the admissions process and adjustments are possible from one year to another according to the changes in the make-up of the admissions commissions and the shifting requirements of the universities.

The guide includes five parts:
I – The statement of purpose (or personal statement): the guide presents an overview of higher education (HE), explains the process of reflection geared towards self-knowledge, sheds light on the choice of programs and outlines the individual training course, personal and professional experience, as well as extracurricular activities. This part also includes information about GPAs, international tests and scholarships for French students. Questions about the form of the statement are also dealt with: the writing process, the level of language expected, the style to adopt to convince without boasting, the grammar and vocabulary mistakes to avoid. Positive and negative (*) examples drawn from experience are meant to show what is acceptable and what is not. A final section focuses on the interview process that certain programs require and offers examples and suggestions for going through this ultimate admission stage.

II – The academic CV introduces the method for drafting a curriculum vitae, details the different parts, offers an appropriate vocabulary and presents a standard example.

III – The letter of recommendation (LOR) offers advice on how to write letters which are part and parcel of the application file.

IV – Useful vocabulary for writing a statement is presented in the form of an English-French lexicon. Grouped according to each part of the application process, each chapter aims at facilitating and nourishing reflection and writing by offering the right word or expression in context, as well as model sentences and expressions (☞) drawn from practice. Examples of collocations (✓) are also present. The applicant's attention is drawn to some points of grammar (➔). Cultural notes (🕮) enlighten the reader on certain facts or words. Part of this chapter deals with the vocabulary useful for translating transcripts from the preparatory program (*CPGE*) or university courses. It is presented in the form of a French-English alphabetical lexicon and brings together the assessments most commonly used by faculty. These transcripts must be attached to every application file.

V – A compendium of statements of purpose and personal history statements written by students (all anonymous). They are in no way models to be copied *verbatim*, but they can serve as examples. We chose the most relevant statements, without adding or subtracting anything.

No guide can ever replace the individual and personal work that every applicant must put in, either on their own or, when possible, with the help of a coach. Nevertheless, the guide intends to provide fundamental answers germane to the general approach of successfully tackling this difficult exercise which will allow students to know themselves better, define their choices more narrowly and thereby follow the path that will lead them to academic and professional success.

Table of Contents

PART II

THE ACADEMIC CV

PART III

THE LETTER OF RECOMMENDATION (LOR)

PART IV

VOCABULARY FOR THE STATEMENT OF PURPOSE/ *LE VOCABULAIRE POUR LA LETTRE DE CANDIDATURE*

PART V

SAMPLES OF STATEMENTS

PART I
THE STATEMENT OF PURPOSE

I. The Application Process

1. The US system of higher education

In the United States, a **college** refers to a higher education institution that offers a 4-year program and grants only bachelor's degrees. A college can be independent, or it can be part of a university. A **university** is usually a larger institution, often made up of specialized schools or colleges, that grants **graduate degrees** as well as **bachelor's degrees**. Americans say they are "in college", no matter which type of institution they attend. Americans will hardly ever say they were at university, but rather "I went to X university/college".

There are over 4,300 accredited colleges or universities (including branch campuses or satellite locations) in the United States (referred to as the American higher education system, roughly speaking, 1,600 public colleges, 1,700 private nonprofit schools, and about 1,000 for-profit schools), all with different entrance requirements, tuition fees and course specialties. Higher education institutions in the U.S. are not centrally organized or managed, but are accredited on a national or regional level by independent accrediting bodies.

They also come in many different sizes from the vast **state universities** with enrollment in the tens of thousands, to small **private colleges** with fewer than one thousand students. Public universities are state universities, whose reputation may not always be as high as private universities. Sometimes the varied naming systems make it hard to tell public universities apart from similarly named private universities. For example, the University of Pennsylvania is an Ivy League university, whereas Pennsylvania State University is a state one. On the other hand, University of California is comprised of a dozen public colleges, the most reputed of which are UCB (Berkeley), UCLA, and UCSD (San Diego). Besides the University of California system, you find the Cal State system. There is some overlap in selectivity but generally it is harder to get into a UC than a Cal State school. In New York State, the State University of New York (SUNY) system has several flagships, including Binghamton University, University at Albany, and University at Buffalo, Stony Brook University, and a very large number of other colleges. Big league universities such as Brown, MIT, Harvard, Stanford, Columbia are private.

Besides the quality teaching, the main difference between public and private universities is the **tuition fees**: tuition fees are much higher for private universities than for public ones. That is because public schools are funded mainly by local and state governments, whereas private colleges are supported primarily by their own endowment funds (Harvard's endowment is over 53,2bn dollars, Princeton 26bn, MIT 127,4bn (2021 figures), for example, compared to University of California's

22,1bn), donations and students' tuition fees. Private universities receive virtually no state or federal money. **Research universities** (which are committed to research as the central part of their mission) can also apply to federal and private agencies for research grants (from the National Institutes of Health, National Science Foundation, National Institute for the Humanities, Department of Justice, Education Department, and other federal agencies). Research universities can be public or private. **Private colleges** may receive contributions from individual donors - perhaps in exchange for getting buildings named after themselves. **Public colleges** also receive donations. In-state residents receive favorable tuition rates at public universities based on the premise that their tax dollars fund the state governments. Private colleges, on the other hand, are more expensive because they rely more heavily on students' tuition payments to cover their operating expenses. Yet, if private colleges and universities may be more costly to attend, they frequently offer more substantial tuition discounts than do public universities. On the other hand, British universities are far less expensive than American colleges.

The **Ivy League** (an athletic conference) refers to eight top private universities in the Northeastern United States. The **eight members** are Brown University, Columbia University, Cornell University, Dartmouth College, Harvard University, the University of Pennsylvania, Princeton University, and Yale University. Ivy League has connotations of academic excellence, highly selective admission, and social elitism. Seven of the eight schools were founded during the colonial period (Cornell was founded in 1865). Those schools are usually viewed as the most prestigious. MIT and Stanford often outperform them, though. Admission rates to an Ivy university is between 4,5% (Harvard) and 10% (Cornell). For instance, for the Class of 2021, 39,506 students applied to Harvard University of which 2,056 students were accepted, yielding an overall acceptance rate of 5.2%. The equivalent in Britain would be **Oxbridge**, a portmanteau of Oxford and Cambridge, the two oldest universities in the United Kingdom. The name has implications of superior social or intellectual status or elitism. At the undergraduate level, candidates may not apply to both Oxford and Cambridge in the same year, with a few exceptions. The term **Loxbridge** refers to the golden triangle of London, Oxford, and Cambridge but is much less used.

The perceived **prestige factor** plays a huge role in the students' admission aspirations. Public universities typically are lower in the college rankings than private schools, and frequently have less selective admissions criteria. Private colleges may employ more distinguished faculty or publish influential academic research more often. The quality of education received at a private institution is not necessarily superior to that which can be obtained at a public school, but graduates of highly-ranked or "prestigious" colleges are typically more sought after in the job market. Yet, students should be aware that what matters is not so much a brand name as the quality of a **specific department**. Some public colleges and universities carry as much prestige as the more exclusive private schools. A case in point is the university of California. Similarly, studying computer science at the University of Washington may be as competitive as gaining admission to Carnegie Mellon University[1].

---

1. I do not have a specific list of universities in mind. Stanford, Caltech, MIT, UC Berkeley, Columbia and CMU are certainly up there, but I am not particularly referring to any particular list of graduate school rankings. In a more general sense, I am writing about schools where the default attitude of the admissions committee is "rejected, unless strongly proved otherwise" rather than "let's give him/her the benefit of the doubt". These schools tend to follow a risk minimization policy, and if in doubt, they would deny admission to a candidate rather than risk diluting the quality of the incoming batch.

An alternative to four-year institutions is the junior or **community college**, an institution that offers two-year degree programs in general or technical education. Students who complete the course of study are such an institution earn an **associate's degree** (A.A.) in either the arts or sciences. These institutions are also much less expensive than four-year colleges. Many students transfer to a four-year institution after receiving an associate degree, as a way of completing their general education requirements more cheaply.

Americans do not **specialize** in a subject until late, often until their last two years at college or university. Getting a master's degree is the beginning of specialization. Therefore, a bachelor's degree from an American institution does not generally represent the same degree of specialized knowledge in a subject area that other bachelor's degrees from other countries represent.

The primary goal of a college education is not mainly to produce brilliantly educated people with narrow, specialized skills. Rather, it is to produce broadly educated people with strong leadership skills who can contribute to society by getting a job. Among the qualities the university values: collaborative spirit, intellectual curiosity, practical intelligence, analytical strength, creativity to generate new solutions to existing challenges, growth in personal and professional endeavors, drive and determination to put one's stamp on the world. These attributes make students intellectual leaders.

The American **school year** usually starts in late August or early September and runs through to early or mid-June. The school year is divided into 2 semesters or 4 terms (the term "quarter" is usually reserved to the business world). Some MSc programs may start as early as August and include what they call math boot camps. In general, 180 days of class time are required by law. In the quarter system, the school year is three periods of roughly 10 weeks (fall, winter, spring) with a summer quarter offered but not required. In the semester system, there are two semesters of 14 weeks each, usually a break for the month of January, when optional short classes are offered.

A college education is almost indispensable for any sort of professional career. After getting a high school education, practically anybody can go to college or university. Once a student chooses a few likely colleges, the application process can begin. A college application gives details of a student academic record and also covers the extracurricular activities and volunteer organizations a student may have participated in, any honors received, and even part-time or vacation jobs he or she may have held. It helps to have more on one's application than just good grades, in so far as Americans value well-rounded people. Having an excellent academic record is one thing, being involved in activities, especially those that serve the community, is added value.

Many universities will look at a student's college exam scores. The college's catalog will tell students the minimum scores necessary for admission. Many colleges will ask a potential student to come for an interview before offering final admission, or entice you with fellowships so that you will accept admission.

In the U.S. (2021 figures):

- There are about 12,000 graduate programs.
- 1.98 million college graduates earn bachelor's degrees.
- 820,100 graduates earn master's degrees.
- 184,070 earn doctorate or professional degrees.

- 18.3% of college graduates earn degrees in STEM fields.
- 1.2% of people in the United States graduate from a postsecondary or postgraduate program each year.
- Worldwide, the United States of America ranks 19th in college graduation rates. Australia has the most educated population in the world. (https://educationdata.org/number-of-college-graduates)

2. The UK system of higher education

The British university system goes back to the eleventh century and has produced some of the major developments in western science, medicine, art and philosophy.

There are some **160 universities** in the UK, the oldest being the University of Oxford (1096). A vast majority are **public universities**, meaning that they receive funding (including budgets for PhD studentships) from the UK Government. British universities are free to pursue their own research objectives, but the amount of funding each receives is partly based on regular assessments of its performance as part of the Research Excellence Framework (REF). The REF examines the research a university is producing as well as its impact on society in general. There is a small number of private universities that tend to specialize in business and law. Note that there might be slightly different systems in England, Scotland, Wales and Northern Ireland. Yet doctoral studies work pretty similarly everywhere.

Most UK universities award their academic doctorates as PhD qualifications. However, some institutions (Oxford) award a DPhil instead. The two degrees stand for the same thing.

UK universities are loosely organized into different groups. The most common ones are:

- The ancient universities comprise seven institutions including Oxford, Cambridge, St Andrews, Glasgow, Aberdeen and Edinburgh as well as Trinity College Dublin (Ireland). Some ancient universities award their doctorates as a DPhil rather than a PhD.
- The Russell Group is a self-selected association of 24 public universities across the UK. The group is self-selecting and represents the country's leading research universities including of the best ranked British universities. They award the majority of UK PhDs.
- The red brick universities (campuses were built from red brick) are another informal grouping based on history rather than collective organization. They include nine civic universities founded during the nineteenth-century industrial revolution, originally designed for the education of middle-class youth and therefore usually nonresidential and serving a large city.
- 'Post-92' is used to describe universities that were originally polytechnics (higher education institutions with a focus on teaching and training rather than research) before being granted full university status in 1992. Many of these 'ex-poly' universities actually have long and proud histories and are now some of the UK's most innovative research centres.
- There are other universities, called **plate-glass universities**, established or promoted to university status in the 1960s. The name comes from their modern architectural design, that includes plate glass in steel or concrete. University of York, East Anglia or Warwick are cases in point, named after the county or wider area they serve.

In the **UK**, higher education often begins with a three-year bachelor's degree. Master's degrees are either taught or by research. Doctoral level research degrees usually take at least three years. Tuition fees for first degrees in public universities are up to £9,250 per academic year for English, Welsh and European Union students. Higher education in England is provided by Higher Education (HE) colleges, university colleges, universities and private colleges. Students normally enter higher education as undergraduates from age 18 onwards, and can study for a wide variety of vocational and academic qualifications.

The UK academic year runs from September to June, but the lack of formal teaching in British doctoral programs means that PhD students can, in principle, start at any point in the calendar year. At the **University of Cambridge**, for example, the academic year commences on 1st October and finishes on 30th September each year. The year is divided into three terms, with a Long vacation: Michaelmas term (October – December) – Lent term (January – March) (also at Lancaster University and LSE) – Easter term (April – June) – Long vacation (July – September). At the **University of Oxford** (and the University of Dublin), you have the Michaelmas term (roughly Oct-early Dec), the Hilary term (called Epiphany term at Durham University) (Jan-March), named after St Hilary of Poitiers (c. 310 – c. 367) and the Trinity term (Apr-June).

Also note that Oxford and Cambridge have a collegiate structure. When you apply to a postgraduate degree, you will have to select one college where you will live, socialise and do most of your studying. The college you choose won't affect your chance of getting a place. If your department makes you an offer of a place, you are guaranteed a college place as well. You can express your preference for a college or let the program choose one for you. For more information, see each college website.

In the UK (2021 figures):
- 817,340 students graduate from postsecondary and postgraduate programs annually.
- 418,700 annual bachelor program graduates.
- 253,670 annual master program graduates.
- 29,470 annual doctoral program graduates.
- The most educated people aged 65 and older live in the United Kingdom.

3. A few definitions

An **undergraduate degree** is a bachelor's degree.
Graduate degrees comprise master's degrees and PhDs.

Postgraduate programs (UK term) (**graduate programs** in the U.S.) are undertaken after completing an **undergraduate degree** (*i.e.* BS degrees), or, for some careers, on the basis of relevant work experience.

A **postgraduate degree** (**graduate degree**) is an academic title that students earn when they have completed their **bachelor**. In the UK a postgraduate degree is a "catch all" term for all degrees higher than undergraduate degrees. Postgraduate programs include graduate certificates, graduate diplomas, masters and doctorates.

In the U.S., you go to **graduate school** (grad school) for an MSc or a PhD. A **freshman** (UK **fresher**) is a first-year student. A **sophomore** is a second-year student. A **junior** is a third-year student and a **senior** a fourth-year student.

There are three types of postgraduate degree: MS and MA degrees, doctorate degree (PhD) and specialist degrees and MBAs meant to broaden your knowledge in a given field. Masters courses are usually one year long either in the U.S. or in the UK (with some exceptions, like architecture, for example, which are 2-3 years long).

A **course** is a set or series of classes on a particular subject or one area of study, leading to an exam or qualification. Required courses are also called **core courses. Elective courses** give students a chance to deepen or learn about other subjects that interest them in a given curriculum. In the United States, a course is named after an abbreviation of the major and then given a 3- to 4-digit number (FIN289, for example). This is called **course numbering**. Some courses can be taken online. In the UK (and in Australia), a course is the entire program of studies required to complete a university degree. Words such as **unit** or **module** are then used to refer to an academic course as used in North America and the rest of Europe. This corresponds roughly to an academic **major** in the United States system.

A **major** (US) (degree course, UK) is a specialized area of study. Another word for major is **concentration**. A **double major** combines two areas of interest. A **minor** is related to an academic subject and requires fewer courses than a major. It is a secondary subject that complements the major.

Class is used to describe a particular instance of a course. Most of the time, class is used to informally describe a course. For example, students may ask, "How many classes are you taking?" A class is the particular time and day that a lesson takes place. Class (UK) may also be short for **classification**, the level of award of a degree (eg 2:1 or Upper Second). Last, a **class** (US) may refer to a **cohort** (UK) (=*promotion*).

Lessons are taught within class. They are the building blocks of a course that are taught during class.

A **lecture** takes place in a large room (lecture hall) with theatre-like seating. A professor stands in the front and talks for most of the time. Students take notes.

A lecture can be supplemented with a **discussion**, also called a **section**. It is a small setting that is more like a classroom. In discussions, you talk with peers, go over homework, ask questions and work with a teacher's assistant.

A **seminar** is when a faculty meets with a small group of students. Seminars are typical in graduate school.

In a **tutorial** course, a small number of students work on a topic and meet with the instructor weekly for discussion and guidance.

A **lab** is where students apply what they learn in class by practicing hands-on in a lab setting. A laboratory **rotation** (US and UK) allows students to conduct research in a lab of a faculty member.

Rotations last between six and eight weeks and help students, especially PhD students make informed decisions regarding the research group they wish to join.

A **studio** (arts and humanities) is where students apply theory from class to their work.

A **syllabus** [pl. syllabuses or syllabi] is a guide to a course and what is expected from the student. It is usually handed out by a professor at the beginning of a course. It includes course policies, rules and regulations, required textbook and assignments.

A **curriculum** [pl. curriculums or curricula] is the subjects comprising a course of study in a school or college and the learning objectives. This is the academic content taught in a course or program. (*cursus* in French).

In the U.S., a **credit** is roughly equal to one hour of class time (in general 30 credit-hours per academic year). In the semester system, the word **unit** or **semester credit hour** (SCH) is preferred. Most UK universities use the European ECTS system (European Credit Transfer and Accumulation System or the Credit Accumulation and Transfer Scheme (CATS).

In the UK, a **dissertation** is an extended subject on a topic as agreed between the student and the faculty. It is an extended piece of writing done at the end of a master's degree. It is normally applied to a doctorate. It is to be distinguished from the **doctoral dissertation.**

Both a thesis and a dissertation are considered as a final project and required to graduate respective programs.

Completion of a doctoral program requires submission and defense of a **dissertation** (the **viva**). A dissertation is a piece of scholarly writing that accounts for your research work throughout the doctoral program. It develops a unique concept and defends it on the basis of theoretical and practical results.

In the United States, the definition of a **thesis** [pl. theses] is almost the opposite of that in Europe. It is a critically written scholarly piece of research work. It refers only to the **master's degree** requirement. (Thesis is also used to describe a cumulative project for a bachelor's degree: senior thesis or senior project done in the senior year before graduation). A thesis is supposed to be an original paper presenting a proposition. It is about 100 pages long and shorter than a dissertation. A thesis is presented at the culmination of a master's program and allows students to showcase their knowledge and expertise within the subject matter they have been studying as part of the program.

In the UK, the term **thesis** is usually associated with PhDs and research master's degrees, while dissertation is the more common term for a substantial project submitted as part of a taught master's degree or an undergraduate degree (*e.g.* MSc, BA, BSc…).

A **doctoral thesis** is a focused piece of original research which is performed in order to obtain a PhD. It is about 300 pages long. In the U.S., a PhD consists in writing between three to six published and peer-reviewed papers in A-scholarly journals.

In Europe the original distinction between a thesis and a dissertation has been largely retained. A doctoral thesis is a focused piece of original research which is performed in order to obtain a PhD. A dissertation is part of a broader post-graduate research project.

A **capstone course**, also known as **capstone unit, capstone module, capstone project, capstone subject**, or **capstone experience**, is the culminating experience of an educational program. It may also be referred to as **senior seminar** (in the U.S.) or **final year project** (more common in the UK). A capstone is an independent assignment that serves as a culminating academic and intellectual experience for students, typically during their final year (it is called a capstone because it represents a crowning achievement as a capstone does in architecture).

Faculty (the / a) (American English) are people who teach in a university, college, or US high school, or in one of its departments. To be a faculty member = to be teaching, to be a professor. Also, **academic staff**. A top math faculty = a top math professor.

Rolling admission process. Applicants need to make a difference between rolling admission and regular admission. Colleges with rolling admissions (mostly in the UK) review applications as they are sent in (from July until April) *vs* waiting to evaluate all applications after a set deadline. It is the "first come first serve principle". Other colleges may set priority deadlines (prospective students who submit an application by this deadline are guaranteed to receive an admissions decision by a specific date) and cutoff dates beyond which admissions are closed. Schools will continue to evaluate applications until they have filled all the slots for their incoming class. A qualified candidate who waits until the 11th hour to apply may be more likely to get denied, so it's recommended to not wait too long to submit your application.

4. The admissions committee (adcom)

All applications for graduate studies go through the grinding mill of an admissions committee. An admissions committee consists mainly of faculty members from the department and occasionally a few students already in the graduate program. The applications are split up among the committee members in a way such that each application has at least more than one reviewer. Each file is read by a minimum of **three people**, sometimes including a student member (usually a PhD student), a faulty member, a staff member and the Director of Admissions. If there is no consensus among the reviewers, the file automatically goes to a fourth and occasionally a fifth reader. It is a thorough and fair process. Do not listen to those who say that the SOP is hardly ever read. It is definitely one of the four pillars of your application (along with transcripts, CV, letters of recommendation).

The decision-making process is a multi-stage process. For utilizing the committee members' time most efficiently, there is usually a preliminary round where a lot of the applications are weeded out, based on some requirements that the committee thinks of as minimum expectations for a student at their university. These could be cut offs on GRE, GPA, TOEFL or in some cases, criteria such as not considering an applicant who already has a graduate degree in the same or related field. The ones that go through this filter are the true potential candidates and get reviewed more rigorously by the committee. The review process typically ends with a committee meeting where the final shortlisting is done to reach the admission target for the academic year, with a few more being chosen for the waitlist.

If you mention that you would be interested in working with a specific faculty member, your application might be forwarded to her/him and she/he will be required to provide feedback. Beware of mentioning only one faculty in the SOP as it might be possible that a faculty member has decided to take a sabbatical, or no longer takes students or has transferred to another position elsewhere.

5. The application process

The application process to American or British graduate programs is arduous and **time consuming**. It is more than just writing a personal statement. The decision to apply must be thought out long before the process actually begins. So, start the process as early as you can, and gather together all the necessary material you will need for the application. Naturally, when you apply to a master's degree, you can't apply to a discipline completely unrelated to your bachelor's. Or you can apply, but nothing guarantees you will get accepted. You would be hard put to be accepted into a Biology program if all the courses you followed were in OR, FE or ML. You need the right base to build an education on. You cannot throw yourself into a pool when you do not know how to swim.

You will have to:

- prepare and take the required standardized **language tests** (GRE/GMAT/TOEFL/IELTS). You will probably have to sit them more than once to meet the standards of each program. The sooner you get ready, the better off you will be;
- create an online **application account** with each school;
- create a **CV** that matches the expectations of the admissions committee;
- draft, polish an **application essay**, personal statement, statement of objectives or statement of purpose as well as a personal history statement (many versions will be necessary before reaching an acceptable draft) or a diversity statement;
- get **advice** and **tips** from faculty, students in or graduates from the programs you are applying to. If necessary, you can also ask advice from the departments themselves;
- secure **letters of recommendation** from faculty members, researchers and other people (tutors, supervisors)—and sometimes write those letters yourself because professors and managers will tell you they are too busy to deal with them;
- translate original **transcripts** from your preparatory program or university and convert the grades into letters (on a maximum GPA of 4.0 for US programs. For some UK programs see the relevant classification below).
- sometimes upload your files and/or send paper-based material through snail mail via a guaranteed carrier;
- fill up the **application online** before the deadlines; and given the complexity of the US system *vs* the French system, it takes a while to clear all questions;
- pay the **application fee** (usually $150) for each school;
- prepare for the **videos** and **interviews** in the best of cases; there may be as many as three interviews (technical, behavioral, right fit);

– prepare for the **quantitative assessment tests** mandated by some universities, such as MIT Sloan (MFin program), Princeton's Bendheim Center for Finance, amongst others;
– draft some **additional essays** ahead of interviews or as part of the interviews;
– research and draft **scholarship** applications and possibly prepare interviews;
– apply for a **visa** and meet visa officers. Once you have gained admission to a US program, the university will send an I-20 form for you to fill up that is necessary to have an F-1 visa. You will have to set a date to meet with the visa authorities and pay a fee. (https://studyinthestates.dhs.gov/students)

Naturally, all this will be done concurrently to your present workload, project work, exam preparation, applications for internships, knowing full well that the grades you will have obtained by the end of the semester might well be sent to the admissions offices as additional material or requested by them for your admission.

Keep a careful record of all actions taken in that direction. Do not wait until the last days to apply online as servers tend to be bug prone in the final hours of the application process. If the school uses a rolling basis admission process, admissions staff read and process applications as they come. The longer you wait before submitting the more likely chances are that all the slots will have been filled. If the school uses a fixed date system, the essays may or may not be read all at one time. In any case, it is your responsibility to make sure you have sent all the documents and complied with the deadlines.

Graduate application timeline

April/May	Start thinking about a program abroad, and who the potential recommenders might be – Start securing LORs – Start studying for GRE/TOEFL/IELTS – Reach out to faculty in your university to ask for advice on grad schools
May/June	Draw up a list of potential programs (reach and safety schools) and research relevant faculty – Retrieve and translate transcripts from undergraduate institution – Send them back to school for validation
July/August	Draft SOP and scholarship essays – Take language tests
July/Sept	Talk to faculty – Read papers
Sept/Oct	Applications open – Start them – Provide biographical information – Write resume – Make contact with students and professors at your prospective schools
Nov	Make final edits – Check with recommenders
Oct/Dec	Submit applications and essays – Keep copies of every section for your records – Verify that your recommendations have been sent
Jan/Feb	Quantitative assessment tests – Interview and video process
Feb/March	Admission results (admission/rejection/waitlisting) – Early deadlines
April 15	Deadline for admission selection and your final answer

6. GPA (Grade Point Average)

The academic record is a key component of the application. Since the committee members do not get an opportunity to interview or test a candidate in any way, they have to use the grades as proxy for determining a candidate's competency in their field of study. Having an impeccable academic record (*e.g.* topping the department or being in the top three, etc.) is definitely a surefire way of getting noticed by the committee. Mentioning it in the SOP is relevant (ranked in the top 1% of the cohort, for example).

Letter grades. Most colleges and universities in the United States award a letter grade A (best), B, C, D, or F (fail) for each class taken (potentially with + or - modifiers). These letter grades are then used to calculate a GPA from 0 to 4.0, using a formula where 4.0 is the best.

Grades appear on a **transcript**. A transcript lists all the courses you have taken, or are currently taking during your study program. It also lists the results you have obtained and the credit value you have earned for each course. If you have completed your study, the transcript should show the final degree you have obtained (BSc, MSc, etc.).

Your school or institution should deliver official transcripts in French **and** English. If that is not the case, it is up to you to translate them. This is the case for the preparatory program, for example (see example below). You have to do the translation of the faculty's observations, change the point grades (or marks) into literal (or letter) grades and then into equivalents on a four-point scale. You need then to have them authenticated (stamped) by the school.

Applicants may not be required to mail in an **official** transcript with their application via a secure electronic transcript system so as to verify their authenticity. However, they are required to upload a transcript **online**. If they are accepted into the program, they will be contacted and instructed on submitting an **official transcript**.

For some universities, if you are an international student and your transcripts are not in English, it is recommended that you mail an official notarized translation and separate degree certificates indicating the conferral of your degree. if the documents are not in English you must upload a full translation prepared by a certified translator. Some universities or schools will ask you to go through a dedicated translation service (such as **World Education Services, WES**) which is fee paying. (https://www.wes.org/advisor-blog/wes-translation-services/) or the National Association of Credential Evaluation Services (NACES (https://www.naces.org). Also, many translation or evaluation services can convert your grades to the US scale. An accredited evaluator will accurately determine what your GPA would be on a US grading scale. Do not write on any of the documents before uploading them. The official or original language transcript must be sent in addition to the translated version. There are several sorts of GPA which you might be aware of:

This is the way high schools report GPAs to colleges. Generally speaking, official high school transcripts include both unweighted and weighted GPA, but this can differ between schools. International students should not be concerned with weighted and unweighted GPAs.

An **unweighted GPA** uses a 4.0 scale – meaning each letter grade corresponds to a numerical value. Getting an "A" means you have a grade of 4.0. Most high schools and colleges use the unweighted GPA to best reflect a student's academic performance.

A **weighted GPA** uses a scale that typically goes higher than 4.0 to allow for difficult classes. This usually means a 0 to 5.0 scale but it can go higher depending on the school. In the U.S., students in Advanced Placement (AP) or honors classes that use weighted GPA can expect to receive a 5.0 when they get an "A," a 4.0 for a grade of "B," and so on. This method accurately represents a student's academic proficiency and class rank based on their chosen coursework.

Normal GPA has a top 4.0, Advanced GPAs have a top of 5.0, so those students get the credit for their advanced learning. Compare unweighted vs weighted GPA:

Letter grade	Weighted	Unweighted
A+	5.3	4.3
A	5	4
A-	4.7	3.7
B+	4.3	3.3.
B	4	3
B-	3.7	2.7
C+	3.3.	2.3
C	3	2
C-	2.7	1.7

A simple way to find your weighted GPA is to take your unweighted GPA and multiply that by the number of classes you've taken. Then, add 0.5 for every mid-level class and 1.0 for every high-level class you've enrolled in. Finally, divide the result by the number of classes you have taken. You can always do this with an online GPA calculator such as https://gpacalculator.net/high-school-gpa-calculator/.

Colleges, such as Princeton, give more value to your weighted GPA than your unweighted GPA. For the school there is an advantage for students that take advanced courses — honors, AP, and International Baccalaureate classes — in high school, pointing out that the strongest, most promising candidates earn high grades and have taken full advantage of the academic opportunities available to them. For more information, see https://thecollegepost.com/gpa-weighted-unweighted/

Advanced GPA is the GPA of the final two years of your undergraduate education (typically year 1 and 2 in France's engineering schools). U.C. Berkeley, for example, requires it.

For applications to graduate studies, **cumulative GPA** or **CGPA** measures a student's performance for all of his or her courses (including all units and semesters) instead of just a given period of time. A cumulative GPA is the cumulative grade from all the courses you took during your four years whereas GPA measures the performance of a single unit or semester.

You might provide the mean between both the preparatory program and *grande école*/university programs. In other words, you should take into consideration the preparatory program GPA **and** GPA during the first two years (=four years of undergraduate studies, *i.e* equivalent to a BSc). Some schools may offer to submit a document with the CGPA.

The undergraduate GPA can be thought of as being similar to the GRE since it acts as another negative filter. A poor GPA is a compelling reason for a reject, but a stellar GPA by itself might still not be a good enough reason to win admission.

It is recommended that you submit the GPA of the first semester of your third year as additional material for admission. Some universities may not like it, yet, if you are a strong student, you will want to put all chances on your side. There are two reasons for that: one is that submitting third year results is sometimes mandated by universities (especially in Britain where some programs ask for first class honors as a prerequisite for admission[2]); the other is that it might reflect positively on the results gained in that semester, especially if those results are trending up. There is a final, hidden reason: some students will submit those results come hell or high water and you do not wish to be left behind or disqualified because your next-door classmate did so and you did not.

A cause of concern while comparing students from different universities is the variation in the curriculum and in the weightage associated with non-technical courses. In general, the committee goes through the transcript of the candidates, focusing mostly on courses related to the program they are applying to. The transcript also gives insights into how the candidate has fared over time. Obviously, an increasing or a consistent trend in the grades looks more favorable than a declining one. In fact, being consistently good is the safest option. A candidate might have had one or two poor semesters (or terms) and made a very good comeback, but all else being equal, one candidate would still lose out to another who always maintained good grades. The only exception is the case where there was a genuine reason for the dip in the grades, something that is explained via the statement of purpose, optional essay, letter of recommendation or elsewhere in the application.

Your GPA should be as close to 4.0 as possible. Getting a 3.9/4.0 will definitely be looked upon much more favorably than getting 3.6/4.0. Some preparatory programs consider that you deserve a 4.0 if you have been admitted to the École Polytechnique, no matter what. Other French schools are more captious.

Here is a guide that you might use to calculate your GPA. In general, limit yourself to the A+/A/A- letter grades. The admissions officers appreciate if the university's official transcripts have an appendix that clearly spells out the mechanism behind the assignment of grades and the final GPA calculation.

Bear in mind that some programs indicate the cutoff for admission. Another way of benchmarking your chances of admission is to compare with previous admissions cases, even though other factors come into play. On the other hand, strong recommendation letters from professors who can com-

---

2. A bachelor's degree can be an honours degree (bachelor's with honours) or an ordinary degree (bachelor's without honours). Honours degrees are classified, based on a weighted average (with higher weight given to marks in the later years of the course, and often zero weight to those in the first year) of the marks gained in exams and other assessments. First-Class Honours (70% and above) are usually referred to as a 'first' or 1st. It is the highest honours degree you can achieve.

ment on the candidate's academics can help in levelling the playing field. In particular, it helps when a professor clearly states that the candidate did indeed top the department (or a particular course) and also provides some background regarding the usual range of grades for courses taken at that university.

Ranking in subject	Letter grades	Grade for GPA
1-5	A+	4.0
5-10	A	4.0
10-15	A-	3.7
15-20	B+	3.3
20-25	B	3

The British system is somewhat different from the French or the American system. UK degrees are classified out of **100**:

- **A First-Class Honours/a First/1st** - 70 or above (typically awarded to 30% of all students at British universities). It is the highest honours classification and indicates high academic achievement. The percentages of graduates achieving a first vary by university and course studied. Students of law are least likely to gain a first, while students of mathematical sciences are most likely to gain a first. It is commonly accepted that the top 10 UK universities give out more Firsts than other universities, for example Oxford University was mentioned as having given out 30% of grades as firsts, which is a greater proportion than the average university (according to the Higher Education Statistics Agency, HESA). Approximately 15% of all degree candidates graduate with a First while the figure for attainment of a Third was stated as only 7.2%.
- **An Upper Second-Class Honours/2:1 (or II.i)** (pronounced two-one) – 60 to 69 (upper second). The 2:1 is a minimum requirement for entry to many postgraduate courses in the UK.
- **A Lower Second-Class Honours/2:2 (or II.ii)** (pronounced two-two) – 50 to 59
- **A Third-Class Honours/a 3rd** (also referred to as a "gentleman's degree") – 40 to 49. It is the lowest honours classification in most modern universities.
- **An Ordinary Degree (or Pass)**
  There are variations in classification at the University of Cambridge, where undergraduate Tripos examinations are split into one or more Parts, which span one or two years. At the University of Oxford, a formal degree Class is given, and this is typically based on the final examinations.

US/UK equivalents:

British degree	US Grade	US GPA	US Grade (WES)
First	A	4.00	A
Upper Second	A- / B+	3.33-3.67	A- / B+
Lower Second	B	3.00	B
Third	C+	2.30	B-
Ordinary	C	2.00	C

How to convert UK Grades to 4.0 GPA Scale

There's no set standard, but according to Fulbright US UK Commission, here's the comparable scale to convert UK grades to a 4.0 GPA scale.

UK Module marks	UK degree classification	GPA
70+	First class honours	4.0
65-69	Upper-second class honours	3.7
60-64	Upper-second class honours	3.3
55-59	Lower-second class honours	3.0
50-54	Lower-second class honours	2.7
45-49	Third class honours	2.3
40-44	Third class honours	2.0
35-39	Ordinary/Unclassified	1.0
below 35	Ordinary/Unclassified	0.0

(source: https://gpacalculator.net/grade-conversion/united-kingdom/)

UK classification	UK percentage grade	US equivalent grade
First	80-100% 70-79%	A+ A
Upper second	65-69% 60-64%	A- B+
Lower Second	55-59% 50-54%	B B-
Third	46-49% 43-45% 40-42%	C+ C C-
Fail	0-39%	F

GPA scale

Percentage	Grade	GPA
75-100	A+	4.25
71-74	A	4.00
67-70	A-	3.75
64-66	B+	3.50
61-63	B	3.25
57-60	B-	3.00

Percentage	Grade	GPA
54-56	C+	2.75
50-53	C	2.50
48-49	C-	2.25
43-47	D+	2.00
40-42	D	1.50
38-39	D-	1.00
35-37	F+	0.75
30-34	F	0.50
0-29	F-	0.00

7. Transcripts

It is your responsibility to translate the transcripts according to a standard model provided by the school. Here is an example:

Student's name: first name/last name SCHOOL NAME
Date of birth: mm/dd/yy (US)/dd/mm/yy (UK)

ADVANCED MATHEMATICS, PHYSICS AND CHEMISTRY/ ENGINEERING SCIENCES /COMPUTER SCIENCE CLASS

Year 1 – 2021-2022

	FIRST SEMESTER		SECOND SEMESTER	
Subject	**Grade**	**Professor's comments**	**Grade**	**Professor's comments**
Mathematics				
Physics				
Engineering Sciences				
Computer Science				
Philosophy				
English				
German				

Average grade for the year:
GPA:
General Observation: The Principal (US)/Headmaster (UK)

Grading system: A+ = outstanding student – A = very high honors – B = high honors – C = with honors – D = passing – E = conditional failure
Name of High school – Address – Telephone – Fax – email

Beware of how you translate the professors' observations: some universities require a **literal** translation, others do not or will require the original once you have been handpicked for admission. The transcripts should be validated by your own preparatory program, university and school. As for the *grande école*/University GPA, it should be provided with its translation by the Dean of Studies Office. Make sure you have written copies, and that some of them are provided in a sealed envelope.

8. The international language tests

Most academic graduate programs require that you should take two kinds of tests when you apply: the GRE and the TOEFL or IELTS.

- The GRE (Graduate Record Exam) is conducted by ETS. It can be GRE **subject** or the GRE **general**, or the **GMAT** (which is more oriented towards MBA programs). The GRE subject is required for PhD candidates and in certain programs (Biochemistry, Cell and Molecular Biology, Biology, Chemistry, Mathematics, Physics). Sometimes it is ***highly recommended***, so you'd better take it than sit it out.

The GRE general is required for Master's programs. It is **valid** for five years. You can re-sit the exam up to five times a year (each test a minimum of 21 days apart).

Be aware of the **dates** for the test. Whereas the GRE general is administered virtually every day, the **GRE subject test** is administered twice a year in France. Do not miss the date. You may take **subject tests** as often as they are offered. Naturally, you need not take those tests in France. If you happen to be abroad, it might be cheaper to take it there.

The GRE subject test is administered on paper whereas the GRE general is computer-based. Also, note that some departments at such universities as Princeton, Brown, Yale, Cornell, U of Penn and even Harvard (Philosophy), life sciences programs in particular are opting out of the GRE (nicknamed the GRExit movement), which the 2019 pandemic is bound to accelerate as most admission test scores were waived for 2021). So, check the requirements when you apply (UK universities do not require the GRE).

When selecting a test date, make sure your scores will be reported in time for your application deadlines. Score reports are sent to the score recipients **you** designate (count 11 days). Allow time for delivery of scores and processing by the institution. Beware that some schools require that all test results be sent, so doing well the first time round is highly recommended.

Opponents object to the GRE for many of the same reasons that they are against the SAT and ACT: the GRE hinders inclusion and diversity efforts, tests are expensive (paying for training and taking the test – which costs $200+ a pop, plus travel in some cases – can be a burden for low-income students); on average white people and Asian Americans do better than black and Latino test takers do. It is also said that the scores do not speak to how well you can do in graduate school. Critics also point to the small size of doctoral programs, which means that admissions decisions must be made on a personal basis. Yet, diversity tends to be the primary argument. The long reign of the GRE may be drawing to a close...

The GRE general has three major sections:

- Verbal reasoning (130-170 score scale) (two 20-question sections),
- Analytical Writing Assessment (AWA) (0-6 score level) (two 30-minute essays, Analyze an issue task + Analyze an argument task),
- Quantitative reasoning (130-170 score scale) (two 20-question sections).

The verbal reasoning section consists of only four types of questions: Text Completion, Sentence Equivalence, Reading Comprehension, and Critical Reasoning. The test assesses your ability to analyze and evaluate written material and synthesize information obtained from it, analyze relationships among component parts of sentences and recognize relationships among words and concepts. The quantitative reasoning section tests your knowledge in Algebra, Arithmetic, Data analysis and Geometry. It assesses your basic mathematical skills, understanding of elementary mathematical concepts and ability to reason quantitatively and to model and solve problems with quantitative methods.

At a testing center, you are allowed one break during the exam. Take a snack as well as a bottle of water. Get rest the night before and wear comfy clothes for the test.

What are the scores you should aim at? Schools typically have an admission rate below 10%. So, anything above 90th percentile is a safe bet even though if it is a math-heavy program 95th is even safer. Actually, the GRE scores are mostly used as a negative filter for rejecting candidates. A poor GRE score can get the candidate rejected, but an exceptionally high GRE score will still not be enough (by itself) to guarantee admission. Candidates with full (or almost full) marks in the quantitative section are viewed favorably. Being proficient at math, 170 is the expected score. For the verbal, a score of 160 is what you should seek. As for the written part, no less than 4 is expected (out of 6).

Low scores might definitely slam the door to quality programs. You can re-sit the GRE (once every 21 days, up to five times within any continuous rolling 12-month period). A consistently bad percentile in each of the three GRE sections definitely stacks the odds against a candidate. However, a slip up in the Verbal or the AWA section might be overlooked, provided the rest of your profile is genuinely stellar.

The test is about 3 hours and 45 minutes long, so brace yourself for a hard morning or afternoon. Schools will not see if you choose not to send scores from a particular test date, so if you have taken the GRE three times and chosen to only send your best scores, they would not know you have taken the GRE two other times since they would only see one set of scores. Retaking the GRE multiple times will not hurt your chances of admission. Many people take the GRE more than once in order to get their highest score.

Check the website of each program to have an idea of the expected scores you should achieve to have a fair chance of admission. A low score may well ruin your chances, but a score within or even above program expectations will not help you a whole lot if you lack some essential components sought by the admissions committee (such as research experience or strong recommendations from faculty). A high score may shore up a comparatively minor weakness, like a GPA a little below the program average, but it will not make up for any truly glaring deficits in your application. In general, successful PhD candidates are going to have higher GRE scores than master's candidates. Not all programs, even within the same discipline, consider GRE scores to have the same weight, nor even have cutoff scores. Some place great stock in them, while others only see them as an ancillary or supportive piece in the application. The more competitive the program, the higher the GRE score needs to be. So, have a holistic approach to your application, and even though you might think your scores are too long, rest assured that this is but one element in the application. So, do not overplay, or downplay the importance of your score. If a GRE is optional, only send the results if you are taking it and if you have obtained strong scores.

Last, make sure you take the test in person so as to remove any issue regarding **questionability**. Also, stick to the rules when taking the tests. If you are suspected of fraud, your test scores will be withheld and possibly way beyond the deadline you have to submit.

The other mandated tests are the **TOEFL IBT** (also conducted by ETS) or the **IELTS**. The TOEFL is 3h30 minutes long. Four skills are tested: reading, listening, writing and speaking, on a 30-score scale each (120 altogether). Given the nature of each skill, we recommend you should train thoroughly. Use the study preparation courses: however expensive they may be, they are also useful. Experience has shown that the writing and speaking tests are the more difficult for students. Therefore, I suggest sending essays to your language professor, as a matter of practice, and ask for one-on-one training for the oral part.

The test covers a set of basic knowledge and concepts not in-depth or specialized fields. Therefore, brush up on your math and vocabulary, train and take the practice tests offered even though they are usually easier than the real tests.

Section	Number of questions	Time given
Reading	36-56	60-80 minutes
Listening	34-51	60-90 minutes
Speaking	6 tasks	20 minutes
Writing	2 tasks	20 minutes

The (academic) **IELTS** is 2h45 minutes long. It is administered by the British Council. It has four parts – Listening (30 minutes), Reading (60 minutes), Writing (60 minutes) and Speaking (11-14 minutes). Reading and Writing tests are done in one sitting. The Speaking test is held on the date you choose during your registration. The score is measured on a scale of 0 or 1 to 9. The higher the score, the better understanding and ability to communicate in English you have. Results can be sent directly up to five organizations.

TOEFL/IELTS scores hardly carry any weightage (in fact, might even be neglected altogether) as far as the admission decision is concerned. If the university has clearly spelled out a cut off (sectional or aggregate) for the TOEFL score on its website, it is then necessary to just clear that cut off, but the actual overall score (be it 120/120 or 100/120) does not matter once the minimum score has been obtained. It would almost never be the case that a candidate is rejected only on the grounds of having a poor TOEFL score. In some cases, when the TOEFL score is low and the rest of the application is strong, the candidate might be given admission, but asked to take an English proficiency class and/or pass an additional English test after joining the university.

Another test, **Duolingo**, has been gradually accepted by US and UK universities. The test is much cheaper than others ($45). It is 45-60 minutes long. Results are given within 24-48 hours. Duolingo assesses candidates on four criteria which are reading, writing, listening and speaking. The score is on a scale from 10 – 160. A Duolingo test can be taken anywhere, anytime and you just need a reliable internet connection. (See: https://fr.duolingo.com)

Do not take those tests cold. They should be **prepared well ahead of the application process**, typically in the summer preceding the start of the process (count 1-2 months of preparation depending on your level in English). You will then avoid the stress of last-minute applications and be able to fully focus on the application in itself. Do not hesitate to train with the official test guides for those tests, the most popular being ETS (*Official Guide to the GRE*) or Kaplan (*Prep Plus*) (buy the year's edition). There are specialized guides as well (verbal, math) and preparation programs such as GregMat (https://www.gregmat.com)

Also double-check the name variation when you sign up for those tests; the matching process is done by **exact spelling and variation** in application and the exam(s). So, the name given for application AND tests should be the same.

You need to make sure the tests scores are forwarded to your schools of interest (**four universities** are included – free – in the GRE fee, $19 for each additional school; if you re-schedule it will cost you another $60).

Those tests are not cost neutral (respectively 140€ and 150€ for the GRE subject and general, 220€ for the TOEFL and 240€ for the IELTS). The GRE is valid for 5 years, the TOEFL and the IELTS for two years. (http://www.ets.org/gre / http://www.ets.org/toefl / https://www.ielts.org/for-test-takers/test-format). Some schools require the GMAT whereas others may accept either the GRE or the GMAT (https://www.mba.com/exams/gmat).
Most programs have minimum scores that the applicant is supposed to comply with.
See also https://kaplan.com, https://www.princetonreview.com

Both GRE general and TOEFL/IELTS tests are computer-based except for the IELTS Speaking section: it is a face-to-face discussion with a certified examiner. The GRE is a graduate school entrance exam while the TOEFL is a test of your English language skills. Schools want to see GRE scores to make sure you can handle graduate-level coursework, and they want to see TOEFL scores to make sure your English skills are strong enough to do well at an English-speaking school.

Metrics such as GPA and test scores give an admissions committee an idea of a student's qualifications. They are impersonal and do not indicate whether a candidate would be a good fit for a given program. Metrics only show one small part of the entire picture. In general, those scores are used as a cut-off even though it is hard to figure what the cut-off is going to be. It depends on many external factors such as the size of the applicant pool to the level of competition.

9. Reasons for applying

Before committing time and money to the application process, you need to ask and answer some **tough questions** about why you have made that momentous decision.

- What are the scientific reasons why I want to pursue an education abroad?
- What will an education abroad provide me with that I cannot find in my home country?
- Do I enjoy spending long and hard hours studying?
- Do I have a passionate interest in a subject area that I will want to explore further abroad?
- Will graduate studies offer a chance to advance my understanding of those topics I have grown fascinated with as an undergraduate without regard to any immediate industrial or economic benefit?
- Do I like to do research (in case you are aiming at a PhD program)?
- Am I resilient/agile enough to leave home and family and spend one year or more abroad?
- What profession do I desire to pursue and what degree does it justify as a credential?
- What are the geographies where I aspire to work, once I have completed the US/UK program?
- What are my career goals, my short-term goals as well as my long-term goals. (Naturally, as time goes by, those goals may change). What attracts me in this career? What do I hope to gain?

Remember that earning more money might be a good reason as well: as statistics show there is a lockstep relationship between education and income. A bachelor's degree increases lifetime income by $1.2 million more than a high school diploma in the U.S., for example. High-income people have more education than lower-income people. Higher education has a strong negative impact on unemployment too. In other words, graduate school is a sound investment in your future. Investing in your education is a capital no one can take away from you. Also, going to graduate school is probably a finer use of your time than wasting a few years in an entry-level job.

Now, there are **negative reasons** why you should not go to graduate school.

- The first of which is **peer pressure**: you feel obligated to do it because your classmates do it. If the only reason is to test whether you can outperform them or at least be as good as them, it is **not** a sound reason.
- The second reason is you do it **to please someone else**: for instance, your grandpa went to UCSD, your mum is a Yale alumna, so you feel duty bound to follow in their footsteps whereas you'd rather get a job straight away, start your own company… or keep sheep. You need strong internal motivation to strive in graduate school. Align your interests with your own instincts and follow your intuition.
- The third is you are **clueless about a subject to study**. One way of solving the issue is to talk to your professors, or an academic or career counselor. Take time to explore your options.
- The fourth is you are trying to **prolong the academic journey** for fear of getting on the job market, because unemployment is running high, you are afraid of being rejected and would rather pile up debts than face the music.
- The fifth is a **cultural** and **hedonistic** one. You enjoy London, you like the American way of life, and plan to go surfing at Steamer Lane and snowboarding at Squaw Valley while studying in California. Your **love for foreign cultures** or an **education abroad** are no motives to apply.

> *There are several reasons for my motivation to study abroad in a campus like Ann Arbor's. My living in London for four years, which was a priceless experience, gave me an enlightening overview of its rich cultural diversity, and furthered my will to further travel outside France.

> *Because I was a pupil in a French-German high school in France, I consider myself as a genuine European citizen. That is why I want to discover the scientific culture of another great European country, the United Kingdom.

Studying at the graduate level is tough and similar to the pace of work you went through in a preparatory program. There is a hefty load of homework, team work, assignments, every week. So, if you expect to take a break, bask in the sun, hit the slopes and enjoy campus life, you'd better reconsider your options.

There are ways to lift the barriers of uncertainty and set you on the academic road. One question you might ask yourself, is, when was the last time in my undergrad years I got excited about a subject? What would you like to do for a living if money was not an issue? Have you ever fantasized about the life you would like to live? Who are the people you admire and that inspire you, and why? What recent scientific papers have I read that pointed to research I would like to undertake? If you raise the question of how you will finance your graduate program, this is of course a no-brainer. Should you want to go, you would find a way to pay.

10. The financial onus

American universities are in for the money… and the prestige. Make no mistake about it. An American education is not a free ride and therefore finances loom large in your decision and motivation. Universities charge high **tuition fees**, to which you might add the cost allowance, bearing in mind that you might not benefit from on-campus housing and that you will have either to share digs or rent your own. In New York City, renting a flat can cost an arm and a leg. In any case, do not let financial fears prevent you from pursuing the degree of your choice. On the other hand, do not choose a program because the tuition fees are cheaper than anywhere else.

Students need to beware of applying for **financial aid in the U.S.** At the graduate level, financial aid usually means a loan, and usually with interests much higher than in your own country (France, for example) where interest rates are low.

It is often cheaper to go to a well-known school. Schools such as Harvard, MIT, Princeton, Stanford, Yale have huge endowments. These schools have deep pockets and usually will provide financial aid if only to retain the best candidates. The tuition is offset by grants and fellowships, or any other financial aid package, for example in some departments, but not in others. In addition, some projects carried out with the industry, part of the program, will offset part of your tuition.

– Public universities charge lower tuition fees than private universities. For example, the University of California, which gathers together some 11 campuses across the state, charge less than

Stanford. At UC Berkeley, the 2020 graduate school tuition & fees were $14,131 for California residents and $29,345 for out-of-state students. By way of comparison, graduate school tuition & fees were $49,617 at Stanford. To which you need to add room and board ($15-17,000) and the health insurance plan ($3,500). On that latter issue, it might be cheaper to hunt for a health plan in France that will cover as much as in the U.S. but will cost way less.

– It is cheaper to pursue a PhD than an MS/MA. PhD students are generally fully funded, sometimes partly. Tuition waivers for PhD students are common. Yet, it is not uncommon that a department will offer a PhD berth in its program, yet the first two years will be on you. A student may be offered a slot at MIT's Department of Economics but the department will not pay for the first two years. If the student is part of the elite *Corps des Mines*, the Corps may choose to fund the two years.
  Do not apply for a PhD and drop out after two years with an MS/MA under the pretext that your education will have been free then. A PhD is an iron-clad commitment. Do not break it. Besides, a **'bailout' MSc** is not counted the same in industry or academe as a regular master's degree. Plus, if you choose that strategy then the admissions committees will look twice before admitting a student from your school or university next time. So, if you are not sure of going in for a PhD, it is preferable to start with a master in the first place.

– Some schools offer TAs and RAs (under the guidance of a faculty member) that help defray the cost of your education in the U.S. during your MSc program. Competition for such positions is fierce. Before you become a college teaching assistant (for undergraduate students), you must also go through a TA training session. Teaching assistantships require you should teach undergraduate courses or labs (typically a few hours a week, under the authority of a professor). You will be selected according to your eagerness to teach but also your results in the course you have attended and will later teach. You need grades good enough to be selected. Sometimes a letter of motivation will be required, as early as the admissions process. Sometimes too, the university will look at your teaching experience (this is when having been an oral examiner in the French preparatory program or any such teaching experience matters).

On the **open days**, set up by the university and reserved to successful applicants once the admission process has been completed, you will have an opportunity to meet with the professors and (re-) state your willingness to TA or RA. Therefore, it is **always** useful to visit the university on those occasions. Nothing beats face-to-face conversation. When you are invited to a meet-and-greet with a department faculty, it may be a serious *faux pas* not to appear, all the more so as the university can help you towards your traveling expenses. Assistantships are routinely assigned during those tours, formally or informally.

In exchange for your RA or TA, you will have your tuition or part of it waived and you might receive a **stipend**. A TA is a nice addition to your CV if you wish to become a college professor. It is even more prestigious if you have been TAing for a professor that eventually got the Nobel Prize! Conversely, the workload can be harrowing as well as the hours of preparation and grading, plus the office hours in which TAs answer questions to the undergrads who need help. Also bear in mind that your performance as a TA will be assessed by the students at the end of each term.

You get a **research assistantship (RA)** by applying to a professor or a laboratory. You should indicate your interest in the research under way. You are under the obligation to carry out around 20h of research per week. You are paid $2,000-3,000 a month. You will be hired at the university, not before. Many US universities have offered RAs to students, such as MIT, Berkeley, Columbia, Stanford, Carnegie Mellon, Johns Hopkins, UCLA, Illinois-Urbana Champaign, Georgia Tech, Brown University. Yet, pay close attention to your visa status, be it F-1 or J-1, depending on each university. For example, at UCB, "students on F-1 visas do not require permission to hold University employment or academic appointments for 20 hours per week or less if they are registered during the semester. They may also work full-time on campus during the summer break if they will be registered the following semester. All J-1 students, however, must have permission from their program sponsors to hold any employment or academic appointment. Students on F-1 and J-1 visas may not work more than 20 hours per week during the academic year; there are no exceptions to this federal regulation."

Fellowships are awards that come with no strings attached. There is no requirement to perform any job or task to earn the award. Generally, scholarships and fellowships are reserved for graduate students with special qualifications, such as academic, athletic or artistic talent and whose academic potential is so great that they should not be distracted in their studies. Awards are also available for students who are interested in particular fields of study, who are members of underrepresented groups, who live in certain areas of the country or who demonstrate financial need. Fellowships are two-fold: internal and external (the equivalent of a scholarship). In the latter case, inquire in your home country.

Some fellowships have instant name recognition and having them on your CV will further your career (Examples: AAUW International Fellowships for Women (USA), World Bank Robert S. McNamara Fellowship Program, Rotary International Peace Fellowships, Knight-Hennessy Scholars Fellowship, William Randolph Hearst Endowed Fellowship for Minority Students, depending on fields of study and nationality). There may be international conferences which the fellows are required to attend. Check finaid.org and fastweb.com. Unlike student loans, scholarships and fellowships do not have to be repaid.

Grants are smaller fellowships, in the range of a few hundred dollars to a few thousand. You can find them the same way you find fellowships.

As a general rule, American students can apply for **loans** to the federal government (about $20,500 a year). In any case, once a school has made a fellowship offer, you can always ask another university where you have also been admitted to match the offer. It cannot hurt, especially if you claim that their program is better than the other.

11. Scholarships for French students

No matter what, when you go study abroad, you have a lot of options in terms of scholarships for MSc or PhD applications which can ease the financial burden. Even though applying for a scholarship (or a **studentship**, UK word) in France is a time-consuming chore it will lighten your financial load once you have drafted a personal statement. A few guidelines:

- Pay attention to **deadlines** that can vary from one year to another and be as early as December 1st and extend into the following year. Many scholarships of fellowships require a personal statement describing the journey that led you to your field of study, the obstacles you have overcome, whether you belong to an underrepresented minority, the kind of research you want to carry out, or your career goals.
- Make clear how the scholarship will **support** you.
- The **amount** granted by a scholarship can vary from one year to another.
- You need **not** have an answer from a graduate program to apply to a scholarship.
- Mention the scholarship which has been awarded on your **resume.** If you have declined one, mention it 'declined'). It will show how strong a candidate you are and that you can bring in money.
- The selection is based on a **written application letter** (a statement of research/study), **letter(s) of reference** and often followed by one or two **interviews** (including one in English) with the members of a commission (as is the case for Fulbright). You can use your personal statement for a scholarship application: both are usually similar. It will save you precious time in the application process.
- Several scholarships can be combined (typically the Arthur Sachs dotation). You can apply to as many scholarships as you want.
- Some schools offer their own scholarships, be it needs-based or merit-based. But some schools do consider all applicants for a merit-based one (see MIT MFin program, for example) that might help offset the cost of tuition but will not cover the full cost.
- Note that in the UK, a **commoner** is a student who does not have a **scholarship** or **exhibition** (a lesser student scholarship). In the UK, **fellows** are senior members of a college who, together with the college head, constitute the governing body of the college. There are also other categories such as honorary or emeritus fellows.

Here is a list of some scholarships you can apply to if you ambition to study in the United States:

- The **Association for American Women in universities** (AAWU) offers scholarships to women who are pursuing degrees in fields which are currently underrepresented by women. These degrees include computer science, math, scientific study, and engineering. The amount of funding provided is between $18,000 and $30,000 for each scholarship award recipient depending on level of studies. (https://www.aauw.org/resources/programs/fellowships-grants/overview/).
- **Commission franco-américaine (CFA) Fulbright**. Valid for one year only and with the *caveat* that you must return to the home country after one year. Typically, the Fulbright Program offers full scholarships in the U.S. for international students who want to pursue a graduate degree. The scholarships can also be awarded for non-degree postgraduate studies. The grant covers tuition fee, textbooks, airfare, a living stipend, and health insurance. The exact amount awarded depends on the nature and length of your project, as well as the host country. Fulbright also looks after the visa requirements. The most important part of the project proposal is that it can feasibly be completed in less **than one academic year** (and in no less than six months), and that it will benefit the host community. Projects that are innovative and unique, addressing topic in which there is little current research, have a greater chance of being accepted. (https://fulbright-france.org)
- The **Jérôme Lohez 9/11 Scholarship Foundation** for French students applying to programs at Columbia University, Stevens Institute of Technology, Harvard University, Princeton Univer-

sity, New York University. Not much information is provided as to the amount, to be determined by the board. (https://www.jl911.org/scholarships-2)

- The **Harvard French Scholarship Fund** provides financial aid through grants to gifted French students enrolled at Harvard University. (https://www.linkedin.com/in/harvardfrenchscholarshipfund/)
- Fulbright France, **Dotation Arthur Sachs** (6-8 $5,000-$35,000 scholarships) for Harvard applicants (whatever the field). French nationals or students with French and American citizenship can apply. The Sachs scholarship can be combined with other scholarships. (https://fulbright-france.org/fr/qui-sommes-nous/fondations-partenaires/dotation-arthur-sachs)
- There are at least four scholarships available each year for students in the domains of medical research, sciences and law (selected fields). The amount is $50,000 maximum. (http://www.fondation-monahan.fr)
- **Fondation Carnot**, *Bourses d'études* Carnot. Five scholarships every year, $7,000 for PhD or MSc students admitted to a US program (one or two for X students). It can be combined with financial aid provided by the *Fondation de l'X*. (http://carnot.org)
- ***Fondation École Polytechnique*** provides financial aid to students willing to study abroad (the *Fondation* pays the interests of any personal loan up to 20,000€ loans taken out with some banking establishments to study in the U.S., UK and Japan (15,000€ in any other countries). (https://www.polytechnique.edu/fondation/aides-financieres). Students paid by a Corps are excluded. In the same way, the **CentraleSupelec Foundation** provides financial aid to students (up to 25,000€, interest rate around 0,6%).
- *Fondation École Polytechnique*-California Institute of Technology (Caltech)-Master Aéro, PhD. Free tuition for one year to X students plus $10,000 living expenses. Only top students need apply…
- **Jean Gaillard Memorial Fellowship Fund**. Jean Gaillard Fellowships are awarded each year to citizens of France for graduate study at Harvard University or MIT. Applications are made to the Board of Directors of the Ecole Centrale des Arts et Manufactures in Paris, who nominate finalists to the Committee on General Scholarships. 1,000-30,000€ that can be combined with other scholarships. (https://scholarships.harvard.edu/international-students/france and https://worldwide.harvard.edu/jean-gaillard-memorial-fellowship-fund-france). See also: ninon.vinsonneau@centralesupelec.fr
- The ***Fondation Monahan*** for merit students. About 2-5 scholarships (maximum of 50,000€ each, according to the website) are given to scientists, researchers, physicians willing to study in the United States. Medicine, physics, chemistry, math, environmental sciences, intellectual property law and law in general, biotechnology, law. You need to have an M2 or be a doctor in medicine to apply, be French or have dual French/American citizenship. (http://fondation-monahan.fr/)
- **Leonora Lindsley Memorial Fellowship** (administered by the Fulbright Commission). Its "purpose is to assist deserving French students in attending institutions of learning in the United States. Students must be those who participated in the French Resistance movement during World War II, or are the children or descendants of those who took part in the Movement." One or two fellowships a year (between $6,000 and $12,000). Reserved for French students applying to master's programs in the U.S. There is no interview. (https://www.iie.org/Programs/Leonora-Lindsley-Memorial-Fellowship).
- The **UK government** offers hundreds of scholarships, bursaries and additional financial support to students from several countries. You can visit the UKCISA (UK Council for International Student Affairs) website to find out if you are eligible for a scholarship. UKCISA is the UK's national advisory body serving the interests of international students and those who work with them. (https://study-uk.britishcouncil.org/scholarships)

- The **British Council** offers scholarships as well. For instance, inspired by COP26, the British Council is offering four **Entente Cordiale for the Climate Scholarships** for the academic year 2022-2023. This program is aimed at postgraduates (master degree and PhD) studying in a UK university in environmental studies. All disciplines are welcomed, as long as there is a relevant link with environmental issues (environmental law, physics, engineering, environmental economics, environmental history, etc.). The funding scheme supports one whole year of studies and amounts to 10,000€ per student. (https://www.britishcouncil.fr/en/scholarship-climate)
- **Erasmus + Mundus scholarships** (BS, MS, PhD). The EU (European Commission) provides scholarships through its *master commun* **Erasmus Mundus** (*MCEM*) for one or two years for application to European universities for all international students. Students will be able to study in 3-4 different countries in Europe and get a chance to do an internship during their two years of study. There are some 2,500 scholarships available. All educational and living expenses are covered by Erasmus (monthly stipend 1,100-1,500 euros). Sadly, the UK has also opted not to take part as an associated third country in the new Erasmus+ program 2021-27. The UK will therefore not be taking part in the new program as a Programme Country. Yet, Erasmus Mundus students will be able to study at UK universities which jointly deliver joint master programmes. (https://erasmus-plus.ec.europa.eu/fr/bourses-de-masters-communs-erasmus-mundus) and (https://www.eacea.ec.europa.eu/scholarships/erasmus-mundus-catalogue_fr)
- **Zonta International.** Zonta is dedicated to achieving gender equality in education and supports scholarships, fellowships and awards for women and girls pursuing education and careers in these traditionally male-dominated fields. Includes **Amelia Earhart Fellowship** (Zonta International Foundation Amelia Earhart Fellowship Fund): "The $10,000 Fellowship is awarded annually to up to 35 women pursuing PhD/doctoral degrees in aerospace engineering and space sciences. It may be used at any university or college offering accredited post-graduate courses and degrees in these fields. Women of any nationality pursuing a PhD/doctoral degree who demonstrate a superior academic record conducting research applied to aerospace engineering or space sciences are eligible. It is imperative that students be registered in a full-time PhD/doctoral program and have completed at least one year of that program or have received a master's degree in an aerospace-applied field at the time the application is submitted." (https://www.zonta.org/Web/Programs/Education/Amelia_Earhart_Fellowship.aspx)/). There is also the Jane M. Klausman (JMK) Women in Business Scholarship program which helps women pursue undergraduate and master's degrees in business management and overcome gender barriers from the classroom to the boardroom. (https://www.zonta.org/Web/Programs/Education/Women_in_Business_Scholarship.aspx)
- **MIT Legatum Center**: Legatum Fellowship/MasterCard Foundation Fellowship for students applying to a graduate program at MIT. The Legatum Center for Development and Entrepreneurship at MIT is a community hub for students, alumni and faculty who seek to accelerate social and economic progress through innovation-driven entrepreneurship. The Center runs a competitive fellowship program for MIT students with a commitment to building and scaling their ventures through principled entrepreneurial leadership **in the developing world**. (https://legatum.mit.edu)
- The **National Science Foundation (NSF)** has a graduate Research Fellowship Program (NSF Graduate Research Fellowship Program (GRFP) for American-born students seeking to pursue research-based MSc or PhD programs in STEM (Science, Technology, Engineering and Mathematics) disciplines at accredited US institutions. The five-year fellowship includes three years of financial support including an annual stipend of $34,000 and a cost of education allowance of $12,000 to the institution. (http://www.nsfgrfp.org/resources)

- **Society of Women Engineers (SWE)** offers scholarships ($1,000-$17,000 with most below $5,000) for those who identify as a female/woman and are pursuing an ABET-accredited bachelor or graduate student program in preparation for careers in engineering, engineering technology and computer science in the United States (PhD or MS/PhD track in most US universities. ABET (Accreditation Board for Engineering and Technology, Inc) is a nonprofit, ISO 9001 certified organization that accredits college and university programs in applied and natural science, computing, engineering and engineering technology at either the undergraduate or graduate level. Very few MSc Programs and no PhD programs are ABET-accredited, though. (https://swe.org/scholarships/) and https://www.abet.org/accreditation/find-programs/). For other scholarships for women, see https://www.scholarshipsforwomen.net/engineering/
- Fulbright France, **Georges Lurcy scholarships** for master's level students. Valid one year. Amount is roughly $20,000. Six scholarships are given each year. Reserved preferably to students studying Political science, Law, the Humanities related to American history and civilization. (http://www.lurcy.org/bourses.html)
- The **Diamonstein-Spielvogel Foundation**. "With this focus, deeply rooted in inclusiveness, social equity, and community service, the D-S Foundation creates and supports original projects based on results-driven and innovative strategies. The D-S Foundation funds projects which demonstrate creative promise in four priority areas: projects focused on civic leadership, public affairs and diplomacy; projects of cultural merit; original educational initiatives; and science and medicine, in support of the advancement of the field of health. All funding initiatives are through an invitational process only; we are unable to accept unsolicited applications." They fund projects that demonstrate innovative approaches to strengthening public and civic engagement and democracy in the United States and abroad. They support projects "undertaken by proven leaders in the civic, urban, and governmental areas, who are working to support the development of critical thinking, analytical, and leadership skills in the public sector; or who have promoted strategic diplomatic engagement to produce positive change and advancement. Consideration will also be given to young innovators with creative promise." They also fund projects of cultural merit (including Visual, Performing, Literary, Film and Electronic Arts), innovative education initiatives, projects advancing medical science through scientific research. For example, The Columbia Climate School, inaugurated in Fall 2021, has received a grant to support two Diamonstein-Spielvogel Fellowships for graduate students.
 (https://www.diamonstein-spielvogelfoundation.org)
- **Stanford University - Knight-Hennessy Scholars**. The program concerns 80 to 100 graduate students enrolled at Stanford (out of 3,000). All Knight-Hennessy Scholars have to apply to (and be accepted by) a graduate program at Stanford at the same time they apply to Knight-Hennessy Scholars. The graduate program, however, may admit you to Stanford even if you are not selected as a Knight-Hennessy. Review of applications are done separately but in parallel. About one third of applicants are from the U.S. *vs* two-thirds from countries outside the U.S. The education of Knight-Hennessy Scholars is funded for up to three years for any graduate degree(s) at Stanford to which you are admitted at the time you are selected as a scholar. If your degree program exceeds three years – such as a PhD program – then your Stanford home department(s) will fund the remainder of your education to the extent consistent with its standard funding commitment for that program. During each of the first three years of graduate study, Knight-Hennessy Scholars receive: a fellowship applied directly to cover tuition and associated fees – a stipend for living and academic expenses (such as room and board, books, academic supplies, instructional materials, local transportation, and reasonable personal expenses) – a travel grant intended to

cover an economy-class ticket for one annual trip to and from Stanford. Knight-Hennessy Scholars also may access supplemental funds to support academic enrichment (*e.g.* conference travel). (https://knight-hennessy.stanford.edu)

- Some **regions** in France, such as Ile-de-France, Champagne-Ardennes, Hauts-de-France provide financial aid, which is means-tested (dependent on family income). (https://www.etudionsa-letranger.fr/bourse-etudes-france-regionale/ile-de-france-aide-a-la-mobilite-internationale-des-etudiants-amie or https://www.champagne-ardenne-guide-des-aides.fr/lesaides/Pages/Mobilite-internationale.aspx or https://generation.hautsdefrance.fr/envolez-vous-avec-mermoz/)...
- The **Global Study Awards**, launched by SIC Association, Studyportals and British Council IELTS. The Award prize (10,000€) will be applied toward the cost of tuition fees in the first instance, paid directly to the Higher Education Institution that the successful candidate will attend. The Global Study Awards is designed to support highly motivated, talented individuals who can actively demonstrate their potential to contribute to society through their studies; a strong commitment to developing their career; their sincere interest in increasing intercultural understanding and exchange. The Global Study Awards will be available to prospective students in all countries worldwide. The Global Study Awards enables the successful candidate(s) to study abroad, on any chosen undergraduate or postgraduate program at a higher education institution. (https://www.mastersportal.com/pages/the-global-study-awards/#fflt:SP_GSA1)
- There are also scholarships in Canada, such as Sauve Scholars (https://www.sauvescholars.org). See also https://www.educanada.ca/scholarships-bourses/non_can/index.aspx?lang=fra
- For further information, see https://www.etudiant.gouv.fr/cid135449/les-autres-bourses-et-aides-pour-etudier-a-l-etranger.html
- **Schwarzman Scholars**, founded by American financier Stephen A. Schwarzman and inspired by the Rhodes Scholarship (1902), is designed to meet the challenges of the 21st century and beyond. Schwarzman Scholars supports up to 100-200 Scholars annually from the U.S., China, and around the world for a one-year master's in global affairs at Beijing's Tsinghua University (over 4,000 applicants). Scholars chosen for this program will live in Beijing for a year of study and cultural immersion – attending lectures, traveling around the region, and developing a better understanding of China. Admissions opened in the fall of 2015 (inaugural cohort in 2016). Schwarzman Scholars are selected from an international pool of distinguished candidates. Prospective Scholars are expected to demonstrate academic excellence, exceptional results in their field and outstanding leadership qualities. Schwarzman Scholars has an acceptance rate comparable to the Rhodes and Marshall scholarships, making it one of the most competitive scholarships in the world. (https://www.schwarzmanscholars.org/about/)

There are scholarships available for (summer) internships as well at the national or the local level. There are some criteria such as being a scholarship student, for example. Scholarships must be filed with the university or school you are a student of. Amount: 400€/month. Duration of the internship varies between 2 and 9 months. (https://www.service-public.fr/particuliers/vosdroits/F380). At the local level, one example is the **Mermoz scholarship** (up to 400€/month), funded by the Hauts-de-France Region, and that is meant to encourage students who wish to study abroad. (https://www.hautsdefrance.fr/bourse-mermoz/)

12. Choosing a school or a program

Choosing a program abroad is a decision that is not to be taken lightly, or blindly. Even though magazines list the best programs according to departments, there are several criteria that need to be considered in your quest to find the right fit.

The first step is to build a **list of possible schools**. Select a wide range of schools. Make a list of about 10-12 programs at most and winnow down that list to five possibilities (check your school's policy for the number of programs you are allowed to apply for). Divide the schools you are interested in into categories according to your chances of admission (from the most to the least probable). By applying across the board, you will maximize your chances of gaining admission to at least one program, especially when competition in your own school or college is tough. The number of programs American students apply for is between 4 and 15. In medicine, it is about 14. (See comments on how many schools you should say you are applying to below).

Look for **people** and **research**, not schools, while you are puzzling over programs. Reading the literature will help you pinpoint names of faculty and their teaching residences. Avoid the trap of prestige-chasing. It all looks glitzy and ritzy to apply to MIT, Harvard or Stanford, but there might be no one there that fits what you want to study. On the other hand, there might be lesser-known schools but which have exactly the program you are seeking.

Avoid applying to **two different programs** at the same university (unless it is explicitly allowed, or possible when you apply to two different schools within the same university). That would send a wrong signal about the depth of your commitment. If you hesitate between a statistics and a data science program, then apply to statistics programs at some universities and data science programs at others. Yet, it is acceptable practice to apply for an MSc knowing that you will go on with a PhD. Some universities offer PhD tracks that involve starting with an MSc first. Some PhD-bound students will apply to a PhD program at some and an MSc at others too. By the way, you do not need to have an MSc to join a PhD program. There are some exceptions of course as some fields require that you should start with the MSc before applying for a PhD. Conversely, some MSc programs will count towards a PhD if you decide to extend your studies beyond the master's level.

The following resources should be tapped in order to find out about graduate programs:

- **Faculty**. Identify the professors in your present degree course that have studied in the U.S./UK, published with American/British colleagues, or taught in the U.S./UK.
- **Scientific papers** and **academic journals** might be a source of information on the state-of-the-art and the type of research coming out of those programs. When you read papers germane to your present program, check out the authors' names and find out where they teach or do research.
- **Alumni** or the students you know who are currently enrolled in your subject area are another useful source of information. When and if you write for clues, be to the point and ask them which professors/courses would they recommend and whether they have any hot tips for a prospective student. Also, use LinkedIn databases to find them yourself. Write them and ask about the quality of the program (and whether it is worth investing $60-70,000 in a one-year MSc program). Gossip is one of the surest ways of getting informed.

- **YouTube** and various tutorials, virtual information sessions, alumni panels available online are also useful sources to create a successful application. You might glean interesting tips on various aspects of the program (which is likely to change from one year to another) as well as application advice. It is a helpful way of getting updated about programs.
- **Academic advisors** in each department of your present course. They ought to have precious information or at least refer you to the relevant professor that might provide the info you need.
- **Annual business magazines rankings** are a decent source of information. Yet, rankings should be considered with a pinch of salt. There are not always truthful nor relevant as they lump programs together. Do not put too much weight on the rankings alone and do not confuse rankings with "fit". Fit takes precedence. As said, departments are more important than universities. For an objective analysis of the ranking system, read *The Order of Things, What College Rankings Really Tell US*, by Malcolm Gladwell (2011), which debunks rankings; his thesis: determinations of 'quality' turn on relatively arbitrary judgments about how much different variables should be weighted. It is extremely difficult to measure the variable you want to rank because of differences in how a specific metric can be compiled by different people at different schools in different countries. Rankings turn out to be full of 'implicit ideological choices' by the editorial chef who cooks up the ranking's methodology.
(https://www.newyorker.com/magazine/2011/02/14/the-order-of-things)
  - https://www.gradschools.com
  - http://www.phds.org
  - https://www.usnews.com/best-graduate-schools

There also exists a website for those interested in worldwide programs of study at all levels: https://www.topuniversities.com

- **Peterson's guides** (on every accredited graduate program in the U.S.) are a useful source of information in book form or online (https://www.petersons.com). Actually, there are thousands of guides related to all sorts of sectors, including sports medicine.
- Some websites specialize in certain areas as well (law, medicine, dentistry…).

To explore your options, you should take the following elements into consideration:
1. The academics. Ask your own professors about the quality of the research being conducted in your targeted program. They are the best sources of information. Inquire about the faculty there, and whether they know some of them. You can always approach the professors in the U.S./UK through email, stating who you are and how you have developed an interest in their work, inquire about their present research projects or ask about recent papers or lab. Keep your inquiry as concise and specific as possible.

```
Dear Professor XXX, I hope this email finds you well. My name is… and I am a
senior at…, majoring in…
I have done research in… I will be applying to a PhD program this Fall and I
would be interested in joining your group, should there be any openings.
I have come across some of the papers you have published on… I have attached my
CV below. I would be interested in talking about your research and my interests
if you have a chance.
I look forward to hearing from you soon. Regards.
```

In the same way, if you intend to intern with a researcher or a professor, propose a study topic related to their own specialty:

```
Dear Dr/Professor XX. Currently an MSc student at…, I am interested in continuing my graduate work at XXX's IEOR Department. I recently graduated with a BSc in OR and completed a year-long project on… under the direction of Professor XX. My main focus is supply chain management; in particular I am intrigued by the methods to integrate and optimize various operational, tactical and strategic decisions in large-scale supply chains so as to help managers deal with the uncertainty inherent in the real world.
In the course of my studies and research I came across your name and read some of your papers. I would appreciate the opportunity to further explore and analyze the topic under your direction and I was wondering whether there might be some possibilities to intern at your lab for the Spring quarter.
```

If a professor or researcher does not reply, do not take offence or be discouraged. They get oodles of unsolicited emails. Should you elect to insist, wait a couple of days after the first email and resend it with the following introduction:

```
I am not sure you received my recent email. Here is what I emailed you (…)
```

If such a strategy failed to elicit an answer, you may well resort to snail mail your e-mail message, with the following statement:

```
Perhaps I do not have an accurate email address for you. Here is my query printed for you. I look forward to hearing from you by email or regular mail at your convenience.
Thank you so much for taking my request into consideration.
```

If that fails again, better leave it alone. The professor/researcher may be on sabbatical, may be retired, out of the country or may have a perfect rationale not to answer you. Of course, the best way of catching their attention is through your own professors who might be able to put in a good word for you. You can also go through the Department's secretarial staff and ask for assistance in having your message delivered to the right person.

Do not forget that a school's reputation may be overdone and that what may have been true 10 years ago is no longer so. Professors come and go. Some retire, leave or transfer to other positions. Likewise, it is sound to know what a department will look like in 5-10 years' time, and therefore look closely at the professors' long-term research.

2. The locale. The location of the school actually should **not** matter in your choice of a program, unless there is a direct relation between the program and specific geographical features (Berkeley's Structural Engineering, Mechanics and Materials program in a highly seismic hazard zone).

Whether it is on the East Coast, the West Coast or the Midwest – to name a few – what matters is the quality of the program, not the state or the city. Yet, if you believe you will be miserable in Pittsburgh or Sioux City, better find another destination. Yet, if for some reasons you'd rather study in the Sunshine State rather than on the Last Frontier, in London rather than Lancaster, then location takes center stage in your choice of programs.

One factor that might be taken under consideration is the big city location and the job market. Actually, studying in New York City, Boston or the Bay Area will make it easier for you to land a job, whether you want to work in finance, in tech or if you aspire to become an entrepreneur. Now, the cost of living in a big city, and therefore the area around the school will have a direct bearing on the cost of your own education. Yet, when all is said and done, cost of living in itself should not be a factor in your selection. But no matter where you are, you are likely to forge bonds of friendship that will survive long after you have graduated.

Naturally, you can always **go and visit** the schools you are aiming at. Some schools may welcome visits from prospective students. You will see for yourself the campus, have a taste of the department's atmosphere, meet some of the students there and get a feel of the place. A personal interview with a professor, a meeting with some of the faculty may make an impression that is deeper than an essay and a file. However, you do not wish to reveal more of yourself than you intend. A successful visit should be planned and prepared well ahead of time and given due consideration only. In particular, if you intend to meet some of the faculty give them a heads-up as they will certainly be busy. If you decide to go, respect a certain decorum, be courteous and dress properly. And make sure you have intelligent questions to ask.

13. PhD programs

You have first to determine which program suits you best: PhD or MSc? **A PhD** (Philosophiæ doctor translated as Doctor of Philosophy) is a top option, reserved to the best students who have a definite bent for research.

- The material you need for your admission includes academic transcripts, academic references, a personal statement and, sometimes a research proposal. Samples of a paper you have written or a project you have worked on may be required. You have to provide evidence of language proficiency as well and deal with the visa process.
- The number of students who apply far exceeds the number of students who get admitted. The selection level is high given the long-term investment made by the university that pays you a stipend over several years.
- You will need to find a **professor/advisor** that not only does research in your field of interest but also, in some cases, has the funds to finance you. Some departments admit you and give you a chance to explore who you would like to work with once you have taken your quals, for example. In other departments, it is the professor that hires you directly for your PhD and who will finance your studies. That is why PhD candidates, especially in many social sciences and arts and humanities subjects, are encouraged to actively seek expert academics in their field prior to applying. As stated, reading papers and publications relevant to your project, will help you identify the researchers you might be interested in working with.

The reputation of academics hinges on their ability to closely monitor your research and supervise your work. Enquire about a professor's reputation and you will soon realize whether that professor is tyrannical, hands-on, or hands-off in following up on her/his students. Even though it might be premature to pass judgment at this stage, visiting the department and meeting with the faculty – when that is possible – is a useful step to take in order to check whether their research matches your interest, but also if you will be able to get along. When you commit to five years of doctoral studies, you want to make sure that you will be able to work with the faculty and fellow students and vice versa.

- A PhD is on average **five years long**, even though it might be four, or sometimes six years full time. In the UK, a full-time PhD usually lasts for three or four years (while a part-time PhD can take up to six or seven). However, the deadline can be extended by up to four years at the institution's discretion. In France, it is three years' long.
- A PhD involves students independently conducting **original** and **significant research** in a field or subject, before producing a publication-worthy thesis or papers (usually three to six). A PhD therefore requires qualities and potential of someone that is fit to do **research.** This is what the admissions committee need to see through the various elements of your application.
- A PhD student will often work alone or with limited collaboration, and he may feel isolated or demotivated at times.

In the **U.S. and Canada**, doctoral programs typically include a series of required and optional courses at the beginning of the program. Education in the latter portion of the program tends to consist of informal discussions with the thesis advisor and the student. The program can thus be separated into two portions (**doctoral student** and **doctoral candidate**) with a required doctoral examination (the **quals**, or **qualifying exams**), sometimes also known as **preliminary examinations** ("prelims"), **general examinations** ("generals"), or as **major field examinations**. Upon successful completion, students are formally admitted to a **doctoral program** and students are considered as "PhD candidates".

Alternatively, a student may be admitted to the program, but still be required to complete a **comprehensive examination** ("comps") in her or his field before advancing to the dissertation state. Comps are not linked to any particular course, but rather test knowledge across one or more general fields of study. They are often based on a reading list agreed upon by the student and his or her committee, which is staffed by the primary supervisor and several advisors, normally professors at the university, but not necessarily in the same faculty. The comps, which are stressful and time consuming, usually come after the student has completed required coursework and before starting on the dissertation.

Other programs will require students to take a General Examination once they have passed the Qualifying Examination and completed all of their program requirements. It is comprised of a research-oriented (RO) paper and a presentation of a research paper.

Once you have passed the quals, the remainder of your time will be spent looking for the right advisor with whom you will do your research. Ultimately, you will publish papers (three or more) and secure the highly sought-after title of Doctor after a *viva* in front of a jury.

The **PhD (ABD)** (not an official degree) serves to note when a PhD student has completed all graduate coursework for the doctorate, has passed the cumulative and/or qualifying examinations, has been formally advanced to final candidacy and may have conducted original research, but has not submitted a dissertation to satisfy the final requirement for formal conferral of the PhD degree.

In the UK, universities are free to admit anyone to a PhD programme (UK spelling), with admission generally conditional on the prospective student having successfully completed an undergraduate degree with at least upper second-class honours (UK spelling), as well as a master's degree. A research proposal is required by students when applying to study for a PhD. The proposal should clearly address the research you wish to undertake, how you will do it, and why it is important.

It is common for students in the UK to have two supervisors. The **primary** supervisor provides expert academic advice on the best direction for your project and offers feedback on drafts and other work in progress. This person is sometimes referred to as a 'director of studies'. Your **secondary** supervisor provides more pastoral support and general mentoring. They may not be as closely related to your research, but will help with professional development and training. It is not rare for students to be **co-supervised** by two academics who both offer academic advice and more general support.

It usually takes **three years** to complete doctoral research under the guidance of an academic supervisor or supervisory team. Programs tend to be located within an existing research group. The PhD in the UK has traditionally been a **research-only degree**, with no taught classes or exams. You do not normally have to take classes either as you do in the U.S.

In the first year you will meet with your supervisor to discuss your research proposal and agree an action plan with deadlines. You complete your literature review or study, in which you evaluate and critique existing works to inform the direction of your project and make sure that your research will be original. A **Certificate of Postgraduate Study** (CPGS) is normally taken as the probationary year of a PhD. In the second year you start gathering results and developing your thesis, and potentially begin writing chapters of your thesis. You also jump into the academic fray, attending academic conferences to present your findings, teaching, collaborating with other students on similar projects, going to workshops, lectures and presentations, or submit work for publication in an academic journal or book. In the third and final year you write your thesis, though your research may still be a work in progress. After receiving your supervisor's green light, you submit your thesis before undertaking a one to three-hour oral exam (*viva voce*) in which you discuss and defend your thesis in the presence of at least one internal and one external examiner. Both will have read your thesis and will question you about it. It is your responsibility to 'defend' your findings and conclusions in order to prove the value of your research and confirm the PhD is your own work. The defense takes place in a closed room setting (unlike European universities where it is public).

In the UK, there are alternative routes to gaining a doctorate. A **Higher Doctorate** (reserved to those with several years of academic experience and in some fields only such as Law, Divinity, Literature, Music, Science) is granted on the recommendation of a committee of internal and external examiners, which assesses a portfolio of published, peer-reviewed research you have undertaken over the course of many years. The **Integrated/New Route PhD** is four years long. It is offered by over 30 universities and involves taking a one-year MRes before studying a three-year PhD. It combines taught elements with independent research, allowing students to learn different methodologies while building their transferable skills. The **professional Doctorate** is geared towards students of vocational subjects such as medicine, education and engineering. Professional Doctorates are focused on teaching and involve smaller research projects and thesis components. They are often sought by those aiming for a career outside of academia.

PhD students in the UK are partly or fully funded through scholarships, bursaries and Research Council grants. The main funding body for UK PhD research is UK Research and Innovation (UKRI). UKRI is made up of seven **Research Councils**. Each covers a specific academic discipline. They provide full studentships covering fees and living costs. Funding can also be provided by professional bodies, or charities, foundations and trusts. Studentship recipients should be aware that they may have to do some teaching as well. Some PhD students will be automatically considered for financial support once they have been accepted by an institution, but many are required to make separate funding applications. These are usually made directly to the university – even for those studentships.

Doctoral Training Centres (DTCs; also called CDTs, Centres for Doctoral Training or Doctoral Training Partnerships) manage the Research Council-funded PhD degrees. DTCs fund students to support their technical and transferable skills training, as well as research. Each DTC involves a university (or a small number of universities) in delivering a four-year doctoral training programme to a significant number of PhD students organised into cohorts. Each Centre targets a specific area of research, and also emphasizes transferable skills training.

British universities offer first a one year's or two years' master degree (sometimes called MPhil) where one studies a field in depth. At Cambridge, there are two types of **MPhil**: the MPhil by Advanced Study (9-12 months), which includes a taught element, and the MPhil by Dissertation (12 months), which is a research-only program leading to a dissertation. Both types of MPhil provide a transition to full-scale PhD research and a doctorate which is called a DPhil, although this is not automatic. Actually, an MPhil dissertation is a valuable introductory experience in the preparation of a research thesis. In fact, in some subjects, an MPhil is a prerequisite for continuing on to research work yet a new application must be made and a suitable supervisor must be identified. If an offer of admission to the PhD is made, it will be conditional on your performance in the MPhil, as well as on providing evidence of your ability to fund your PhD studies.

Not all UK PhD applications require a formal **interview**, but this is more common for funded positions or programmes with limited space. Interviews can often be conducted online. You may be asked to answer some questions about your application and/or give a short presentation on your intended research.

14. Master's degree programs

An **MSc (Master of Science) (MS, M.S., M.Sc., SM, S.M., ScM or Sc.M.)/MA (Master of Arts)** is contingent upon holding a bachelor's degree. Most of the US universities refer to the Master of Science as MS and in the UK they term it as MSc, which I will use for clarity's sake.

A **Master of Engineering (M.Eng./Meng/M.E.)** is awarded for study programs that are more practice-oriented. An MEng is structured with technical coursework and focuses more on application. It corresponds in France to the *Diplôme d'ingénieur*. Contrarily, an MSc specializes in theories and studies. It is more research-oriented. In the **UK**, the Meng is an integrated degree. Instead of studying for a Bachelor before a postgraduate master you enroll in one four-year undergraduate degree. The MEng is a BEng degree with an extra year, in which the final degree is graded on both the bachelor's and the master's level. It can be a 'sandwich' five-year course with the last year spent in industry. The degree of Master of Engineering (MEng) is the highest award for undergraduate studies in engineering and leads to the title of chartered engineer. In the **U.S.** the Master of Engineering is academically equal to the Master of Science and Master of Arts. Yet, it is common practice to award the Master of Engineering for technical programs at universities of applied sciences or universities of technology but not only (See UCB programs, for instance).

A **Master of Research (MRes)** degree is designed to provide training in how to become a researcher. It prepares prospective PhD candidates for doctoral research in a specific area. The Master of Research (MRes) and Master of Philosophy (MPhil) are the most common types of research masters degrees.

A **taught Master's degree** includes a series of modules following a set timetable of seminars, lectures, assignments, exams and other activities. Students are responsible for studying independently in their free time. Most taught master's degrees generally require you to complete a final dissertation or a major research project. In taught courses you will be learning alongside classmates, whereas a research-based degree entails independent work.

A **Master of Public Administration/of Public Affairs (MPA)** and a **Master of Public Policy (MPP)** are public policy degrees with a focus on policy analysis and management. Other specialized master's degrees include the Master of Public Health (MPH), Master of Laws (M.L. or LL.M, *Magister Legum* or *Legum Magister*), the Master of Fine Arts (MFA), etc.

A **Master of Business Administration (MBA)** is designed to provide students and professionals with the tools and skills to advance their careers. Related degrees include the Master of Science in Information Systems (MSIS), for example.

In the UK, a **Master of Advanced Study (MAST)** (Cambridge) is the equivalent of a fourth undergraduate year.

In the UK, a **Master of Letters (MLitt)**, (Cambridge) like the MSc, is a research degree requiring six full-time (or ten part-time) terms of research. Terms of research are normally consecutive, and, for full-time students, require residency in Cambridge. Not all departments offer part-time research degrees.

A **Master of Studies (MSt)** is a part-time master's degree, designed for individuals who are typically studying in addition to working full-time, allowing students to develop their professional and academic interests for career progression or diversification and personal development.

An MSc is **usually one year long**, sometimes **18 or 24 months**. In the UK, it is a one-year degree in full-time study.

In the U.S., credit hours vary depending on the university as well as the program. In general, you need **36-45 units** (=72-90 ECTS) to graduate with an MSc. Each course counts for three units, which means you have to take **12-15 courses** in all. Yet, once you are in a given program, you can always choose a course outside the track that might interest you (for example you are following a data science program and wish to enroll in a *Cryptography* class that is not part of the mandated curriculum): your faculty **advisor** (who is assigned to you by the graduate program at the start of the academic year) will either give you the green light and count the course towards the 45 units or deny your request. In the latter case, you can still take the class for which you will pay additional fees. Similarly, you can extend the program beyond the three or four quarters necessary to graduate. Often students may stay two quarters longer and choose to do a 10-week internship in the Summer (mid-June/mid-August) rather than graduate after one year and study during a quarter when the course offer is slim and professors are on leave or on holiday.

In the UK, and across the European Higher Education Area, a master's degree (Bologna second cycle qualification) requires a minimum of 60–120 ECTS credits. (1 ECTS credit = 2 UK credits), which is 1-2 Academy years of study.

- Master's degrees assessed purely by thesis (MPhil) take 2 calendar years, *i.e.* 180 ECTS credits.
- Most taught and research master's (MA, MSc, etc.) are a full calendar year (90 ECTS credits/180 UK credits).

An MSc is about science (STEM), whereas an MA spans fields as diverse as linguistics, history, communication studies, diplomacy, public administration, political science, or other subjects within the scope of the humanities and social sciences. Some **Harvard** degree abbreviations follow the tradition of Latin degree names: A.M. = Master of Arts (M.A.), is Latin for "artium magister"; and S.M., = Master of Science (M.S.), is Latin for "scientiae magister." In the UK and Ireland, an MA is typically a "taught" postgraduate degree, involving lectures, examination, and a dissertation based on independent research. Taught master's programs involve one or two years of full-time study. A Master of Arts may be given in a scientific discipline, common at Ivy League universities. In the UK, students typically must first enroll in an MPhil program and are then admitted to doctoral study only upon successfully defending their research proposal.

What are the **differences between an MSc/MA and a PhD**? A key difference is that an MS/MA is about the **consumption** of knowledge whereas a PhD is about the **production** of knowledge, *i.e.* a work of research. The second difference is **financial**. Whereas a PhD student receives a stipend, usually in exchange for teaching undergraduates, an MSc student usually pays full tuition, which means between $60,000 and $100,000 a year. Conversely, MSc students might benefit from a scholarship in their own country (or not). Yet, the MSc opens the door to a job or a career in the U.S., with the added advantage that, should you remain in the U.S., for example, the hiring bonus (golden handshake) might take a big chunk off the student debt you will have incurred by studying in the U.S. Therefore, choosing between a PhD or an MSc program is no trivial matter. It needs careful thinking out. Another factor to take into account is the cost effectiveness of studying abroad, compared to a home program that is usually much less expensive, if not free.

Note that the BSc doesn't exist at the University of **Cambridge**. Undergraduate courses lead to a single degree, the Bachelor of Arts. When you graduate successfully, you are awarded a **BA Hons.** (Cantab) (Cantab is short for Cambridge[3]). In Computer Science, Engineering, Mathematics and some Science subjects, you can study for a fourth year and obtain a second degree in addition to

3. Cantab is derived from Cantabrigia, a medieval Latin name for Cambridge invented on the basis of the Anglo-Saxon name Cantebrigge. A Cantab is a graduate of Cambridge University in England. It can also refer to an alumnus of Harvard University (Cambridge, MA, USA) or a resident of Cambridge.

a BA; these integrated masters courses lead to either a Master of Engineering (MEng), Master of Mathematics (MMath), or Master of Natural Sciences (MSci).

Cambridge undergraduate courses are assessed through examinations in broad subject areas called **Triposes**[4]. The Mathematical Tripos is the oldest. Each **Tripos** is divided into one or more **Parts** and you need to complete a number of Parts in one or more Triposes to qualify for the BA degree. There are some restrictions on how you can combine Parts together to make your degree. As of 2018 the **Mathematical Tripos** course comprises three undergraduate years: **Parts IA** provides much of the basic knowledge requisite for mathematics. This includes algebra, analysis, methods in calculus, and probability;

Part IB has no mandatory content but recommended coursework in pure and applied math (geometry, complex analysis, group theory, for example, in addition to quantum mechanics and fluid dynamics);

In **Part II** students are free to choose from a large number of courses over a wide range of mathematical topics. The Tripos qualify a student for a BA degree. An optional one-year master's course (**Part III**) qualifies a student for a **Master of Mathematics** (**MMath**) degree (with BA) if they are a Cambridge fourth year student or a **Master of Advanced Study** (**MASt**) degree if they come from outside just to do Part III.

At Oxford, the MA is a higher degree. In Scotland, the first degree in arts is an MA at three of the four older universities. Some British universities, including York, Oxford and Sussex refer to the PhD degree as the DPhil.

As for all those who hesitate before continuing with a PhD but wish to test their research skills, it may well be possible for them to mention it in the statement. This is what I usually suggest, to be put in the introduction or in the conclusion:

At this point in time, I have not ruled out going on with doctoral studies. In that respect, I expect the MSc program to provide the tools and methods to narrow down my choice/to define my choices further/to help me make an informed decision/and help me make an informed decision/in the matter.

Although I am applying for a Master's program, I am seriously thinking about continuing my studies with a PhD program, and your strong theoretical courses would allow me to leave that door open for the near future.

4. The word **Tripos** is a 16th century alteration of Latin tripus 'tripod'. It is a reference to the three-legged stool candidates once used to sit on when taking oral examinations (see tripod). Legend has it that students used to receive one leg of a stool in each of their three years of exams, and the whole stool at graduation. At Cambridge, the candidate who has obtained first-class honours in Part II of the mathematics tripos is a **wrangler**. The wrangler with the highest marks is called the **senior wrangler**. The wooden spoon was presented to the student who had achieved the lowest exam marks but still earned a third-class degree (lowest honours classification) in the Mathematical degree.

Once you have made your mind about applying for a PhD or an MSc, you will have to choose among several programs. One website (*US News and World Report* https://www.usnews.com/rankings) ranks programs by department (roughly 1,400 schools are taken into account). This is a source of information for whomever seeks the best programs, and not necessarily the top names. This is what you want to look at first. This so-called Best College ranking system includes each educational institution that participates in an annual survey that every school receives. Additionally, these rankings are based on opinion surveys from faculties and administrators who do not belong to the schools. To be included in the rankings, each school must offer four-year undergraduate degree programs and be regionally accredited. A college can't be ranked if it only offers associate degrees programs or has a student population of 200 or less.

What you might bear in mind is that well known universities may not have the best programs you are looking for whereas small name universities might have the best programs, even though they are much less known than Harvard, Stanford, Princeton, or MIT, Cambridge or Oxford.

II. Statement of Purpose & Personal Statement

1. Introduction

Graduate programs (all American universities and a growing number of European institutions inclu-ding British or Swiss universities) require a (detailed) letter of motivation known as **statement of purpose (SOP)**, **personal statement (PS)** and a **personal history statement (PHS)** in certain cases (see infra). Because requirements vary from one school/program to another, it is essential that you should read the personal statement instructions for each program. These guidelines will tell you what to include in your essay (and what to leave out), thereby clarifying what your overall angle needs to be. They will also recommend a word limit (in general **my recommendation** is 1,000 words, absent any guidelines in the matter). For example:

MIT, Mechanical Engineering:

> Please explain why you are a good candidate for graduate school. You should describe why you wish to attend graduate school, what you would like to study, and any research experience you have. Describe one or more accomplishments you are particularly proud of that suggest that you will succeed in your chosen area of research.

MIT, MBan:

> Please describe your reason for pursuing the Master of Business Analytics degree. What do you hope to gain from the program? What are your career aspi-rations? (500 words or less)

This is what **CMU** mandates for some of its programs:

> - *Part I: Briefly state your objective in pursuing a professional graduate degree in MSBIC. Tell us if you have a particular reason for applying to this degree program.*
> - *Part II: Describe your background in fields particularly relevant to your objective. List here any relevant academic, industrial or commercial experience.*
> - *Part III: Include any additional information you wish to supply to the Admissions Committee.*

This is what **UCLA** mandates for its MS in Financial Engineering:

> **Essay 1**. Financial engineering requires a combination of mathematical/quantitative abilities and creative thinking. Describe a project you worked on, either as a student or professional, then demonstrate your analytical and creative problem-solving skills. Tell us why this project was interesting to you (Maximum 750 words).
> **Essay 2**. Why does a career in quantitative finance appeal to you? Based on your abilities and what you know about careers in financial engineering, why do you think this is the right career path for you? (Maximum 750 words)
> **Essay 3**. Please feel free to provide any information you think would help us evaluate your potential to succeed in the program. (Maximum 375 words).

This is what **Oxford's** Department of Statistics requires (UK):

> *Guideline: Your statement should be written in English and explain your motivation for applying for the course at Oxford, and your relevant experience and education. You should explain why you are interested in studying for the course. The statement should summarise your background as it relates to applying for the MSc and the advanced mathematical and statistical content you have covered (or are in the process of covering, if you are currently completing a degree). This will be assessed for your reasons and motivation for applying, evidence of motivation for and understanding of the broad area covered by the MSc, capacity for sustained and intense work, reasoning ability, the ability to absorb ideas at a rapid pace.*

Chicago University:

> *Please discuss your academic and career objectives, why you want to attend the University of Chicago Financial Mathematics program, what you hope to do after completing the program. You may also use this space to clarify or provide additional information about your application materials and/or overall candidate profile that would be helpful to the committee to know.*
>
> *There is a 750-word limit on the Candidate Statement.*

The **LSE** (London):

> *For each programme you apply for, you must upload a statement that describes your academic interest in, understanding of, and suitability for that programme, as well as your purpose and objectives in undertaking this graduate study. The statement of academic purpose is an important part of your application, and selectors are looking for evidence of your academic motivation and suitability, and of what you can contribute to the programme. If you are applying for two programmes, you will need to submit two separate statements, both clearly and fully addressing why you are applying for each programme. Please make clear in each statement which programme it refers to.*

Your statement(s) should be typed and no longer than two sides of A4 paper. There is no fixed word limit, but we expect statement(s) to be no longer than 1,000 – 1,500 words.
In your statement(s), you may wish to discuss the following:
- *Motivation for undertaking the programme(s)*
- *Academic interests, strengths and background relevant to the programme(s)*
- *Areas of specific interest within the programme(s)*
- *Academic ambitions and/or research interests related to the programme(s)*
- *Any professional aspirations, and how academic work within the programme(s) might help you realise such aspirations*
- *Other relevant information, such as additional reading or research, work or other relevant experience that has informed your decision to apply for the particular programme(s)*
- *Please note: some programmes have other specific requirements for statements – these are outlined on this page.*

NYU/Stern, MSc in Quantitative Finance:

Essay 1: Professional Aspirations
(maximum 500 words)
1. Why do you wish to pursue this degree?
2. What do you see yourself doing professionally upon graduation?
The admissions committee gives great weight to this essay in evaluating your preparation for the program and enables us to understand your professional focus and commitment to the program. Before writing your essay, you should research the program and make sure you understand the different components, and be clear about your professional short term career goal/s post graduation. You may consider including details regarding your preparation plan to reach your career goal/s and how the program would contribute to achieving such goal/s, taking into account the program's China and Asia focus.
Essay 2: Personal Expression
Describe yourself to the Admissions Committee and to your future classmates using six images and corresponding captions. Your uploaded PDF should contain all of the following elements:
- A brief introduction or overview of your personal expression (no more than 3 sentences).
- Six images that help illustrate who you are.
- A one-sentence caption for each of the six images that helps explain why they were selected and are significant to you.

Note: Your visuals may include photos, infographics, drawings, or any other images that best describe you. Your document must be uploaded as a single PDF. The essay cannot be sent in physical form or be linked to a website.
Essay 3. **Additional Information** (optional)
(maximum 200 words)
Please provide any additional information that you would like to bring to the attention of the Admissions Committee. This may include current or past gaps in employment, recommender choice (for working professionals without direct supervisor recommendation), further explanation of your undergraduate record or self-reported academic transcript(s), plans to retake the GMAT, GRE, IELTS or TOEFL, or any other relevant information.

Other programs (such as Imperial College's Master in Climate Change, Management and Finance, for example) will even be more specific. In addition to the personal statement, applicants have to answer questions regarding professional experience (duties and responsibilities), career planning (*What key criteria does your target company use in their recruitment process?/What gaps in your skillset will you need to develop to prepare for this career?*) in a limited number of characters. Questions about your teaching experience are not to be ruled out:

Essay 1. Please describe any teaching experience you have had, in any subject, at any grade level. This can include but is not limited to experience as a teaching assistant, lab assistant, grader, tutor, or any other role in which you interacted with students or mentored your peers. 250 words max.
Essay 2. For those with teaching experience, describe a specific instance when you helped your student/students overcome a misunderstanding or understand a difficult concept. If you do not have any teaching experience, please describe an oral presentation or talk you gave that explains a particularly difficult concept. 250 words max.

When you have an optional question, asking for additional information, I suggest you fill it in. There are plenty of interesting things in your life that the mainstream questions do not allow to mention, be it the arts, competitive sports, teaching, volunteering activities, etc., and this is the place to do so. It will show another side of your personality and prove that there is more than just studying that matter for you.

– A graduate school **statement of purpose** is about what you want to do. Typically, it will showcase:
– professional/academic background;
– research interests;
– classes you wish to attend and professors you wish to work with;
– why the program is a good fit for your interests and academic goals;
– career goals.

An SOP is formal and academic. It looks forward, and focuses on what you intend to do with the degree you plan on acquiring.

– A **personal statement** is about who you are: it highlights your personal motivations for applying and why you are a good fit, your accomplishments, your motivations, the challenges you have faced and overcome. It allows the reader to get to know you (background, expectations, challenges and possible hardships you overcame).
– A **personal history statement** is more concerned with you as an overall person. Personal history statements allow you to be more personal.

There is definitely some overlap between the three. "Personal statement" often means the same thing as "statement of purpose": both the SOP and the PS serve the same overarching **purpose**: to make the admissions committee think you are a good fit and will be successful in the program for which you are applying. Both expect you to address your goals and interests in the field. Note that some departments call their statement neither statement or purpose nor personal statement but **statement of objectives**.

Statement of Purpose	Academic and professional background, skills, and accomplishments; research interests; academic/career goals; why this program is a good fit for you
Personal Statement	Personal motivation for applying; how you developed your research interests; any relevant experiences, challenges, or accomplishments

Which one will you have to actually write for your grad school applications? The answer to this question depends on what documents the school requires and how it defines the two types of essays. While some grad schools distinguish between the SOP and the PS, other schools **do not distinguish at all between them**. In fact, many grad programs use the terms **interchangeably**. So, I suggest combining qualities from both statements into one comprehensive statement.

Yet, to sum it up (and given that there is no hard and fast rule that might hold forever):

- statement of purpose = tight focus on academic work/research (may include a PH paragraph for MSc application).
- personal statement **only** = a snapshot of you as a person (priorities, judgment, self-reflection, overcoming adversity, diversity); in the UK, a short piece of writing about yourself and your interests that forms part of your university application.
- personal history statement = you as a person, motivation for applying, potential as a graduate student, educational, familial, cultural, socioeconomic, or personal experiences or challenges; gender identity; community services, outreach services, first-generation college status and struggles in life. Please note that the personal history statement is not meant to be a general autobiography.

Whatever you call them, statements are required whether you apply for an MSc/MEng/MA/AM or a PhD program. Yet, there is a marked difference between MSc/Meng and PhD applications. In the former case, the statement will include a **personal history paragraph** whereas in the latter personal references will seldom if ever be included in the letter (except, perhaps in the conclusion and in passing). In the former case, the statement will be divided into five parts whereas in the latter, four parts will suffice.

Sometimes the **personal statement** is what it portends to be: an essay on your personal and not academic life. It may be optional. It is focused on the themes of diversity, family background, personal challenges, etc.

Johns Hopkins is such a case:

> The Personal Statement is optional for all programs; check the instructions on your degree program website for specific criteria, if available. When included, this statement will help programs gain a more holistic understanding of you as an applicant.
> Provide a statement describing your personal background that is no more than one page in length. Elaborate on personal challenges or opportunities that have impacted your decision to pursue a graduate degree.

No matter which program, the SOP is one of trickiest components of the overall application since it cannot be easily and objectively evaluated. In the entire application, the statement of purpose is perhaps the only opportunity that the applicant has to ***intellectually arouse*** the admissions committee. For example, a novel research idea or problem that the applicant has been working on or would like to pursue, or a groundbreaking and useful application that you plan to develop or have been developing, a purposeful internship you have carried out are things that will get the committee excited and make them want to admit the candidate to their university.

American universities expect **more** than a letter of motivation in this statement. It **is** an **essay**, not a letter. The admissions committees want to know about your professional goals, but they expect a larger, global picture. Here is the opportunity to **explain yourself**, to open your personality, competencies, knowledge, skills, talents, vision and spirit to the admission committee.

The ***purpose*** part of the statement is central to the essay. The statement must prove a candidate's worthiness not just through their prior work, but with a detailed discussion of why the candidate chose the particular program, what they intend to do while pursuing the program and what they will do after having gained the education.

Chances are that you will probably apply to several graduate programs: choose just **one** to begin writing. Of course, the application deadlines might decide for you which that first program will be, yet if you take early steps you will have a wide array of programs to choose from. In general, I would recommend that you begin the writing process with a full statement rather than one that requires only 500 or 1,000 words.

This first statement will be the **backbone** for all other applications following. You will work on it carefully and thoroughly and once it has been drafted it will provide the fundamental elements in terms of choices and wording. You will keep it throughout and change only **one paragraph**, the one concerning the program you are applying for and that you will customize according to each school. Naturally, for the universities that require a tailored down statement (say, 250-500, 750 or 1,000 words) you will cut down the cheese and stick to the essential, that is the academic part or this one-off project you have in mind.

One of the challenging steps will be **to choose the program in which you want to specialize**. There are plenty of possibilities and one field might encompass several aspects of the science you want to study further (typically what if I enjoy operations research, optimization, statistics, machine learning and data science?). To help you along, here are a few steps you need to take:

- Write down the areas which you want to study in graduate school. It is the thought process you are developing, not a strait jacket. How will taking up this course of study help you achieve your long-term career goals?
- When and how did you become interested in that field of choice? What has stimulated your interest and strengthened your conviction that you are well suited for this field? How has your thought process evolved over time?
- How have you built your knowledge in this field (class, readings, conferences, seminars, project or lab work, conversations or meetings with experts already in the field)?
- How and what do you know about the program you are applying for and specifically how will it help you reach your goals?

– What has prompted you to choose a program/university/department? Give examples.
– Check the reputation of the teaching staff (NOT: `"they are well known", but rather: they focus on my favorite subject, ie "working on applying derivatives to the multiplication of purple frog eggs…"`; in other words, be specific or do not talk about them.)
– Check the lab facilities offered by the department.
– Check the research teams in the department.
– Explore the parallel programs with bridges.
– Find a program which is complementary to your studies.
– Check the location of college as it might be of some interest. In other words, the Bay Area, the Silicon Valley or Route 128 – close to universities – might foster your goal of becoming an entrepreneur.
– Why study abroad? How strong is your motivation to study abroad? (Professionally speaking. They don't care if you want to see Mt. Rushmore.)

2. Guidelines

The statement is your chance to show you can think about your goals (the purpose part) and that you can write clearly about your thoughts.

- What should a statement look like? It should be a **good story well told**, but not a romance.
- It should be **your story**, not someone else's. There is **no magic recipe**, no book of spells that contains the miracle expressions, phrases or vocabulary to draft a successful SOP. In the same way, attempting to draw your inspiration from reading reams of SOPs is a no-brainer. The only source of inspiration is **you**.
- In particular, NEVER PLAGIARIZE: US/UK programs check carefully for repeat with the help of their own detection software. In particular, **do not attempt to copy any part or sentence you will find in this guide**.
  Programs "take active steps to scrutinize and verify documents received during the application process. If they are unable to verify independently the accuracy of information supplied, your application may be cancelled and any offer or subsequent registration withdrawn. This also applies if we discover that your personal statement and any writing sample you submit is not your own work." (LSE guidelines)
- Nothing you write should be invented or made up. **Be truthful** and stick to the facts. You **are** a good story waiting to be told; you simply have to uncover it. There should be **passion** and **sincerity** for your essay to come off the page a bit, but never try to be something you are not. The essay must reflect your core, obviously with your **strengths**, pertinent weaknesses, and above all the desire to make the learning community stronger by your contribution. It is rare, at your age, to have lived through dramatic circumstances, but it will not hurt if the story you tell has drama.
- Favor **substance** over **sheen**. Your goal is not to impress the admissions committee with your writing but with the clarity of your intentions. **Content** does matter, yet **style** will be taken into account. **What is written without effort is generally read without pleasure**. In that respect, try to make a fresh, lively and unique statement. By distinguishing yourself from other stories you will put yourself ahead of the pack, you will make your personal statement **memorable**.

- **Edit** to make sure you get the message across. Do not worry about writing a piece of poetry or the next Pulitzer Prize novel. In particular, do not over-worry about transitions, as the French do when writing an essay for a philosophy class. Language is a means, not an end in itself. The end is the message you want to get across.
- **Be selective** about what you say to the admissions committee. You need not tell everything about yourself, only that which is **relevant** to your story. Remember that not only must a statement be well written, it should have **punch** and **impact**. Pick and choose in telling your story. What you choose to tell shows the committee what your **priorities** are and what you consider to be important.
- The admissions committee cares about what they call the "**sparkle quotient**" in their classes. They also want to know what students do with their free time, what makes them tick outside of class hours and whether they have demonstrated the ability to work with and help others – this is especially true for applications to MSc programs. This will be obvious in the **way** you talk about your activities. You do not describe "**sparkle**", it is found between the lines as you describe your motivation.
- There is **no magic formula** for admission, there are no right answers. Admissions officers attempt to get to know the prospective student as an individual and they want that student to provide sufficient context for an appropriate evaluation. They try to get to know the applicants as people, why they chose to do what they do, why they chose to go to their previous school, what they value most about their individual experiences and the impact of those experiences on their development as people. Explaining the **WHY** is more important than the **WHAT**.
- Last, the SOP is but **one part** of the application file. Along with transcripts, CV, LORs, it needs to be dealt with earnestly. An outstanding SOP may not get you there, but a poor one will certainly doom your chances.

3. Thinking it through: Who am I?

"Who you are" is reflected in the choices you have made in your life. If you have already written a resume (the US word for CV), you know that the facts you choose to write about give a brand image of yourself to the reader. A resume, however, is a picture lacking depth and breadth. The admissions committee is looking for "the core of the onion", they want to know **you**, not just what you have done. They want to know "**what makes you tick**", what your personality is and what it would bring to them. Your job is to open the door to your motivation and to let them inside. The problem, often, is finding the door yourself. You will need to do a great deal of self-assessment and reflection on your life and on what is important for you.

It would be helpful for you to pull out a notebook and use it as a **personal journal**: here you will jot down your thoughts and collect memories from the past. Note **facts** (events, experiences, achievements) which are relevant either to your choice of study or your future career choice. **Personal journaling** will help you develop a thought process which should put you beyond superficial, vague platitudes, to a more meaningful, personal vision of you not as a scientist or an engineer but as a unique individual. You will not necessarily write about these personal qualities, but being aware of them will help you make more pertinent choices for your essay, hopefully turning you from writing about the "what's" to describing the "why's". It would be useful to deepen this thought process throughout the summer preceding the application process. As you think of your past experiences and choices, keep asking **WHY** you chose that. Talk to those close to you about how THEY see you. Get closer to the heart of WHO you are and WHAT motivates you.

- Consider your own life and possibly that of your forebears, your origins, your upbringing, your travels, your homeland...
- Write about what your **intellectual influences** have been. What writers, scientists, professors, books, papers, have had the greatest influence on the development of your thought process. I suggest reading biographies or autobiographies to get a feel of how people became who they were.
- Write down all your **past accomplishments** – academic, extracurricular, social contributions, volunteering, military duty, teaching, sports – whatever you've done well in life.
- Make a list of **personal qualities** these events have helped you develop. In particular, find out the qualities you have discovered through your studies and activities (competence/creativity /dedication/enthusiasm/international vision/leadership skills/open-mindedness/potential for team work).
- Write down the things that you strongly **care** about.
- Think about educational **milestones** or **guideposts**: the seminal essay you wrote, the project you carried out, the lab work that you took part in.

> During my second year, I spent several months in the University's laboratories carrying out experiments aiming at detecting the emission of anti-matter by a radioactive source. This experience gave me a first overview of the work done by a research team. It confronted me with the technical problems that arise when using experimental devices.

- What is special, **unique, distinctive or impressive** about you or your life story? Write the story in your journal.
- Have you had to **overcome unusual obstacles** or **hardships** in your life?

> My dad is Turkish and came to France as a child with his parents, who were guest workers in the 1960s. My mother is German. Even though I was born and raised in France, there is the constant assumption that you do not belong, or that you do not identify with France like others around you. This in a way becomes a self-fulfilling prophecy – if people tell you that you do not fully belong often enough, you start wondering whether you do actually belong to the place where you were born and have lived your whole life. However, I have determined that I do not want my identity to be defined by national categories.

- What details of your **life** (personal or family history, notable accomplishments, people and events that have shaped or influenced your goals) have developed your character? Tell how.

> My kid sister is developmentally delayed. The twist of fate sensitized me early on to learning to live with disabilities. I grew up with a strong feeling of social responsibility and of obligation to help others. Not one to sit passively in anguish watching my sister grow, I went to work and find solutions to address her situation, among which occupational therapy. That led me to take an interest in painting, drawing and sculpting as a way to help teach basic skills

```
to the mentally impaired. My choice of Berkeley as my program of choice is not
exactly neutral, because of its reputation for commitment to handicapped access
and engagement in the fight for a more inclusive society.
```

- Make a list of your **strengths and outstanding characteristics**. Do a little research about yourself: ask parents, relatives, friends, and teachers what your strengths are. Next to each trait, list **evidence** from your life – things you have done – that prove your point. Demonstrate everything **by example**; do not say directly that you're a persistent person, **demonstrate** it. **The proof is in the pudding**.
- What makes you a stronger candidate for graduate school, more successful and effective in your field or profession than any other applicant? Look for **patterns** in the material you have brainstormed. Group similar ideas and events together. For example, does your passion for numbers show up in your performance in the state math competition and your summer job at the computer store? Was basketball about sports or about friendship? Was it about competition or integration?
- What **personal characteristics** do you possess that would enhance your prospects for success in completing the program and, more generally, in the field or profession you have chosen for yourself?
  - clarity of focus
  - commitment to others
  - compassion/empathy
  - creativity
  - determination
  - energy (adj. energetic)
  - generosity (adj. generous)
  - intellectual curiosity
  - integrity/honesty
  - maturity (adj. mature)
  - motivation
  - persistence
  - resourcefulness
  - risk-taking
  - seriousness
  - vision
- What **intellectual** or **scientific skills** and **abilities** do you possess?
  - ability to inspire others
  - analytical mind/strength
  - challenging the status quo
  - communication
  - critical thinking
  - goal-centered (motivation to pursue goals)
  - leadership
  - logical thinking
  - management
  - problem solving (ability to seek alternative solutions)
  - reasoning

– rigorous mind
– sense of organization
– sense of initiative
– team-working (ability to collaborate)

All those elements will provide a pool of information from which to draw the first draft of your essay.

4. Beginning to write your statement

Writing a personal statement is like constructing a building: you must first lay a solid foundation on which to place your creation. That foundation is your vision for the future, the motivation which drives you towards your choice of graduate programs. At the moment you may not have a vision for the future. You may be thinking: "I don't know what I want to do in five years' time, much less in ten years' time, I do not even know which specialization I want to choose". If you have not yet chosen your third-year BS/BA classes, then it is probably too early for you to start writing a statement. Yet, you will have to address your ambiguous future at some point, even if you know you will not make a concrete career choice until the end of your master's or doctoral program. Your most efficient tools will be the questions: What? Why? and So what? Use them at every fork in the road.

The juries in the application process are not asking you to sign a contract binding you to one field or one vision, they want to see if you have a **coherent project**, and if their institution truly has the keys to open the door to that pathway you are describing. A lack of vision will definitely be a hindrance to writing a good statement. If this vision is still foggy for you, then you will have to treat statement writing as an intellectual exercise, going through the process with what is a **potential** choice. Once your thought process about yourself is in place, it will transfer to other programs, other passions. That is why, starting a statement in the following fashion is **not acceptable** because of its fuzzy life vision:

*I built my first windmill at the age of sixteen. With my best friend, we found it entertaining to construct a thirty-centimeter-high model, using an old car fan, a plastic pipe and a bike dynamo to light a small bulb and cheer up a sophomore oral presentation. At that time, I did not know what to do with my life at all. I was only subconsciously obsessed by existential questions, asking myself how I could contribute to improving what I saw in the world around me. Too young to find convincing answers, I decided to study subjects I was good at, mainly Mathematics and Physics.

If, on the other hand, you have been acquiring expertise in several areas for the past five or six years, you are in a position to make some practical choices for the future. There is nothing vague about looking for the program that you want to apply for, judging its depth and rightness for you. However, this search will take time and personal questioning.

What the admissions committee reads **between the lines**: motivation, background, competence, intellectual curiosity and passion, capacity to work autonomously, team work experience, potential as a graduate student/scholar.

If you wish to re-orient yourself in graduate school, do not throw away your past education, but, on the opposite, use it as a strength by highlighting the skills you will be able to apply in graduate school.

```
Because I am an applicant from a non-traditional background, I can provide dif-
ferent perspectives to problems encountered in... and can even introduce vastly
different but equally effective approaches to solving these problems.
```

The way to address the applications is the following:

- **General**: Find no more than five or six institutions, read their general sites, then their graduate school sites, find the graduate programs which appeal to you.
- **Specific**: Compare the different graduate programs. Make a list of their strengths and weaknesses. Choose the one which attracts you the most. Write your first statement for that program.
- **More specific**: Find out as much as you can about the program: Which courses? Which professors? Which research groups? Which field of research? Do they offer bridges to other domains? Most graduate schools do not make it easy for you to find the details. You are going to have to be very clever, like a good detective, to find concrete aspects. Find names of teachers, but do not limit yourself to one or two, for some may be on sabbatical just the year you will be there or about to retire as you apply, three or four is a good number.
- **Details**: If the program site does not offer enough in-depth description for you to react to, google the professors. Find out what they have published, look for a subject that attracts you, and go so far as to read the papers you find interesting, if not the abstracts.
- **Write**: now write a paragraph explaining why this department has the keys to your future.

This research will give you thoughts and vocabulary to describe your motivation. You must **be specific**. Generalities and vagueness will get your statement eliminated faster than you can blink.

III. The Opening Paragraph

1. General

"You've got to be very realistic about where you are, but very optimistic about where you can be."
(Steve Ballmer)

The lead or opening paragraph is the most important. It is here that you grab the reader's attention, or you lose it. Once you figure out this first paragraph, the remainder of the essay will be less problematic because you have the framework of what you are going to say. If there is drama in your story it will be introduced in the opening paragraph.

As a general rule, the introduction ought to include the **following elements** as can be seen in the following example:

- Source of your interest for the domain;
- Current academic status (senior student, taking a gap year...)
- Ambition (short and mid-term vision);
- The tools, skills, knowledge you are seeking at the XXX University...
- ... which fully justifies why you should apply for the program.

> In a 2019 conference *(source)*, Mark H., GE's Europe CEO spoke at length about the strategic impact of Big Data in today's companies' operations. Learning that every corporate decision can be influenced and optimized by computational methods was extremely inspiring. I was then a second-year student at the Ecole XXX, where I had been admitted in 2018 and the interest stirred by the speech shed light on avenues of study and research that I soon decided to embrace, eager to explore the myriad methods and strategies to help bring change to these organizations. I am currently enrolled (*status*) in the Entrepreneurship master's level program, with a major in Applied Mathematics and a minor in Innovation Management. My ambition is to acquire new skills (*justification*), so as to start a career in the advisory business services or the hi-tech, possibly in the automotive industry (*vision*) a domain at the cusp of innovation. Those are the reasons that have led me to apply to Stanford for its MS&E program.

The introduction, and particularly the first sentence, must be carefully thought out as it is supposed to whet the admissions committee's appetite for more. They must feel the need and the urge to go on reading your statement and check out who the author of the SOP is, her/his skills and background, ambition, purpose in applying.

To get readers past the first line, you must catch their attention: you need an introductory line or paragraph which announces your intention and makes them want to keep reading. A strong SOP should start like a thriller, or a detective story. It should be a **page turner**, something you **do not want to put down**. Therefore, it deserves particular care. If you have journaled long and deep enough, your opening line is written on the pages of your journal: it is a thought you have had, a word which was spoken to you, a line you have read, a passion you have lived… and it has a direct, or indirect, connection with your field of study.

Your opening line should connect with the reasoning behind your choice of studies, and light a clear path for you to describe your motivation in applying to this graduate program. Within this paragraph you might want to indicate your **status (year/level of studies)** and the **program** you are applying for and why. For example, the following introduction **does not meet** those standards.

> *When I was younger, I used to imagine myself as a scientist developing new technologies in a laboratory. About four years ago, I experienced a change of heart, when I began to view science in a much more multifaceted way. While many events contributed to this shift in my perceptions, I remember, in particular, my reactions after watching a fascinating documentary film on a solar electrification project in rural Brazil. What was most striking to me in the film was that although everybody would obviously benefit from this clean and inexpensive source of power, the project had to overcome numerous obstacles. The issues here were not technological, however, but involved the attitudes of the people affected by the project—their fear of change, mistrust, and greed. I understood at that point that technology is only one part of any solution to an environmental issue, and that scientists must be able to negotiate the human and economic aspects of new environmental policies and technologies in order to make them work.

In the following example, we have tried to show how an **unfocused lead** can be strengthened and turned into a **purposeful statement**.

> *The scientific education I have received at XXX, where I was admitted in 2015, rests on cross disciplinary courses, providing a general view of science yet helping to define a path where they all merge and are borne to fruition. That path for me pointed towards Mechanics, Physics and Computer Science that I chose to explore in my second year. The knowledge obtained in these three subjects allowed me to continue in the field that fascinates me: energy systems. Thus, currently a graduate student, I am majoring in a master's program called Energy of the Future. There are many issues around energy such as the development of these new energies, but above all the optimization of their implementation, the regulation of the electricity grid in a context of renewable energy strongly dependent on the meteorological conditions, and the understanding of

consumption trends for setting up smart grids. By choosing this specialization, I wish to improve my ability of analysis and bring computing solutions in applied problems in Energy. Second year classes complemented my knowledge in Flow Motion, Dynamic of the Atmosphere and Statistical Physics, and the comprehension of energy systems. Besides, Fundamentals of Programming and Algorithms class and the Machine Learning skills I learnt during my second-year internship gave me the opportunity to have technics and tools useful to the management and logistics of energy resources. One article in particular on the collection of the main issues for wind farm optimization in complex terrain led me to think that, although many new tools are at our disposal today, there is a vast technological field of multi-disciplinary investigation. MIT's Master's in Operation Research is the ideal fit to expand my knowledge in those fields, and that is why I have resolved to apply.

☞ Now a punchier and more impactful introduction would read like this:

I grew up in Brittany where wind power and shipbuilding combine to give the region a dynamic economic pull that, in a way, influenced my studies and the direction I want to take them. Following a program that embedded my knowledge in Math and Physics, I gained admission to XXX where I rekindled a long-standing interest for Mechanics (my father, a marine engineer may have had some influence here), expecting to build a career in civil engineering. The wind caught up with me and after an exciting second year internship in which I discovered and relied on machine learning and neural networks, I decided to mix my solid and fluid mechanics background with the more applied side of math, computer science, and machine learning. Several problems such as how and where to install wind turbine farms for maximum efficiency or energy production and consumption forecasting or flaw detection in energy devices have been promising fields of investigation and specialization I want to explore further so as to build a career as an expert in renewable energies, thus addressing topical issues and contributing, in however small a way to mitigating the carbon footprint. The MIT OR program, with its variety of classes is bound to strengthen my background, and that is why I am applying.

Another example:

*The landing of Philae on Churyumov–Gerasimenko, 12th November 2014, was a watershed of how I project myself into the future: studying Rosetta mission, my childhood dream has evolved into making concrete plans. Scientific missions are life-time projects with fascinating challenges: exploring space may bring the answer to 21st century issues such as pollution and overpopulation and improve scientific knowledge and technologies. This year, which is my final year at XXX, I am following a master's program in Mechanics and my ambition is to go on exploring the world of aerospace engineering and subsequently work on space exploration missions to develop innovative technologies that would ease the discovery of the solar system. I believe a Master's program in Aerospace/Astronautics in Stanford is the next step to pursue the development of my own ambitions.

☞ It was while competing for the 2017 Mars City Design Challenge that I grasped some of the key issues at stake in space exploration and the place still vacant for innovation and discovery in the aerospace industry. I headed a one-year team project whose aim was to design a Martian balloon for tourism. To do so, we used hydrogen and re-thought the balloon structure as well as the taking off and landing procedures. This project was forward looking but relevant at the same time: Martian balloons are now studied around the world. As the winner of the contest, I was invited to visit the Jet Propulsion Laboratory, SpaceX and Virgin Orbit, which further strengthened my interest for the field. This year, which is my final year at XXX, I am following a master's program in Mechanics and my ambition is to go on exploring the world of aerospace engineering and subsequently work on space exploration missions to develop innovative technologies that will contribute to the understanding of the solar system. Stanford's Master of Science program in Aeronautics and Astronautics is the next best step to fulfil my ambitions.

Here are examples of how a somewhat **weak introduction** can be turned into a **cogent one**:

*At the time of the adoption of the euro in France, I began concerning myself with the economic consequences of money policies. I was then studying high-level mathematics, physics, and computer science. I gained strong analytical skills and enjoyed great success in my scientific courses. Then, during my first year at XXX, I shifted focus from mathematics to economics because of my growing interest in macroeconomics, particularly my interest in exchange rates
☞ The advent of the euro was a game changer that immediately caught my imagination for the boundless challenges and promises it could bring. I was then studying pure sciences and, upon my enrolment at XXX, I chose to shift my sights towards economics so as to grasp the intricacies of monetary policy, while leaning on strong analytical and reasoning skills gained in my undergraduate studies.

OR:
*I have travelled a lot around the third world, where I have seen the bad effects of ecological catastrophe. When I was in Bangkok, I never saw the sun because it was covered by a cloud of pollution. In Tanzania, the inhabitants totally ignore the dangers of waste, and I was shocked to see everybody innocently leaving old batteries on the ground. I will probably never see the snows of Kilimanjaro again, since they might well have disappeared in the next twenty years. It is impossible for me to remain unaffected by such tragedies. I have a strong desire to work as an environmental consultant in countries of the third world, so as to concretely improve environmental practice and awareness. I want to develop the skills I need to be effective in this field, which is why I am applying to enter the Atmosphere/Energy program to obtain a Master of Science at Stanford University.

☞ Extensive traveling around the world has been instrumental in exposing the harm wreaked by environmental disaster. Be it the pall of pollution shrouding Bangkok, the heaps of waste piling up in Dar es-Salaam or the use of biomass-fueled cookstoves in Nairobi, they are all evidence of man's wanton neglect of a planet whose resources are getting scanter by the year. Trained in the hard sciences and endowed with strong quantitative skills, I believe it is the duty of the scientist I aspire to become to tackle head-on the problems brought about by rampant urbanization and unregulated industrialization in countries stricken by the scourge of underdevelopment. My ambition is to contribute to take up the challenges at the origins of global warming and climate change in the third world, possibly as a consultant with an international organization. Eager to round out my training, I am applying to Stanford for its Atmosphere/Energy graduate program.

OR:

*The coin collection that I started when I was young was my first step towards the world of finance. Indeed, even if I started it to keep elements that would remember me the countries I had visited, I realized later that my motivation was, in fact, that coins were a perfect materialization of the link between mathematics (their numerical value), today's world (engraved in the heads side) and concrete results (money is a key to make things happen). In order to have this motivation throughout my life, I engaged myself on the path to financial mathematics which is also a bridge-material linking those three elements, and a 2017 research project dealing with the correlation factor in high frequency trading strengthened my decision to become a financial engineer.

☞ Who could have surmised that the step between numismatics and the world of finance was to be so short? When I started collecting coins along the various journeys I would take abroad with my family, they were reminders not only of the story of the travel but also insights into the history of the countries we were visiting. Specie was the perfect materialization of the link between mathematics (the numerical value), geography (engraved on the heads side) and a medium of exchange (doesn't money make the world go round?). Today, I see financial mathematics not only as a continuation of an early interest but also as a bridge merging those different elements into one: the link between advanced sciences, geopolitics and concrete results is clear and appeals to me.

The introduction might also be the place where you mention your **origins**, **education** and **values**. Quite often, those elements might find their way in the PHS, but highlighting them straight from the start does not hurt.

A Lebanese student at Sorbonne University in the Financial Engineering department, brought up on my culture's old values of dignity, loyalty, care for others and the search for wisdom, my ambition is to create, or at least help to work towards, a safer global financial environment where the preservation of the public interest takes precedence over private greed. As I go back and forth to

Lebanon, meeting with the underprivileged people who yearn to escape unemployment and poverty, I am convinced I have a role to play in rebuilding my country and making it a better place for all.

2. Elements to include in the introduction

There are a certain number of things that ought to be included into the paragraph, although, once again, it is all a matter of personality and originality.

- I recommend you should tackle the subject directly. Do not waste time and words: an SOP is short, and the admissions officers have a thousand of them to process before making a decision.
- You may start with a question, or a couple of questions that will pose the problem you are intent on working on straight from the start.

How much can the study of one type of waves tell us about the ocean? This is a question I became able to answer to a certain extent thanks to a research project I have done this year on the stability of internal gravity waves in the ocean. Understanding that specific phenomenon might partially explain the mixing observed in the ocean and therefore help with modeling the global climate. Working on a particular technical point actually makes it possible to better comprehend more global issues. This project, supervised by J.M. C. in the hydrodynamics laboratory of University XXX, has definitely made me want to contribute to solve complex environmental issues in studying the scientific problems they raise. This is why I am now applying for the MSc in Environmental Engineering at Imperial College.

- If you have a **theme**, or a **thread** that you want to include in the SOP, here is the place to start. Building an essay around a theme is eminently difficult. A theme strings all paragraphs together into a comprehensible whole. Yet, it confers a coherence and cohesion to the whole statement. Thus, what was said in the introduction...

The rigor, exactness and rationality of science have always attracted me. It probably started with my grandfather's numerous stories of managing constructions, such as the Basilica of Yamoussoukro (the largest church in the world), for I had "caught" his energy and enthusiasm for engineering.

...can be echoed in the conclusion:

Needless to say, the proximity to the most important financial center in the World would be an enriching and exciting experience. In the future, I will never build the world's largest church, but with your help, I might just become a financial engineer who makes a difference.

Or, in the introduction…

> When I saw the Millau Viaduct for the first time, I was struck by the combination of hugeness and elegance of this cable-stayed bridge. The design and technological solutions adopted in its construction enable the structure to fully integrate into its environment, as if it had been there forever. This unique construction will stand for centuries and, from day one, has proven useful to a multitude of people.

…and in the conclusion:

> The idea of being part of a team that works together on the creation of a unique and lasting structure like the Millau Viaduct is thrilling to me. The constant search for technological and environmental innovations, to improve the solidity, efficiency and elegance of structures, makes the construction industry a challenging one. Each project is different, because of client expectations, environmental, social, and economic issues, or simply due to the architect's creativity. As a project engineer in a construction firm, I will put all of my energy and training into overcoming the unique challenges involved in bringing a construction project to life. A Master in Construction Engineering from Stanford will prepare me fully for this task.

- Not all life stories can be dramatic obviously. The most difficult is probably **to find an angle explaining the origin of your interest for the science in question**. Ask yourself: when and how did you become interested in that field of choice? What has stimulated your interest and strengthened your conviction that you are well suited for this field? How have you built your knowledge in this field (class, readings, conferences, seminars, work, conversations or meetings with experts already in the field)? The question is thus how to make your story interesting? Finding an angle or hook is vital. Among the possible angles:

  – The **science** itself:

> Computer science took on its full meaning in the course of a collaborative scientific research project on railway scheduling which I carried out last year at XXX, where I am currently a final year student. Having committed to a rigorous training in theoretical sciences—among which mathematics played a major role—it was exciting to find out that abstract tools could and would bring about concrete solutions to real-life problems.

> Living in Indonesia and Burma for five years, I experienced frequent power outages, due either to insufficient electricity production or to obsolete and incomplete electric networks. The memory of these events took on importance of its own when I began deepening my scientific vision and realized that the electricity that comes out of our power sockets is a product that, unlike any

other, can hardly be stored efficiently and requires continuous transportation. This is a domain where good decisions go unnoticed, but where every mistake has a huge impact on society. I felt grateful then that I had been building strong foundations in mathematics and physics in the undergraduate program, for I was beginning to realize this was the field in which I wanted to specialize. The concern for carbon-free energy came later, when I learned more about electricity production in France.

While preparing for the International Physics Olympiads, my professor explained that modern physics appeared at a time when people thought they knew it all, except for a couple of spots that did not seem important until they evolved into relativity and quantum physics. It is this potential explosion of knowledge, this discovery of unsuspected solutions that attracts me to the field. Mathematics and physics became passions during my studies. I found it fascinating to study normal objects from different points of view, such as the physical qualities of a vibrating ideal string compared with a piano string (an instrument I knew well because I had been playing it for ten years), but the passion came when I saw how many bridges could be built among the different domains to solve concrete problems. I slowly came to realize that my dream of being a researcher was actually a project for the future.

Although I have been drawn towards the hard sciences since early on, many events in my life have shaped my particular interests. Discovering what lay at the frontier of computer graphics was one such life-changing event. It happened in 2009, when I had just begun to wonder about the possibilities of 3D movies in the future. Square Picture sent me a powerful response: it was possible to reproduce reality. This was what I thought after I had viewed *Final Fantasy: The Spirits Within*. Graphic arts engineers had successfully created skin whose texture seemed real, with all its imperfections, and had made a quantum leap in facial animation. Since that day my passion for these kinds of images has grown endlessly, both in a technical and in an artistic sense.

– A **high school** or **college course**:

A class in kinematics when I was in 12th grade piqued my curiosity and opened my eyes to how essential a role physics could play. We had to study the movement of a tennis ball from the moment it left the racket after a smash. We found the analytical law behind the ball movement by computing the equation of the trajectory. However, limited that experiment was, it showed the power of science governing the laws of Nature. That interest gradually bloomed into passion, which was strengthened further when I visited the GANIL (Great National Heavy Ion Accelerator) and discovered particle physics. I was shown around facilities, and had lengthy discussions with physicists on site. Today, it has become the field I definitely want to work in.

With hindsight, I can say that my interest for networks grew after I attended a class on *Probabilities, Protocols and Algorithms in Networks* at the beginning of this academic year. I was then looking for a field that would enable me to combine my theoretical knowledge in various subjects but also one with a strong emphasis on applied research. Actually, after two years of pluri-disciplinary studies at XXX, I am now determined to go further into the specialized field of networks and that is why I am applying for an MSc degree in Electrical Engineering.

I discovered my interest in the field of robotics and artificial intelligence last year during a course I was taking–in the humanities and social sciences department, ironically–on "brain and cognition." The class examined how, among other things, the human brain manages to precisely and rapidly analyze the information of "pixels" of light seen by our eyes, so as to retrieve forms and objects and thereby understand the 3D world around us. Studying this process made me better understand my growing passion for robotics and artificial intelligence, transforming this passion into an actual career goal.

– A **conference** you attended:

Last year, listening to a conference speaker talk about his life as a quant for a bulge-bracket French investment bank, I realized that this was a job that would allow me to use my math and computer skills in a stimulating environment. The diversity of tasks truly spoke to me: using modeling in long-term research projects, talking with traders and structurers, from whom I would learn much.

Professor Ivar Ekeland's speech on Nobel Prize winner John Nash made me realize that mathematics has a key role in today's developments. Indeed, this experience was pivotal in my academic curriculum and encouraged me to study different mathematical fields, such as game theory, signal processing, operations research, finance, and "econophysics".

It was in 2013 that while I was listening to Cécile Renouard(1) it all started to make sense. In a conference on the theme of "Being helpful rather than helping oneself", she spoke of climate change, and explained in a crystal-clear manner that there was no other choice but look squarely at the problem, decide on an action plan, and commit oneself to acting on it. All the dots connected: since my childhood, I had spent my time marveling at nature, hiking and bird spotting in the Swiss Alps, and feeling a strong concern for the environment. At the same time, my curiosity had driven me to walk down a scientific path which was to lead me to the Ecole XXX, where I am currently a third-year student. There, while I acquired broad-based scientific competences, my interest for nature study grew. Eager to know how science at the forefront can help in the fight for the preservation of the environment, I am applying to UC Berkeley's Environmental Engineering MS program.

(1) Cécile Renouard, Doctor in Social Ethics, Institut de la Recherche et de l'Enseignement sur la Négociation en Europe (IRENE)

In 2017, Thomas Pesquet, an ESA astronaut, gave a series of lectures about the future of space exploration at the Paris-Saclay University, where I was a final year undergraduate student. I was carried away by the impassioned recounting he made of his space flights, as well as his presentation of the breakthroughs and challenges arising in Aeronautics and Astronautics. Those events were defining moments which definitely convinced me that those were fields I wanted to explore further all the more so as they combined my strong interest not only for science and technology but also for cultural and intellectual adventures. That is the reason why I am applying for a Master of Science at Stanford's Aeronautics and Astronautics Department, my objective being to carry on with a PhD.

Listening to French astronaut Jean-François Clervoy talk about life on the MIR station last year not only confirmed my interest in the study of space, it convinced me that I was capable of succeeding. I grew up in an aeronautical environment, basking in the excitement of discoveries and a pioneer spirit, but I preferred the more challenging field of astronautics as I know it is a strategic issue for the future of Earth. I chose the French Air Force for my first-year leadership training, where I was granted the exceptional opportunity to fly in a fighter plane and fighter helicopters, thus encouraging me to pursue a vocation in designing high-technology flying objects. Clervoy's words stating that "becoming an astronaut is a matter of both encounters and motivation" rang true to me, but I knew I would have to persevere before I actually reached a career in the aerospace industry.

"If the rest of the world consumes as Americans do, we will need five additional planets to survive" said Professor Jean-Marc Jancovici, a well-known French engineer and energy and climate expert. He was invited to give a conference at my university during which he impressed by the bluntness of his speech; above all, he triggered the reflection that led me to my actual interest, developing smart grids.

– A **science article** you came across by chance or that you read on purpose, in class, for example or for a project:

I especially appreciated the quantum physics classes. I was fascinated by the fact that there are only a few equations that describe every single phenomenon we can observe. However, what amazes me even more is the fact these equations do not lead to a simplistic world, mainly because it is impossible to know the exact behavior of a very large system. Reading P. W. Anderson's paper More Is Different confirmed my choice to study the physics of large systems through a statistical physics class and interacting systems through a condensed matter class. I enjoyed both classes for they allowed me to understand common devices, such as semi-conductors, through both fundamental physics and mathematics.

– A **science book** or **textbook** that raised your awareness:

Last summer, while reading Steven Shreve's opus on *Stochastic Calculus for Finance,* I had an epiphany. Shreve's implementation of abstract theorems to practical and concrete issues led me to realize that I had finally discovered what I had been searching for—something that makes me passionate. As I continued through the textbook, I felt like an explorer, discovering not only theory and models but also their applications to the world of financial markets. For example, I learned how traders make decisions and strategies to build portfolios that are immune to market trends. The glimpse into this vat of knowledge only stimulated my curiosity.

I recently came across *Quarantine*, a novel by Greg Egan, in which he describes a world where nanotechnologies are used in daily life. For example, nanorobots are deployed in the human brain to rearrange neurons. Of course, this remains fiction. But, for how long? Reading Egan's work led me to ponder about the future, and raised an intriguing question: how to develop nanorobots for medical applications, and unlock the potential of such technologies to improve human life.

"If morality represents the ideal world, then economics represents the actual world" (*Freakonomics*). When Econometrics Professor Franck Q. advised me to read Stephen Dubner and Steven Levitt's book, he could not foresee how much it would change my perception of science. Indeed, following the two-year intensive scientific undergraduate program prior to my admission to XXX in 2018, I had acquired theoretical tools which I imagined could not connect directly to real life. It dawned on me then that science, through rigorous mathematics and economics, could apprehend the way people behaved and could help us improve everyday life by making the right choices. Actually, science can bring ideas to life by successfully channeling creativity towards innovative projects. My goal is to explore those venues further and take part in that process, which is why I have chosen to apply for the MS&E program at Stanford.

– A **professor** that inspired you:

One of my first teachers of science was the German physicist Carl von Weizsäcker, who had been an apprentice to the quantum theorist Werner Heisenberg. Dr. Weizsäcker was kind enough to give me some formal tutorials on scientific topics. I confess that while listening to him I could grasp the intricacies of the full argument, but when the sessions were over there was often not a great deal of his explanation left behind. Goaded by his advice and intrigued by his intuitions, I chose to probe the field further and apply to selective programs that would take me to understanding better a field I found more and more appealing, if not alluring.

– An undergraduate **school project**:

My interest for computer science was aroused while doing an undergraduate project in which I implemented the BSP tree hidden surface algorithm. The objective was to study and understand the algorithm and the influence of its parameters, which eventually led to drawing up a statistical study on the size of the obtained trees. My knowledge of computer science has broadened since then, and after several years of scientific studies that have led me to raise more fundamental questions, I have narrowed my interest to programming languages, which is the exciting field of research I definitely want to explore.

My interest for Statistical Genetics arose while I was doing a three-month research internship at the Cambridge Research Institute in the summer of 2016. My research project, which I carried out under the supervision of Prof. Carlos C. and Dr. Oscar R., consisted in finding ways to improve the analysis of DNA microarrays data. The newest generation of DNA microarrays, which contains both polymorphic (SNP) and non-polymorphic probes, has been used to investigate DNA copy number aberrations in breast tumor samples. I was faced with two kinds of challenges: first, microarrays contain two types of probes; second, the samples were made up of an admixture of normal and tumoral cells, making data interpretation difficult. Yet, to my knowledge, no existing algorithm had been found to address tissue heterogeneity and handle both probe types. I eventually came up with a two-step method to solve this problem, which uses change-point analysis and maximum likelihood estimation. This is exactly the type of strategies I am eager to investigate in order to better understand and explain how tumoral cells mutate and proliferate. This is the reason why I have decided to apply to the Genomic Medicine and Statistics Programme, hosted by the Wellcome Trust Center for Human Genetics, for a DPhil in Statistical Genetics.

My first experience of industry goes back to the Shell Eco Marathon Challenge in 2009 when a team of eight students, which I was in charge of, led a project whose goal was to create a car-prototype, which would be as fuel-efficient as possible. We worked in collaboration with the staff from the PSA Peugeot-Citroen car maker, comprising aerodynamicists, as well as design engineers and technicians. The former helped us in the preliminary legwork, to determine the best shape possible taking into account the body constraints, the latter machining the body mold with the help of a 15-foot-high digital mill. Throughout the project we discovered the different industrial stages, from the conception of the car on paper to the completion of the final product, the car itself, via wind tunnel testing, the computer-aided design of the vehicle, the manufacturing of the mold, as well as the creation of the carbon-Kevlar body. One of the most significant moments in the project was the 40-hour machining of the streamlined mold as we could see with our own eyes the project gradually come to life and, in a way, a dream come true. As leader of the year-long project, I kept an eye on all the different phases, first defining the objectives and making sure the deadlines were met, but also raising funds from PSA and managing a $20,000 undertaking. There were technical glitches that required quick solutions and compromises so as to be operational on D-Day, and human problems too—which is natural when you deal with people from various backgrounds—so as to make sure the team worked harmoniously at the same pace and in the same directions, whatever the assignments and the tasks. It was highly rewarding because it actually involved building something from scratch, with some knowledge and not much know-how at the beginning but above all a learning experience in which we could apply what we had studied in class to a concrete objective. It was all a fascinating process, in which I did put into practice my scientific background (I am a third-year student at one of France's premier universities for sciences) and which has clearly given an impetus to a career which I want to pursue in manufacturing management by applying to the University of Cambridge for an MPhil in Industrial Systems, Manufacture and Management.

– An **internship** you carried out recently or relevant **work experience**. Note that an internship is professional (and paid) work experience and will be considered in your application.

Working for Zorrino, an NGO that coordinates humanitarian programs in South and Central America and of which I am the president, I flew to Guatemala in July 2014, to build a greenhouse for a Mayan community. Monitoring the $13,000 project, in collaboration with our local and European partners, spending several weeks overseeing the construction, and managing a twenty-people team reinforced my ambition to become a leadership professional in the construction industry. After such a rewarding experience, I have made up my mind to broaden my training. Not only do I want to use my scientific skills to master construction concepts but I also intend to gain a strong background in engineering and management methods. I do believe that Stanford's Construction Engineering and Management MSc program can help me fulfill my goals.

– Recent **research experience**:

The opportunities to address challenges in computational biology through novel machine learning methods were made evident to me when I interned at Prof. Nir Y's lab at UC Berkeley in 2019. During these six months, my research focused on a modeling problem central to the analysis of scRNA-seq data. Spurred on by Prof. Michael I. J's enthusiastic comments about the model that I had developed and the acceptance of the paper[1] as a spotlight talk and a poster to the 2019 MCLB conference in Vancouver, Canada, this fruitful research experience further motivated me to expand my knowledge in fields related to machine learning and apply it to challenges in biology and health. This is why I am applying to the position of Doctoral student in Machine Learning in Computational Biology" at KTH.

1 XXX *et al.*, "Detecting Zero-Inflated Genes in Single-Cell Transcriptomics Data", 2019.

– **Observation** from past experience:

My interest for nature is not recent. As I belong to a family from France's corn belt, I was introduced to an early age to all the problems that farmers meet in managing their agricultural estates. I remember vividly how, after heavy rainfalls occurring once the fields had been manured, the runoff water laden with toxic waste turned orange and flowed into the nearby lakes and killed off all the fish. That ecological disaster, however small its scale, left a deep impression in my teenage mind and aroused my concern for the environment. It also showed me that one of the main concerns of a scientist must always be for the long-term consequences of her or his discoveries and the stakes that such discoveries raise.

I was repelled at first, but finally moved my hand toward the wet, rough skin of the snake, just to see how it felt, surprisingly soft and warm on my skin. A few days later I came across a giant spider web, and was fascinated by its original design and amazing resistance, able to retain enormous water drops. My interest in materials stemmed from this experience in Amazonia, whose diverse and extreme natural environment still lives vividly in my memory. If my passion for materials was first built on observation of nature, it is fitting that environmental concerns play a major role in fueling that passion. Emerging ecological constraints require very efficient materials and open the door to creative developments in material science to meet this challenge.

I was made aware of water issues when my family moved to Rambouillet, which is my hometown. Shortly after our arrival - I was then 11 years old - the poisoning of the aquifer led us and the whole community to use bottled water only, the authorities having forbidden to drink tap water. My concern for water safety was to grow over the years, during the walks I would take in the region, watching lakes getting increasingly eutrophic. It became acute when, doing a work placement in Egypt, I watched the damage pollutants had inflicted to the legendary Nile and attended disquieting lectures on the exhaustion of the country's water resources. There are crying needs for safe water in both developed and developing countries: it is my desire to address those problems and apply new solutions, especially by way of biological techniques and methods. So as to specialize in water issues and its treatment, I have decided to apply to Stanford for an MSc in Environmental and Water Studies and more particularly for the subprogram Environmental Engineering and Science.

– **Volunteer work experience**:

I was first confronted to the problem of water shortage two summers ago, as I was doing volunteer work in a primary school in Burkina. To cope with the water crisis, the government had to resort to special canon on the capital to trigger rainfall and relieve the inhabitants. Later, traveling to Mali, I realized the water problem was also acute as there was no equipment, not even wells, to meet the water needs of the communities. Such experiences made me aware of how precious a commodity water can be, especially in developing countries. After a two-year program for the entrance examinations to the *grandes écoles*, I was admitted to XXX and this year I have chosen to specialize in chemistry to explore the field of water management further. An additional trip to Guatemala last Summer stiffened my resolve and that is why I've made up my mind to apply to… for an MSc in…

– Exceptional **military duty period**:

Beyond the world of academia, my life has enriched me in different but none the least exciting ways. One of the most memorable experiences is when I served as a cadet officer on the *Charles de Gaulle* aircraft-carrier. The microcosm on board makes social relationships more intense and therefore forces you sometimes to compromise, sometimes to defend your opinions with strength and authority, and overall, helps shape your personality in both an assertive and open-minded way. Another aspect of life on board is the on-going activity and agitation, as hundreds of people work together, day in, day out, for the boat to fulfil her mission. This is the kind of stimulating and intense environment, in which you have to give the best of yourself and that I would certainly cherish in my professional life.

During my year of leadership training, I chose to be a lieutenant in the French National Gendarmerie. I was appointed first to the Child Abuse & Exploitation unit and later to the Narcotics unit. The thrill-seeker that I am was turned on by the investigating, but the overall experience proved to be frightening in many aspects. In the child-abuse unit I faced psychological dilemmas. Collecting the testimony of sexually abused kids was heart-rending, often unbearable, but I had to learn to get a grip on myself when it came to questioning their remorseless torturers. It was harder than I expected it to be, and I learned the importance of team support. In the narcotics unit, I was confronted with other kinds of misery. Watching drug-addicts suffering withdrawal symptoms was troubling, but it was harrowing dealing with frightened innocent children who did not understand why you had smashed into their home at 06:00 AM and why you were handcuffing their parents. I had to explain to them why they had to go with social workers while their parents had to be in police custody. Fortunately for me, I discovered how a real team spirit can be helpful in those situations. I was relieved to be able to talk about my feelings with them and from that moment I became an efficient team member able to listen and share with teammates.

I had the incredible opportunity to play an active role on the warship *Dumont D'Urville* based in French Polynesia. As a security officer, I was given the chance to carry out a study about the buoyancy of this ship. First, I calculated the vessel's reaction to flooding and found the best way to stabilize the structure. Secondly, I found the optimal configuration of the ballast tanks to set the tilt angle for the critical beaching stage. Then, I went a step further and looked into another area I found fascinating, discovering the best ballast management to optimize fuel consumption. Not only did this experience allow me to apply the mechanics I had already learned, it revealed my interest for the fields of aerodynamics and energy.

I chose to enter the French Navy Commandos to learn if I could meet the challenge, and actually experienced a defining moment in my life. I learned that, given minimal physical training, mental strength was a major quality to achieving my goals. However, in this highly competitive environment, it took a group of cooperating individuals to succeed.

Actually, not being cut off from reality is one of the reasons why I chose to do my military service in the Police Force. I taught Math, French and basic military rules to help young gendarmes prepare for their examination. I did investigative work, attended post-mortems, was part of rescue teams and participated in several arrests. I also did a shift on the vice squad where I had to deal with the harsh realities of battered and abused children. By coping with painful situations, it developed my interest in working with and among people.

Following my high school studies, I joined the Naval Academy and subsequently the Navy as a midshipman. At some point, I had a crew of twenty under my orders during navigation and watch time, duties that made it both technically and humanly demanding considering my limited experience. I learned how to command, make quick decisions in crisis time and build balanced relationships with subordinates. On a daily basis, I tutored a dozen young midshipmen from deprived backgrounds who had found in the Navy a way to build a career of their own. Teaching them the basics of military discipline along with some math showed me how valuable knowledge is.

– A **personal experience** that has sensitized you to a problem (travel, injury, disease, trauma, war) might also be used:

Last winter, I signed up for the France/Morocco 4L Trophy Raid, a team effort to deliver school and sport supplies to disadvantaged families in remote parts of the Sahara Desert. It was my first humanitarian experience. At one point during the raid, I installed a solar panel on the roof of a mud hut. I will never forget the smiles on the faces of the family when the light bulb hanging from the ceiling inside lit up. It was the first time they used electricity. This experience convinced me to pursue graduate studies and undertake a career dedicated to the environment and renewable energy.

August 2006. For two weeks now, war has been raging in the South of Lebanon and around Jounieh, the town I hail from. As gas and electricity were cut off, as roads were closed, I received a call from a friend working for the Red Cross

> pleading to come and help. Without a flicker of hesitation, I entered the fray. The following day I joined the few volunteers in downtown Beirut, packaging and delivering food, medicine and clothes to helpless refugees whose homes had been destroyed in the shelling. This experience left a lasting memory and, in an uncanny way, has today steered my academic path in the direction of humanitarian supply chain management. Now in third year at XXX, a leading college for theoretical sciences, I am specializing in Operations Research. I am eager to deepen my knowledge and experience by pursuing my graduate work in MIT's Operations Research Center's Master of Science program.

> Six months ago, a close friend of mine passed away after fighting an undiagnosed illness. The difficulty of physicians to formulate a diagnosis showed me how far we still are from understanding the human body. Recent advances in technology were powerless to help doctors detect what ended up killing my friend then. As an aspiring scientist trying to decide which area of the engineering profession to strive in, witnessing this situation was an eye opener. I decided that I wanted to be part of the project of developing more advanced, cheaper, and more effective medical tools and biotechnologies to combat diseases. In order to put my scientific abilities to work for these ends, however, I first need to obtain graduate level training in the field of bioengineering, and I see no better place to do this than in the Department of Mechanical Engineering at the University of California at Berkeley.

3. The PhD application

When considering a PhD application, start with **seminal problems** you have been faced with in the course of your recent studies or research and in the field you are interested in. You can raise those problems under the guise of questions (a couple of those problems will do, not a list and even less a catalog). Mention some **broad but scientific issues** that you are eager to explore or investigate, and which are naturally in relation with the program you are applying to. Say that those problems take time to be explored/investigated and amply justify why you are applying for a PhD program. Note that what is true for a PhD can also be true for an MSc application.

> The pursuit of a PhD has become a necessity given my need to satiate my intellectual and scientific curiosity for seeking deeper knowledge in the area.

> In the course of my undergraduate years, I have become convinced that a doctoral program is core to the fulfillment of my intellectual interests and to serve as the foundation of a career I envision at the top of the profession. My objective is to serve in a leadership role while contributing to research and education.

Naturally, you can also start with a research experience or internship in which you were confronted to tractable problems that need time to parse and plumb. (See examples in Part V)

4. Avoiding the pitfalls

- The introduction is a statement, showing a **direction**. All the information inside must be relevant. Which is **not the case in these examples** as no information shows any purpose in the statement if only vaguely.

> *For the time being, I have been quite fortunate. I think I have succeeded in almost everything I have undertaken in my life. My success is linked to my natural taste for competition. My competitive nature has not only been honed through rigorous academics, but also through sports. At the age of fifteen, after winning the French Junior Show-Jumping Championship, I almost chose to become a professional rider. Instead, I elected to focus my competitive spirit on academics. In fact, I have always sought out the most challenging academic opportunities. Today, this facet of my personality, coupled with a strong desire to gain international experience, has led me to apply for the highly-selective Master of Science in Financial Engineering at Columbia University.
>
> *The unknown fascinates me. How to deal with it, where to take hold of it, how to become part of it are challenges I seek. It may seem like a tame beginning, but living with a Californian family for three months when I was younger, completely transformed me. I came back to my provincial France knowing I had acquired a taste for adventure. I then had to wait until I started studying physics to be completely thrilled: I had found the science that offers the keys to understanding what is around us. I knew physics would help me find the path I would take in the future.
>
> *Applying for an MSc degree in Environmental Engineering at Stanford University is a decision that I have carefully thought through. Today more than ever, the environment is at the core of everybody's preoccupations and is, by its implications and universality, both a fascinating and crucial field of study. Saying that the future of man relies on how well he will manage to cooperate with the world he lives in is not an exaggeration but a reality. That is why I want to be part of making changes in the way we are dealing with our environment.

- Do not write a **résumé in prose**. In particular, do not include information that is found elsewhere in the application. Your essay should not sound like an autobiography, travelogue or laundry list.
- Do not include information that doesn't support your thesis. All you have said should be **proved by example**.
- A strong introduction is one that avoids the pale, **bland and child-like story** telling format. Do not start your essay with a banality:

> "I was born in…", "My parents came from…", "I have always loved science", "I was born a scientist", "I have always wanted to become an engineer", etc.

If you insist on starting with a personal anecdote, these are acceptable beginnings:

> The smell. The persistent acrid stench of dirty water in stagnant pools. The opaque wastewater contrasting with the gaudy colors of floating plastic bags scattered along the open gutters. The stifling humidity of the equatorial climate, almost unbearable in the rainy season. And the market place, only a few yards away, where women in brightly-colored garments sell coconuts without even seeming to notice the overflowing water, carrying away the scraps indiscriminately discarded day after day.
> The sight of the open gutters of the town of Port Novo that my father, a Beninese civil engineer, was charged with renovating greatly impressed the twelve-year-old girl that I was then. Though young and still unable to grasp the technical aspects of this clean-up project, I was nevertheless acutely aware of what was at stake: being able to provide people with a reliable source of water and sanitary conditions, though often taken for granted in modern societies, is one of the first and most important steps in a country's development.
> On that June day in 2015, I resolved to acquire the scientific skills necessary to tackle these vital social problems. Following that goal, I left my family at the age of fifteen to study in France.

> At the foot of the Sainte-Victoire Mountain, one of the most typical sights of the Provence region in the south of France, the Bimont dam holds back 15 million cubic meters of water from the valley below. Climbing this mountain with my family year after year, I became impregnated with the dam's strength and harmony. Strength? Because civil engineers have tamed nature so well. Harmony? Because the dam merges perfectly into the luminous landscape of the region. This is where my passion for construction was born, and when I began making study choices that led me to Ecole XXX. If I am applying to the MIT MS program in Civil Engineering, with an emphasis in Structures and Materials, it is because my vision to become a design engineer has grown stronger with the years.

> Little did I know when I went to Spitak three years ago for the summer to build the roof of a school that this experience would spark my interest for solid mechanics. After Armenia was struck by an earthquake in 1989, it took time to rebuild, not only because of new stringent regulations but also because the town – which had been leveled to the ground – was displaced further east for reconstruction. It dawned on me that civil engineering was not only about structures but also about supporting the local economy. When one year later, some of the local children sent me their school results, it also proved that civil engineering affected both the physical and the social environment. In other words: no building means no education and hence no social or economic progress.

- Avoid anything **trite**: hobbies, events too far back, impersonal statements are no-brainers.
- Avoid **vague references** that smack of superficiality:

*My interest for the power of data to treat disease stems from a conference which I attended.

That is a no go as we will be wondering: *what conference, when, who delivered it, what was the topic?*

- Avoid the **banal** and **naive**:

*Today more than ever, the environment is at the core of everybody's preoccupations and is, by its implications and universality, both a fascinating and crucial field of study. Saying that the future of man relies on how well he will manage to cooperate with the world he lives in is not an exaggeration but a reality.

*My desire to work in the financial industry derives from the dynamism and unpredictability of this world.

*As I have shown throughout my career, I am someone who is not afraid of taking on heavy responsibilities and making difficult decisions—qualities that will help me to succeed in the world of finance.

*There is little doubt that particle physics and high energy physics are likely to be the fields in which physicists will achieve great breakthroughs in the years to come.

*More recently, the scarcity of fossil resources and global warming made me even more convinced that energy production is now a real challenge and that it is high time we developed alternative, more sustainable and less pollutant, sources of energy. I am thrilled at the idea of taking part in this challenge because it is vital to the survival of life on Earth as we know it. I have chosen to help the world get through this crisis by becoming a nuclear science expert. Indeed, I am convinced that nuclear power is one of our greatest assets to produce energy massively and progressively reduce carbon dioxide emissions.

*The increasing price of oil and the surge in energy demand throughout the world urge us to find solutions to meet the needs of developing countries such as China. The recent contracts signed by Areva in China confirm that nuclear energy will likely play a big part in the future energy picture. This is a crucial moment for the people who believe that nuclear energy is the solution, and, being one of these people, I look forward to playing a role in this trend.

*Actually, Dominique O., my professor of Physics before I entered University XXX, a gifted storyteller of Physics and also an admirable man, is the one who transmitted the virus to me. The virus of a whole life dedicated to the pursuit of truth.

- Avoid listing **impressive icons** who have graduated from your school blatantly placing yourself amongst their ranks.
- Avoid **references** to your childhood experiences, high school years; death of a grandparent, second-grade teacher, yourself at an early age, an experience when you were a teenager: the image of immaturity may stick in the minds of the admissions officers. Here are some examples **NOT** to follow:

*When I was 10 years old, I remember feeling more joy in opening a toy car and understanding how it worked than playing with it.

*In the *Three Little Pigs*, the Big Bad Wolf crafts a pedal helicopter from a bicycle. When I read it at the age of 8, I was fascinated by this invention, and my decision was made: "Mum, I want to be an inventor". It was the beginning of a passion for crafting, discovering and sciences that never left me.

*When I was 11, I was lucky enough to watch the retransmission of an Ariane 5 launch in a command: I was blown away by the skills of engineer that made possible to send a rocket into space, and I was touched by their emotion and their joy when the mission was deemed successful.

*As my mother is a dermatologist and my father a physicist in experimental particle physics, I grew up in a scientific environment. Without pressuring me into pursuing high studies, my father has transmitted me his interest for science and top-level technology.

*From a very young age, I have enjoyed mathematics, because of its reliance upon pure logical deduction.

*As a shipbuilder, my father passed his passion for boats on to me. What started as an unsophisticated pleasure, that of plying the waters off the Brittany coast, gradually turned out to more serious interrogation about flow dynamics of flow and shape design.

*I had an uncle who was a GP and who often talked to me about his patients. Always curious, I paid great attention, even though I hardly understood. I guess I recognized myself in his interest in helping people.

*My desire to work in the nuclear field can be traced back to 2015, when I visited a nuclear power plant, including part of the nuclear core, in the eastern part of France. I've always been fascinated by industrial facilities. My father manages a metallurgy plant and when I was young, I'd spend hours watching the machines, trying to figure out how they worked. In the power plant, I was amazed by the size and complexity of the engine room. The nuclear core was some kind of mysterious and mesmerizing place. I wondered how many people had been involved in the conception, design and construction. I wanted to know how it worked. Most important I knew I wanted to be part of an industrial, scientific and human challenge like this one. It is for this reason that I am applying to the Nuclear Engineering Program at Berkeley.

*Space was a childhood passion. When I was growing up, in Provence, my father bought me a telescope to gaze at the stars, and I never lost interest. After high school, I enlisted in the Army, and served in the Air Defense Command. Then, I enrolled at the University of Grenoble to study physics. I quickly found my way to the frontier of space research. Before graduating from college, I began working at ESA, through a program that allowed students to split their time between classes and the agency.

*My desire to study nuclear engineering is a very strong and old one. I used to live during my childhood not far from the greatest nuclear plant in Europe and since, this kind of energy has kept fascinating me.

*I will always remember the day where my grandparents gave me my first refracting telescope. Soon I would sneak out at night to gaze at the moon, the planets and the Milky Way.

*When at the age of 13 my father bought me my first stock for my birthday, I knew I wanted to become a quant.

*At the age of 9, I had the opportunity, through my dad, to attend the real-time broadcast launch evening of the Thaicom II satellite. This memorable evening triggered my interest in the aerospace domain.

*First, I was naturally introduced to the world of science by my family. My father is a University Physics professor with a PhD in Electrical Engineering and my mother is a chemist with a PhD in Pharmacy.

*My love for mathematics started in 1st grade when my teacher introduced me to the power of figures and numbers through block building.

*My uncle, for whom your main library is named, used to tell me that nothing could compare with an American education.

*When I was six years old, my father would take me along with him to his workplace (he was then working for the Post Office). I remember being fascinated by noisy bustling machines behind which everybody spent the day typing in an undecipherable language, which I had ever seen before. Even though I hardly knew my three Rs, my curiosity was whetted by this unknown language which I was then discovering. I had caught a glimpse of something I couldn't fathom and eventually talked my father into teaching me the language of computers.

*Studying mathematics has always been a game to me, rather than a constraint. When I was younger, in Junior High School, I was fond of small logical riddles or brain-teasers, and I used to devise a few of them every month in the school newspaper.

*When I was a child, there was a TV show called 'It's Not Rocket Science' that I would never miss. It would typically present a scientific phenomenon and explain its consequences thanks to illustrative experiments. This broadcast was one of the triggers of my curiosity and willingness to understand the world in its complexity. Since then, I have constantly been fascinated by the way Science operates.

*But in fact, I have been interested in the world of finance ever since, two years ago, when I was first given the opportunity by my parents to manage my savings. As a consequence, I decided to trade French stocks and shares, and this is still of great benefit to me.

- Avoid starting the statement with a **quotation**, which points out to your lack of inspiration and make the introduction artificial. Besides, such introductions lack in scientific content. They may look apt for undergraduate applications, but are unworthy of the scientific level graduate students have reached.

*"When written in Chinese, the word "crisis" is composed of two characters – one represents danger, and the other represents opportunity". These words, spoken by John Fitzgerald Kennedy fifty years ago have clear meaning for me today. While some people think that the current worldwide financial situation is a good reason not to study financial mathematics, I consider it to be a perfect opportunity to focus on the essence of the field: applied and financial mathematics themselves. Indeed, I hope to become a professional with sound expertise and a solid capacity to meet tough situations with creative solutions.

*"To Be or Not to Be" is the famous line I have dreamed of delivering in my ten years of theater acting and is a keynote in my thought process for the future. All the decisions I have made concerning my education have been motivated by intellectual curiosity. At every step of the way, I have chosen the subjects that attracted me the most and in which I saw the greatest sources of wonder. This reflex has taken me deep into the study of science, and brought me to the best programs I could find.

*FDR's words 'There is nothing to fear but fear itself' ring true to me today, both as a mathematician and a budding orator. My two passions, math and public speaking, are both strong potential tools to calm the waves of fear. Both need logical and rigorous skills. As a finalist in my high school oratory contest, I lost my fear thanks to the rock-solid logic of my speech. I also believe that mathematical and logical reasoning will be a way to get rid of the fear that is currently spoiling the markets. I hope to become one of the mathematical experts who will give the profession a new foundation of confidence.

Yet, the following introduction might do:

> Never has Shakespeare's aphorism "All the World's a stage" been truer to me than when I attended Prof. M's conference on international relations, in which he exposed and took apart the complex interplay of mechanisms that are at work in the global arena today. I have always been curious about the way the world has been ruled but also, and more generally, how things work, from a scientific point of view. Although I have never let life decide for me, when it came down to making choices, I opted for sciences rather than humanities *per se*, aware yet that the scientist cannot do without a conscience. Those choices have led me to XXX where I was admitted—above other schools—after an intensive undergraduate program. Choosing the TPP program is a way of reconciling two extremes, without sacrificing one for the other, but above all to build up on the knowledge I have acquired over the past years to try and become an actor in the technological world whose values I would like very much to adhere to as they are not essentially materialistic but moral as well. Technology is not an end in itself, and studying its stakes can by all means help shape a world in which man is not its slave but its enlightened master.

- Avoid stating the banal **first sentence** that panders to the program and is loaded with empty words. The rule of thumb here is to start with the science, or what triggered your interest for the science.

> *My constant desire to pursue the most challenging academic and personal opportunities, coupled with a devoted passion for automobiles, have led me to apply to the very prestigious Master of ME at the University of Michigan-Ann Arbor.
>
> *In addition to its academic excellence, XXX encourages its students to develop their leadership and teamwork skills through fascinating projects and mind-boggling lab work.

- Include a sentence or two about the school you are a student at, your study level, and what your major is about:

> Currently a third-year student at (name of college/school + date of admission), I am enrolled in a Master's level program in (name).
>
> This year, which is my final year, I have specialized as much as possible in areas that will equip me with the skills to succeed in computer graphics work at the graduate level.

- This is the place to mention your **admission ranking** (overall or in your track) (if it is in the top 1-10%) or your **present ranking** (same). If you are ranked 90th in the class, no need to mention it. If you have chosen, say, Polytechnique over the ENS ULM Paris program, you may state it and explain why.

```
Granted admission to every school I had competed for, I chose the Ecole XXX
because of its reputation for scientific diversity and excellence.
```

```
Now a third-year student at the Ecole XXX where I was admitted in the top 5%
(and which I opted for over the ENS ULM Paris program for the breadth and depth
of its curriculum), I am specializing in…
```

```
I chose the Paris VI university over other schools for its worldwide reputation
for multidisciplinary, intellectual challenging courses. Besides a broad groun-
ding in fields ranging from Chemistry to Statistics, along with various courses
in Math, I have managed to acquire a solid knowledge in Physics.
```

- State what your ambition is. You must take two aspects of the science under consideration: on the one hand the **scientific knowledge** and, on the other hand, **the skills** you have. On both counts your ambition is to enhance them. Therefore, verbs such as **to broaden**, **to enlarge**, **to consolidate**, **to strengthen**, **to deepen**, **to explore further**, **to firm up**, **to investigate**, **to probe**, **to parse** will come in handy in your statement.
- At the **end of that paragraph**, include the program you are applying for as well as the university. This is the end result of the reason for applying to graduate studies in XXX department at the University of XXX, your goal being to start a career in/to embark on a career as/to launch a business in, etc.

```
Stanford University's Statistics program has all the ingredients to answer my
scientific needs and help me design first class decision support systems to leve-
rage green and high-performing solutions. That is the reason why I am applying
for its master's in data science.
```

```
Harvard University's master in Statistics will provide a unique mix between
Machine Learning and Statistics and will allow me to gain top-level insights
in both domains.
```

5. Rotten apples

Here are a few examples of introductions **not to follow**. Please note that the style, typos and grammatical errors have not been changed nor altered. Those are all original masterpieces.

When-I-was-a-child story telling type

```
*Since a very young age, I was driven to understand how things worked. My father
is an engineer and my mother a biology teacher. I was raised in a culture of
```

science and curiosity where I incessantly asked why and how. That is why I want to study engineering.

*As a child, I used to play "Legos" with my younger brother. I remember a "dog-fight" involving the spacecraft that would survive the three-foot dive test with almost no exterior damage and, most importantly, without "sacrificing" the pilot inside the cockpit. Nowadays, a car designer would want his car to be light, yet its structure capable of absorbing most of the energy in case of a crash so as to save the occupants' lives. This paradoxical crash/no-kill problem that triggered my mind as an eight-year-old child must have steered me into studying mechanics.

*Since I was a child, I have been reading scientific reviews in which there was always some articles about climatic changes, amazonian forest disappearance with all its resources. In a way, like lots of children of my generation, I'm a child of Tchernobyl, and I was revolted by this disorganised destruction of the planet.

*At 10 years old, with my little microscope, I used to observe the leaves and wonder how they worked. Since then, I have never stopped. This desire to understand how living things work is part of me. It led me to study Sciences, to enter preparatory classes and then to the prestigious Ecole XXX. In the future, I want to bring this desire to life by becoming a researcher in biology in the fields of health and the environment. I am convinced that the Master of Science in Bioengineering at Stanford University is the best venue now to pursue this objective.

*As a child, I was fascinated by mathematics. Having four brothers that had gone through advanced scientific studies throwing flashes of beautiful pieces of mathematical theory around that I was too young to understand made me curious and hungry to learn it all. Mathematics has always been a source of inspiration for me, the one subject at school that I don't have to, but rather I love to study. I am intrigued and captivated by universal algebra and its unusual yet somehow familiar structures and articulations, and the way mathematics bring order and theoretical rigor to the seemingly chaotic and random events of nature mesmerizes me. If there is one thing that I learned studying mathematics, it would be that everything is connected on a far deeper level than we can imagine, and we only get a few moments to glimpse some of those fascinating, intricate and complex connections.

*When I was a kid, I firmly believed that science could eventually solve all the world's problem. I thought that if one was given enough information or enough time to compute every possible output of every possible experiment one could devise, one would have the key to solve any kind of problems. So, I grew bearing that positivist attitude in me. Yet, as time went on, I discovered that some problems were simply unsolvable, or that one would never be able to predict the spin of an atom. But I also found out that sometimes, the answer to a question would be laying in a vast amount of data, but that one could be oblivious of its existence, let alone set it apart of the rest.

*My first contact with the world of transport dates back to my early childhood, when I was fascinated by the multitude of suburban trains running near my home in Asnières, a suburb of Paris. Later, I discovered French high-speed trains and took my first airplane from Paris to Detroit through London. These striking experiences made me increasingly keen on the idea of acquiring more knowledge about transportation.

*I was once given a computer for Christmas and soon learnt how to print, draw, and process basic calculus. At the age of nine, I was able to master the basics of the BASIC language. Parallel to my interest for computers, I developed a strong liking for mathematics, delving into books so as to grasp the fascinating algorithms, although the word was still opaque to me at that time. Unfortunately, as CS wasn't taught at school, I had to study it all on my own.

*At the age of 15 my father introduced me to the arcane and hitherto mysterious world of finance and more especially to that of the financial markets. He had made some investment on the stock market and was anxious that I should learn more about it. Although my scientific studies kept me away from the subject for a while, I made up my mind to take it up once I was admitted to XXX a few years later.

*A visit to the trading room of UBS in London in 1998, where my elder brother (who holds a PhD in financial mathematics from Imperial College) was then working, was certainly, although unwittingly, the starting point of a desire to learn more about a field, financial engineering, which at that time looked slightly puzzling for the teenager that I was. I remember being both awed and intrigued by the hustle and bustle of individuals running in all directions while curves of various colors would appear on computer screens. That visit left a lasting impression on me. It all was a mystery to me and, many years later, after intensive studies of mathematics, physics and chemistry, I've chosen to specialize in applied mathematics and economics at XXX where I enrolled in 2010. Determined to follow on my idea to understand more about finance, I have made up my mind to apply to… for an MSc in…

*I have been interested in financial markets since high school, when I understood what happened during the financial crisis of 2008. At this time, I did a lot of research on this subject as it interested me to know how a so controlled field could have collapsed. Thanks to these researches, I realized how mathematical this field was, and I became interested in understanding how some bank, insurance and hedge fund could use mathematical models to anticipate the future of the market while preventing the risk of losses.

The "my-father (or grand-father)" introduction

*My whole family has always influenced my very childhood. That is to say that my family background is very tough. My mother's father was to be a pilot in the French army. He died when my mother was 12 years of age. That's why, I think, I had special relationship with my last grandfather who was to be an engineer in the agro-economical sector. He really was the model of the grandfather to me. I was fascinated about the kind of life he had. Thus, if we consider that background, this is all but surprising that I went on studying general sciences. At that period I didn't really know what I wanted to do, or to become, further.

*Mechanics interested me early, well before I could read and write, when I used to draw the details of the gears and belts of my grandfather's tractor. I found engines particularly fascinating, these precise assemblies of metal parts that, put together and fueled with a little gasoline, could produce incredible power. After my grandfather's death, I was the only one in the family who could fix engines. From this time forward, I was designated to repair the chainsaws, mowing machines and tractors that my grandfather had left us. I always loved working with my hands, crafting and creating. Although I found my grandfather's yard machines interesting as a child, my true inspiration for structures, particularly how they are built, comes from my father, who is a former stone-cutter and with whom I spent many hours renovating our house, building stone walls or making concrete slabs. Now, I want not only to understand how structures and buildings are built, but also to become an actor at the design level.

*From a young boy who originated playing football in the streets of Casablanca, I grew up living my father's dreams. He is a strong man who always does everything in order to achieve his dreams. I was quite impressed to see how he was able to go against odds, to defy societal hierarchy because he had the courage to be bold and audacious. He is part of my everyday work, he is the person who always pushes me to continue working, to continue believing on what I am doing, because even if it takes long to achieve, hard work will always pay off.

*In a biology course, in high school, it occurred to me that I wanted to understand those triangles and squares standing out for molecules and put this knowledge to the use of Human beings. My mother is a chemist whereas my father is a professor of mathematics. Thus, I grew up in a scientific background, taking great pleasure to understand life and mathematics.

*A book written by Hubert Reeves which I read at the age of twelve, concerning the history and evolution of the universe, turned into a passion what had hitherto been a mere interest, when my father would take me and the family telescope stargazing to the top of a nearby hill. I remember spending several nights peering into the sky, as he would explain the various types of galaxies, the origins of the Moon craters, and the formation of stars. It was indeed difficult for the young boy that I was to decipher the mysteries of nature but my curiosity had definitely been aroused and pointed me towards a scientific path I was to follow later on in my studies. I enrolled in college in 2019 and decided to devote as much time as I could to the understanding of the physical elements that have shaped the universe. I do intend to explore that field further, hence my reason to apply to the Physics Department of Berkeley for a graduate program leading to a PhD in Astrophysics.

*My amazement reached a new level when my father and I took the car we had inherited from my great-grandfather apart and put it back together again, piece by piece. I will always remember the sound of the motor starting after our lengthy experiment, confirmation that our hard work had paid off. Working alongside my father from age twelve onwards, allowed me to inherit his enthusiasm for mechanics and the automotive industry.

*My desire to work to preserve the environment is coupled with my love of nature. During my childhood, my grandparents transmitted to me their love of the mountains. They have a flat in a small mountain village in the Alps where I used to go hiking with them during the summer and skiing with my family in the winter. Once, there was no snow, only rain, and we were forced to go back home after only two days. I remember being really disappointed when my father told me that, ten years before, there had always been at least a meter of snow at this time of the year. As he spoke, I started wondering about the future long-term outcomes of global warming.

*Since my grand-father explained to me ten years ago the basic mechanism of a nuclear power plant, from the fission reactions to the alternator, I have been fascinated by this way of producing electricity. My grand-father was not a nuclear engineer, but a man passionate about science in general. In addition, engineer Frank Wolf's explanations about the conversion of Uranium into Plutonium in Tintin's album, *Destination Moon*, intrigued me when I was a child. At the time, I was really eager to understand how it worked and what purpose it served. Today, I am able to grasp Wolf's precise description of an atomic battery's mechanics. My child experiences provided me with a strong desire to explore nuclear energy in order to produce electricity.

The "friend-of-my-father" introduction

*When I was 15, I met a friend of my parents: Professor Jean-Nicolas M. (MD, PhD). He was a famous researcher in the field of genetics and also a tremendous entrepreneur who created XXX, the French leading provider of genetic expertise. I was really impressed by his scientific achievements and his humanism. This outstanding man was the major source of inspiration of my professional project, which is to develop computing tools to understand and model human biological systems. For this purpose, I want to remain as closely related as possible to the cutting edge of medical science since I hope these tools to be useful for improving human health and welfare/comfort.

The inspiring professor

*"You don't need any specific reason. It's simply the curiosity. When you realize that you are trying to solve an existing problem or to find the explication for it, you are already doing the research." This was how Mr. Yuan Tseh Lee, a Taiwanese Nobel Prize laureate, answered to my question during his visit to my school when I asked him what was encouraging him to devote himself to scientific research. He added that everyone who is astonished by the beauty of science should be contented by new discoveries. It was a good speech worth chewing, and his words went far in my mind. Since then, I have not stopped expressing my interest in science. It was during my stay at the Ecole XXX that this interest finally transformed into a passion in physics.

The recollection introduction

*Having spent every school holiday for eight years in India, I had become used to power cuts. That is, until a friend of mine almost died during an operation because of just such an accident. I was completely shocked that this could happen in our time, and decided right then that I would be part of solving energy problems in developing countries.

*I remember that dark, cold, moonless and cloudless night of early 1997. My father took me out to a small observatory to let me see the comet Hale-Bopp through a professional telescope. I had been fantasizing about it for several weeks. When I eventually saw the star, looking so amazingly bright and shiny before my eyes, only one question began haunting my mind: "How could I possibly build something powerful enough that could fathom the secrets lying on the surface of this intriguing star?" Time has gone by since this first encounter with space and my motivation for space exploration has only intensified. Starting from that simple question I raised ten years ago, I have now grown eager to explore what lies beneath the surface and reach the core of the complex astronautic problems that motivate me: spacecraft propulsion and design optimization. For this reason, I would like to present my candidacy to the MSc in Aeronautics and Astronautics at Stanford School of Engineering.

*When I was in high school, I visited the Institut Curie. I was struck upon meeting mathematicians who explained how mathematics could be related to an experimental science like biology. They shared with me that in reality, the field of mathematics contributes to many facets of biology, such as biostatistics, imagery and modelization. My experience at the Institut Curie helped confirm my interest in the means through which knowledge from mathematics can be applied to complex problems in biology.

The "I-love-science" introduction

*There was a time when I was obsessed with radio-controlled miniature cars, reading all the magazines before I had my own nitro RC car. I actually loved the building process and understanding how this complex system worked. I have always enjoyed mathematics and science, which led me to enter the undergraduate preparatory program. There I built strong foundations in both mathematics and physics, and overall, I developed my scientific reasoning.

*Sciences have interested me from a very early age. As a child, I remember being awed by a book on scientific experiments which I kept on reading, performing the experiments and trying to understand the underlying reasons behind them. Hence, in high school at the European School in Luxembourg, I chose all scientific classes, participated in the Belgian Mathematical Olympiads, as well as led my class to take part in scientific competitions. After obtaining my European Baccalaureate with high honors, in order to pursue my interest in sciences, I attended preparatory classes at the Lycée XXX in Versailles. There, I followed advanced courses in mathematics, physics and chemistry, reaching ultimately an amazing GPA of 3.99. Those preparatory classes taught me rigor and furthered my ability to study in an academically-demanding environment.

The naïve introduction

*Who needs Spielberg when he has the life span of cathedrals and the size of the Millau viaduct to spark his imagination? Buildings and bridges have always intrigued me. I might have been an architect, but it is much more exciting to become the engineer who works the magic of transforming materials into concrete realizations requested by a community. This vision led me to study mathematics and physics at college.

*One day, my mother hung a small newspaper article in our bathroom which said: "If our societies keep on developing with the same energy needs as today, Man will confront inevitable problems because natural resources are not expandable whereas demography is". I suddenly became aware of the emergency we are facing and our immediate need to care about our environment. Consequently, I am willing to take an active part in solving environmental issues (our lack of water, the energy crisis, etc.) and the best way to do so is to study Environmental Engineering.

*The minute I stepped into SG's trading room in Paris, I was struck by the amount of activity: traders had their eyes riveted on five computer screens, stockbrokers were having heated conversations over the phone, and a multitude of other people were swarming around the room with the same look of promptness on their faces. Seeing mathematics at work in such an exciting environment gave me an adrenaline rush. I had been studying mathematics out of pure passion for the subject, not knowing where it would take me. I am now grateful that the foundations I have built in that field will allow me to enter the realm of finance.

*Five years ago, I had an extraordinary philosophy teacher whose passion and clarity of thought inspired me. In fact, I caught the fire and it changed my whole behavior. If I had been a good student satisfied with good grades, I was now filled by a nascent curiosity and an analytical eye for everything. My interest for philosophy has contributed to helping me make appropriate choices. The reason I am evoking that catalyzing event is to illustrate that my choosing to apply for the Master's program in the Department of Management Science and Engineering (MS&E) is the result of an intense personal reflection, the same reflection that has been driving me for five years.

*"Does the universe in fact have a beginning or an end? And if so, what are they like?" That is the question which has always consumed me. As a child, I read as much science fiction as I could, and often went to science museums where I was struck with wonder by the amazing possibilities science offered. I enjoyed thinking about our universe's history, so much that I created a card game about it when I was 12. Later, I oriented my readings to laymen's books about physics. I found Stephen Hawking's bestseller *A Brief History of Time* and his discussion about the universe's extension, contraction, and its geometrical properties really absorbing. General questions related to physics have always stimulated my imagination in an inexpressible way. Within my courses, the more I delve into subjects like Particle Physics, General Relativity or Cosmology, the more I want to know.

*I was a child when I got a grade of 9 out of 10 in a math test. As a young idealistic pupil, I promised myself to correct this *terrible* grade! But in my struggle to get my revenge on mathematics, I was actually falling in love with it. What followed was ten years of intensive competitions in national and further in international Olympiads, and math turned into my major passion bringing me joy and accomplishments. That grade of 9 is still on my transcript but it taught me to practice mathematics beyond grades, and I'm grateful for it being the starting point of my mathematical career

*As I was having lunch with a Chinese worker in Beijing two years ago, he told me about his youth. His parents were working 12 hours a day and had one day off every two weeks. He still remembers that he was hungry most of the time. He is now in his late thirties and is working for CRTVU, he can now afford to eat in restaurants; he was complaining that I could afford a trip to China whereas he always wanted to visit Europe. It dawned upon me that I wanted to study economics. I want to be one of the economists, like the Stiglitz commission, that blaze new trails for a better sharing of the world's wealth and a fairer world economy.

The I-don't-know-how-to-start-so-let's-BS introduction

*Aeronautics to some people may sound like an abstract and somewhat mysterious branch of physical science, yet for me it was to become a natural field of investigation combining theoretical studies and life experiences. Having always nurtured a keen (and earthly) interest for science and technology - which led me from the preparatory classes to XXX - I would also draw genuine pleasure from flying kites for recreation or reading the history of the Wright Brothers' flying machines. Later on, a paragliding course came to replace the flying tethered objects, which, parallel to my present training to obtain a private pilot's license, conferred on my academic studies not only a meaningful direction to live an abiding passion but also an intense desire to understand the rules that govern aviation.

*A strategic consultant from Bain & Company came to the campus in April 2016 and spoke to us about the qualities necessary for his job: you need to have a truly structural and strategic approach, to be entrepreneurial and autonomous, and to be capable of making rapid decisions in the corporate business world. This excited me immensely. It corresponded exactly to the way I saw myself in the future.

*Not for me the choice of becoming a dotcom entrepreneur or a real estate developer, even less the financial wizard who will have made his first million dollars by the age of thirty. The passion that is mine has been machines of all kinds, taking them apart and putting them together, trying to devise the secrets they harbor or what makes them tick. Actually, blessed with a mathematical frame of mind coupled with an unquenchable curiosity for how things work, I was soon to take advantage of those qualities and immersed myself in the study of sciences and the mysteries of technology.

*When I attended a conference where the BNP presented its banking activities in quantitative research, I realized this was a domain in which I would flourish. The "financial engineering" jobs were fully presented and it echoed my own profile: strong analytical skills, a high level in mathematics, a taste for intellectual challenges. Then, chatting with the professionals, I understood the excitement they felt in their work, and the satisfaction of using their skills to make coherent decisions, and I knew that is what I wanted to do too.

*A pop-up tent: what is it? A good combination of a well-thought-out design and a selection of specific materials to create an innovative technology. In High-School I had the opportunity to meet an engineer who worked on this camping equipment, and he explained how this project was managed. What interested me the most was the challenge of using scientific knowledge and thinking smartly about the shape of an object to produce perfect equipment for the user. The interaction between knowledge and creation appealed to me and interested me in becoming an engineer. Much later, through an elective university course, I discovered the importance of the interaction between city-based infrastructures and its citizens. These interactions have wider consequences for individuals because he uses roads, bridges and hospitals daily and they have an impact on his life. Therefore, the crucial role of Civil Engineering in today's society is a challenge that I want to be part of.

*What do elephants, giraffes and zebras have to do with learning economics? Along with the beauty of the environment, it was poverty and underdevelopment, and the questions these provoked in me, that impacted me on my first visit to Kenya. At the time, I knew very little about economics, but I had read about the animated past of the country and I felt a thirst to understand several issues. What policies had allowed France to reach a higher standard of living and a lower unemployment rate? What modern solutions could Kenyans find to improve their circumstances? I was so interested in those questions that I began making academic choices which would allow me to specialize in this field.

*Not very long ago, I read some articles in a scientific review by IPCC scientists and IEA experts on energy and the environment. The fact that such renowned scientists want to warn us against an on-coming energy crisis and the threat of climate change, backed by scientific proof, opened my eyes to these problems, about which I had previously had a confused opinion. I also once went to the UN Headquarters in New York City, and this visit convinced me that the UN is able to implement global plans to reduce the negative effects of energy use on the environment. Since then, I have not only wanted to work in the domain of energy and the environment at a global scale, but I am determined to become an energy expert attached to an international organisation like the UN or the IEA.

The first sentence that misses the point and discourages the reader

*Passing from the right atrium to the right ventricle via the tricuspid valve, being then pumped through the pulmonary valve into the pulmonary arteries which go to the lungs, returning to the heart via the pulmonary veins into the left atrium, passing through the mitral valve from the left atrium to the left ventricle, being pumped again through the aortic valve into the aorta arteries which go to the body - such is the astoundingly accurate cycle of one of our most fascinating muscles, the heart. I am captivated by the minute behavior of our body and of the knowledge we have managed to get of it. To be able to understand accurately the functioning of a human heart and to study the reality of what is happening in it, is an incredible challenge. To this end, I have hesitated for a long time between studying medicine or engineering.

Bland generalizations about your interest for science

*Among all the fascinating science around me, mathematics has been the one I enjoyed most. From early on until today I see in it an intrinsic beauty, a pure art: the structure of the proofs, the beauty of the objects, the strength of the constructions… I admired it all.

*For long I have thought that sciences were like Life's big instruction book, capable of providing the answers to the many questions on the Universe that my early and intense curiosity was hankering after.

*At the crossroads of many sciences, Aeronautics has for long struck a particular chord, not only because of the intellectual challenge it offers but also for life experiences that started when I built model planes or visited the cockpit of an Air Force jet. Yet I was always intrigued by the hidden forces at work behind the flying machines, as well as the design or command systems that are actually instrumental in making planes fly.

The-fake-change-of-heart introduction

*When I was younger, I used to imagine myself as a scientist developing new technologies in a laboratory. About four years ago, I experienced a change of heart, when I began to view science in a much more multifaceted way. While many events contributed to this shift in my perceptions, I remember, in particular, my reactions after watching a fascinating documentary film on a solar electrification project in rural Brazil. What was most striking to me in the film was that although everybody would obviously benefit from this clean and inexpensive source of power, the project had to overcome numerous obstacles. The issues here were not technological, however, but involved the attitudes of the people affected by the project--their fear of change, mistrust, and greed. I understood at that point that technology is only one part of any solution to an environmental issue, and that scientists must be able to negotiate the human and economic aspects of new environmental policies and technologies in order to make them work.

The video-or-movie-giving-way-to-a-bland-generalization introduction

*My passion for mathematics comes from a very anecdotical yet motivating source: as a student in primary school, I loved the documentary "Tara: A Journey to the Heart of the Climate Machine" so much that I chose to visit the boat and meet the crew upon its arrival in Paris. From this discussion I discovered the passion that can arise from such a long-term project shared by scientists from all fields. In particular, I remember talking to a mathematician trying to draw meaningful conclusions from the data of the salinity of the water at different places in the Arctic. Already convinced of a scientific path, I discovered a few years later the enjoyment that I could draw from probabilities, both for its applications to real-world questions and for the puzzle-like combinatoric problems it offers.

*Since I saw the film *Apollo 13*, the aim of working in the space industry has never left my mind. I have studied since then with the dream to go and study in the USA which sent the first man on the moon and which is leading space exploration in order to take part in the "giant leap for mankind" Armstrong talked about on the 21st of July 1969.

The sport comparison introduction

Such introductions force the comparison in ways that are artificial and unconvincing. The competitive aspect between sports and academic fields or research is too often constrained. There are exceptions when sports have proven personality-building.

*I'm fond of bouldering. I love this sport because in addition to all the physical efforts it requires, it is a challenge you throw to yourself: in front of a boulder you must imagine the way you will climb over it, try anything you can and start again for every new boulder. I love challenges and spending hours to find solutions – and I abandon so rarely a problem without considering all possibilities that it can really take hours.

*When I'm asked to describe myself, I like to picture myself as a samurai. In B*ushido*, they sought to fight none but the strongest. Just like them, I feel honored when I'm given the opportunity to work on sophisticated problems. This explain why I was initially drawn to physics, it was a great challenge but it gave me a tool to comprehend the world.

*For the time being, I have been quite fortunate. I think I have succeeded in almost everything I have undertaken in my life. My success is linked to my natural taste for competition. My competitive nature has not only been honed through rigorous academics, but also through sports. At the age of fifteen, after winning the French Junior Show-Jumping Championship, I almost chose to become a professional rider. Instead, I elected to focus my competitive spirit on academics. In fact, I have always sought out the most challenging academic opportunities. Today, this facet of my personality, coupled with a strong desire to gain international experience, has led me to apply for the highly-selective Master of Science in Financial Engineering at Columbia University.

*Epee fencing and mathematics are two realms I relish, often for the same reasons. They have helped me to become more creative and observant and to develop finesse in some of my thought process. Also, I have learned that I adore meeting a challenge. My love for mathematics is long-standing, but became deeper under the teaching of Claude D., my mathematics teacher at XXX in the undergraduate preparatory classes for the *Grandes Ecoles*.

The music comparison introduction

*The harmonic beauty of music gave me the courage to pick up a classical guitar and to learn how to play it on my own. In much the same way, the perfect elegance of mathematics helped me succeed in the preparatory classes for the *Grandes Ecoles*.

The I-want-to-have-an-impact introduction

*My passion for math combined with a strong will to change the world and make it a better place to live shaped who I am and what I want to achieve. Armed with my passion and my will, my goal is to contribute to changing the world by exploring groundbreaking OR fields. Therefore, I am striving to pursue an operations research PhD

*During my year of duties, I served under the management of the Director of International Relations for the French Military. When I heard him pronouncing the speech I wrote in front of important diplomats and military officers during an international meeting in Addis-Ababa (Ethiopia), I felt proud and I understood that committing myself to reaching achievement was crucial to me.

*The climate change, the generalization of nuclear power, the sustainable development, it would take too much time to list the issues of our times which cannot be reduced to a mere scientific field. Interdisciplinary programs linking the scientific world to the economical and political one are developed all over the world to answer these complex issues quoted above as examples. I have always considered myself as a very curious person who cannot be satisfied by understanding only a small piece of an issue. Of course, it would be foolish to pretend to resolve or even understand such a broad problem as the climate change on its whole, however it would be much more foolish to believe that lowering CO_2 emissions would represent an efficient solution. Therefore, I want to complement my scientific studies with a master that teaches me not to think how a technology could revolutionise society but how it can integrate itself in society.

The I-love-traveling-in-the-United-States introduction

*I have always wanted to study in the United States for two main reasons: on the one hand, I have been to the U.S. several times, particularly in New York where I have family, and always enjoyed the American culture and the openness of people; on the other hand, and more importantly, I strongly believe that Ame-

rican studies are quite complementary to French ones. Having talked to people who have studied in both countries, I understood that American studies tend to leave more room for autonomy, teamwork and practical courses, which is exactly what I am looking for during my last year before work.

*Along my scholarship, I have gone through many countries, such as Morocco, Italy and Puerto Rico. From the latter I learned the north American way of work. Although quite different from the European standards, it adopts a practical approach I am willing to find again. While doing my undergraduate studies in France, the idea that it was the best way to work sneaked in. By going outside for my graduate studies, I want to see how other people work and understand why it is at least as good as the one I was taught.

*I have always lived in an international context. First of all, my hometown is on the Swiss border, my father works at the United Nations in Geneva and my mother is a German teacher, also in Geneva. In addition to teaching me foreign languages at very early age, my parents have considered it important to sensibilize me to the problems of the world. I've always had this dream, a dream that has never left me, that I wanted to understand the world, and do everything I can to change what's wrong with it.

The quotation introduction

Do not start with a quote unless it is somehow directly linked to your research interests. Admissions committees are interested in **your** thoughts and insights; borrowing the insights of others can make you seem intellectually lazy.

*At the end of high school, I was offered a poster of Einstein with the quote: "When I examine myself and my methods of thought, I come close to the conclusion that the gift of imagination has meant more to me than my talent for absorbing absolute knowledge". As I was about to begin further scientific studies, such statement reminded me that I had to remain open to other kinds of thinking.

*Steve Jobs' words in 2005 "If you haven't found your love yet, keep looking. Don't settle." are a fitting summary of my academic life up to now. Indeed, my path towards computer science has been an interesting journey, from practical work in physics labs to the development of software during C++ classes.

*Feynman's quotation that "every theoretical physicist who is any good should know six or seven different theoretical representations for exactly the same physics" makes a lot of sense for me. I strongly believe that the ability to tackle scientific questions from different points of view, to draw one's imagination from knowledge in different fields is a solid asset. This idea has somehow guided my academic curriculum.

*"In physics there may one day be a Theory of Everything; in finance and the social sciences, you're lucky if there is a usable theory of anything", wrote Professor Emanuel Derman in *My Life as Quant*, arousing a curiosity for the financial field which, after my admission to XXX in 2008, has never ceased growing. All along my science studies, I had been taught that each problem always had a solution; I was stunned to discover that scientists, with powerful tools at their disposal, were unable to find "a usable theory of anything". At XXX, I went on studying applied mathematics at the advanced level, finding there the beginning of theoretical solutions which, in practice, did not provide wholly satisfactory results. Eager to learn more about the subject, I have resolved to apply to the New York University's program Mathematics in Finance.

The fake entrepreneurship streak introduction

*The Technology Entrepreneurship curriculum is of particular interest to me as I've been an entrepreneur my whole life, from selling marbles in primary school to launching a start-up in my first year at Ecole XXX through the entrepreneurship program directed by Louise D.

The introduction that reads like a CV

*I am currently a final year student at a top-ranking college for science which has provided me a strong grounding in different subjects including economy, biology, applied mathematics and physics. As an undergraduate, I followed the Classes Préparatoires which provided me a strong pluridisciplinary scientific knowledge. Last year, I followed the microeconomy class of Mr G., which gave me a precise view of the theory needed to understand and implement microeconomical policies in industry. I also attended the cellular biology class of Mr Martin, which enhanced the strong inclination I always had for bioengineering as well as both the scientifical and economical issues it raises. The statistical class of Mr M. provided me strength in a particular field of applied mathematics which I believe to be relevant if I am up to enter a career at the border of social and engineering sciences. I believed it to be also very relevant to have real scientific experiences while attending those theorical courses, because I found it very interesting to think by myself and try to figure out my on models describing particular scientific phenomena.

The story-no-one-understands introduction

*I remember very distinctly, I was in the first grade and we were taking a simple exercise. When the teacher would whistle, we would run and gather around him. After trying this exercise a few times, he added a rule and stated that from now on whenever he would whistle twice we were to freeze. He whistled twice; I froze. In fact, only five children had frozen and most of the class had gathered around the teacher. Slowly, my four classmates changed their mind and joined the others. I stayed still for a whole minute. After a minute had passed, the teacher finally announced that I was right. You may well wonder what this little story has to do with finance in mathematics - it has a great connection to me. After studying for years I learned much about very different topics, but I also came to discover myself. I guess this experience in the first grade was the first time I realized there was something different in my way of thinking. I had a strong affinity with skepticism; whenever I was confronted with an opinion, I instinctively thought that opinion was flawed in some way. My convictions on a point of view are as strong as my skepticism has failed attacking it.

The hodgepodge introduction

*Since high school, I have wondered what research in math could be. I have participated in different mathematical tournaments like Benelux Math Olympics (BxMo) and the International Tournament of Young Mathematician (ITYM) and have worked on different projects. Sometimes it is about theoretical topic (like a collective project on Quantum Computing) and sometimes it is much more about practice and real data like developing a prediction model for French railway system. (during an internship in SNCF) They are not all about math model that we understand well like my third-year research project about modeling biology system with reproduction and mutation, but my instinct has indicated me that, with some angle, the applied mathematics behind those systems have common root and it is nothing else than my own package of knowledge and understanding of the problem.

6. Convincing examples

My passion for computer science bloomed after admission to one of France's premier schools for sciences. Following the preparatory program, during which I got familiarized with some of the basics of the science, second- and third-year courses were to open perspectives on the possibilities of a science that my reasoning and analytical skills contributed to conceptualizing. I thus came to consider mathematics from a point of view of the relations between mathematical objects much more than from their definition or from how to only logically derive their properties. My ambition is to go deeper into the science, explore some of its fields and possibly—through doctoral studies—become a researcher in my own right. The Oxford MPhil program has all the ingredients to fulfill my ambition.

Excitement, thrill, adrenalin: this was the atmosphere I found in the trading room of HSB in Paris last June. Every trader was intent on his screens, updating continuously his positions thanks to complex mathematical tools, and shouting his orders and advice to his colleagues: a challenging world that makes you go beyond your own limits, a work environment that would allow me to give my very best. This is why I am seeking to be at the heart of the financial markets, with a career in a front office where I can be a decision maker, and why I have directed my academic path towards the fulfillment of that purpose.

My interest for applied mathematics grew from an activity I developed in my teenage years when, on my computer, I started scanning and modifying photos taken from the family album. Not only was I interested in the technical aspect of photo editing and organizing, but it was also a way for me to give way to my creative mind, arranging people, inventing characters and restoring old pictures. Being gifted with a scientific mind, it was therefore logical that I would be tempted to investigate the ins and outs of image processing; after taking the arduous path that led from the preparatory classes to the entrance examinations to the *grandes écoles* and being admitted to XXX in 2010, I decided to explore further those fields closely related to what had become a passion in the meantime and took several classes in applied mathematics and CS. I graduated from XXX in 2013 and I am currently in my second year of a Master program in Mathematics, Computer Vision and Learning at the Ecole normale supérieure (France). My goal, after my Master—to be awarded in April 2015—is to go on with a PhD in Statistics and Mathematical Analysis hence my decision to apply to Stanford.

My interest in probability was stirred in my undergraduate years when I undertook a project on Intermittent Search Strategies. This interest grew to include stochastic calculus and optimization models after I was admitted to University of XXX in 2018. I have then found in Operations research a mathematical means to address and solve real-world problems, especially in financial services. I am especially intrigued by revenue management and dynamic pricing problems. How an airline company should price its plane tickets given the fact that online travel sites have created a real-time price competition between every airline, and that aggregate market demands evolve over time? Finally, the main field game theory developed by Lasry and Lions captivates me: modeling a stochastic game with a large number of players as a solution of a system of partial differential equations used in physics is for me a trailblazing contribution to research and paves the way for many other challenges. My ambition is to explore such problems in depth and breadth and Princeton's PhD program in the ORFE Department is in that regard the best fit. That is why I am applying.

During my leadership training with the French Navy, I traveled to Vanuatu and the kingdom of Tonga in the Pacific Ocean. There, I saw countries that have a dramatic need for electric power, but the only cheap solutions they have at the moment, petrol and coal, are environmentally dangerous. I realized, concretely, how life changing it would be if they had access to a mix of wind, solar and geothermal energy and knew I wanted to be part of a solution to help such countries adapt to sustainable energies.

What do cooking and mathematics have in common? They are creative and personal, and for true excellence they require someone with vision. When creating mathematical exercises for my students, or exotic dishes for my family, I experience the pure satisfaction of a successful alchemist. I am looking forward to the day I will see a unique combination of my various competencies, and with the same satisfaction I enjoy in my kitchen, will turn them into successful original business ideas. This is why I ventured so deeply into mathematical studies: I believe they are all about creativity and competence, two ingredients I have been seeking to develop and which I hope to find in the Stanford MS&E program.

A three-month internship with a subsidiary of the *Caisse des Dépôts et Consignations* (one of France's largest public banks), in 2003, gave me a first-hand opportunity to apply my knowledge in mathematics to finance. I designed and developed software that improved the company's decision-making process in order to invest in venture capital funds. Besides deepening my analytical skills, this experience provided an invaluable opportunity to learn more about the complexity of finance. Not only did I enjoy modeling a complex system, I was also excited by the idea my software could help the managers make the right choice in investment. At XXXX, where I had been admitted after three years in the intensive preparatory classes, I therefore decided to choose courses dedicated to financial modeling. I have now made up my mind to study further the field of Financial Mathematics, hence my reason for applying to the Master in Financial Mathematics at NYU, which will give me the academic foundations to become a researcher in finance.

As a child, I often roamed Canada's old-growth forests with my siblings, building forts from fallen branches, foraging mushrooms and huckleberries. My grandfather and uncles worked nearby as horse loggers, using low-impact methods to selectively harvest cedar, Douglas fir and white pine. They took so few trees that I never noticed much of a difference. The forest seemed ageless and infinite, pillared with conifers, jeweled with raindrops and brimming with ferns and fairy bells. I experienced it as "nature in the raw" – a mythic realm, perfect as it was. When I began attending the University of XXX, I was elated to discover forestry: an entire field of science devoted to her beloved domain. It seemed like the natural choice.

I have always thought that some students fail to invent or do original research for the same reason computers fail to pass the Turing Test. Mircea Eliade, the Romanian philosopher and longtime University of Chicago professor, thought that human experience could be divided into two categories: sacred and profane. Using the same dichotomy, the concepts learned in undergraduate education can be separated into 'self-discovered' and 'explained-and-understood'. Inferring a new idea strictly within the latter concept space is like a computer understanding the sacred part of human experience. The path to an original idea must pass through the 'sacred', self-discovered space where blind-deduction is replaced by rational-intuition. And this is what I am looking for from graduate school.

While Ecole P. and Politehnica Bucharest did a very good job of instilling many valuable concepts, I am now ready to make the transition from internalizing and applying 'profane' concepts, from examples and laws, to expressing those 'sacred' concepts that are in me to create. MIT's Master program in Computer Science is the perfect environment for this transition.

Unlike most students who specialize in finance late in their study program, my experience in this field dates back to my first year, when I was doing a part-time internship with H, a French OTC-pricing software development startup. My first task was to implement the Black-Scholes pricing model on the VOCTA software, something I learned by immersing myself in John Hull's seminal book on options, futures and other derivatives. Yet, Hull did not provide all the answers I was seeking, such as, why should the price of an asset be equal to the expected discounted future cash-flows under risk-neutral probability? What might happen to the pricing models if the underlying assets did not follow the Geometric Brownian motion or, how to examine this Brownian motion assumption? I thought the financial models were not presented in a rigorous enough way according to the Bourbakian standards taught in the preparatory program where I had studied for two years after leaving China at the age of 18 and before my admission to Ecole XXX in 2007. The questions I raised then have kept puzzling me even after taking several advanced applied mathematics classes in my second-year at XXX. Eager to find answers, a PhD program is the logical link to expand my knowledge base in financial theory. That is why I am applying to Princeton's Department of Operations Research and Financial Engineering for a PhD in Financial Engineering.

I had the good fortune to hear J.M. J. deliver a conference on peak oil this semester. At the end of his presentation, a student asked whether he considered the development of fossil fuel as a boon or a bane, to which Prof J. answered that it was man's duty and responsibility to balance technological progress vs man's well-being. This statement, a mind-opener for me, led me to mull over the energy transition we are going through and the direction we are taking, in particular whether in the long term the building and deployment of wind turbines or solar panels will not harm more than they will help. Goaded by the lecturer's remarks, I re-oriented my focus on energies and sustainability with a minor in economics.

Working with model trains, is one of the reasons I have been attracted to the field of transportation engineering. In fact, building a model rail network, involves various steps like drawing the circuit plan or defining various landscape areas. Since then, my personal experience has shown that transportation planning is a fundamental condition for local development and thus for prosperity. My home region of Alsace is for example believed to be richer than other French regions because of its linear shape, making the highway, the rail tracks, the Rhine and other lines of communication cheaper and more effective. I am convinced that transportation planning and engineering have very important consequences in people's daily lives and can improve their quality of life and this is the way I want to use my scientific background professionally. My current curriculum has in a way fulfilled my scientific ambition with its strong scientific theory-oriented program, yet without fully nourishing the early interest for transportation network designing and building. So, studying Transportation Engineering at MIT would allow me to round off my training and that's why I am applying to the degree program in Transportation.

In February 2012, as my military service in the Air Force was drawing to an end, I was given the unique opportunity to fly a Jaguar fighter plane (the Jaguar is a two seat French-British aircraft). Although the flight was only two hours long, it left a lasting impression upon me, all the more so as I was able to be at the commands for a short while. That flying experience, which, incidentally was not the first, was but one aspect of my passions, which is basically science, and more particularly aeronautics. My interest for science led me quite naturally to XXX, and today to apply to Stanford for an MSc in aeronautics.

Although I have been drawn towards the hard sciences since early on, many events in my life have shaped my particular interests. Discovering what lay at the frontier of computer graphics was one such life-changing event. It happened in 2012, when I had just begun to wonder about the possibilities of 3D movies in the future. Square Picture sent me a powerful response: it was possible to reproduce reality. This was what I thought after I had viewed *Final Fantasy: The Spirits Wi- thin*. They had successfully created skin whose texture seemed real, with all its imperfections, and had made a quantum leap in facial animation. Since that day my passion for these kinds of images has grown endlessly, both in a technical and in an artistic sense. In the process of learning more about what was behind such masterful work, I have also come to realize that a solid theoretical background was the key to doing innovative work in computer graphics. After beginning the process of acquiring my theoretical foundations at the Ecole XXX, I now seek to build upon this base with advanced study in the MSc program in Computer Science at CMU. Such training will move me closer towards my main ambition of doing leading edge work in the field of computer graphics.

While preparing for the competitive entrance examinations to the *grandes écoles*, I chose to do a research project on the re-enactment of a historical experiment carried out by Milikan in 1916 on the photoelectric effect. That experiment, coming on the heels of Einstein's 1905 article, along with Planck's black body radiation, gave birth to Quantum Physics and helped pave the way to its development. However hard it was for me to find the right equipment, this experiment, under the guidance of Prof. H. (University of Strasbourg) was successful enough to attract the attention of the Society of Physics and was eventually presented to the national Physics Forum which took place in Paris in 2017. That first brush with physics in the raw developed in me a strong taste for science as a general rule and quantum physics more particularly. That is why I have chosen to take the next logical step, which is to apply for an MSc/PhD in Applied Physics at MIT so as to further strengthen my knowledge in that field.

Mathematics and computer science are two fields I have been attracted to from an early age. However, it was during my year of leadership training with XXX that I began to define my professional objectives. Indeed, being in a regiment from the Signals Corps made me fully aware of the technical and strategic issues concerning communication and signal processing in our modern technological world. Doing simulations of wartime field communication, I was struck by both its complexity and its simplicity. It was impressive to see the amount of technological knowledge required to build the headquarters, for in a very short time, an important variety of complex fields, such as networking, space communications and cryptology, were connected. The final result was a system which was easy to use and which could command and coordinate thousands of soldiers over a vast area. I realized how exciting the true application of this technology could be, and I knew I would learn more about signal processing.

In 2002, I was confronted for the first time in my life with the havoc a disease can wreak, in that case AIDS, while I visited Namibia. Driving through the capital city, Windhoek, I saw dozens of AIDS sufferers wandering aimlessly, some begging for money to buy what little medicine they could in order, so they hoped, to survive. Besides the shocking sight, that experience was an eye-opener to me: why could not the pharmaceutical industry manufacture drugs cheap enough so they could be affordable by the poorest? Why could not medical laboratories develop generic brand drugs to help HIV-positives? It was only two years later that I could grasp in their complexity the challenges of designing, developing and marketing new drugs, in the course of a scientific team research project I was in charge of at college under the supervision of Professor Z. The aim was to study and synthesize molecules similar to duocarmycins, and to check whether they might be effective in the fight against cancer. I discovered that synthesizing molecules was a non-linear process, as experiments carried out in a laboratory do not always work as easily as on paper. From that point on, I knew that I wanted to work in a field related to new chemical technologies which could have applications to medical research. Indeed, I believe there is ample room for development and implementation in that domain. For all these reasons, I have decided to apply to MIT for a Master of Science in Chemical Engineering Practice.

A tour of the Cadarache center for nuclear research in January 2017 (part of the Silk Roads Program which I am a member of) was a unique opportunity for me to discover in the raw the various cycles of energy generation through uranium enrichment and fission as well as the retrieval of thermal power; but beyond the sheer scientific interest, the technological achievement of building a plant from scratch as well as the safety measures surrounding the facilities offered a challenge to the mind that I almost instantly wanted to take up. Not that nuclear energy was entirely foreign to the family where I grew up (both my parents work for EDF, the French utility), but the studies I had followed up till then had gradually aroused my curiosity as well as strengthened my knowledge in the different fields of sciences, especially in the intense undergraduate programs of the preparatory classes and, more decidedly at the Ecole XXX where I was admitted in 2004. Cadarache has been the designated site of the future international tokamak fusion power reactor ITER and the economic side of research—finding clean energy resources by means of fusion—is also one of the stakes of the 21st century, a topic which has struck a chord in the environmental-friendly attitudes of most young people today, me included. My ambition today is to build upon the knowledge I have acquired but also apply it to designing cutting-edge technologies that will help find solutions to the twin problems of clean energies and nature preservation. That fierce ambition which has led me to take the hardest and most demanding examinations to college is the same that has now steered my path towards the United States and Stanford, whose Master in Nuclear Engineering I have resolved to apply for.

One of the defining moments of my education happened during my six-month science research project at the Ecole XXX. With five other students, I elaborated a computer-video program that modeled oil spills, the shores affected and the cost of depolluting them. Using the geographic situation of the wreck of the *Erika*, the quantity of fuel released and the weather forecasts, we worked with mechanical equations to predict the drift of fuel towards the coast. We also calculated the wealth of each coastal region in flora, fauna and professional activity to quantify the total expense. We then designed a computer program to help the authorities choose between sinking the wreck at sea or giving it shelter in a harbor. I enjoyed dealing with both the mechanical and economic modeling to find concrete solutions to a real-life problem, but the defining moment was realizing the fabulous challenge that lies ahead in coming up with concrete solutions tapping into the ever-increasing knowledge that is being gained in environmental sciences. This is an adventure I plan to join, and I have chosen all the courses I can to get me there.

Martial arts and sciences. They seem to be worlds apart, but they both have played substantial roles in my life and for reasons that are significantly similar. They both offer challenge, require great discipline and call for a goal-oriented approach. Whether you are dealing with the model of a phenomenon or your adversary, you have to permanently call into question your representation. In both disciplines, making mistakes is just a learning process: humility is a key quality, at the very root of progress. In all those aspects, karate and sciences have greatly contributed to the building of my personality.

IV. Why your Program Appeals to me

1. General

The goal of this paragraph is to explain why the US/UK program appeals to you. It should show that you have done your homework and that you know exactly why you are interested in them: courses, professors' research, lab and project work should figure high in this paragraph that is meant to convince them of your motivation.

Researching a university program takes much time and effort but it should prove how motivated you are. So, take careful notes and find out whether the program is a good fit or not. Make lists and compare programs before drawing up your priorities.

Admissions officers will be looking for you to show genuine passion for your field and area of interest and why you plan on devoting your energy to this field. Remain professional, but communicate your excitement. And do not just say that you're interested in epidemiology because you want to help people or save the planet. It is fine to mention an altruistic motive, but you should be specific and particular when articulating what you're passionate about within your field.

2. Go straight to the point

Read about the general philosophy of the program. Go **straight to the point** and say why the program appeals to you in a couple of introductory lines. Do not waste words. You may use the "**would**" or "**will**" (more assertive) when you describe how much you will gain from following the courses:

```
The Master of Science in the Operations Research program at Columbia University would allow me to maintain the broad multidisciplinary approach which my university has given me, and to become the mathematical expert I want to be, with enough knowledge about the industrial world to be strongly socially responsible.
```

```
I am now looking for a graduate program that will use my multidisciplinary foundations and lay the professional competencies to solve problems and help society. I believe the ICME at Stanford fits exactly with the choices I have made over the past five years.
```

The wide range of courses in the MS&E program particularly appeals to me for it would allow me to continue building cross-scientific competence for the future. In addition, it would give me the opportunity to apply my theoretical foundations to the real problems of enterprise.

The MSc in Environmental Engineering at Imperial College will enable me to further deepen those subjects I have started exploring. The *Urban Hydrology, Environmental Fluid Mechanics,* and *Air Pollution* modules would perfectly complement the Fluid Mechanics courses I am following this year, and the environmental issues I have studied besides.

I would like to play an active role in the renewal of nuclear energy and help to find new applications to this extraordinary field of physics. To do so, I am looking for the missing brick in my training: the professional tools to become a full-fledged engineer. I believe that MIT would bring this final touch.

With this vision of becoming an international researcher, I realize that I need to strengthen my fundamental knowledge in the materials involved in nanotechnologies and to develop the wider scientific vision which is necessary for cutting-edge research where sciences overlap. The PhD program in the Department of Materials Science and Engineering at Berkeley offers exactly what I am looking for.

I especially look forward to the case studies: listening to professionals, learning how to translate problems into mathematics and finding innovative solutions, actually catching a professional vision. The work experience of these teachers would allow me to gain a global vision of the financial mechanisms involved.

Thus, I am looking for a graduate school which will allow me to build on the theoretical foundations I have acquired so far, deepening the theory, but giving me the tools to take the creative steps towards innovation. The Master's program in Nuclear Science and Engineering at MIT offers exactly what I need to meet my goals.

During my time in France, I have been exposed to a strong multidisciplinary and theoretical curriculum based on mathematics, physics and economics. Being able to put this theoretical knowledge to practical use by performing applied research would be a great way to complete my education. It is for this reason that I wish to study at MIT.

A Master of Science in Aeronautics & Astronautics would be a logical extension of my academic pursuits and a major step towards achieving my career objectives. The academic courses will allow me to continue my theoretical Mechanics studies at a more advanced level, while experimental courses and laboratory research will provide the experimental knowledge I will need as a Research & Development engineer.

3. The program coursework

Look up the courses you are interested in and select **4-5 courses** within the core program but also the electives. The selection of so many courses should thwart the possibility that a professor has retired, gone on sabbatical leave or transfer to another university. You need to justify your choice of such courses. So, get some information on the course, or the professor. It is advisable to ask the former students of your school about the quality, the interest and the content of the course especially if the website offers scant information.

Check whether the courses you have selected will be taught the following year. It is usually indicated on the Department's website and in the course catalog. When in doubt, email the Department and ask for the relevant information.

Mention the course title in ***italics***. When you mention the name of a class or course, **capitalize** each first letter (*Markov Chains and Martingales, Statistics in Action, The Art of Regression, Math 101*, etc.).

For the courses you plan to attend, mention the **numbers** (such as COS 654) (not in italics) and write the title in full. It will make for easy and faster reading by admissions officers.

> UC Berkeley's program is the ideal fit in addressing these challenges. STAT 210A-B *Theoretical Statistics* will teach the statistical background necessary to provide a refined analysis of a model's outcome and provide accurate decisions. CS C281A *Statistical Learning Theory* is bound to consolidate my knowledge in various theoretical aspects of probabilistic models in machine learning. CS 294-150 *Machine Learning and Statistics Meet Biology and Chemistry* will help me find a broad range of problems in biology and medicine that can be solved with machine learning, whereas STAT C245E-F *Statistical Genomics* will be instrumental in applying statistical tools to topics in genomic research.

When you talk about a professor, mention **her/his first name and last name** (Professor Bill Martin). If you are to repeat the name, just say Prof. Martin. Now, if you mention a class, just say: in a class on *Optimization* taught by Bill Martin (no need to put in Professor in that case).

> I would like to keep my multidisciplinary vision, and understand the physics underlying the design of aircraft, including aerodynamics and propulsion. *Aerodynamics of Viscous Fluids* would allow me to study laminar and turbulent flows and their influence by boundary layers. *Aircraft Engines and Gas Turbines* would help me understand the characteristics of engines and turbines, with a focus on noise reduction, a major issue in the aerospace industry.

> Searching for the best university at which I could pursue my education in the domain of networking, I especially noticed Hector G.-M's class dealing with distributed databases and parallel data management: it would perfectly supplement the knowledge I have gained during my previous peer-to-peer networks class.

I need graduate training in the field, which is why I am applying to the Master's program in Financial Mathematics at Columbia University. Your program would complement my current studies and would allow me to acquire all the necessary elements to become an excellent professional. Indeed, courses such as *Introduction to Stochastic Differential Equations* and *Continuous Time Stochastic Control* would strengthen my mathematical tools; courses like *Credit Risk: Modeling and Management* and *Dynamic Asset Pricing Theory* would teach me to apply these technical tools to real financial products. It is this broad understanding of financial mechanisms that I will need in the future. Having done so much theoretical work at XXX, I am attracted to courses like *International Financial Markets and Monetary Institutions* and to the Master's project, which will give me hands-on experience and allow me to acquire a more "intuitive" feeling of financial notions. I would be honored to work with Darrell Duffie and Kenneth J. Singleton and learn from their insights in credit and liquidity risk research. Indeed, I am very interested in the field of risk management, as I believe much can be improved in the present financial situation with more precise quantification.

Professor Friedrich P's work in the Rapid Prototyping Laboratory ideally matches my taste, and I would be thrilled to follow his courses. The development of fuel cells is source of many problems and considering its huge potential impact on society, I find it intellectually challenging. I would be pleased to join the research team working on the "ion highway" project. Other research programs attract me: I would like to improve the electrolyte and electrode reactions in order to lower the SOFCs' operating temperature. The "thin film processing techniques" and its application also appeal to me, since it would allow me to combine my interests in materials and energy. In addition, I would like to take courses from Professor Kenneth F. in heat transfer and Professor Peter M. Pinsky in finite element analysis, for I need to acquire enough specific background before starting research. I am also interested in participating in a project with Professor Fu-Koy X. in the Structures and Composite Laboratory, working perhaps on design and damage tolerance of composite structures. Because these enlightened materials have fantastic outcomes in energy savings for the transportation sector, I could easily see myself as part of team testing their reliability and durability.

Columbia will help me advance both the technical and managerial side of my dual skill-set with courses like *Deterministic Models* and *Managing Technological Innovation*. The program's wide range of courses and high degree of flexibility fits perfectly with my desire for broad and multidisciplinary expertise.

Try **linking the courses** you are taking this year or next semester with those you will follow abroad. Show coherence, logic and purpose.

> At Duke, I would choose the *Advanced Engineering and Corporate Economics* course taught by Steve K. to understand how the financial performance of a firm is assessed and link it with the ethical criteria Socially Responsible Investment (SRI) funds are based on. I believe this will be a concrete application of the game theories I am learning, but also in keeping with the interest for corporate finance I developed during my *Finance, Strategy and Organizations* classes.

4. The faculty

Do not just mention the **names of the professors** (anyone can browse a website). Say something of substance about each professor by name, something that reveals you know and appreciate that person's work. Do not necessarily pick the most famous professor at the grad school; chances are many other applicants will do the same, and the admissions committee members will be unconsciously filtering those mentions out. Besides, the most famous professors do not necessarily work with all graduate students.

Check the professors' **research**: **read their papers** and make a link with the courses you plan to attend. The papers should be recent, if possible. Try to make the research interest resonate with your own experience and knowledge, be it in the classroom, the lab or a company where you have interned.

As you may well understand little in a paper, focus on the **abstract** and, at best, read the **introduction** and **conclusion**. The idea is to get a general drift of the recent trends in the research being conducted there. Of course, it is always positive to be one step ahead of the research and suggest some directions which you might be party of in case you fully understand the paper.

Footnote the papers you have read (title, source, date of publication) when you mention them in the SOP. Alternately, you can put the references at the very end of the SOP. Therefore, admissions officers will read the SOP in a fluent way, focusing on its content and general trends.

> Parallel to that, environment-targeted computational methods are a wide field of exploration, into which I hope to delve with courses like Pr. Fotini K. Chow's on Numerical Methods for Environmental Flow Modeling. I was struck by her work on complex-terrain weather simulation, and would be eager to take part in her research whose applications range from mountain weather forecast to wind turbine design(3).
>
> (3) Investigation of model parameters for high-resolution wind energy forecasting: Case studies over simple and complex terrain, N. Marjanovic, S. Wharton, F.K. Chow

I read with interest Kathleen E's paper on "How firms navigate cooperation and competition in nascent ecosystems"[1], in which she identifies three strategies for companies, namely *component*, *system* and *bottleneck*, exhibiting tipping dynamics or dialectic tension at the interplay of competition and cooperation. I look forward to attending her *Strategy in Technology-Based Companies* class in which she analyzes competitive positioning and resource-based perspectives for high technology firms. I expect the content of the course to strongly resonate with what I know of McKinsey's approach on this subject.

1. Hannah DP, Eisenhardt KM. How firms navigate cooperation and competition in nascent ecosystems. Strat Mgmt J. 2018;39:3163–3192.

5. The course content

Make sure you say something about the **content of the coursework** and how relevant to your experience or career it will be. You need to show that your decision to apply is fully justified.

I plan to take Olivier T's course in *Water Science and Environment* which will allow me to explore some concrete problems in environmental fluid mechanics and to learn the modeling approach in this field, an excellent tool to understand the natural environment. It was a one-month internship in Playa del Carmen in Mexico that led me to choose this course. Due to wild hurricanes, the sea has been taking away the sand from the beaches and left hotel owners looking for solutions. One proposal was to build an undersea wall, a thrilling challenge, but one that might destroy their environment and the biodiversity of the Caribbean Sea. During this month, I observed some of the concrete problems in sustainable development, including water issues, and became determined to seek scientific solutions.

I believe the *Continuous Time Asset Pricing* course would fortify my theoretical knowledge, but would also present different numerical techniques and expand my competence. The *Monte Carlo Simulation* course would clearly build on the foundations I will be acquiring next semester and show me the ins and outs of these simulations. Then, *Optimization Models and Methods for Financial Engineering* would teach me how to choose the most appropriate optimization method, and to code and apply it. I appreciate this program for its combination of theory and practical skills, but also for allowing the development of analytical skills. This I would do in *Advanced Engineering and Corporate Economics* by tackling economic evaluations of firms and projects, an essential step to be ready for managerial positions in the corporate world.

Technological innovation linked to strategy and entrepreneurship is what I have most enjoyed at college, a knowledge base I would now like to build on. When Kathleen E. talks about the view researchers have about ventures, or Tom K.

describes his creative view on the same subject, I feel I am looking through the right window, catching an extraordinary glimpse of the variety and passion that can exist in my future entrepreneurial projects. This is exactly what I want to develop, the capacity to "see the world with fresh eyes", and know which strategies to choose. Working in MS&E with today's and tomorrow's successful entrepreneurs would be the nourishing and challenging environment I need in order to become one of the top movers who will be answering the energy issues of the future.

I would now like to understand not only technology, but also business issues such as investment, management and strategic planning. I am currently able to understand scientific aspects of new technologies, but this is far from being enough: courses such as *Organizational Behavior and Management* and *Strategy in Technology-based Companies* would teach me to make cutting edge technologies credible for the marketplace. I would acquire the ability to take a promising theoretical concept and turn it into technology that people can use all over the world.

Professor X's research, whose class I plan to attend, has laid bare how complicated and captivating computer graphics can be, deepening my understanding of concepts I have encountered before, like vertices and meshes. Moreover, next semester I am also looking forward to my first specialized class on animation, which will combine theoretical aspects such as differential equations and practical sides and therefore pave the way to a solid grasp of the Cornell-Technion program. In addition to such technical study, I have taken more artistic courses such as drawing, architecture and computer graphics. The drawing course helped me improve my perception of light, patterns and shapes, and to be more observant, while the introductory architecture course trained me to become more familiar with 3D software such as Blender and Maya.

6. Lab work and project work

You can insist on the **practical aspect of the program** you are applying for:

However, beyond the theoretical study, I am working on a financial project about pricing algorithms for American options. I am enjoying the connection between theory and the real issues, and would like to continue developing a practical approach to technical problems along with strong theoretical tools to solve them.

Having acquired a solid foundation in numerical theory and general mechanics, I would now like to apply this knowledge to learning how to design aerospace products. Being theoretical and mathematical, I am interested in learning to compute problems that include several disciplines; for instance, computations that could combine structure and fluid interactions, as well as large deformations. Thus, my research interests are mainly numerical analysis and computational mechanics and their application to aerodynamics and fluid structure interaction. I am particularly interested in the powerful finite element method which applies to several cases in fluid dynamics, as well as solid mechanics. The Aerospace Computational Lab seems to be the perfect place to do research in that domain. I would be honored to work in the 3DG group under the supervision of Professor Jaime P.

In the same way, check the **labs** in which you might be able to design research or participate in a project. You can also link it with an internship you will do prior to joining the program.

I am quite interested in the research work that is being led at Berkeley. In particular, Professor F.G's research on the microbial degradation of emerging contaminants, using molecular tools to understand and optimize how microbes detoxify certain pollutants is exactly the sort of study I would like to get involved in. For that reason, I have set up a four-month research internship, beginning in March, at the Laboratory for Environmental Biotechnology (LBE) of the Swiss Federal Institute for Technology in Lausanne. The use of living organisms to detoxify water is both an ecological and economical solution to water pollution in developing countries and is, therefore, the technology that must be further developed for these contexts. Under the direction of Dr. J. D., I will work on the biodegradation of xenobiotic and recalcitrant compounds that pollute water, using molecular techniques and methods to better understand the physiology and interaction of the microbial populations involved in pollution degradation.

The Aerospace Computational Lab seems to be the perfect place to do research in that domain. I would be honored to work in the 3DG group under the supervision of Professor Jaime P. Indeed, I am fascinated by the higher order methods they are developing, especially the Discontinuous Galerkin Finite Element method, which stands out for its high accuracy with minimal dispersion. It is amazing how it can produce stable discretization for advection schemes, no matter what the order, something I have not yet seen in my coursework.

I would very much like to help build an intelligent robot that can move like an animal, have complex interactions, and learn behaviors. Thus, I would take Oussama K's courses on robotics. I am also fascinated by his research projects on humanoid robots, which could lead to the totally new world that we have seen in science-fiction literature. I would be honored to work on any of these projects, as I am convinced that this kind of research will bring one of the most important future revolutions in our society.

Check whether the programs include a **capstone project**. The goal of this task is to challenge a student to carry out significant research over an extended period of time. While similar in some ways to a thesis, capstone projects may take a wide variety of forms, but most are year-long investigative projects, in collaboration with an industry or not, that culminate in a final product, presentation, or performance. The capstone must be in line with a student's topic, issue or problem of interest. Students conduct research on the subject and give an oral presentation on the project and their findings to a panel of professors, and experts. The successful completion of a capstone project can be used for an employment portfolio.

Alternatively, students may be required to write an MSc thesis in the subject / field that they are interested in working on. Whether it is the capstone or a year-long / semester-long project, it should be mentioned in the personal statement. Be inspirational. For this, you might want to check which are the problems that PhD students enrolled in the program actually work on or the research professors are focusing on. It will give some sense of direction and purpose. Above all, don't be vague, and avoid writing that you want to have an impact or change the world or that you are interested in working in the energy or healthcare fields. An example of relevant capstone you might want to work on goes like this:

```
Building on my experience in computer vision, and due to my personal history
and severe eyesight problems, I am particularly enthused by Brian B's project
of a Vision Correcting Display. I found the idea of incorporating a person's
own optical aberrations into the computation, to compensate for the optical
blurring on the target image by a process of prefiltering with the inverse blur
particularly inspiring and would be thrilled to contribute to such a project.
```

7. Visit to the campus

If you have **visited the campus** and met with professors/researchers there, or corresponded with some in the targeted program, this is the place to mention it.

```
In the course of a discussion with Prof. Martin while visiting the Johns-Hop-
kins campus, we mentioned the possible idea of being part of a genomics project
which my programming and biology skills might contribute in a meaningful way.
```

8. Highlight your career vision

You are encouraged to link the graduate program with your own **professional aspirations** and your **career vision**. Remember that this is a statement with a purpose and the admissions officers will consider whether your prospects warrant admission. In addition, they want to have students with a focus in life. That vision may be expressed right at the beginning of the paragraph "Why your program appeals to me". It can also be mentioned in the conclusion.

My short-term goal is to start my career working for a management consulting firm in order to acquire practical experience dealing with business problems. Later, probably quite a bit later, I aim to set up my own company using all the knowledge that consulting will have taught me. To do any of this correctly, I still need a graduate program which will give me realistic approaches to business. Having attended high school summer sessions in the United States, I believe the American pragmatic approach to education is highly complementary to the theoretical training I have had in France, and is exactly what I now need.

My project for the near future is to work in a financial institution as a quant or a statistical trader, using mathematical reasoning to take measured risks and turn them into profit. Then, later, my dream is to set up my own financial company, for waiting inside me there is an entrepreneur who will someday urge me to start my own business. That time has not yet arrived, for my current goal is to obtain the best education in the field of finance. Thus, I am looking for an MSc in Financial Engineering, and the Fu Foundation at Columbia University offers the program that best fits my needs.

In a variety of disciplines at my school, my curiosity and enthusiasm have risen every time we have taken another step into deeper and more complex scientific knowledge. Working at the threshold of what is unknown in the subject which fascinates me the most, nanomaterials and their environmental applications, is what I want to be doing for my life's work.

In the future, I expect to begin my career as a researcher on industrial projects for commercial aviation or aerospace companies. I would then like to evolve into being a project manager with a strong scientific approach. I am convinced that UPenn has the perfect program for my professional goals, and I, in turn, would bring my multidisciplinary background, my international culture, and my intense interest in aeronautics to contribute to life on the campus.

In ten years' time, I see myself working in industry, creating new materials to meet tomorrow's needs in medical products. Allowing myself to be inspired by Nature, I want to create materials that will help restore vital abilities to dysfunctioning bodies. With this goal in mind, I now need a wide and professional understanding of the properties of industrial materials. The Master's Program in Materials Science and Engineering at the University of M. is offering exactly that. Here, I would gain the multidisciplinary training I seek in physics, biology and chemistry. This is not only complementary to the background I have gained at school, it is specifically the path I want to take towards my future career. I am especially interested in taking the courses in *Polymer Physics*, *Biocompatibility* and *Materials Chemistry* for they would show me how physics is related to the medical sciences. I am also very interested in David M's research on polymer coating for biomedical devices for it would allow me to combine and deepen my knowledge in both biology and material coating. Biology and Physics together are uncovering amazing new solutions for mankind, such as restoring sight and hearing. This is the kind of adventure I aim to join, and with your help I will develop much more than a hat and a whip.

Years from now, I would like to look back on my career and find that I have made a substantial contribution to new generations of reactors which have exceeded expectations, that my efforts in construction include the implantation of safe and efficient power plants in less developed countries, and that my achievements include a major breakthrough in energy collecting on the ITER project that will then be built and operational. With your help, this dream would become reality.

9. Don'ts

Avoid giving the impression of writing the **course catalog** when you mention your interest for the program.

*First, I would be very pleased to follow the core curriculum. The courses *Atmosphere and Global Environment Change and Air Pollution Modeling* would answer the questions that have been nagging me this year. Because I would like to deepen my knowledge in climate change adaptations, the course *Climate Policy Analysis* would give me a clearer view of the current situation. Then, *Fundamentals of Energy Processes and Energy Resources* would give me a broad vision and understanding of the energy sources I hope to be dealing with. Add the course on *Energy and Environmental Policy Analysis* and I would have a complete set of essential tools for my career. I am convinced that the Atmosphere and Energy program is where I need to be next year if I am going to make a difference to society. In return, I would bring my theoretical training, adaptability and dedication to enhance my class.

*But working in an international organization requires also a certain knowledge of international laws and economy. So, I would be able to take courses in truly useful fields such as "Alternative energy resources", "Energy, sources and conversion" and "Carbon sequestration". But I would also take courses dealing with more economic or legal topics such as "Economics of Earth resource industries" and "Production of inorganic materials", involving skills I will need if I want to work in an international organization. Finally, I would strengthen my background in ecology by taking courses like "Industrial ecology".

*I would, for example, choose the class on Dynamic Entrepreneurial Strategy to acquire a rigorous approach to market analysis. Next, I would take the class on *Capital Deployment* for it would be an ideal way for me to connect theoretical stochastic skills with more concrete business plans issues. Then, *Engineering Risk Analysis* would allo me to delve into the mechanisms and problems when creating a high-tech business.

Do not be a sycophant. The adcom will see right through smarmy students who think fulsome compliments are the road for admission. They will not fall in for blandishments. So, do not be a **toady**, do not **polish the apple**:

> *My interest in your department is due to its international reputation and the fact that it can boast academically renowned professors such as Professor S. Bernstein, as well as strong links with industry and research laboratories.

> *Europe may not be the best place to be trained in acoustics, and the United States is more dynamic in the field. Penn State University is indeed the only institution that owns a specific Department of Acoustics.

> *Finally, in a world going global, where the aerospace industry is a strategic sector, only top-ranking universities can help me achieve my dreams, only Stanford can train engineers able to conduct projects such as Apollo missions.

> *Last but not least, I regard this year abroad as an exciting challenge and I am eager to find myself in an environment where emulation will encourage me to give my best.

> *I am keen on having a go in the US world of science. Starting at Princeton, framed by top scientists in the domain I hold dear, is an opportunity I would cherish. Becoming a graduate in your M.A.E. Department is the exact environment where my taste for hard work, collective effort and long-term vision could be fully expressed.

- Do not be a **panderer**:

> *The United States appears as one of the most challenging environments in the field. Brown University would be the perfect starting point because of its unique human and geopolitical resources.

- Avoid the **self-evident statement** when describing the program or a course.

> *Moreover, the SLAC is an incredible instrument on this subject because it is one of the most prolific colliders currently in use.

> *And the race for more and more brilliant theories is going to be even more intense, since we will be able to test their consequences with the LHC. Thus, working now on the latest improvements of the split supersymmetry theory will be an immensely worthwhile endeavor.

- Do not be a **Mr. Know-it-all** in order to gain admission. Admitting you is their decision to make, not yours.

> *By studying at your university, I consider that my theoretical academic background in mechanics, applied mathematics and computer science would benefit from a more pragmatic experience than I could not expect to gain here in France.

> *I have a strong belief that a graduate degree from your department is the most valuable training for me to succeed in my chosen path. I strongly hope that my background and qualifications are found suitable to pursue a graduate program at the University of Michigan and I am eager to hear your advice.

- Avoid mentioning the **international make-up of the student body** for a reason to study abroad. After all, most HE institutions are host to international students today, including in France.

> *The international nature of the student body and staff in the MSc is a major attraction for me, since I have travelled and backpacked extensively for many years, developing and nurturing a growing interest for foreign cultures and ways of life.

V. My Academic Background

1. From the baccalaureate to college/the preparatory program

The academic background paragraph can chronologically be the second or the third one in the statement. It may look more logical to put it in the second place, and then follow up with the 'Why your program appeals to me' paragraph. Nevertheless, for admissions officers pressed by time, putting 'Why your program appeals to me' in the second position shows clearly why you want to join the program.

The question you need to answer in this paragraph is the following: Do I have what it takes to follow your program? Do I have the prerequisite background to be an active member of the program you offer? How well have I prepared myself to succeed in graduate school? What body of relevant knowledge will I take with me? What skills have I honed? What intellectual characteristics make me particularly likely to succeed? What research have I completed to date and what role have I played in the projects I have carried out? A short introductory sentence will do:

- I feel confident that my undergraduate studies have prepared me to effectively take on the challenges of graduate study at MIT.
- I feel confident that I have acquired a strong basis for advanced study in engineering during my undergraduate years.
- From a youthful contemplation of nature in Southern France, and a will to have a lasting and positive impact on an increasingly globalized world, I have thus acquired multidisciplinary scientific skills in order to be prepared to deal with the issues of atmospheric pollution and energy consumption.
- In the course of my studies, I have gained familiarity with approaches in fundamental science and applied science alike. It is for this reason that I am convinced that I am well-equipped for Harvard's School of Engineering and Applied Sciences.
- I am confident that my coursework over the past several years has provided me with the kind of scientific background I will need for graduate study in mechanical engineering at a rigorous program like that of MIT.

The French academic program (US spelling) includes what we call the ***baccalaureat***, prior to admission to the **Preparatory program** (=*classes préparatoires*) or **college** (also called university in Europe). It is not necessary to mention the *baccalaureat* in the SOP when you apply for graduate studies. The *baccalaureat* is a little-known notion in the United States. There is no equivalent. American high school students actually receive a diploma once they have completed high school. There is no nationwide exam, similar to the *bac* in France. In the U.S., high school is typically a four-year program that starts with ninth grade and ends with twelfth grade. Students start high school at the age of 14. High school students complete a program of general education courses, but they can also choose from a series of electives, in more specialized subjects such as computer science, music, art, and foreign languages.

The question remains of how to translate the word *baccalaureat* for those who wish to include it in their statements. The easiest and simple way is to leave the word as it is and give a British equivalent in brackets (=A levels). You will also add the mention **in sciences**. A **baccalaureate** in the U.S. may be a speech, a sermon or a religious service for the graduating class of a high school, college or university, held shortly before commencement. It is also a bachelor's degree.

If you have been awarded a *mention*, here are some ways to translate them:

- *mention assez bien*: don't mention it!
- *mention bien*: with high honors/distinction
- *mention très bien (avec felicitations du jury)*: with highest honors/distinction (avoid the summa cum laude!)

Please notice the US spelling **honors** in comparison with the British spelling **honours**. Also, remember the distinction between **taking** and **passing** an exam. To take an exam/to sit an exam: *passer un examen*; to pass an exam: *réussir un examen*. Syn. to be successful.

The **preparatory program** is typically French. It should **not** be translated by preparatory classes or prep school. In the **United States** a preparatory school, or prep school, is usually a private secondary school (or high school) designed to prepare students for higher education. In the **United Kingdom** and some parts of the Commonwealth of Nations, a Preparatory School, or Prep. School is a private school, designed to prepare a student for fee paying Public Schools. The age range catered for may be only eight- to thirteen-year-olds, or it may include younger pupils as well.

Only four percent of French students make it into the public *grandes écoles*. But the *grandes écoles*, along with a swath of semiprivate preparatory schools, absorb 30 percent of the state budget.

The preparatory program is where students acquire some rigor and discipline in their work habits. They also gain reasoning and analytical skills. Students choose several tracks:

- scientific (it can be physics, math, chemistry, engineering sciences tracks)
- business (economics or math)
- engineering (engineering sciences, SE in French)
- literary (literature and the humanities)

It is not necessary to tarry too long on the preparatory program or college: what matters is the hard core of your undergraduate studies there. There is no need to explain what the preparatory program is about. However, it will be mentioned if only briefly as it represents the first two years of undergraduate studies, which cannot be ignored. Similarly, there is no need to mention the elite preparatory programs of *Lycée Ste Geneviève* or *Lycée Louis-le-Grand*.

If you have chosen the **university track** (=*voie universitaire*) to get into a *grande école*, mention which university you come from. The heart of the matter is what you did at college/*école*/university XXX, how well you perform. If you chose to enter a *grande école* after the university program, justify your choice.

> Upon completion of a BSc in Physics at University Paris V, I chose to broaden my intellectual horizons and explore other avenues of science. The Ecole XXX appeared then as the next best step to do so.

The **entrance examinations** to the *grandes écoles* are highly challenging. You may say that you were admitted through competitive written and oral exams/after tough examinations which select the best and brightest students amongst 3,000-4,000 candidates. Yet, there is no need to explain the French system of education.

> I feel that my academic background has prepared me to take this next step. After obtaining my scientific baccalaureate (high school diploma), I spent two years training for the competitive entrance exams to enter France's leading institutions for scientific study. During this time, I focused on the disciplines of mathematics, physics and computer science. The extremely competitive nature of the exam forced me to work under pressure, an experience that I feel has prepared me for the challenges ahead. Although it was hard work, I enjoyed this education, as it gave me a sound scientific background that now serves as a steppingstone to more advanced study.

> My scientific training began during my years in the preparatory program studying a range of fields for the national competitive exams to enter the *grandes écoles*. These intensive and stimulating years enhanced my ability to learn new concepts rapidly and to use them efficiently. It was during this period that I developed a deep interest in computer science which has grown continuously ever since. Thanks to hard work, I obtained results that qualified me for a place at the Ecole XXX, one of France's leading institutions for scientific study. Upon entering the Ecole, I was most interested in physics and computer science, and was eager to explore the theoretical possibilities of both these fields.

> After passing my *baccalaureat* with highest honors, I chose to spend two years studying mathematics, physics and chemistry in a preparation program leading to competitive exams to enter top-ranking science universities. I also took English, German and Philosophy courses. This period was crucial for me as I was compelled to work an average of fourteen hours a day, under a lot of pressure, taking three or four tests every week. Thus, I learned how to work efficiently, how to cope with stress and sometimes failure, so as to be among the best in my class.

> After obtaining my *baccalaureat*, I spent two years of intensive training in order to pass the national competitive entrance exams. During that time, I focused on the disciplines of mathematics, physics and computer science. The extremely competitive nature of the exam (top schools offer 400 berths for 3,500 students registered for the exam) forced me to work under pressure. Although it was hard work, I enjoyed this educational experience, as it gave me a sound scientific background that now serves as a steppingstone to more advanced study.

> Blessed with a mathematical mind, it was natural that, once I had passed the *baccalaureat* in sciences, awarded with highest honors, I should enroll in the intensive and demanding undergraduate program of the preparatory program which was to lead me to the Ecole XXX in 2019.

> I worked hard in order to be admitted to Ecole XXX, the only science school that also offers students courses in economics and the social sciences. Its entrance examination is extremely competitive and the depth of the program is such that it requires perseverance and the ability to work under a great deal of pressure.

> My scientific training began during my years at preparatory school studying a range of fields for the national competitive exams to enter the *grandes écoles*. These intensive and stimulating years enhanced my ability to learn new concepts rapidly and to use them efficiently. It was during this period that I developed a deep interest in computer science that has grown continuously since. Thanks to hard work, I obtained results that qualified me for a place at the Ecole XXX, one of France's leading institutions for scientific study.

> I am confident that I have acquired the right kind of training to that next step. I developed the foundations of my scientific background after high school, when I spent two years of intensive study in mathematics, economics and history to prepare for the entrance examination for business schools. The extremely competitive nature of this exam taught me how to work efficiently under pressure.

- **Awards**. Some may have performed outside the realm of the preparatory program. They may have taken part in the **Olympiads**, whether at the national or international level. If you have been the recipient of a bronze, silver or gold medal, it is worth mentioning it. The **International Science Olympiads** are a group of worldwide annual competitions in various areas of science. The competitions are designed for the 4-6 best high school students from each participating country selected through internal National Science Olympiads. You have the IMO (International Math Olympiad), IPhO (International Physics Olympiad), IOI (International Olympiad for Informatics), etc. Olympiads are held annually. Up to 100 countries are represented.

> Given my passion for physics during this time, I earned the chance to represent France in the 39th International Physics Olympiads in Hanoi, Vietnam in 2008.

```
My passion for problem solving goes back to the mathematics and physics compe-
titions I took part in during high school. I was among the five students selected
to represent France at the 2019 International Physics Olympiads, where I was
awarded a silver medal. These experiences convinced me to follow the French
preparatory program that led me to the ENS (Paris Ulm) where I was admitted in
Mathematics (ranked 10 in the nationwide entrance exam).
```

After I was awarded my third gold medal in the Brazilian Mathematical Olympiad for Public Schools at the age of 13, I went on studying for the IMO, in which I participated two years later and where I was awarded silver and bronze medals. I went on to win awards in other international contests while studying at the *Instituto Tecnologico de Aeronautica* (ITA). As a freshman, I was ranked first in the Brazilian Mathematical Olympiad for Undergraduate Students, the Brazilian equivalent of the Putnam Competition, while competing against more advanced college students. By seeking to excel in these competitions, I proved that perseverance, autonomy and ambition were not hollow words.

In the same way, it is worth mentioning if you have been awarded a prize in the ***Concours general*** (a national academic contest/competition, which is open to France's top math/physics... 11th or 12th grade students), whatever the field. In a subject, up to 18 prizes can be given. So, make a difference between prize/*accessit* (honorable mention)/regional award. If you have been selected but earned no rewards, you may indicate your selection. Being a *lauréat of the Concours général* is a prestigious award for any high school student. Many well-known French scientists, artists and literary figures have won the *Concours Général* in one or even several subjects. Note: **avoid mentioning the Kangaroo Math Competition** (KMC):

*I have never felt stressed when competing in mathematics contests, such as the French "Concours Kangourou", in which I ranked sixth in 2012.

2. Undergraduate/college/*Grande école* curriculum

The **rank of your school** might play a role in the U.S. (where graduating in the top 10% at Stanford is preferable to being in the top 1% at an unknown college). In general, graduate schools compile and keep a list of good universities in different parts of the world. This helps the committee to an extent, especially when they are unfamiliar with institutions. If worse comes to worst, admissions officers refer to current enrollees whom they can turn to for information about the school of origin, or they go through faculty research to assess the level of the foreign schools. The committee might also resort to doing a web search about the applicant's university or looking at its website to gauge its reputation. The list of foreign schools however is by no means exhaustive and often might not get updated frequently enough to reflect the current state of affairs. That is why French schools are not always well known to the Americans and therefore they will make little difference between the ENS programs, Polytechnique, Telecom Paris, Arts et Métiers Paris Tech or any other engineering school, or business schools such as HEC, ESSEC, ESCP, EDHEC..., let alone the universities. Which may explain why some students from one school are denied admission while students from other schools will get in. For example, a student ranked in the top 1% of a medium tier engineering school may have more chances of admission than another student who went to a top school, yet was ranked overall in the top 40% only. When taking the GPA into consideration, a 3.9 in one school may qualify a student who, at Polytechnique, only got a 3.7.

When dealing with your undergraduate education – post-preparatory program – you will divide your paragraph into three parts:

3. Coursework

You need to write about **relevant coursework** only (do not talk about the *Architecture* studio when you apply for a data science program, for example).

Do not mention courses you have taken unless you have something interesting and consistent to say about them.

Do not use **empty words** to describe a course, a project or a field as in the following examples:

```
*It was then that I developed a passion for mathematics: I loved the elegance and efficiency I found in real analysis and group theory, my favorite topics.
```

```
*To strengthen my programming skills, I also took a fair amount of computer science classes.
```

```
*One of my research projects dealt with the fractal compression of images, proving the convergence of the algorithm and then implementing it. Seeing the connection between the theory and the concrete results was a source of tremendous satisfaction.
```

– Do talk about a professor's approach which stimulated your interest, or thrilled you to your toes. Describe in detail both what was taught and how you reacted. What choices has this led you to make? Be specific. Do not produce a catalogue of your courses (admissions committees have your transcripts). Remember: you are sending transcripts of **all** the courses you have taken, here you are talking about the **few** that have really mattered.

```
Once I have a good understanding of a domain, I like to see how it interacts with other, new fields. When the time came to choose a specialty, I knew I needed to find a path that would invariably keep me moving. I searched for an innovative science which constantly progresses, offers challenges and is on the cutting-edge. When Roman B. talked about the impact of material science, the way its evolution has modified peoples' lives and what were the new challenges, I was stunned. It was exactly the creative and promising science I was loo-
```

king for. The only thing missing was the link with medical science, for I had long wanted to work in its interface with physics. I discussed my project many times with Professor B., who pointed me in the right direction: biomaterials. Although this science has a strong basis in physics and chemistry, it is a field which is wide open, with unanswered questions to last me a lifetime. This is my definition of adventure.

This year, I am specializing in biophysics and electronics. The course in *Physics of Biological Structures* explains the cellular metabolisms that I am learning in the *Cellular Biology* course. I am enjoying the creativity in building theoretical physics models that describe objects in the world of the living cell. In the course on *Active Materials*, I am studying conductive electro-active polymers, working to use them to propel a "swimming" microrobot. Defining our research plan with the resources we were given has been motivating and required inventiveness and breadth of vision. Then, in *Physics of Electrons in Solids*, as well as next term's courses on *Spintronics*, *Optoelectronics* and *Nanomaterials and their applications in Electronics*, I am enjoying a growing understanding of nanoscale electronics and the current trends that motivate research in this field.

This year, I am enjoying the cutting-edge math used in the world of finance in Pierre T's class on stochastic calculus and finance. The first time I was successfully able to price a European call option with the Black-Scholes model felt like a real personal achievement, a concrete application of the mathematics I have been studying for so long. Having learned that a number of asset pricing topics, such as market manipulation models, had been influenced by game theory, I chose the course on that subject taught by Kurt W. I have found his pragmatic approach fantastic, for it is enabling me to understand new concepts such as Lyupanov stability in the replicator dynamic.

Nicola K's course on *Random Walks* attracted my interest to the field of quantitative finance. It was discovering Markov chains and martingales which allowed me to model strategies in random environments, such as perfect stopping time in decision making. I loved using theory to impact real decisions and felt pulled to study this field in depth. This theoretical approach was complemented by Pierre L's course on *Mathematical Modelling* focusing on numerical methods. Seeing the concrete aspects given by the use of computer simulations was fascinating, for the results of my projects were not abstract theorems, but solutions built on the methods and parameters I had chosen, and could change.

Last year, I started specializing in economics, taking courses in fields such as microeconomics, macroeconomics and game theory. These complementary approaches have helped me gain a broader perspective of the economic world. I finally understand major concepts, such as the role of central banks, the relationship between growth and interest rates, and the impact of increased competition on prices. I especially enjoyed the economic history course during which Professor G. developed original interpretations of historic events such as the American

Civil War. Seeing the impact of economic factors on political decision-making was fascinating.

Antoine G's course on *The Theory of Distributions* showed me that function generalization is an impressively powerful tool. I love seeing the technical simplicity brought to the manipulation of non-regular functions, thus permitting the modelling of non-continuous natural phenomena. When I realized that distribution could be interpreted by average values, it made perfect sense; in fact, we deal with averages in most situations. This idea was re-enforced by Jean D's course on *Quantum Mechanics* where the concept of probability was associated with every possible state of a microscopic system, basing acceptable observations on averages.

– You can mention the choice of your school based on the **broad-based** or **cross-disciplinary curriculum**, and more, generally, its advantages.

- The curriculum at XXX introduced me to a wide range of subjects, both in and outside the field of Mechanics.

- The XXX program has enhanced my capacities to deal with abstract problems while opening vistas on new fields of science.

- At University XXX, the diversity of the curriculum has allowed me to expand my knowledge and understanding of mathematics across several domains.

- At college, I have had the opportunity to acquire a broad, multidisciplinary scientific background, upon which I have developed my focus on environmental issues. The training is very demanding, as students are required to study many different disciplines. But such a program was advantageous for my particular career goals, since it allowed me to combine my technical training with coursework in economics.

- The school's cross-disciplinary and broad curriculum strengthened my knowledge in fundamentals, while opening the door to other avenues that I followed with the eagerness of the adventurer that is never satisfied with what he knows.

– Say something interesting about the **courses you have followed**. In particular, **avoid the "catalog" aspect** such as in this example:

*My coursework there has been multidisciplinary and mainly theoretical. Last year, in addition to advanced classes in physics, I also studied biology, mechanics, chemistry, economics, and both pure and applied mathematics.

But this is acceptable:

- Last year also allowed me to acquire an acute capacity for problem-solving in several domains ranging from mechanics, economics, biology, pure math and quantum physics to architecture.

- At XXX, I started off by following a multidisciplinary curriculum, with electives that gave me some training in the area of architectural engineering. My classes in mechanics and numerical analysis, for example, provided me with the tools for understanding and predicting how structures will behave over time in the face of erosive forces.

– Try to link the curriculum with **future coursework** when possible.

My courses in *Nuclear Physics* and *Astrophysics* (taught by Martin L.) and my class on *Energy and the Environment* have provided valuable instruction on the potential and environmental impact of different energy sources—an introduction that will allow me to progress rapidly in developing this key area of expertise at the graduate level.

The course I enjoyed the most was *Condensed Matter* taught by Richard E. It has given me the basics to the description of the quantum mechanics of electrons in solids. For instance, I learnt that the Josephson Junctions are integral in superconducting quantum computing as qubits, such as in a flux qubit. I look forward to my coming courses on *Quantum Field Theory* and *General Relativity*, which will help me understand the most recent Information theories further.

I am currently taking Professor Olivier D's course in *Geometric Computing*, which focuses on Delaunay tri-angulation. This class has revealed to me how complicated and captivating computer graphics can be, deepening my understanding of concepts I have encountered before, like vertices and meshes.

Among all my courses, *Statistical Physics* in particular amazed me by the quantity of fields it can influence, including economics. As I was studying micro- and macroeconomics at the same time, it was fascinating to see the accuracy of scientific methods applied to actual people. Even though this has been partly undermined by the subprime crisis, I still think that economics represents an interesting meeting point between science and humanities.

Similarly, Professor Christian F's course in *Fluid Mechanics* familiarized me with the Navier-Stokes resolution, thereby helping me to understand significant coefficients, such as viscosity and the Reynolds number, which I am now able to use effectively. From interactions between solids to particle systems, my coursework in mechanics helped me understand how software and algorithms work, and made me eager to participate in the creation of new algorithms.

– Mention relevant coursework from **first, second and third year**, showing how you **built up your knowledge base**. If not, try to link the years in this way:

> These years of comprehensive overview gave me the keys to explore the vast scientific world, and choose the right path. This year I have specialized as much as possible in areas that will equip me with the skills to succeed in computer graphics work at the graduate level. Hence, I am currently taking...

> I am following *Quantum Optics*, with Fabien B., which introduces lasers. I am thrilled at the way transversal physical notions are being put into perspective, bringing new interpretations of physical phenomena. The striking applications (such as atoms cooling to the nano-Kelvin) have encouraged me to have a daring thought-process, to challenge some well-established hypotheses to obtain creative results.

– You may mention the **classes you are going to study next semester** (and that will complete/complement the program) (all deadlines are usually from December to February, that is before the end of the year).

> In addition, in the Spring semester I will be taking such critical courses as *Development Economics*, which will equip me with the theoretical skills to tackle the economic aspects of environmental issues. The training I would bring to Imperial is thus strongly multidisciplinary.

> Next semester, I will be able to deepen my mathematical knowledge of stochastic processes during the course entitled *Processes and Estimations*. The *Stochastic Simulation and Monte Carlo Methods* is another course of great interest to me for, once again, I will be acquiring techniques used in the practical implementation of theoretical models.

> Next semester I am looking forward to my first specialized class on animation, which will combine theoretical aspects such as differential equations and practical sides.

– Show how those courses will resonate with what you will be studying in the U.S./UK, in other words how the US/UK program will add up to your knowledge.
– Try to regroup the coursework under some headings (for example, Applied Math + Computer Science for a Data Science program, Fluid Mechanics + Solid Mechanics + Optimization for a program in Aeronautics, International Macroeconomics and History for a geopolitics program…). It will show how structured your thought process is and how focused you are.
– Only mention the **names** of the **professors/supervisors/researchers** that will recommend you and put them in bold letters so the admissions officers will connect them with the recommendation letters easily. Some students are prone to slip in the names of Fields Medal recipients, Nobel Prize winners or other luminaries into their statement, if only to impress the jury. This

is called **name dropping** which no admissions committee will fall for. So, avoid it. It is common knowledge that Nobel Prize recipients and others are no longer put in charge of teaching and therefore have little connection with the students. Yet, there are exceptions when they hire students to carry out research for them. In that case, a letter is always welcome.

– If you have complemented your formation through online courses, and provided you have obtained a certification for those courses, you may mention it in the SOP (as well as on the CV).

```
To round out my knowledge in machine learning and update my knowledge in the field, I signed up for online courses for which I got a full certification.
```

– Do not mention present **course numbers** (such as INF422). Write the title of the course in full.
– No need to explain how your school system works. Thus, such an introduction sentence is not mandated.

```
*All second-year students at the Ecole XXX are required to enroll in courses in different fields in order to enlarge their knowledge and contribute to their open-mindedness.

*Once at XXX, students are required to take at least nine different subjects during their two first years, a situation that was well suited to my desire to acquire the interdisciplinary approach that is essential to productive work in the environmental field.
```

– You do not want to make excuses, but you can talk about the **mistakes you have made as a learning experience**. Americans want to see you as you are, but more likely they want to see through you. Therefore, if you have experienced a drop in grades or failed at some point in a project or an exam, if you have grades or test scores that do not reflect your exact potential, do not conceal it but explain it. If you have earned less-than-stellar grades during your undergraduate education, you might provide some context in the personal statement. Conversely, highlight upswing in grades if applicable.

```
Studying the Fourier Theory in physics class, I was so fascinated by its tremendous potential that I chose to follow a separate math course on the subject. I was disappointed to see that the course was bogged down by dry math instead of showing the vast potential of the theory. I found computer science more satisfying for these courses have allowed me to develop my skills in new technologies and understand the tools I use every day.
```

Students may not feel this is necessary or be comfortable with this, but it is an option. Do not make long and involved excuses, but keep it simple and devoid of drama (two lines maximum).

– If **setbacks** have been learning experiences and helped you to rebound, then you might want to mention them. Do not shun from addressing potential shortcomings, deficiencies or blemishes. But do not give mealy-mouthed, weak excuses for your course results, GPA or test scores. Also, if you address weak points, do not be apologetic but explain how you rebounded.

> The professors were thrilled with our academic work, but our grade was not as good as it should have been because of communication problems between team members. This misadventure also taught me the importance of communication as a key element in teamwork for collaborating more efficiently.

If something **untoward** happened to you (poverty, illness, injury, excessive work, etc.) and affected your grades (a **C or D** in one of the major courses in the field you are interested in) state it, write it affirmatively. Be honest. Better explain than let the admissions officers fantasize about what happened. Draw lessons from failures and difficulties instead of whining and complaining. Focus on the positive and do not blame the system or circumstances in your life. An explanation should not sound like an excuse but should be framed in a way that demonstrates perseverance, capacity to overcome obstacles, improvement or the lessons learned that followed those challenges. The core idea you want to give is this: Is it a true picture of me? Admissions committees are quick to detect a phony, so do not cheat.

More examples

> It was simple logic that took me down the path to the post-secondary preparatory program for the *grandes écoles*. I then chose XXX because of its wide variety of advanced scientific courses. I have taken every physics class offered in the last three years and every hour has been a delight, for each has taken me a step deeper into the core of the subject and offered me the keys I was looking for. From mechanical determinism to quantum physics, I was interested in every theory for each one added a new point of view. I knew I would specialize in physics, but I wanted to study other sciences to widen my way of thinking, to see how they function and how they interact with physics. I have especially enjoyed studying biology and economics. The complexity of biology has allowed me to apply the theories I have been learning in chemistry and physics, which has been satisfying, and even exciting at times. I also like its link with medical science and, last year, I participated in an experimental project on this subject. My partner and I studied antibodies, their structure and specific applications. It was truly stimulating to prove by ourselves, step by step, absolutely everything we had learned about antibodies. The Cartesian side of me was thrilled, while the Indiana Jones in me was thinking ahead to more such experiences.

> I am now studying biophysics and materials coating. I am especially enjoying the first class because it is giving me the chance to apply the theories of physics to the behavior of microscopic organic structures. Organization and transport within cells are the main topics of this course and I have been thrilled to see how the laws of physics always lead to an answer. *Materials Coating* is teaching me how to modify surfaces in order to give them new functions. This course is

```
also convincing me that most of the time, properties we seek can be found in
Mother Nature. Our job is to understand the mechanism underneath. It has been
truly fascinating to see, through these two courses, how imitating nature can
lead to industrial solutions.
```

4. Project work/Research work

You would have to have an amazingly unusual reason not to want to develop this theme. A candidate's research background might hold the key to her/him being chosen over someone else.

Research or **academic project experience** (especially the final year thesis or project) should naturally be mentioned at length, especially when it is **relevant** to the program you are applying for and particularly if they are significantly research-oriented instead of being purely implementational. It is advisable to get one recommendation letter from the professor or researcher who supervised the work. Name the **supervisor** (supervised by/under the supervision of…).

An applicant's research background can be inferred from the **research papers** published in journals and conferences (always provide the full references, or footnote them). A paper published anywhere will carry some weightage. Of course, the committee is more likely to be impressed if the journal or conference is a highly reputed one. The adcom usually maintains a list of first tier, second tier (and other respected) conferences/journals in different fields of studies and refers it to evaluate the value of a publication. Having relevant publication(s) to your name is a safe way to convince the committee members of potential research capability. Though not as crucial as in the case of PhD applications, having research publications for a Master's candidate definitely helps in setting an applicant markedly apart from the rest of the pool. Often, universities ask for a list of publications to be attached while filling the application form. Therefore, it is advisable for the applicants to talk about their publication(s) in detail in the SOP if it is relevant to the program you are applying for. If not, mention it/them in the résumé. If your research has been published on the web, if it is a **working paper**[1], put it in the résumé, or set up a **GitHub site** where you will give further information about a project or give the links to a paper. Bear in mind that a strong research experience may offset some of the unimpressive grades you may have received, especially if they are not in the field of the chosen program.

When mentioning research experience, you should go from the more relevant to the less relevant. Do not use the chronological order when writing about the projects. The admissions officers should see immediately what matters to you.

1. A working paper, or work paper, is a preliminary scientific or technical paper, released by authors who want to share ideas about a topic or elicit feedback before submitting to a peer reviewed conference or academic journal. A working paper can also be a technical report, an official report on a particular problem or situation. It provides suggestions or suggests improvements.
Also note that a **preprint** is a version of a scholarly or scientific paper that precedes peer review and publication in a peer-reviewed scholarly or scientific journal. Both working paper and preprint are available free of charge. Once it has been peer-reviewed, a preprint becomes a **postprint**.

Graduate admissions programs also take into account the following activities that are persuasive to them, such as serving as a **research assistant** to a professor and/or **doing research in a lab** where original research is under way.

How far into the past should you go when referring to research? First, recent research experience matters. Second, that research may have been conducted at university or in the preparatory program (typically some *TIPEs* may be viewed as research). Three, if you plan to carry out a research project in the present year of application, mention it, and provide some details.

How you tackle research problems matters for admissions committees as well. Many students will have or have interesting projects during their majors. Mention them.

Have a word of **introduction** such as:

- The Aerodynamics experimental project I carried out with another student last semester was actually my first advanced experimental approach.
- As engaging and valuable as my coursework has been, it was during my second-year team research project that I truly discovered the field of sustainable construction.
- In addition to these classes was a seven-month team research project, which I chose in electronics to sharpen my programming skills.
- In the course of my studies, I have gained familiarity with approaches in fundamental science and applied science alike.
- Reinforcing this rigorous classroom training were the various research projects I have engaged in at XXX. Last year, for example, I joined a team of four other students on a scientific project that involved studying the behavior of windswept droplets running over inclined planes.
- In addition to the coursework, I have participated in a range of research experiences over the past several years that have helped to reinforce my theoretical background and develop a range of useful research skills.
- A team-based research project under the supervision of Pierre-Jean B. gave me an insight into the mechanisms of marketing in Second Life.
- During my second year at XXX, I took part in a research project with four fellow students to better understand the current financial situation. Our goal was to find potential solutions to avoid another such crisis.
- Part of the curriculum, I have undertaken several research projects. Last year, I did an eight-month group project focusing on the impact of a carbon tax on the market produce sector and the tomato business.

- Being innovative, creative and thinking out of the box is an essential approach that current and future defenders of the environment must take. For the past four years, I have developed my own innovative spirit while working as a researcher within the context of several long-term scientific projects.

When writing about research projects, always give the impression that you are **on top of things**. In other words, avoid mentioning that you **"have to do"** a project (or an internship), that it is mandated by the school, etc. Turn the curriculum into an **opportunity to do research**. You need to impress the jury with your sense of initiative and commitment. Do not give the impression that doing a project is a chore, or a burden. Rather, show what a splendid experience it all was and what scientific vistas it has opened. Thus, introduction sentences such as the following are to be shunned:

*Course requirements included a research project in which I **had to** study heat conduction in a bi-material radiator.

*Second year requirements at XXX also include a group research project which **we have to do** in the third year.

When you talk about research work, your **scientific analysis** is, of course, pertinent: you want to **sound like a scientist**, so describe what you did in detail. Do not second guess the committee thinking they will have trouble understanding your research.

Currently, I am conducting lab research in biology involving the manipulation of genetically modified bacteria in order to understand how the Methionyl-tRNA synthetase recognizes the transferRNA Methionine among the other tRNA. Even if the mechanism of selection is already known, this work provides me with an opportunity to familiarize myself with experimental procedure, as well as methods used in biology laboratories such as fluorometry, DNA sequencing, and radioactive marking.

Projects and lab work have been conducted in keeping with my theoretical studies. First projects addressed the prediction of chromosphere's solar spots (Levinson-Durbin), and stock option evaluation on the financial market (Black-Scholes-Merton model), the related reports of which can be consulted on my website...). In parallel, for the purpose of an experiment in CS, I programmed a Gnutella client-server in Java, with the aim of exploring peer-to-peer networks and draw their graphs. More importantly, my second year's experimental module really fulfilled my passion for image formation. A colleague and I studied thin film transistors (TFT), an indispensable component of image sensors and LCD screens. We even managed to implement 4 nine-pixel displays in the clean room of a startup (XXX, Optics Valley, Paris). In the framework of my MSc, I also completed a four-month scientific internship at the *Laboratory of Modeling and Calculus* of Grenoble, under the supervision of Pr. Valérie P., a researcher at INRIA. The objective of the project, carried out in the Summer 2003, was to implement and improve active contour methods in the case of medical radiographies of vertebras, in collaboration with one of the lab industrial partners, XXX, a start-up developing surgetic systems (computer assisted surgery). I published a multi-scale extension of traditional methods, that are much too sensitive to noise, and a more efficient solution based on global minimization.

My research project consists in a study of the spatial organization of a microbial community that can detoxify aquifers contaminated by chlorinated solvents. With the use of the T-RFLP method (Terminal Restriction Fragment Length Polymorphism), we will compare the relative density of the microbial communities such as Dehalobacter restrictus and Desulphuromonas chloroethnica in different samples from polluted sites in the commune of Suss in Switzerland to determine which are the relevant parameters (temperature and pH, concentration of dissolved oxygen, organic (CO2) and inorganic (Ca, Mg, N, S, P, Fe) compounds, geology, concentration of pollutants, etc.) that influence the structure of the microbial community. Knowing which factors are important in the development of these communities could help us to better understand and predict their functioning in the biodegradation of contaminants.

College has offered splendid opportunities to conduct long-term research projects. For example, I led a year-long team-based research project on mineral separation and purification by flotation. We produced a laboratory-sized flotation column that we used to purify mineral talc. Our choice in appropriate surfactants was made using the Gouy-Chapman-Stern model. Applying my knowledge of surface chemistry to systems broadly used in industrial processes was a great experience. It gave me the taste of industrial challenges in a team environment, and this is something I look forward to doing as a graduate student in chemical engineering.

In addition to my coursework, I have participated in a number of research and extracurricular activities over the past few years that have prepared me well for the challenges ahead. One of these was an eight-month team project on slash and burn agriculture, under the supervision of a researcher in ethno-biology. Our objective was to study the sustainability of slash and burn agriculture in Equatorial Africa, an interdisciplinary task that forced us to understand the ecosystem of the area (from a biological perspective) as well as the behavior of the inhabitants (from an ethnological perspective) in order to create an effective mathematical model of a village of cultivators. Theoretical models had not yet explored this subject thoroughly enough, and it was thus thrilling to create our own model using data from the ground and bits of theory we could find. This project made us realize the parameters we have to take into account with any subject dealing with the interface between the environment and human society are numerous and varied. This experience also taught me valuable lessons about collaborating and communicating effectively with colleagues.

Insist on the importance of **teamwork** if you have carried out a team or a paired project. What role did you play? What insight did you gain? About your subject? About research in general? About yourself? About teamwork? Choose to describe only the pertinent details. And this is not a checklist where you have to answer every question.

> My part of the job was to develop and implement an indeterministic procedure to compute a solution, the main obstacle being that we needed algorithms efficient enough to compute solutions to real-scale problems within a reasonable time frame.

> In addition to my coursework, my participation in research activities during my years at a life science school has helped prepare me for the challenges of advanced study in environmental policy and technology. Last year, for example, I carried out a yearlong team research project entitled "Halieutic Resources: the Hake Market." After substantial work gathering data and analyzing it, we developed a biological and economic model from which we drew conclusions about the efficiency of quota policies. While it was both useful and fascinating to apply our skills in mathematics and modeling to such an important issue, our methodology did not consider the social dimensions of the problem. This experience made me realize how much I wanted to work on more concrete projects that involve confronting ground-level realities.

You may even hazard some comparison between teamwork and sports with research work.

> Working in team on those different projects was highly enriching and stimulating, rewarding me with the unmitigated pleasure that I have only found in mountain climbing (another of my favorite activities beside image editing) when the roping party are slowly but surely gaining ground and are nearing the top. An experienced mountaineer, I have climbed the most arduous summits in the Alps and therefore know that effort and determination are no hollow words.

Naturally, it is essential to show the **lessons** that you have drawn from research or project experience. What you learned from it matters as well as how you did it. For example:

> A different kind of scientific experience I have enjoyed was the eight-month team research project I did in economics. Supervised by Malcolm K., the team I was on studied how a soccer club can efficiently manage its financial capital and its manpower. First, we studied the current research, and then applied econometrics theory to our data: we carried out statistical research to determine which criteria can explain good sports performance and their correlation to this performance. We examined over twenty aspects, answering questions such as: Is it profitable to invest in training young players? Or for a club to be placed on the stock market? One of our conclusions was that stable and experienced manpower is essential to continuing sports success. This very complex subject, where

> each detail is linked to many others, helped me develop stronger skills in analysis and logic. With each team member bringing their own expertise, vision and interests, the sharing was extremely enriching. It was also challenging, for we had to learn to listen to each other and find compromises that worked.

Methodology. When you mention the project put it in that order:
- **name** of project,
- **goal** of the research,
- **findings/rcsults** you have obtained,
- **process** (methods, tools, technology) to reach your goal. Be to the point.

You can add a couple of lines about the **non-scientific aspect** of the project, more specifically the **soft skills** you developed while carrying out the project as leader (typically: task distribution, streaming of the work or organizing the various streams, working under deadline pressure, liaising with the authorities/outside institutions, setting up the planning, the hurdles/obstacles you faced and overcame…).

> I was put in charge of the team and responsible for assigning the different tasks. There were seven of us each focusing on different domains: we had to assess the direct and indirect costs of the antennas, study electromagnetic wave transmission, and use a new type of nature-inspired algorithm: particle swarm optimization, to solve the optimization problem. What I found highly fascinating in this project was to share and transmit information between each group. As every team member was getting deeper into their research, it was becoming increasingly vital and challenging to handle and master the flow of information among the team.

Naturally, they do not expect you to be a full-fledged scientist or researcher yet, and tamping down your skills is acceptable.

> In addition to its all-round academic training, the University made me more familiar with research and lab-work. The first scientific team project was on the site-specific effects of seismic waves due to soil inhomogeneities. I was in charge of the experimental model designed to create and measure a microseism. Professional-level accuracy was beyond our technical capabilities, but this experience was enriching because I was privileged to meet various researchers, compare different experimental options and finally make a choice in accordance with the team's resources. In 2019 I studied with another classmate the Rayleigh-Plateau Instability in Fluid Mechanics; this turned out to be quite challenging because we designed and developed our own experimental device in order to measure the length of drops along a line. We built our own theory, including two models for drops, and managed to define a typical formation time for the drops based on our observations. The experiment was highly successful since our mark was near the top of the cohort.

In the same way, if you have met with failure or if you struggled while doing the project, it is OK to mention it. What matters is the lessons you learned. If you have a **C or D in one project** in the field you are interested in, explain briefly why. It may be for health reasons, for lack of coordination, focus, motivation or supervision, incomplete data, because the project was over-ambitious, etc.; one or two lines maximum.

> Along with this education I did some experimental work. I studied the alpha disintegration of radionuclides. To that end I built a Wilson cloud chamber, a detector allowing to materialize the 3D trajectories of charged particles. It actually took me several months during which I went through cycles of hope and despair, depending on my ability to make the device work, not an easy task given the parameters I had to control. After the device was set up, I carried out experiments on the mean path of the alpha particles in methanol and confronted my findings with previous results. My efforts paid off after six months when I could observe that the results were in agreement with the theory of interaction of heavy charged particles with matter. Because of the many different fields of knowledge required to build the detector I had, for the first time, to use all the skills I had been taught.

Of course, if you have mentioned a project in the introduction, do not repeat it in this part. But you can very well develop it at length here after sowing some hints in the introduction.

List the projects by order of importance or relevance, not in chronological order.

If your supervisor writes a letter of recommendation about one of the projects, no need to expatiate and write at length about it. Yet, you need to mention it as well as the name of the tutor.

Having your own **work published** is a sign of intellectual and academic promise. If you are working closely with a professor on a research paper, make sure your name will be included as coauthor even though it may mean an increased workload on it. If your university or college has a research journal in which undergraduates can publish their own work, and that you have submitted a paper, mention it even though the range of such research is somewhat limited. At least it will show that you have grown familiar with publication formats and practice. Finally, if your research is a working paper on the Internet, mention the site it can be accessed.

Write a short conclusion on the project itself, if necessary.

> However complex that project was, it convinced me that in computer science I had at long last found a way to express my natural bent for all things theoretical and in line with thought processes nurtured in the French educational system. Above all it proved that I was capable of yielding concrete results, that I could actually be both productive and innovative in that field.

5. Internship experience/Work experience

Experience outside the classroom should be factored in in the application file. Internships are carried out while you are a student whereas work experience refers to full-time positions taken after graduation (rather than part-time jobs or internships). Unless you are applying for an MBA, work experience is not required when applying for an MSc or a PhD. And having held positions in the world of work while studying does not make you more qualified.

Mention only the relevant internships regarding the program you apply for. If an internship is not directly related to the program you are applying for, yet was important for you or them, mention the tools, methods, skills you acquired, stressing the aspects that are essential to a researcher's work, for example. The committee will look favorably at an internship done in artificial intelligence in an R&I lab when you apply for an MSc in computer science. Likewise, gaining some solid programming experience, even more remotely linked to AI, will earn you the attention of the admissions officers. However, working in marketing, as a sales representative, even in the computer industry, will cut no ice with the committee.

Naturally, some companies are better known than others: admissions officers may be more familiar with Facebook, Apple, Microsoft, DeepMind, Google Brain, or Owkin, but deep inside, what will give weightage to the application is what you did during the internship and the results obtained.

```
In the same vein, the two internships I have done since I got into University XXX were matchless opportunities to developed complementary skills.
```

– Link internship with your **program**.

```
My work experience has confirmed the deep interest I have in computer science. Last summer, I undertook an internship on the Actuary team at the consulting firm Deloitte.
```

– Link internship with your **program and career goal**.

```
Another concrete application of financial engineering, which I have wanted to understand better since my internship at DZ Bank, is risk management. I would very much enjoy taking Credit Risk Modeling and Credit Derivatives to strengthen my knowledge in that field. My career goals can only be achieved if I have been allowed to build practical experience on strong theoretical foundations, exactly what you would allow me to do.
```

– Put in: name of company/institution/lab you worked in and where.
– Describe the missions you did.
– Use the following order: goal, findings/results, process (methods, tools, technology). Be to the point.

– Some of your missions may have been confidential, so remain vague on goal (you can say you signed a non-disclosure agreement, though), but insist on the skills you learned or the scientific method.

> During the Summer of 2019, I worked for one month in a Los Angeles hotel. There, through the spirit of involvement of the managers and the numerous discussions with the owner of the hotel, I caught a glimpse of the technical issues and management decisions involved in a company. The variety of these experiences helped me understand that developing my skills in management, economics and entrepreneurship was a prerequisite if I wanted to bring a true added value to any future job as a consultant or an entrepreneur.

– You may insist on the essentiality of **teamwork** in internship experience.

> My scientific, but also my life experiences have been carried out in team. During my freshman year in college, I was elected student representative, sat on the board of trustees and fought to further my classmates' interests. Last summer in London I was employed (along with many immigrant workers) in a waste collection and street cleaning company. However arduous the job was, I realized that each position is essential inside a team and deserves the respect and attention of management, which were unfortunately not always forthcoming. A summer internship, on a law enforcement team, also taught me respect for others and dedication, both of which are key components to motivate people.

– At the end of this paragraph you may mention a **coming research internship**, showing thereby that you will have built up more experience by the end of the present program: if this is still a blank space in your brain at the moment, simply leave some directions which you will develop when the details become clear to you. What matters for the admissions committee is that you will have gained some long-term research traction by the time you join the program. Research experience, especially if it is long term (a few months) right **before** joining a program will show that you will be better armed to meet the standards of an MSc program.

> This Spring, and for five months, I will be interning with… focusing on/under the supervision of…. Upon completing the present program, I will have thus acquired solid research skills.

> This Spring, I am planning to do a research internship where I will be studying biological phenomena with tools developed by statistical physics, probably with Mara P. at Harvard, whose work on the mechanical properties of DNA would match my interest in biology and my skills in physics.

> Next Spring, I am looking forward to a six-month research internship at Saint-Gobain, studying the hydrophobic properties of tropical leaves in order to improve the coating for car glass. I expect this practical and industrial

```
application of the theoretical knowledge I have gained to confirm my vision for the future.
```

```
This Summer, I am looking forward to my four-month internship as a quantitative analyst. This will be a foretaste of my future career, and an opportunity for me to apply my theoretical background to a professional sphere in banking. I am excited to work with other quants on interesting research projects. I will be looking to pinpoint my strengths and weaknesses in the real world of financial engineering, which should help me define the fields I need to focus on next year.
```

How you organize the two paragraphs ('Why your program appeals to me' and 'My academic formation') depends on what has influenced you the most. There is no **right** or **tight** formula or answer. You can very well invert the order of the three subparts and start with project work, if you think that it says more about you and your skills than classwork. Some programs such as Stanford's MS&E may insist more on project work than classwork.

```
As of my second year at XXX I chose to merge exacting theoretical courses in mathematics and physics, with more applied classes or projects.
```

When introducing **project work**, write a relevant sentence. Here are some examples:

- The different projects I have been working on and the classes I have taken so far have walked me through the main steps of the science from understanding the problem, data cleaning and visualization to building consistent models to achieve results.

- Project work has been a litmus test of the theory, helping validate the equations, algorithms and paradigms studied in class.

As with project work, do **not** give the impression that the internship was an onerous burden as in the following example but turn every opportunity as a way of nourishing your experience and sharpening your skills.

```
*During my second year, I was asked to do a blue-collar internship, anywhere in the world provided I worked with my hands/research internship and provided it was 5 months long at least.
```

VI. The Personal (History) Statement (PHS)

1. General

The **personal history statement** is a less formal essay than an SOP. It is typically more flexible than the statement of purpose, with a bigger emphasis on storytelling. Schools often encourage applicants to discuss (relevant) challenges in their lives and how they have overcome them. In the same way, you will describe achievements outside the classroom or the lab, and how extracurricular activities have shaped your personality.

Typically, you will include the following elements:
- a **self-portrait** of who you are, what you bring and how you may contribute to the student community;
- **achievements** outside the curriculum;
- addressing issues of **gender** or **racial** inequalities;
- advancing **equitable access** to higher education for women and racial minorities in fields where they are underrepresented;
- **cross cultural** abilities;
- **leadership** experience among students from groups that have been historically underrepresented in higher education;
- life **experiences**, struggles or accomplishments;
- **motivation** for entering the field;
- overcoming **barriers** (economic, social, educational);
- **personal** reasons for choosing the program;
- **research** interests focusing on underserved populations.

Through the PHS, schools can get to know you on a deeper, more intimate level and learn about you in ways they can't through transcripts and letters of recommendation alone. The PHS can tell the compelling story of your life, but not in a chronological order. It will be centered around experiences, values, lessons learned. The PHS explains what personally motivated you to explore your interests. It is a chance to equalize the playing field by giving you full rein to explain yourself and emphasize your success over any struggles you've had.

Many schools require just one essay (and it will usually be the statement of purpose, as it is the more academic one). Yet, I suggest including a personal statement, called **personal history statement paragraph** in the standard statement of purpose.

2. A stand-alone document

Some graduate admissions committees mandate that you should write two statements, a personal history statement, and an academic statement. The objective of this paragraph is to introduce yourself not so much as a scientist as a person, *i.e.*, your values and life principles, even your ethics. For example, for those applying to UC Berkeley. The university gives some hints as to what to write. (See https://grad.berkeley.edu/admissions/apply/personal-statement/)

> *In an essay, discuss how your personal background informs your decision to pursue a graduate degree. Please include any educational, cultural, economic, or social experiences, challenges, or opportunities relevant to your academic journey; how you might contribute to social or cultural diversity within your chosen field; and/or how you might serve educationally underrepresented segments of society with your degree. Such a paragraph will figure in each and every of your statements. Bear in mind that universities are seeking a diverse student body and therefore who you are, and above all, what you have done matters.*

Application to the Robotics Department of the University of Michigan requires a **personal statement** and a **statement of academic purpose** (approximately 1-2 pages). all applicants submit two separate documents for the statement of purpose and personal statement. And they mention: "Many, many applicants talk about LEGOs. If you choose to take that risk, be sure to make it your own, unique, compelling, and personal storyline."

> **Personal statement**
> Talk about your inspiration, background, and academic or project pursuits.
> Indicate how your personal background and life experiences, including social, cultural, familial, educational, or other opportunities or challenges, have motivated your decision to pursue a graduate degree at the University of Michigan. This is a discussion of the personal journey that has led to your decision to seek a graduate degree in Robotics.
> Include your motivations to take your robotics career further. What concrete examples can you share of your academic and non-academic activities that might have prepared you for graduate study? Don't be afraid to name collaborators in the field-our faculty often know many of them! But also talk about the work you did with those collaborators. Think of this as a story about your personal and professional development, and a proposal for your graduate school career.

> **Academic statement of purpose**
> Talk technical, go deep, and talk about your engineering background.
> Include your academic and research background, career goals, and how this graduate program will help meet career and educational objectives.
> Applicants often don't go deep or concrete enough into describing their engineering experience, whether an internship, project, or research. Showcase your technical writing, and your enthusiasm for your work. After describing one or more experiences in detail, including your contributions to the projects or tasks, discuss why graduate school is the next step for you. Make an argument for your unique qualifications and professional preparation, and what you hope to contribute to the field.

New York University has a more original way of getting to know you, what they call Personal expression (for example, for the MSc in Quantitative Finance):

> *Describe yourself to the Admissions Committee and to your future classmates using six images and corresponding captions. Your uploaded PDF should contain all of the following elements:*
> – *A brief introduction or overview of your personal expression (no more than 3 sentences).*
> – *Six images that help illustrate who you are.*
> – *A one-sentence caption for each of the six images that helps explain why they were selected and are significant to you.*
> *Note: Your visuals may include photos, infographics, drawings, or any other images that best describe you. Your document must be uploaded as a single PDF. The essay cannot be sent in physical form or be linked to a website.*

Be it as it may, the PHS is about how an applicant's background and life experiences, including cultural, geographical, financial, and educational or other opportunities or challenges, motivated the decision to pursue a graduate degree. For example, if an applicant grew up in a community where educational, cultural, or other opportunities were either especially plentiful or especially lacking, they might discuss the impact this had on their development and interests. This should be a discussion of the journey that led to the decision to seek a graduate degree. Sometimes there is a word limit. In general, the PHS should not exceed 500-1,000 words. One page is plenty enough (longer essays tend to be skimmed over rather than read thoroughly). Therefore, use space efficiently.

3. The diversity statement

Many applications now include a question – sometimes optional or supplementary – that encourages applicants with minority backgrounds, unusual education, distinctive experience, or unique family histories to write about how these elements will contribute to the **diversity** of their target school's class and community. **Underrepresented minority** (URM), first-gen students to attend university would mostly benefit from writing a diversity statement. URM is defined as a US citizen who identifies as Black/African American, Hispanic/Latino, or American Indian. All other Race/Ethnicity categories or Non-US citizens are considered as a Non-Underrepresented Minority (Non-URM). **First generation** (first gen) is defined as a student who reported both parents as not receiving a baccalaureate degree. All other students are considered as Not First Generation. If you fit neither category, a good angle is to describe how you invested in helping URM and diverse students. Volunteer experience, giving back to the community, making the environment more inclusive must be supported by strong evidence though. One thing is to say, another is to do.

As it is optional, it does not affect your admission. Actually, diversity statements are reviewed **after you have been admitted** and will affect whether you are considered for a diversity fellowship or not.

Diversity refers to things like ethnicity, social class, or gender, and more generally the perspective you might bring to campus life. Admissions officers do believe diversity in the classroom improves the educational experience of all students. Learning and growing in this multicultural environment will prepare students for working in our increasingly diverse and global world. Sometimes a diversity statement might be required if you apply for a scholarship, as is the case for Cornell University, for example.

Stanford, for example, will ask you for an **optional** diversity statement of about 700-1,000 **characters** (and **not words**), according to the IDEAL (Inclusion, Diversity, Equity, and Access in a Learning Environment) policy.

> *Stanford University regards the diversity of its graduate student body as an important factor in serving the educational mission of the university. We encourage you to share unique, personally important, and/or challenging factors in your background, such as work and life experiences, special interests, culture, socioeconomic status, the quality of your early educational environment, gender, sexual orientation, race or ethnicity. Please discuss how such factors would contribute to the diversity of the entering class, and hence to the experience of your Stanford classmates. (700 characters max.)*

Caltech's diversity prompt:

> In an increasingly global and interdependent society, there is a need for diversity in thought, background, and experience in science, technology, engineering, and mathematics. How do you see yourself contributing to the diversity of Caltech's community? (Your response should range between 250-400 words.)

Duke's optional diversity prompt:

> *Duke University seeks a talented, engaged student body that embodies the wide range of human experience; we believe that the diversity of our students makes our community stronger. If you'd like to share a perspective you bring or experiences you've had that would help us understand you better, perhaps a community you belong to or your family or cultural background, we encourage you to do so here. Real people are reading your application, and we want to do our best to understand and appreciate the real people applying to Duke. (250 words maximum)*

I suggest you write something when it can add to your application and if you feel strongly about it. Since it is optional you do not have to write anything at all, and that is acceptable. Yet, it's an **opportunity to help yourself stand out** from other applicants. So, take that chance to show who you are, beyond grades and test scores. If you choose to write it, be honest and tell your story, whether you were born with a silver spoon in your mouth or you walked five miles to school each day in a blistering sun. Link the essay to the values and insights shaped by experience. For example, build the essay around your involvement in a community you contributed to.

You can also mention some activity in which you identify (piano player, jazz lover, team captain, feminist movement, etc.). You can also mention a health struggle, academic struggles, struggles with identity. One aspect I would not mention is your struggle with mental health problems for there seems to be a stigma attached to it in academia. Focus on the **positive**, not so much how often you fell and failed, but how successful you were to pick yourself up and kept running. Focus on your ability to overcome.

4. UCAS application

UCAS stands for Universities and Colleges Admissions Service. It is the centralised service that students use to apply to university (online). Basically, those who want to study an **undergraduate** degree in the UK will have to apply through UCAS. They have a thorough monopoly over the university application systems in the UK. The personal statement you have to write when applying through UCAS is your chance to show universities and colleges why you want to study the course and why you'd make a great student. Your personal statement should explain what you like about a particular field, and why you want to study this subject at degree level to enter a career or one of many more other options. Admissions tutors want to know what makes you a great candidate, and what skills and experience you can bring to their department. Here are some ideas to help you get started:

- Look at course descriptions and identify the qualities, skills, and experience it requires – you can use these to help you decide what to write about.
- Tell the reader why you're applying – include your ambitions, as well as what interests you about the subject, the course provider, and higher education.
- Think about what makes you suitable – this could be relevant experience, skills, or achievements you've gained from education, work, or other activities. Include any clubs or societies you belong to – sporting, creative, or musical.
- Mention any relevant employment experience or volunteering you've done and the skills you have developed. If you took part in placement, or summer school, or something similar, include it.

5. Personal history: a paragraph inside your SOP

Since the end goal of American education is to produce well-rounded, broadly educated individuals who can function effectively in society, academic achievement or metrics is not the only measure of success in school. Personal history statements will help the admissions officers determine whether you are a good fit. Gauging the fitness of a candidate for a program, they will wonder whether you can deal with stress and persevere, whether you have grit, *i.e.* what it takes to succeed in the program. Among the other questions: have you overcome adversity, and does that give us confidence that you will be able to handle the demanding years of graduate school? Will you receive and be opened to feedback, or will you drop out after the slightest bit of challenge or criticism? Can you tolerate differing viewpoints and be open to growth? Considering these questions can help guide students through the writing process.

There may be an explicit prompt, or a set of instructions to guide the applicant. Yet, there are some constraints: a personal essay cannot squeeze your whole life into one single page, or two. It is **NOT an autobiography**. Nor is it or a long-form reiteration of an applicant's resume. The applicant must take care not to go overboard and write a detailed biography, because a long statement is more likely to irk reviewers than to impress them.

Your personality will be reflected in your experiences **outside the program**. What you have done outside the curriculum will also define who you are. Students are encouraged to participate in extracurricular activities such as sports, student government, drama clubs, debating teams, etc. All of these things are taken into account and considered when someone is applying for admission. Many of these activities allow students to learn valuable lessons in leadership, teamwork, and effective communication.

Before writing this paragraph, here is some advice: think first about your identity (who you are), then what you have accomplished, how you approach things, what drives you, what influences you.

Read the instructions. Some applications provide little or nothing in the way of guidance, asking prospective students to expand on why they want to apply or to supply information on their backgrounds and interests. Others, however, give guidelines on content, format, word count and submission method. It is crucial that applicants read and understand what is expected of their personal statements. It won't matter how beautifully crafted the statement is if it doesn't address the prompt or disregards stated length requirements.

Do a great deal of self-assessment and reflection on your life and on what matters to you. Soul-searching will allow you to understand yourself better. Think about your strengths and what you want to convey to admissions committees. Ask yourself the question: what makes you special? What qualities do you bring to a cohort of graduate students that this program does not know they need? What value do you bring to the table? Provide the reader with insight into what drives you.

Be you. Personal statements are individual. Do not second guess the admissions committee: **there is no one-size-fits-all essay**. Essays are designed to give the admissions committees a glimpse into a candidate's personality. Be yourself, not the ideal applicant.

Try to remember and include facts (experiences, events, achievements) that are relevant either to your choice of study or your future career vision. Evaluate experiences instead of just describing them. Include the life-derailing, throw-you-for-a-loop challenges you have faced and overcome.

Strive for depth rather than breadth. Narrow focus to one or two key themes, ideas or experiences. Review your life carefully (get help from friends and family for feedback on who you are and what they have observed about you, if necessary) for facets and experiences that reveal an unusual dimension. Ask them to define you in five adjectives, for example, what sets you apart.

Be authentic, honest and truthful, even candid. Do not make things up. Use concrete examples from your life experience to support your thesis and distinguish yourself from other applicants.

Be careful not to provide information that is no more than a recitation of information available elsewhere in your application, especially your résumé.

Think about how you are going to contribute, to make the program stronger, to make an imprint on the classroom and the-out-of-classroom experiences. The question here is not what the school can do for you but what you can do for the school. Students should not be overwrought over the fact that there may be a couple of C's from their first year or that they are not off the charts in terms of standardized tests. They should focus on their strengths and what they can contribute.

Finally, do not underestimate the weight a personal essay can carry. Allowing for time to write multiple drafts, edit and thoroughly proofread is a must. Have other people proofread and check for grammar before sending in the application; they may catch errors that were glossed over in earlier drafts.

Here are some convincing introductions:

> A good look at myself will certainly reveal someone very determined, believing in the strength of the will to accomplish different things in life. Paying respect to my own limits, I have already attained many of my goals, some of them as an active member of associations such as...

> I also developed other skills through extra-curricular activities. I am convinced that personal rigor combined with determination, mastery, and true, deep and original thinking leads to achieving goals and producing seminal work.

> Life has taught me many lessons outside the academic realm as well.

6. What to put in the personal history statement

Your background, your influences, your origins, your ideas, your work environment, your community experiences, your commitment to student life and the community in general all of these factors and many others come together to create a unique individual, an individual who can contribute to a diverse class and a diverse world. What matters here is how you stand out and what events have shaped your personality.

a. Origins. If you have a cross-cultural background (born and bred in Morocco, but educated in France, for example), this will be the moment to emphasize that difference.
If you are an immigrant, the child of immigrants, or someone whose ethnicity is a minority, you may find your response to this question to be helpful to your application effort. Why? Because you can use it to show how your background will add to the mix of perspectives to the program you are applying for.

> I am the descendant of Chinese nationals who came to France expecting to build a better life. Drawing upon their behavior was an apt lesson in the value of meritocracy. Even though I spent my childhood in one of Paris poorest neighborhoods, I have always strived to do my very best. However, I have never forgotten to help others. Willing to commit myself to society, I tutored underprivileged children during my first undergraduate year and chose to intern with the Gendarmerie Nationale during my first year in order to give a hand to those who need it. There, I sat on interviews of children who had been abused and saw then a reality that my experience had never exposed me to.

Mention which **values** each part of your education has brought to you (typically the attention paid to education in Asian countries *vs* the Cartesian mind trained in the French system).

> Attending top schools in two different countries, and working in those respective countries, has taught me to adapt quickly and easily to cultural differences. I have learned how to integrate quickly into new academic environments, to communicate clearly, to exchange ideas efficiently. Studying in the United States at Yale would provide me with a third 'cultural pillar', enriching my vision of the world, and I can give in return the culture and ideas of two distinct corners of Europe. If I have the cultures and concepts of Eliade and Sartre to offer, I hope to receive those of Emerson in exchange. Indeed, Yale will help foster in me that most Emersonian of qualities: conceptual self-reliance. For, aren't both research and entrepreneurship Emersonian in essence?

> When I was fourteen, I was given the opportunity to take an academic year abroad through the Weicker scholarship, a nationwide competitive award, based on academic record and a series of essays and interviews. This offered me the opportunity to study one full year at Saint Paul's School in Concord, New Hampshire. At only fourteen, this unique experience taught me autonomy, responsibility, pragmatism and integrity, which are all values that would contribute to my studies at MIT.

If you come from **humble origins** (a small and remote village in the heartland, for example) and you overcame academic obstacles, if you are the **first in the family to go to university**, if you pulled yourself up by the bootstraps and, breaking with tradition, you won over your mother who would rather you had married and raised children, if you decided to travel the road not taken, this is the place to write about it. It will say much about you without you having to say that you are determined, willful, that you have a mind of steel, etc. Thus, the story of the little primary school pupil that would plod her way to school and back every day, walking 15 miles both directions to attend the only school of the region in the Grand Atlas Mountains, speaks volumes about her determination.

> I was not fated to become an engineer. I grew up in France's corn belt where my parents have been farmers for several generations. Once I had passed my *baccalaureat* (with honors), I had to make a choice between following in my father's footsteps and taking over the farm or pursuing scientific studies by entering the prestigious preparatory program. Agriculture offering a somewhat uncertain future, I chose the latter path fulfilling my need for understanding how things work by studying physics, mathematics but also economics.

> I grew up in a place where isolation was not a choice but a way of life. We lived in a remote hamlet, at the far end of a dirt road with very few outlets to civilization: one was across the creek bed, mostly dry in the summer and frozen in the winter, another over a small brook and the third a low water bridge over the river. Whether I would go to school would depend on the vagaries of the weather and the threat of freak flash floods. When it rained abundantly—and this

could go on for several days—rivers were swollen, roads impassable and there was no way to get to the nearest logging town. As a result, I missed many days of school over the years. Despite the long odds facing a first-generation kid going to school—both my parents were farmers with no education—I always trained my sights beyond the waters and struggled to build my own bridge to a better future, nail after nail, plank by plank.

Oddly enough my pursuit of knowledge has followed a winding road, taking me from one school to another across several regions, following my father's assignments to various air force bases across Europe. In a sense, this might be compared to the life of a migrant family: always on the move, I never had a chance to forge strong bonds with my classmates. Yet, far from souring me on school and driving me into a shell, I threw myself wholeheartedly into school work, striving to distinguish myself and shine, but above all aware that I was building a capital of knowledge that no one, not even time and distance, would deprive me of. I read anything I could lay my hands on, burnt the midnight oil poring science books and journals, went against my parents' decision to get me into apprenticeship in a culinary school, and pushed myself to eventually earn admission to a preparatory program and, ultimately, in the science school I am studying in today.

Life will test you in ways you cannot imagine. And one of the ways it will test you – over and over – is how you treat others who do not look like you, talk like you or earn like you. My grandparents came to France from Nigeria looking for a better life. Their leap of faith made it possible for my dad to raise his family running a filling station in Northern France. His hard work and sacrifice paid off and allowed me to do what I am doing today: studying science.

b. If you are an **international student** who has built an academic career across several continents, mention it.

One definitively cannot claim I have chosen the easiest road: having left home three years ago, I have been trying to get samples of ways of learning and teaching Physics in several countries, besides having my eyes opened and my hands ready to experimental work done in the field of Quantum Information Science. And it all has been worth it to fulfill my ultimate goal, that is to become a researcher and professor at university level in physics.

Typically, you will bring with you **values** such as hospitality and sharing, two social values high on Morocco's agenda, for example.

In my home village, for instance, back in my childhood, I still vividly remember when some well-off families would invite all the villagers over for lunch, especially after Friday prayer. At the time, villagers still vied with each other to host a new visitor at their homes.

Distinguish between what is proper to the culture you hail from. The family is the most significant unit of **Tunisian** life and plays an important role in all social relations. The individual is always subordinate to the family or group.

The traditional cultural values that influence the psyche of the **Chinese** people are harmony, benevolence, righteousness, courtesy, wisdom, honesty, loyalty, and filial piety. Benevolence, the core value of Confucianism, extends from the importance of family ties and blood connections and is held in high esteem by the Chinese. Benevolence, although based on familial ties, extends to friendships and social relationships, producing a full set of values that include justice, courtesy, wisdom, honesty, loyalty, self-discipline, and commitment. Righteousness refers to justice and correctness. Courtesy stresses modesty and prudence. It is about respecting laws and preventing misconduct. Wisdom requires that one distinguish right from wrong, place capable people in suitable positions, know oneself, and be resourceful. Honesty refers to trustworthiness, integrity, and credibility. Loyalty stresses service to the motherland.

In **Brazil**, personal values are key. In their relationships and families, people appreciate honesty, respect, trust and patience. Warmth and compassion are valued, along with respect for all family members, including children. Brazilians, as a nation, focus much importance on the family structure and the values that are entrenched within that institution. The tendency towards compassion is one central element that keeps the family closely-knit.

You may mention how, after you left your home country at the age of 17 to go to university, you were struck by the individualism of the French system of education, marred by a fierce competitive spirit. Yet, your home values are here to stay…

```
The pull of my home country remains strong, like a spell. I go back at Easter
and during the school breaks.
```

…and you added up to them by discovering the Cartesian way of thinking. Now you look forward to consolidating your education by immersing yourself into a culture that prides itself on self-reliance. In this way, the admissions officers will realize that you have built your personality around three cultural pillars that contributed to make you whole, drawing on the best experience of each culture.

c. Gender. US programs do pay close attention if you are a young woman studying STEMS, as they seek to balance their student body within every program. In addition, if you have been involved in spreading sciences amongst high school or undergrad female students in science, all the better. Mention your action, how you encourage them to take up sciences, that they are as good as and even better than their male counterparts.

In the same way, some universities will ask whether you have been discriminated against for your race/ethnicity/sexual orientation and how aware you are of the necessity to fight prejudice and bias.

```
Annie Ernaux, a French working-class novelist once stated that she had at some
point believed that education was a land of equality, fraternity and liberty.
She quickly realized that some girls were more equal than others and that those
like myself who started at the bottom had a harder time climbing up the acade-
mic ladder and finding their way out. That is why, brought up in a working class
```

> *banlieue* of Paris, I have always sought to reach out to all those young women in high school, encouraging them to take up sciences as one of the likeliest paths to professional success and job security.

d. Minority. If you are a member of a minority group and you wish to mention it in the essay, you need to be subtle about it. Do not say anything outright but mention somewhere in the essay that, for example, you are part of the Moroccan Association of Students or affiliated with the Asian political caucus. Such a statement does not explicitly state that you are either Moroccan of from Asian origins but sends the unofficial code that it amounts to the same thing.

On the other hand, you can write about things you have done to help students from underrepresented backgrounds succeed. Highlight any programs for underrepresented students you have participated in as mentor, advisor, etc. Write about your commitment to working toward achieving equity and enhancing diversity. Describe ways you are willing to contribute, be it pre-existing programs on the campus or in creating new programs based on models at other campuses.

e. Leadership training, military and alternative civilian service. For *Polytechniciens,* this is the place to mention your leadership training as an **officer cadet** (*EOX*) with the *BSPP* (Paris Fire Brigade)/French Navy/Armed Forces/Air Force/National Gendarmerie/French police forces/Foreign Legion/elite mountain infantry or mountain infantry brigade (*chasseurs alpins*)/Civil security unit. Alternately, you will have chosen to work in a civilian service such as a mentor or tutor for a youth organization, a teacher in a detention center, for example.

Not everyone will develop the theme of leadership training in military or alternative civilian service. To choose to do so means you have gained something that will serve you in the future: management skills, a desire to serve, conviction for specific action, a professional vision which has inspired you. In some way it has changed you and may help explain in a backhanded way, your personal motivation. A background in the Army, Navy, Air Force, Police, or Marines shows leadership ability and a strong work ethic.

> In New Caledonia I worked in a program that aims to provide job training and other social services to at-risk youths. My role was to assist the troop leader in charge of a group of thirty people, and to take charge of the training of a subgroup of twelve of them. This was quite a different kind of leadership experience that forced me to adapt to a new environment and to learn a great deal about myself.

> I chose to do a military internship at a Civil Security Unit because its values, symbolized by the slogan "Serve to Save", matched my ethical values of solidarity and social responsibility. I was thrilled by the ability of the leaders to take quick decisions under uncertain and stressful conditions, such as storm, fire, emergency, often with lives at stake. The diversity of the personalities I encountered fascinated me and pushed me to explore more unfamiliar horizons.

> Curiosity and a sense of responsibility are values lying at the core of my leadership training. While doing my military service I spent six months on the

frigate *Prairial* on patrol in the Pacific Ocean. I was part of a unit in charge of counter narcotrafficking, liaising with American intelligence services to help monitor international sea routes. On board, I was given the responsibility, as a security officer, of leading a twelve people team whose task included maintenance work and safety operations. Carrying out such daunting assignments for a junior officer was a unique testing ground to develop my leadership abilities while honing my communication skills within a crew made up of sailors from various backgrounds. Sailing far and wide across the Pacific was all the more rewarding because I was able to discover other cultures too. On call in the Philippines, Micronesia, French Polynesia or Mexico, I took time to explore and reflect on how the ways of life differ from one place to another and how lagging in development some countries still are.

One of the most defining adventures in my life was my leadership training carried with the Paris Firefighters Brigade, where I was first lieutenant. For seven months, I learnt how to cope with emergencies and handle stressful situations. Careful analysis of the situation and strict procedures are the keys to efficient and speedy resolution when a human life is at stake, particularly in suicide cases. Such operations made me realize how self-centered my life had been up to then. That stint with the Paris Firefighters Brigade was instrumental in shaping my personality. In all due respect it was a sobering part of my existence in which I grew more mature and developed a sense of responsibility, both features which I also had a chance of working on last summer when I served on a trail maintenance crew at Redwood National Park.

My internship with the Paris Fire Department exposed me to life in one of Paris' most deprived *banlieues*. I saw from the inside dire social situations. I experienced the daily suffering of people who live 30 miles away from work scraping out an existence below minimum wage. We would rush to help when they had no one to turn to, listen to their problems and try to alleviate their burden if only for a few too short minutes. I grew fast. This experience has changed my vision of life, turning me into a more reflective man, more attentive to and considerate of people's plight and predicament at a time when the great recession has left many on the wayside struggling to make ends meet.

I did my eight-month internship with the non-profit organization *Tremplin*, tutoring more than 75 students from disadvantaged schools. My goal was to help them succeed in the baccalaureate, and to motivate them to undertake high level scientific studies afterwards. I learned to be flexible, to adapt to unusual situations, including student strikes. I was extremely pleased when all but one of my students succeeded in their exams, and 60% chose to enter high level universities.

My time at the Ecole XXX has also provided a unique opportunity for personal life experiences. In the year 2012 I was at the same time a student and a deputy supply officer in the Navy for almost a year on a dispatch boat in the Middle

East. From November to March, my operational role consisted in gathering intelligence for a NATO task force in the Strait of Hormuz by calling on commercial vessels by VHF radio. For the first time I was asked to be a leader, which was all the more challenging as I was one of the youngest crew members, most of whom were parents' age; they were sometimes lower ranked, complicating my cause.

I have been given unmatched opportunities to develop my management skills and my sense of responsibility. As Lieutenant in the French Army, I served as section chief for the military instruction at the fourth Regiment in Reunion Island. **I** was in charge of a thirty-five-recruit unit, including more experienced NCOs. The regiment aims at reinserting into society underprivileged young men and women, many of whom have dropped out school or even served time. I instilled in them a sense of responsibility by giving them key roles in the group. For me, motivating people is essential to successful management, as well as establishing trust between the layers in a hierarchy. Incidentally, I hope to be able to extend my various life-experiences by joining Professor P's Habitat for Humanity program.

Twenty months ago, I ended my eight-month leadership training as second commander of the platoon in charge of Security and Intervention for the French National Police in Burgundy. I remember the moment when the weight of my responsibility to lead such a versatile unit dawned on me: It was 4:00 a.m. and I was about to brief the team when the silence filling the room struck me. I looked up and realized that the fully armed 200-pound stalwarts sitting in front of me were listening to my every word with rapt attention, totally relying on them and waiting for me to transmit both comfort and energy. After months of effort, I had finally been integrated into the unit. It had taken commitment to the group, bringing others forward as I myself matured. This equilibrium between self-mastery and commitment to others has always given me a sane and balanced strength that I use to be successful in my projects.

Justify your leadership training through your **value set**: defense of the homeland, attachment to principles of the French republic, sense of service to the community, family tradition, discovery of the world, its people and cultures.

One of my forebears served as a general in Napoleon's armies, and his attachment to the country runs deep with me. My joining the Armed Forces was therefore a way of honoring a family tradition and doing my parents proud.

My time abroad was rife with new experiences, but it also buttressed many of the values that I already held dear. Volunteerism, service, commitment, integrity, faith. These are things that I identify with on a personal level, including a sense of community, a value that trumps all others.

> I chose to join the Navy, eager to serve my homeland abroad and test my mettle, pushing myself physically and mentally. As a member of the military, I honored a cause which I believed gave me a sense of purpose, was bigger than me and affected the whole world. Serving my country is part of serving humanity.

> Serving in France's overseas territory was a splendid way of exploring the world and experiencing cultures and people different from my own. Going off overseas was the best way to gain perspective and come back with a worldly perspective. At the same time, it provided a new appreciation for the comforts many students like me take for granted every day.

> My time in the service instilled in me a strong work ethic. The military does not believe in quitting, and laziness on the job is never tolerated. At the same time, it was all about a complex combination of selfless missions, tasks and responsibilities – all in constant motion. It was hard at times, but always worth it.

> In the Army, I developed a comradeship unknown outside the Forces. I became part of a tight-knit band of brothers, and acquired a confidence and determination to contribute and succeed that I never imagined could exist given my sheltered upbringing.

> My passion for research and discovery, and my sense of responsibility can be illustrated by three recent achievements. The first one is my eight-month training period in the French navy as an officer during my first year at the École Polytechnique. I chose the navy over the army because I wished to discover new places and people. I used every opportunity to sail to foreign places and interesting missions. The frigate onboard which I served went to the Middle-East to enforce security on the Red and Arabic seas, and called at Djibouti, Dubai and Abu Dhabi then sailed to the Maldives for humanitarian purposes after the tsunami. I enjoyed plying the seas and the voyage abroad and likewise I wish to discover America. Moreover, during exercises involving ships, aircraft and submarines from all NATO navies I was in charge of explaining the system of safety zones to the captain of my ship in order to avoid any collision or crossfires during the exercises, which let me think about the responsibility I had toward the 240 people onboard my ship.

For some people, **serving in the Armed Forces** can be a game changer:

> My stint in Mali changed me forever. It opened my eyes to poverty, oppression, and human need. I saw children standing barefoot in the sand, begging for a bowl of rice. I saw old villagers hunkering down, afraid of terror. I saw bravery, resilience, kindness, and evil up close. I saw suffering on a scale I had never encountered before.

f. If you have served in an **NGO** or a **non-profit organization** committed to raising the academic ambitions of young people, such as *Apprentis d'Auteuil*, this is where you will mention what such an experience has brought to you: love for teaching, getting out of your comfort zone, discovering the other side of France, returning in kind some of the benefits of your privileged education and talents.

> Those fortunate enough to obtain a formal education have a role to play in the social well-being of people. As a treasurer of MicroFinance, a school association providing microloans to the Mayan population, I went to Guatemala in the summer of 2010 and worked in the field, participating in the loan process. I worked with two other members in complete autonomy in our area. Since the beginning of the campaign, I followed the loan payments and adapted our policies to face extreme situations such as illness, death and natural disasters. We also worked to develop a sense of community in the villages, so that people could share their knowledge and know-how about crop cultivation and animal breeding. Our goal was to encourage a sense of initiative in these people, who had a strong desire to progress in spite of the dire poverty they were wracked by. Our association allowed us to make a small gesture that often had a dramatic impact on their lives. I learned how satisfying it is to participate in actions that help others progress.

g. If you have faced a particular challenge in the course of your life or education, it may be to your benefit to let the admissions committee know about it. For example, if you have **overcome an illness or an injury** that has left some deep imprint on you and tested your resilience, adaptability, determination, you may mention it. If you have been victim of a car accident and that it took you two years to get back on your feet again, recounting that experience will show your fierce resolve not to let life take the better of you but to make sure that you take your life into your own hands. If you have been in charge of your siblings and taken over some of a parent's responsibilities, mention it.

> On a more personal level, my father died during my freshman year. Coping with this loss was all the more difficult since I had to deal with the psychological pressure of preparing for highly selective competition exams at the same time. Succeeding in these exams – I was ranked 4th in the nationwide competition – was both a way of overcoming my bereavement and of honoring my father's high expectations of and trust in me.

7. The supplemental question

It is to be noted that MIT's TPP graduate program asks for an additional letter, called **supplemental question** (that comes on top of all the other application material).

> In your Statement, you have described for the Admissions Committee your motivations for, and the goals underlying, your application to the Technology and Policy Program.

> In this Supplement, we want you to reframe the presentation of your goals. Instead of speaking to an academic admissions committee, you should address a decision-maker who has authority and agency in your area of interest. We'd like you to describe how the kind of work you'd like to do at MIT will inform the policy problems they are facing.
>
> This should NOT be a simple recapitulation or rephrasing of your Statement. Rather, your statement should (1) identify a specific decision-maker and address them directly, (2) concisely identify a problem that should concern them, and (3) describe why research at the intersection of technology and policy is useful to address this problem.
>
> Please limit your response to 750 words or less.

I suggest writing a letter addressed to a government official, a member of the cabinet, a government official, a CEO, the head of an NGO, a superior in the organization you have worked for...

As for the **cover letter** that is required by MIT's TPP program, it should be a written recap of all the documents you have sent for your application.

Other programs, such as MIT's MFin program have an optional question as well.

> *The Admissions Committee invites you to share anything else you would like us or your future classmates to know about you. This may be in written or multimedia format. Written essays should be 300 words or fewer (limit of 2,000 characters).*

Such a short essay might include experiences outside the curriculum you have not mentioned in the statement, or any extra activity that you have developed. It might be related to music, the arts, writing a novel, a textbook... Here is an example:

> My experience with ASPE (*Association de solidarité et de protection de l'environnement*), a non-profit organization based in the Rif (Morocco) was a game changer in the carefully crafted academic path I had carved for myself. The association's mission statement is geared towards promoting solidarity, protecting the environment and boosting the local economy by offering job opportunities. The organization works in partnership with international and local institutions, willing to earmark money for development projects. I had passed the baccalaureate with flying colors and naturally was primed for higher education. Eager to use my vacation time in a purposeful fashion, I volunteered to work for ASPE in the summer 2008, one year after its creation. I had grown intrigued by massive immigration to Europe of young and able-bodied young men from that region with no job prospect in Morocco and lured by the promises of a future abroad. Actually, the whole region was in the grip of cannabis growers and, outside that field of activity, there was little job prospect. We took it upon ourselves to find other ways out of the pot business and offer fresh perspectives. Among

several on-going projects, I chose to join a team that were persuading farmers to convert their fields and grow wild aromatic plants for medical purposes. The carrot was that they would be guaranteed minimum revenue that would exceed the profits made on cannabis. To do so, I suggested first setting a bottom price for the harvest, and second buying the whole crop that we would personally move to market. Yet, because we were short of farmers participating in the project, I added a 5% bonus to each farmer that would sign up another farmer on the project. From the initial five people in the program, we ended up with 30 farmers, an apparently modest figure, but a personal achievement.

Some programs may ask for supplemental information that will not be present in the application material. Here's an example:

If names are anything to go by, mine are evidence of some of my personality traits. Zheng, my last name, calls to mind the era of the famous Chinese explorer Zheng He who travelled to East Africa 600 years ago. Qiao, my first name, refers to big trees with strong roots and branches. These images, spirit of exploration, a solid foundation and great ambitions—have blended together with my passion for adventure. I have been away from home for study since the age of 14, and ready to take the next step. A well-known Chinese proverb claims travelling ten thousand miles is more useful than reading ten thousand books. For me, traveling to meet and to learn is not only a means in itself but also an end.

VII. Outside/Extracurricular Activities

1. Definition

You are defined by what you have done. That is why your significant extracurricular activities should be included into the PHS part of your statement. Such activities need not be sponsored by your school. They will showcase your strengths and soft skills.

Therefore, you should consider:

- Community work (Habitat for Humanity, the Golden Heart restaurant association, advocacy, RSPCA...)
- Cultural and language activities (European Week, Languages and Cultures Week, Chinese club, African Forum...)
- Entrepreneurial activities (Entrepreneurs' Club, Career Fair, Tech Fair...)
- Government (student government, student council, community youth board...)
- Media (yearbook committee, local radio or TV station, working on a movie, school newspaper...)
- Sports activities (climbing, skiing, soccer, mountaineering, adventure racing club...)
- Music (school choir, musical, chamber music, jazz band, your own rock band...)
- Performance art (comedy club, dance, film production, puppetry, theater group...)
- Social activism (animal rights club, environmental club, fair trade club, gay-straight alliance, women's organization...)
- Special interests (boy/girl scouts, chess club, model railroads, social entrepreneurship club...)
- Speech and political interests (debating society, foreign affairs club, forensics team, Model United Nations (MUN)...)
- Technology (YouTube TedX, social media, AI club, robotics society...)
- Volunteer (Outreach, mentoring, tutoring, volunteer fire department, local charity, local soup kitchen, hospital volunteer, Red Cross...)

In a word, include whatever teaches skills, gives value to people, has a meaningful impact, either in your own development or that of the community. Do not include activities that are self-centered.

```
Aside from my coursework and research projects, I have also participated in
several extracurricular activities that have enriched my understanding of envi-
ronmental issues and helped me to develop important personal skills.
```

```
In addition to research work, I have engaged in a number of activities outside the lab or the classroom that have served to develop some important personal qualities.
```

Now, there are some professors who emphasize extracurricular activities because they want to have well-rounded students who are not just defined by academic or research work. Others won't give a toot whether you are a surfing instructor or whether you have rowed across the Atlantic. For programs that tend to put a word limit, typically Columbia University FE, or MIT's MBan program, there will be little room to mention the extracurriculars. I would therefore mention one or two personal features in the conclusion, in passing and if possible. Anyway, such activities will be mentioned on the resume.

2. Activities

a. Student associations. Do not develop too many of them, select the strongest and clearest experiences: taking responsibility for a team event during a music festival, the career fair, equestrian events, or the Sustainable Development Week… shows what you learned from the experience as an officer (or member) of the association.

```
One of my commitments has been to the eight-member video student association, filming main events on campus, editing and producing memories for the university. Meeting technical challenges, managing the photo opportunities and debating about the artistic vision has helped me develop a different kind of creativity.
```

```
I am also concerned with my future professional career and the best way to get prepared for it. This is the reason why I was an active member of the association that organizes the school's career fair. My central operations coordinator role provided me with a unique experience of organizing a meeting that gathered hundreds of national and international companies for one day. Of course, it also gave me the possibility to get accurate information about positions in the telecommunications field. The privileged relationship I had with some of these firms helped me understand what the main issues are in signal processing.
```

```
Last year, as treasurer of the integration week-end for the incoming class, I learned how to handle a budget of 150,000 euros. Along with improving my leadership skills, I realized that I was led to make choices based on economic efficiency rather than ecological concerns. I became fully aware that adapting to climate change or protecting the environment needs to be economically efficient, a concept that had been in the back of my mind since the age of 17, when I was a volunteer sailing instructor and co-treasurer of our sailing association.
```

```
I participated in consciousness-raising events, such as the "Sustainable Development Week," to educate my schoolmates about environmentally friendly forms of behavior. Organizing and participating in these activities provided many
```

> occasions to meet people working in the environmental field (consultants, researchers, water distribution and waste processing professionals, senior officials at the Department of the Environment). It widened my vision of environmental problems and confirmed my desire to work in this domain.

> The diversity of backgrounds in finance upheld my interest in cultures. I have been involved in several cultural clubs, including the university's International Club, organizing events cooperating with 74 universities from 29 different countries. I am also the treasurer of two societies representing the Middle Eastern cultures on campus, organizing cultural conferences and evenings, in an unending effort to bring understanding and cooperation between two distinct poles of culture, which actually have many similarities. I was recently responsible for organizing an oriental dinner for 300 students and professors, dealing with planning, logistics, negotiating with caterers as well as dealing with the day-to-day problems of management and organization. Not only did I develop and solidify my leadership and teamwork skills, it was extremely rewarding to see how smoothly everything went, and the general satisfaction of a happy crowd.

Even a confidential club that fights for values that are dear to you can be mentioned.

> Another aspect of our vision is to build cohesion within the student body by remembering tradition: we organize several ceremonies, two of which confer the symbols of the school uniform, our hat and our sword, on incoming students.

> My stint in the Army has also instilled in me values which I cherish such as humility, and solidarity, sense of attachment to the homeland, which I have tried to pass along to other students through a club. Its mission is to foster a class spirit which defends not simply traditional values such as freedom, tolerance, respect for the flag while at the same time trying to adapt to a fast-evolving world in which some of those values have come under criticism and are being questioned.

Student government is highly regarded, as well as serving as the student member on the board of trustees. An applicant who has held a major office on campus, has sat on the board of regents (=the Council, UK, principal executive and policy-making body), for example, will want to include this fact. Your involvement in campus life may account for some of your less than honorable grades… yet, do not overextend yourself, unless the admissions committee think that student life is more exciting outside the classroom than inside.

> The most manifest example of human personal growth for me, though, concerns a particular experience in France. I was elected to represent my fellow students in the Academic Board Council, and dealt, for one-year time, with the studies-related problems of the 1,500 students on campus; besides, I played an advisory

role in the liaison Ecole-students, by analyzing and, above all, proposing adaptations to capital measures concerning the educational policies. Some of them have already been applied, and in however small a way, I am honored of having contributed to the evolution of such a respected school, and to a better integration of the international students, since I have been the first international student to hold the post.

In 2019, I was elected External Affairs representative and since then have carried out several missions in that capacity. The campaign, prepared for many months with a team of fourteen students, was both creative and challenging. Since being elected, my task has been to manage the relations between our student body, firms and universities. With firms, I negotiate budgets to help finance student events, and help organize professional conferences on campus. I also develop the connections with other student councils to create shared events. This year-long team experience focusing on common goals and working together to live up to our campaign promises has been a fabulous leadership experience. However, my commitment to others has never dwarfed my eagerness to excel in class. Indeed, I have done everything to complete both successfully.

One of the life experiences I am most proud of was when I stood for and was elected student representative in charge of academic affairs. As such, I had to deal with the various issues pertaining to the curriculum, examinations, the ranking system, among other duties which also included facilitating relations between students and staff. Sitting on juries, I had to defend the students' interests, meeting with the board of research and academic life, I discussed course content, working with professors, I addressed individual problems that were at the core of student life such as grade distribution. It therefore boosted my self-confidence and brought the added satisfaction of serving the community. I did make some concessions but, by putting duty above self-interest, I also got to know myself better by helping the others. And I gained in autonomy and in organization as I did not wish to sacrifice my own studies. It was also an enlightening experience as I discovered the reality behind the admission of international students, their struggles to adjust to the vigorous system of the Ecole as well as to integrate an entirely new culture.

My experience as class president has given me the tools that will be necessary to the project manager I aspire to become, such as time management, interpersonal and conflict resolution skills as well as the ability to effectively deal with crisis situation. Having to juggle my responsibilities as a student, a class president and an athlete has enhanced my organizational skills by orders of magnitude. I learned to be more assertive and gained valuable leadership skills in the process.

Your action as member of the board/VP/President/Treasurer/General Secretary/officer of a **club** (managing on a shoestring budget of 1k€), a **society** (UK term), the **Junior Enterprise**, the **Student consulting club**, **Cabinet Start-Up**, is to be included in this paragraph. Such activities enhance the intellectual, social and cultural development of its members. Societies and clubs develop talents and leadership qualities, help students to work in teams and facilitate integration. The activities should be explained in that order: missions, results, process, lessons learned, including from failure.

> However, it is without doubt within XXX-Consulting, a student organization providing strategic and technological consultancy services, that I best expressed my will to help companies in building the future. Consulting matched my thirst for exchanges and diversity: our team grouped students from the famous business schools, thus allowing us to cover a large scope of missions, both technical and commercial. In record time, I learned to manage a team and keep an eye on several large projects simultaneously. As president this year, I am in charge of a complete overhauling of the associative organization, giving more responsibilities and regrouping each member by professional areas. Furthermore, the strategic decision to corner start-ups and small highly competitive companies, gave all twenty of us better insight into the reality and stress of business creation. As for me, the six missions I carried out for high-tech companies allowed me to gain full awareness of the need for cutting-edge technological advance and real added value to penetrate such a highly competitive market. Business creation in new technology is a harsh and demanding path. Yet, the challenge of operating in a time-scarce environment where decision-making rubs elbows with initiative, the credence in high technology and the risks it supposes, and most of all, the excitement and enthusiasm of working alongside brilliant, smart and dynamic people, gave me the certainty that I would one day be part of the process myself.

Working for a student club or such group experiences helps you develop **communication** and **organizational** skills, but can also show your **creativity** and **dynamism**.

> Then, as treasurer for the Franco-British Student Alliance, under the aegis of Queen Elizabeth II and the President of the French Republic, I have tripled the membership of the association and launched the organization of an international meeting of students, academics and leading executives for next Spring. Our goal is to build academic and business bridges between the best graduate schools in France and England. This experience has confirmed my desire for a career involving people. Those responsibilities strongly developed my sense of organization and my ability to work under pressure.

Yet, it is not a good idea to mention student clubs which might be associated with the organization of **bacchanals**, the promotion of **hedonism**, or whose **carousing** is the untold norm on Thursday nights. Officers will not be impressed by activities such as revelry. Yet, if you belong to the oenology club, that will show tangible evidence of your attachment to the *terroir*, its produce and traditions. Conversely, do not appear as over-Spartan, over self-disciplined and self-restrained in your lifestyle and activities. Open-mindedness, commitment and character-building matter.

Working in **youth movements**, the scouting movement, summer camp counseling, teaching or tutoring, any experience which helped you become aware of your capabilities matters. Describe **what** you did and **evaluate** what you learned from the experience.

- As a youngster, I learned about responsibility, social cohesion and environmentally-friendly behavior thanks to my activities as a boy-scout. Building a log cabin, for example, taught me how to fit in with a group working toward a common goal without giving in to selfish interests and attitudes. The solidarity I benefited from through that experience has become a significant component of my approach to social life: while I was in high school, I volunteered to help and support a classmate who suffered from muscular dystrophy. Later on, as an undergraduate, I coached a secondary school pupil in math, which also trained me to articulate my knowledge. Both experiences taught me how to include others in my working and reflection process.

- A boy scout for ten years, I was eighteen when I first organized summer camps as a scoutmaster. Teenagers can be a handful at the best of times, but supporting those who are at a stage in their lives when they are making important decisions about their futures is reward enough.

- As leader you have the chance to travel, meet inspiring people and form friendships that will last a lifetime. I have been to Belgium, and done more glamorous trips to jamborees in farther-flung places such as Australia. Some of my proudest moments have been with the Scouts, helping young people to achieve so much more than they thought they could, and realizing that sometimes all it takes is for them to believe in themselves.

- The need to plan and calendar events and activities, group work and team sports, managing and holding meetings through the weekly commitment to troop meetings, liaising with parents, are some of the skills I developed and which have also defined my academic work.

- I have picked up practical and leadership skills myself, but the real joy lies in helping young people to grow and develop. I have learned how to cook, how to communicate with a team and, most importantly, how to effectively lead a group of strangers. It was challenging at first but it will prove very useful in the workplace.

If your university/école have granted you an **Outstanding Leadership/Investment award** as a consequence of your actions, you can mention it.

For all my commitment to student life and the many events I have organized on campus, the school has bestowed upon me an Outstanding Investment award/the school has conferred upon me an Outstanding Leadership award.

b. (Educational) traveling. Do not use this theme unless you have something interesting to say. Admissions committees do not care if you have peripatetic impulses, how much of the world you have seen or how badly you want to spend a year in the United States. They do want to hear about any experience which is influencing your career choices or saying something about your personality. Did you work in India during the summer and feel frustrated because you could not build a clean water system for the village, which then led you to fluid mechanics as a major, and now to their department? It is rarely quite that strong a link, but there must be a reason for you to describe your experience.

> My classroom has been a world without wall. Travelling runs in the family. My great grand-father was a cobbler in Poland, my grandfather was forced into exile to the United States when the country he had called his home was overrun by the forces of evil in WWII. One of my sisters married a Scotsman, and worked on an oil rig off Aberdeen for two years. The other is a war photographer who has visited many fields of operations. I have spent my early years in Moscow, studied in Cambridge (England) before enrolling in one of France's engineering schools. Wherever I go, I put down roots immediately, exploring the city's nooks and crannies, becoming familiar with the neighborhood people. Not content with visiting, I have held summer jobs, done trail maintenance in Yosemite, cooked in Saigon and picked apples in Alsace and strawberries in Brittany. My traveling has gone hand in hand with a curiosity for cultures and their languages. The world is my oyster, and the future mine at Berkeley where, I am confident, I will be able to share my experiences with a cosmopolitan and travel-seasoned student body.

> Travelling abroad, speaking foreign languages, interacting with local populations are maturing experiences I definitely feel passionate about. Travelling has been a wonderful lesson (another one) in learning how to adjust, how to adapt to new environments and, more keenly, how important it is to respect the other people. And the wider the gap between the civilizations I have encountered on my road to adulthood, the more respectful you must be towards uses and customs that are the hallmarks of man. Having a fairly positive idea of multicultural campus life in America (our university opened itself up to other nations much more recently but in no less a cogent way than US colleges), my experience will by all means serve as a yardstick in imposing respect while learning from others.

> I also spent two months in China in order to improve my Chinese and to experience daily life there. During my stay I worked in a bookstore where I was able to speak with average Chinese people and learn more about Chinese culture. With my French background, my familiarity with China, and now the possibility of studying in the United States, I feel that I will possess the kind of global outlook that is now demanded of leading professionals in the field of nuclear engineering.

> I consider that, today, being open-minded to other people and the world is essential for a future high-qualified executive. Which explains why I travel a lot around the world. From European countries to the U.S. and Japan, I have learned to understand different ways of thinking, to live with different cultures and to experience the sparkle created by the melting of persons from different countries. That is why I do believe that studying on an international campus, such as Brandeis', is certainly the best way to be in the heart of scientific breakthroughs.

> Another part of my interest in life is traveling. Actually, I have visited many countries all over the world and have been most impressed by the sights I have seen and the people I have met. For me, traveling is a way of broadening not only my geographical horizon but also my spiritual life as it has given me many insights into the lives and thought of the people I have met. It is by meeting other people that you really get to know yourself. And what people add up to your experience contributes to the building up of your personality, but in a good way. It makes you more human, more acute to the pain and sufferings of the people and it also makes you wiser.

c. The arts also should figure prominently in the personal paragraph. It may be theater, dancing, singing, or music (you have played the guitar for 12 years, played in an orchestra, performed in front of packed concert halls or in more intimate venues, toured Europe's main capitals, be a thespian in a Shakespeare comedy…). Music (another school of life) will say much about patience, rigor, discipline, working together (in a band), conquering stage fright, etc. What music represents for you is also relevant. Learning or teaching oneself how to play an instrument is another school of rigor.

> I inherited my creativity from the family of musicians and artists I was born in. I was initiated to music at an early age. I have been playing the piano for over 15 years. I am part of my University's brass band and sing in the choir as well. Those activities have been an outlet for a sensibility that, together with academic rigor, has led to a balanced and harmonious life. Yet, if I often practice alone, I do enjoy participating in the communal activities for the benefit of all. Allowing others to discover, or rediscover long lost pieces of music and sharing them with an audience is a way of prolonging the commitment that I have shown while thinking up and putting together devices for others.

> I am part of the student improvisation theatre company, an activity I enjoy immensely because of the creativity in letting my imagination duel and collaborate with those of my partners for the pleasure of the audience, and of the comradeship that results.

> What compels a young boy to dance? In my case, it was an uncontrollable longing. Dance has always been so healing for me, no matter how many hours I was putting in, no matter how many cuts and bruises, the rejections, you're not as good as so and so. To me, dance made sense. Dance is a language that I am trying to

understand. But because it has given me so much insight, I feel as though when I dance, I'm sharing who I am. It's not a facade. It's me.

If you do (or have done) **painting**, **photography**, **drawing**, mention it and show how it has developed your sense of observation, tested your patience, and above all taught you to see the world through a different prism while you train your lens.

In addition to such technical study, I have taken more artistic courses such as drawing, architecture and computer graphics. The drawing course helped me improve my perception of light and shapes, and be more observant, while the introductory architecture course trained me to become more familiar with 3D software such as Blender and Maya. The virtual museum I developed during this latter class gave my teacher a new way of perceiving what I first drew on paper. I was able to simulate the effect of light on the structure, while also coming to understand how useful it could be for an architect to visualize and modify his project in real-time.

My desire to look for original solutions and be creative in my approach to problems owes much to my background. I come from a family of painters and entrepreneurs and was brought up in an environment that fosters the expression of the self. I have given free rein to those skills since an early age through drawing and more recently through photography. Last summer, I worked part time as a photographer and graphic designer for a German hotel in Berlin. I took pictures of the surroundings and the rooms for their blog. I had the opportunity to hone my creative skills while attending a computer camp at UCLA six years ago. I have complemented those skills with graphic and web design courses and applied them to different projects and school events around the campus. I do intend to further those skills at the d.school, should that be a possibility offered by the Stanford program.

If you have developed an interest in **languages**, enhancing your work experience and opening wider your horizons, you may mention it.

I have especially enjoyed the cultural richness the school has allowed me to develop; for in addition to English and German, I have been able to study, and learn, Chinese. Spending two months working in a restaurant in China at the end of last year allowed me to discover a new country and a new way of thinking. Learning to adapt to an unknown cultural environment was thrilling, and I will be looking for other international work experiences. I hope to continue developing my linguistic and cultural skills, and look forward to using them to impact tomorrow's worldwide economy.

Also included in the arts is your passion for **cooking**, if that is the case, that says much about a country's culture and your desire to share a communal activity with friends and foes alike.

If you have been involved in **movie making**, mention it. Even better, you can link it to your passion for computer graphics, for example.

> This year, in addition to my classes, I will be working with a colleague to produce a short animation film. This project will allow me to use the skills I have recently developed to create the best-looking animation I can achieve. I am a perfectionist and the time I spend directing short movies and performing real-time video mixes emphasizes this side of my personality. It also shows that computer graphics is not merely a career choice for me; it's my life's passion.

Debating also makes for a fine argument. If you have taken part in Model United Nations (MUN), or be on your university's debating team, it is worth mentioning. Show the skills you have developed on that occasion.

> My membership in the MUN and competing in the final of the Debating tournament have provided me with the skills of impromptu speech, oral communication and the art of persuasion using sound facts as the basis for arguments.

d. If you have nurtured a passion for **geopolitics**, and **history** (through helping your grandpa write his memoirs, for example, or inviting personalities from the political sphere within the framework of a European Week that you set up on a team of two), here is the place to mention it.

e. Mention **volunteer work**, be it with a non-profit, an NGO, a charity or charitable organization, the Red Cross, assisting the homeless, tending a soup kitchen or the golden heart restaurants, visiting the destitute on Christmas Day, organizing summer camps for low-income youths, taking mentally impaired adults to a day at the seaside or on a pilgrimage… A standard example is that of the outreach missions that students have taken part in, feeding the homeless, bringing a word of comfort and being just… human. Volunteering in public service areas demonstrates social commitment, in addition to the maturity you might gain from the experience. In general, do not overlook opportunities to make unusual contributions, whether it be launching a soup kitchen (or soup run, UK), taking part in science outreach programs in high schools and providing science outreach activities, performing as a puppeteer or clown in a cancer ward for young patients, day care center, etc., or volunteering for whole summers at a wildlife rehabilitation center or the society for prevention of cruelty to animals.

> My outside activities reflect the type of scientist that I aspire to become, one sharing experiences and with a taste for team working. Last summer I did a work placement in Portland (Oregon) where I worked as a mentor for an association, *Friends of the Children,* which looks after troubled children and at-risk kids. Besides daily tasks, I helped the 5-13-year-olds improve their learning abilities, assisting the teachers in their work or giving cooking lessons. I also supervised field trips to the science museum and the aquarium and two remarkable geological sites close by. The experience was all the more rewarding as it contributed to building my self-confidence while discovering another, less

spoken-of side of America. The friendly attitude of people striving towards a common goal in a hierarchy-free structure was conducive to creating an atmosphere where we could actually see the children improve and, hopefully, get prepared to adult life.

f. Teaching. If you have chosen to go and **teach**, at home, in an **emerging country** or in a distant land, it is worth mentioning. Say where you went, what you did and how much the experience has enriched you.

If you have taught in a **priority action school** (ZEP or priority action zone), a **non-profit association** such as *La Main à la Pâte*, which aims at improving the quality of science and technology teaching in primary and middle schools implementing inquired-based learning and stimulating a scientific spirit, or being an **oral examiner** in physics, math, etc., it should figure in this paragraph too. Again, emphasize what teaching means for and brings to you. Do not just say, I have been an **oral examiner** for two years. Rather say:

My passion for transmitting knowledge concretized when I was selected to assist my Math teacher in preparing undergrads to the grueling exams I had gone through myself. The teaching position proved challenging, preparing lessons and assessing students several hours a week over the whole year. Catching their attention, arousing their interest forced me to be creative in my style and thorough in my explanations. Yet, I believe such an experience has made me grow more confident in my capacities to get the message across and strengthened my capacity to pass on knowledge while giving a meaning to the theory.

My interest for local development led me to participate in internships, counselling and teaching in underdeveloped areas in Mongolia, China, and the Reunion Island, where I learned first-hand the importance of a solid educational system as the base of any sustainable social progress. Education is also fundamental in microfinance, a field that I have explored through my participation with other students in creating a microfinance association.

I chose to do community training with the association *La Main à la Pâte* ("hands-on"), whose goal is to help children to understand—and love—science through concrete experiments. I taught science in disadvantaged primary schools in Troyes (in the east of France). This confirmed my opinion that scientific knowledge should not be kept to just the bright pupils, but shared as widely as possible. When most of the class is of immigrant origin with parents who do not master the French language, science is an ideal way for them to shine in a subject which does not focus on language skills. I could see children, who had given up on school, become motivated through the activities we organized.

Helping other people has always been part of a personal philosophy which I have learnt to master over the years. Actually, I have been teaching mathematics and physics for quite some time to youngsters from high school and undergraduates.

> I was also a private tutor to servicemen trying to climb up the military ladder. As a member of an Internet forum (*Intermaths*) on which pupils and students ask questions in mathematics I have tried to help them along to find the proper solution to their problems.

> Giving remedial classes in scientific subjects to teenagers who have failed to meet their high school science requirements has been extremely gratifying. Teaching is not easy: I have had to learn how to put myself in someone else's place to understand their difficulties. But, in the end, the reward is making science more accessible to a wide range of people.

g. Sports is generally what students easily fall back on, especially given the huge number of hours spent doing sport in some schools. Now, what needs to be stressed here is not so much the quantity of hours but what the sport you play says about you: character building, fighting spirit, competitive spirit, endurance, the art of strategy, composing with the body, knowing your limits, testing your mettle…, more than the rush of adrenaline it provides or the risk you are ready to take, even though skydiving is an exercise in pushing yourself and exploring the extremes (as is scuba diving). If you perform sport at the regional or national level, it is worth mentioning. If you are a nationally ranked tennis, chess or golf player, your commitment to excellence in this domain might be highly regarded by the admissions officers.

> My greatest love, however, is sports, and I participate in everything, from competitive tennis to scuba diving.

> I enjoy volleyball a lot because, in addition to its technical dimension, the team with the strongest morale and cohesion almost always comes out on top in the end.

> Swimming, which I practice at a competitive level, has been more than a sport: it is a way of life in which values such as discipline, hard training and consistency play a role akin to that of the scientist who will not let go of the experiment as long as the results are not satisfactory.

> When you play a sport, you become part of a family that will always be there for you, even in the worst of times, because they know what you have been through.

> From captaining the team, I have understood how to motivate, how to create a spirit of solidarity among the members, how to show resolve and never give up. I believe a captain must lead by example while at the same time exhibit a sense of the game, the ability to plot strategy, act swiftly on it and make sure that even though victory might elude you, fighting to the end is what matters.

> However, the most important aspect of my non-academic life has been sports. Whether soccer, handball or competitive sailing, sports have significantly shaped my worldviews. In team handball competitions, I have learned about human

interactions. During sailing sessions, I came to understand the importance of focus and precision. On the soccer field, where I spent much of my childhood and still feel at home, I discovered diversity; those fields were unbelievable melting pots. Nowhere else did I encounter so many kinds of people as on those 50x100 meters of grass. It was my first window onto the vastness of French society. And, it is on this aspect of human activity that I want to apply my technical abilities, designing new and better sporting equipment.

Sport is and has always been part and parcel of my life. I have been practicing tennis, scuba diving, parachuting and doing some hiking and trekking as well in regions as remote as the Atlas Mountains in Morocco or the Rockies in Colorado. Sport is for me a means of self-fulfillment. I have oftentimes found in sports what school or life has denied me: it has been for me a way of expressing my personality, like painting for the artist or the piano for the musician. It is also a means of escape, enabling one to travel and see the wide world. It is a means of achievement in a life too much devoted to academic goals. It is also a nice way to meet people from various backgrounds and diverse horizons, as well as learning to know myself (as Socrates would say). Besides, it has brought additional experience to me since I have sometimes been in charge of organizing sporting events in my university. But it is also an essential way of learning about team work. Actually, in sports it is not the individual that matters as much as the team. The only way for a team to win is to rely on the individual capacities and skills of each. But only when each member sacrifices a part of himself or herself to the common good, can the team be assured of success. In that way it is an excellent lesson in courage and abnegation.

Among all my extra-curricular activities, the one I always return to is rock climbing, which I have practiced since the age of six. Rock climbing is an activity involving managed risks. You have to progress upwards from hanger to hanger (metal loops fixed in the rock), in which you place gears called quickdraws and then the rope to ensure your safety, while the belayer is ready to secure the rope in case of a fall. But even if you are belayed, a fall remains dangerous. Therefore, you have to maintain your focus and concentration at all times. The risks of overreaching have always to be measured against the imperative of advancing further up the face. Climbing has taught me perseverance, how to push myself further, through my fears and weaknesses, beyond what I thought were my limits. This is why I love this sport so much. By striving to reach the top of a rock face, I am driving myself to reach my full potential, making it physical and tangible: I know I've succeeded when I arrive at the end of a climb. All these qualities will serve me well in my future career in an R&D department working on new technologies development.

Sport can also be a way of observing your surroundings, and its ominous changes for the worse, when you go fishing or you do adventure racing. If you play a team sport, it might be interesting to mention your position on the pitch/field/court, which may say something about your leadership skills, goal setting, the necessity to strategize, your vision of the game, for example. Remember that whatever sport you practice it is more about team spirit than solitary effort!

> Throughout my second year, I was involved in the organization of the Student Yachting World Cup. As chairman of the association, I managed a team of fifteen people and a budget of $120,000. The first step was to find a host city and sponsors, then to organize the logistics to take care of 120 people for a whole week: accommodation, transportation, food, evening activities, and, of course, sailing regattas organized in partnership with a local sailing association. This was a fabulous experience: making plans, motivating the team, meeting the challenges and coping with unexpected events at every stage. Again, my communication skills grew enormously, as did my self-confidence, and my ability to meet tight deadlines.

> My fighting spirit and physical stamina are surely emphasized by the importance I give to sport and music. On a volleyball court, I forget about science and work and only focus on positioning and game strategy. Face to face with my piano, I can translate my feelings into positive creation and travel in my own world. Thanks to these beacons, blessed with a high work capacity, determined to live at full-speed, I can then dedicate my time to projects I believe in, cross new thresholds and stray beyond common thoughts and opinions.

But avoid the banal explanation to justify your sporting activities.

> *During my free time I am also quite an active person who enjoys doing sports. I jog a lot and I am keen on this sport because it is a permanent challenge.

h. Hobbies and pastimes. What do you do with your leisure time? Do you have a passion that might say much about you, such as cooking, philately, book-binding, building model airplanes or trains? In what ways do pastimes soften the stress of graduate studies, take your mind off problems, train your attention outdoors rather than indoors, make you see the world from a different perspective?

3. What to leave out

- Avoid **controversial topics**. For example, if you were an ordnance explosive disposal specialist during your leadership training and you are applying to the Department of Aeronautics, it may raise more than an eyebrow with the committee.

- Subjects concerning **religion**, **politics** or **money** ought to be avoided, **unless** your experience on a city council or in a Minister's cabinet turned out to be decisive in shaping your personality and ambition. But no names of parties or political opinions should be mentioned. If you have run a Christian student association you may mention it:

```
I am also president of my university faith-based students' club: my role is to ensure that catholic students can live and think about their beliefs through spiritual and conscience-building seminars.
```

- It is not a good idea to mention that you are motivated by **money**. Neither is it worth mentioning how much you love **traveling** and are eager to return to the U.S.

```
*My trip to the West Coast of the United States three years ago remains unforgettable, not only due to all the scenic wonders I saw but also because I discovered a different attitude towards work, more open-minded, direct and team-oriented. Since then, I have wanted to return, to discover more of this country for myself.
```

- It is not a good idea to mention the **French-American relations**.

```
*As a result, I am very enthusiastic at the idea that I may take part in the elaboration of future technologies at Stanford in the USA because as French President Macron recently said: "The state of our friendship and our alliance is strong".
```

- Such an introduction is awkward, to say the least.

```
*Of course, my intellectual passion for science doesn't prevent me from having more humane feelings.
```

4. Convincing examples

```
Outside my academic curriculum, my personality has been shaped by values such as openness, empathy and devotion. Volunteering has always been part of my own ethos. I took part in medical caravans sent to the remote Atlas Mountains to help the local population in dire need of care, an eye-opening experience on the pressing necessity to help the vulnerable in society. Furthermore, sport has proven a relentless school of rigor. Thanks to the stamina and the perseverance that tennis nurtured, the desire to go beyond my limits has become second nature. In addition, my cross-cultural profile has helped me to adapt to change and interact easily with people from different backgrounds. Being educated in Morocco in the French school system and later in Switzerland, I have learned how to adjust and be attuned to the subtle hues that distinguish one culture from another, yet, put together, make us richer for it. I am thus convinced that a diverse and inclusive community can be built by inspiring one another thanks to our unique background.
```

This coming internship will not be my first experience in management. Two years ago, I did an eight-month leadership training in the French Armed Forces. I trained two platoons of recruits, finding the relevant words to motivate them to become integrated in the Army by the end of the training. I was pleased when this goal was achieved for all of them, and I realized that I wanted to acquire more management tools. Thus, back on the campus, I became involved in organizing many conferences, including one with the 2012 Olympic champion, which attracted all 500 students in my class. Managing these conferences with professional people often brought unforeseen complications, and I came to realize how much I enjoyed these challenges. I also became a member of the committee for the annual cohesion week-end for the incoming class, with a budget of $130,000. Along with the general organization in this team of twelve students, I was in charge of the security of this event. Those responsibilities strongly developed my sense of organization and my ability to work under pressure. Last year, I was also elected class representative for three courses. By introducing an internet-based survey, I was able to communicate with any student who did not understand any aspects of the course, and convey these grievances to the faculty during our weekly meetings. I also worked as an International Volunteer in the Redwood National Park last summer to help protect endangered species, but also to immerse myself in a different culture. I was extremely pleased to become well integrated in this team, for it required physical strength and cultural adaptability. Having lived in or travelled to over ten countries has given me a certain understanding of cultural differences which will be helpful in the international career I would like to have in the field of energy.

During a four-week Summer internship in Costa Rica, I worked on a research program for a non-governmental organization, Earthwatch, aiming at improving the productivity of coffee plants. I actually collected soil samples, counted coffee beans on the trees and then fed this information into the Access database. I enjoyed this international project, working along with American volunteers, Costa Rican scientists and local farmers. I also liked the fact that the project applied to a very concrete issue with results that directly help the coffee growers. The Ecole has given me several other opportunities to develop communication and management skills. During my stint in the Air Force two years ago, I worked as a commando team leader, ensuring the security of an Air Force Base located near Bordeaux. During this five-month period, I managed people who were older and more experienced than I was, sometimes in tense situations. I also worked with people with different academic backgrounds, which taught me to adapt to new situations. This experience strengthened me physically and mentally. On campus, I have been an officer in two student associations: as leader of *Raid*, a team sport including mountain biking, running and kayaking, I helped set up a three-day event for 200 competitors, supervising and coordinating the preparations and the activities. I am also chairman of the Ecole's archery association, which I reactivated by organizing professional lessons and an Archery Night event to promote the sport among a large number of students, and the school staff. For my contributions to student life on campus, the Ecole have given me an *Outstanding Investment Award*.

Extracurricular activities are essential to me as well. I have the honor of being the captain of the soccer team, which competes in a hard-fought national championship. It is a challenging experience, and it has provided me with a strong sense of leadership: I deliver pre-game speeches meant to light the spark in each teammate's heart and to lead him beyond his mental and physical abilities, so that, as a team, we can achieve a common goal. That notion of team-leader in a hostile environment will undoubtedly be of great use for my future career. However, I was already familiar with hostile environments. Indeed, I am used to fighting uphill battles. For instance, when I first entered the French educational system, I didn't speak a word of French, and this forced me to work harder in order to bridge the gap. As a consequence, I have developed a taste for challenging situations, a trait that is confirmed by my attraction to extreme sports: I am a qualified skydiver with over thirty 12,000-foot jumps, and I also run long-distance mountain races. I have always valued experiences that force me to overcome my limits, giving me the adrenalin-packed, fast-paced lifestyle to which I aspire. My mental limits were nonetheless put to the test during my five-month internship in Guadeloupe, where I was faced with the blunt reality of dealing with the disastrous ripples of the January 2010 earthquake in neighboring Haiti. Similarly, during a two-month internship as an analyst for a World Bank project in Madagascar this summer, I met with clients who were poverty-stricken and discovered that small encouragements sometimes produce great results. These two experiences were acute reminders to me of the responsibility that we, as developed nations, have towards poorer countries.

VIII. How to Conclude the SOP

1. General

The conclusion should be rather short (between 5-10 lines). The conclusion might recall the introduction; most likely, it will reaffirm your vision for the future and show your clarity of thought. This is not a thank you note. It is an essay, a good story, so end it like one.

> My next step, in a perfect world, will be Stanford master's program in Management Science and Engineering. Although, my short-term goal is to work in supply chain management for an industrial company, focusing on and with cutting-edge technology, my long-term goal is to set up my own company once I have gained the right experience. The core curriculum of MS&E would give me the opportunity to acquire the knowledge I am missing today in optimization, risk analysis and production systems.

> Driven by my passion for Aeronautics since an early age, I have followed a consistent course of study that has brought me to apply to your Engineering Department. The outstanding preparation provided to me by my university will serve me well as I move on to a Master of Science in Aerospace or a more research-focused doctoral thesis. I bring along a strong grasp of problem solving, aptitudes for team work, a liking for challenge as well as an enthusiastic desire to learn as much as I can. Working in an industry that can boast thrilling developments at the cutting edge of technology in an international context and in my domain of interest is highly exciting to me. A graduate degree from your department is therefore the most valuable training to succeed on such tracks. I have strong hopes that my background and qualification are found suitable to carry a graduate program at the University of Michigan and look forward to joining your student community.

> I am deeply committed to making an impact on living conditions all over the world in this most fundamental way: helping to provide a safe and clean water supply. I plan eventually to work for an international development organization as a technical expert and scientific adviser. The ability to merge both an intimate on-the-ground awareness of the material conditions in developing countries and a high-level knowledge of the relevant science, as well as to integrate easily into local populations are invaluable assets in this work, and

my personal history provides with this unique skill set. Studying water quality engineering at Berkeley is an absolutely essential component of the training I will need to do this work. For that reason, I will bring to my studies at Berkeley all of the personal motivation and intimate knowledge of complex social phenomena I have acquired in the course of my experience in Africa, the rigorous scientific knowledge I have acquired in my academic training in France, and all the passion for science I developed in my studies.

I knew I wanted to pursue my dream path when I watched a TedTalk given by Danielle Feinberg – visual effect supervisor at Pixar and former Harvard student in Computer Science. While talking to her afterwards, she said: "We use math, science and code to create these amazing worlds, we use story-telling and art to bring them to life. It's this interweaving of art and science that elevates the world to a place of wonder, a place with soul, [...] and a world where a girl suddenly realizes not only is she a scientist, but also an artist." I too want to fulfill this dream of combining art and science to a greater purpose. In addition to a multi-faceted knowledge of Computer Graphics, I would bring creativity to Georgia Tech, a breeding ground for innovative ideas. This program would be the perfect way to elevate my voice to the higher level of expertise it requires to share my stories through cutting-edge science and art.

2. What you bring to the program

Write what you **bring to the program**; what experiences or strengths make you unique (think about scientific/technical/experiential features). The idea is to stand out amongst hundreds of applications. So, try being inspirational.

My current studies have provided me with strong working abilities and scientific skills. I would bring to Imperial College these acquired skills to develop them and share them with other students and professors. I firmly believe the MSc in Optics & Photonics would allow me to make the right choices for my future, sharpening my research interests and skills in a challenging international atmosphere conducive to thrilling innovative research.

If admitted to Harvard, I would bring with me several key characteristics for successful academic work and research programs: a hard-working and vivid mind, with a great ability to gather various knowledge into a precise plan. My past experiences have given me an excellent capacity to advance projects with both leadership assets and adaptability, thus enabling me to fit into new surroundings and bring my own perception and dynamism. The challenges of new technology are all the more appealing as much room is still available to bring my own contribution. Having played different roles in past projects, I have developed the ability to take myself off the beaten path, suggest my own tune and compose something new, for both science and business.

I feel confident that the academic background I have obtained over the past several years has provided me with the skills I will need to be an effective student in the Master's Program in Environmental Technology at Imperial.

Gifted with a sense of initiative, equipped with a strong background in sciences, I am looking forward to using my skills in confronting the challenges raised by energetic issues, oil being one of them. My competitive mind, honed by several sports tournaments (I am an avid golfer), my dedication and capacity to work in team as well as an unquenchable curiosity for foreign cultures – I travelled extensively in China last summer – have trained me to be enterprising, focused and resolute when carrying out projects. The multi-disciplinary approach regarding the diversity of the background of your MSc students and research at the cutting edge is exactly what I am looking for to develop my skills. I am confident that, given my abilities, I will be able to make a positive contribution to Stanford's program, should I be granted the honor to be accepted.

My all-round scientific background, my determination to achieve a lifelong dream of working in the aeronautics sector will best be served in the stimulating and exciting environment that your program offers.

Being a design engineer is not just a dream, it is a passion and a vision I will carry forward. Once I have enough expertise in design, I then want to manage building sites, for this concrete experience will give me more than global vision, it will teach me how to handle the natural terrain. I have always sought to have the best professional training possible: my course work has given me strong theoretical grounding, my research projects in economics and numerical modeling have shown me the importance of perseverance and teamwork, and my management training of student associations has taught me communication and organizational skills. I now need the professional tools that the Structures and Materials program would give me, thus allowing me to become a member of a dynamic professional team, adding my own vision of strength and harmony to challenging construction projects.

3. What you expect from the program

Write what you **expect from the program** – in terms of knowledge and skills, how the program will expand your **vision**, consolidate your **knowledge**, sharpen your **skills** and put you on the path of a rewarding and useful professional life.

Ultimately, the breadth of the MS&E program equates the diversity of the research connected to materials science. Consequently, I am confident that this program will enable me to find a subject, and at least will give me the physical culture and the key to successfully reach my goals.

I am convinced that my skills will perfectly fit in a multidisciplinary domain such as nanotechnology. But skills are not enough to succeed in research. One has to be passionate for and enthusiastic about research; and I believe that I belong to this class of people. Should I be admitted, I will put my energy and experience to good use so as to achieve those ends and contribute, thereby, to upholding the standards of excellence of MIT's Department of Materials Science.

In that respect, Baruch College is the right fit. Ideally situated at the heart of a fecund and thriving financial environment, I am confident that it will provide me the missing keys to become an all-round quant researcher, in return of which I will do my utmost to uphold the reputation of excellence of the program.

I am confident that, equipped with a broad and solid knowledge in sciences, a keen curiosity and strong determination, I can make a positive difference in Caltech's Aeronautics and Astronautics Department. In return, I trust that it will provide me with the complementary tools so as to deepen my experience and pave the way towards a fruitful career geared at providing man with the means to explore the far and yonder while pushing back not only the physical barriers but also the technological ones.

This program is the perfect launching pad to pursue a career in the quantitative financial world. I plan on using the acquired technical and analytical skills to create new mathematical tools, but international understanding is also essential to financial progress. I would bring with me my Russian and French cultural and analytical viewpoints, but would appreciate adopting some of that American pragmatism.

Mention the **research groups/labs** you might wish to participate in.

In addition to the rich academic content of the program, I would look forward to participating in one of the research groups which speak to my imagination. I would gladly join Miquel S's team to be able to study and manipulate nanometer scales and, eventually, to design molecular electronic structures. I would also enjoy applying mechanical methods to biomaterials in Robert R's group. What I find exciting about these research groups is the vision they bring in resolutely pushing back the frontiers of medical treatments and industrial practices.

4. The locale

Should you mention the **locale**? Some universities may be touchy about this issue. So, end your essay in the following way:

> In addition to these necessary courses, I am excited by the dream of working within an international community in the heart of Silicon Valley, a location which raises endless hopes of taking part in promising scientific projects, and even meeting future associates. The MS&E program would fill my gaps in economic analysis, decision analysis and management science theory and, ultimately, give me the final competence to make a difference.

> Needless to say, the proximity to the most important financial center in the world would be an enriching and exciting experience.

> The close-knit ties and the synergies UCB nurtures with the Bay Area industries play an important part in my decision to apply, since with my background in science, technology-based companies attract me the most as prospective employers. Studying surrounded by this unique concentration of firms and minds around Berkeley would truly be a dream come true for me.

> Located in the heart of a vibrant metropolis, Columbia University in the City of New York will be the ideal location to start a career that I ambition to build in investment banking.

> The very location of Berkeley at the epicenter of the Bay Area would also allow me to further relationships with newborn start-ups or small hi-tech enterprises.

> The geographical location of UC San Diego, with its local seismic activity, highlights the importance of understanding the properties and behavior of structures as well as the specificities of the site when conceiving bridges. (for UCSD's SEMM program)

> In the heart of the Valley, a hotbed of innovation and entrepreneurship, Stanford University is bound to strengthen my skills and open the doors to a career I intend to embark on in biotech or pharmatech, expecting the program to equip me with the tools that will help me make a significant contribution to the field/ to commit to a career at the top.

> Studying Aeronautics in the United States would be a considerable asset for my professional record all the more so as America is a leading country in this advanced industrial field. A Stanford education would give me the opportunity to benefit from the American innovative spirit, driven by fierce determination and an acute sense of the pragmatic. It is this excellence at all levels that would allow me to become the best professional possible.

Mentioning New York City, for example, is a way for students – and the admissions committee – to be aware that it is an expensive, unsafe and distracting city. Yet, no need to gush about how much you would love to live in the city. And do not say you want to join the program because the city has a hectic night life. Those are examples that you should **NOT** follow:

> *Finally, I would add that I have twice had the opportunity to visit San Francisco and its surroundings. I immensely enjoyed its climate and the open-mindedness of its people. I will thus not be lost when arriving at Stanford. Last year I also went to Los Angeles to visit a friend who was doing an undergraduate program at CSUC Fullerton. I discovered a bit about how an American institution of learning works, and was impressed. I imagine that, given its reputation, Stanford would be even better, and I hope I will be given the opportunity to experience this for myself.

> *While traveling to New York City last Christmas Eve, I had the opportunity to stay one week on 116th and Amsterdam Avenue. Walking through Columbia's campus every day to take the underground, I remember being delighted by the idea of picturing myself as a University student there.

5. The right fit

Use your past experience abroad as a yardstick of your capacity to **fit in** and adjust to your future environment.

> My multicultural background has aided me in my development of a keen awareness of cultural identities and differences. My mother is French and my father is Moroccan. I grew up in Morocco, in a French-speaking household, and attended French primary and high school. Six months ago, I was selected to take part in the Cultura program at the Massachusetts Institute of Technology. I spent two weeks there, attending classes, sharing daily life with MIT students and drafting a report about the cultural differences I noticed. Observing the fecund life at an American university—however short my stay—was another reason I would love to study in the United States.

6. Your professional future

Mention perspectives on your **professional future that justify your application**. Here, you might give not one direction but several directions as you endeavor to see what your position will be in the next 5-10 years. The statement of purpose will not box you into a particular research area or profession. Admissions committees do understand that interests change, especially as you become more immersed in a field. However, having a focused plan reassures admissions committees that you are motivated and will actually be able to complete the program. Therefore, emphasize how the program will facilitate the fulfilment of your (possible) career goals. This is the purpose side of your statement.

I do not rule out the possibility to start my own company. I feel I have what it takes. Entrepreneurship runs in my family: My great grandfather founded a supermarket chain in 1904 which, although it was thriving, was bought out by a big retail in 1996. It is now my turn at the helm, and, should I wish to follow in the family's tradition, I definitely think Stanford's program is the next logical step up my academic and professional career. I hope I will be worthy of your trust and that you will give me the chance to prove my value to you.

I definitely want to work in the field of sustainable energies: my short-term goal is to work for a private company gaining expertise in combining new techniques and new energies; then, later, I see myself founding a start-up using cutting edge solutions to bring this combination of energy to small towns and developing countries. The Master's program in Atmosphere/Energy in the Civil and Environmental Engineering Department at Michigan seems to be the perfect complement to my past studies. There are so many energy issues that I have not yet studied, it is almost frustrating to have to make a choice.

I would gladly see myself working for a mutual fund taking SRI into account in its investing practices, for I believe it is possible to "make a profit while making a difference". However, I will never be the professional who makes that difference without the broader understanding of modern methodological decision making that Columbia University researchers and teachers would provide me. It is their expertise that would allow me to do some outstanding quantitative research in the field of SRI and to become the specialized expert the markets need in the era we have just entered.

I cannot say for certain what I will be doing in five years, but I do know that the dominating passion inside me is the urge to create. I have chosen computer science because for me, creativity is what it is all about: building algorithms in the laboratory, creating software for industry, and founding a startup to provide a flexible outlet for one's work. Through my hard work and commitment, I have acquired technical skills and theoretical understanding. A Master in Computer Science from MIT would give me the opportunity to move beyond mere mastery of received knowledge and into the sacred realm of creativity.

In the future, I see myself working on scientific research and industrial projects. Before I can develop a firm's research strategy, I need to obtain solid knowledge and precious expertise in a field. I am applying to the Master's program in Materials Science and Engineering at Berkeley to obtain more exposure to the diversity of the field and more research experience.

After completing my degree in Materials Science and Engineering, I would like to pursue a career where I can be creatively involved in the design of new

> materials, focusing on biomedical devices. The MIT's Bio- and Polymeric Materials program can help me achieve my goal by providing the advanced tools and knowledge necessary to address critical biological questions and medical challenges.

> My short-term goal is, in fact, to work in a construction company as a site manager. I like the concrete nature of the field, the concept of projects which I would follow from beginning to end, seeing the daily progress and producing something useful for society. I look forward to working on highly technical components but also to having a managerial role. I enjoy motivating people to give their best and meeting the challenge of finding solutions to a multitude of problems. More long term, I would like the issues of sustainable development to be at the core of my professional concerns. I would like to develop a way of building which includes ecological answers and a better use of energy. After gaining experience in a construction company, I would like to create my own business in environmental construction.

> For a long time, I have only been asked to solve equations, not really make those choices. Today, I know what I want: to connect my skills with business related issues, and I know what will be expected from me in the future: to solve complex problems by designing innovative solutions and take the responsibility for implementing them.

> While my professional goals are not yet crystal clear, it is obvious that I do envision a life in which I will be able to devise projects, be it in nanotechnology or telephony, guide them along until they are put on the market. Working in the R&D department of a company would by all means be attractive, all the more so as I have had some previous experience in that respect while doing an internship with Alltel in Little Rock (Ark.) in the summer 2019. But I want to keep my options open. Being accepted to MIT will certainly give me ample time to make the wise choice. In return, thanks to my experience and educational background, I hope to be able to contribute to the excellence of your university.

Needless to say, the prospect of **starting one's own company** weighs heavily in the vision you bring to the Bay Area, San Francisco or Silicon Valley eco-system. This the relevance of the following example.

> There are therefore many reasons why the Stanford program is the ideal fit, in addition to the entrepreneurial spirit that I noticed when visiting the university last summer. It has that special mix of intellectual buoyancy combined with pro-business vibrancy. To someone like me that one day aspires to start her own firm, make decisions, create and optimize value, the program is the logical next step.

If you cannot envision yet **what kind of engineer, physicist, dentist, economist** you will eventually become, do not fake it. If you do not have a carefully thought-out mission in life and in your career, you may state it. No one expects you to know exactly what you will be doing in a few years' time.

> I do understand that in the course of my graduate studies my research interests will be refined and may change. Yet, at the moment, I have developed a marked interest in wages policies and that is the topic I intend to explore in-depth.

> I am not sure yet if the beginning of my career will be in an R&D department of a company, or if I will find the perfect subject and choose the more academic doctoral path.

If you do not know yet whether you will go in for **doctoral studies** but wish to leave the options open, put it in.

> Whether I decide to continue my studies at the doctoral level or pursue a career as a nuclear engineer for a major energy company, MIT's Master's Program in Nuclear Science and Engineering is the perfect next step for me.

> George Washington University holds the keys to my professional choices: I am not ruling out the possibility of pursuing a PhD, if I find a field of passion which would allow me to work on women's issues in an international organization. With the help of your department, I would become a professional decision-maker carrying solutions, both theoretical and realistic, to improve the way nations, like India or Bangladesh, deal with their minorities.

Or you may say something about the **kind of researcher** you yearn to become using comparison:

> From my experience as a paratrooper during my military service, I have learned to overcome many obstacles, the first of which was fear and apprehension. But just as the paratrooper must be well-equipped and well-prepared before a jump, I believe a scientist should be well trained, with a solid background in the subject matters he has decided to tackle; but unlike the paratrooper, the scientist cannot make a leap of faith into the unknown. He must be patient, explore all avenues before experimenting but he can't be afraid of innovation and boldness. I believe I am this kind of scientist, and that, thanks to the rigorous and demanding years of studies I have logged, I can contribute to the excellence of your institution.

7. Working for the common good

A conclusion that emphasizes the **common good** rather than the **personal gain** is to be preferred.

> After earning my PhD in poverty economics, I plan to find a faculty position at a research institution where I can spend time teaching students, both majors and non-majors as well as conducting research, thus promoting the discipline whose ultimate goal is to find solutions to alleviate the plight of the most destitute.

> Stanford's MSc program in Computational Mathematics holds the resources that can enable me to continue my quest to enhance and better life for all.

> CMU's reputation as an innovative and quality program provides the ideal combination of freedom and rigor. As someone with a history of taking up challenging and intensive research projects I believe I will thrive in such an environment where I hope I will be able to build a long and productive career in electrical computer science.

> I am eager to take what I have learned so far and add it to a rigorous education in data science. This combination I intend to use for the greater good as a person of service committed to better healthcare for all.

> I am confident I can make a meaningful contribution to the student body, and with a biomedical degree a useful contribution to the world of science in the years that lie ahead, should I be granted the privilege of admission.

> Looking at my character and the path I have trodden, you might say that I am following in the footsteps of a man I greatly admire, my father. He graduated from a French *grande école* and returned to Lebanon to reconstruct the country and create social associations for the sake of the people plagued by civil war. Even though my father has had to face many calamities impeding his development projects, he is still working at making Lebanon the paradise of the East. He taught me to always consider the long-term prospects of my deeds, and challenged me to become an ambitious dreamer and mountain-climber. Maybe excellence is not enough to get admitted into MIT, but I am confident that my efforts will lead me to success.

8. Returning home

A conclusion that may mention that, upon completion of the degree, you will **return to your home country** or **region** to contribute to or help grow the economy is sometimes well perceived, and will paint you as someone eager to return **in kind** the benefits of a privileged education abroad. But do not bet too much on it.

In the very near future, I ambition to return to Morocco and contribute to its economic development by making the most of the knowledge I have acquired. That is what has been my lodestar since I left home country.

I am interested by the program at Berkeley because planners should have technical notions in order to find out the best solutions possible. Moreover, my studies at UCB would be supported by interdisciplinary institutes like the Institute of Urban and Regional Development. I paid special attention to Professor C's project "Commuter Rail Transit in California: Land Use and Travel Behavior Implications". I am interested in that project because ex-urbanization is one of these pioneering concepts that may have a great impact on future regional development. What is more, Alsace is leading a similar "tram-train" project whose aim is to spread development in the whole region, not only around Strasbourg.

Upon completion of the Princeton program, I plan to return to my home country and work for The Boston Consulting Group on topics such as governments' strategies or revenue optimization for pan-African conglomerates where risk mitigation is crucial. In the long term, I aspire to start my own company that provides technology- and engineering-based solutions for businesses to enhance their risks' assessment and management. Africa is set to be the main source of global GDP growth in the 21st century and my ambition is to be part of it. I am thus convinced that Stanford, through the MS&E program and thanks to its inspiring diverse community will allow me to make a meaningful contribution to the continent's promising development.

9. An uplifting conclusion

A conclusion should be **uplifting**. It should be like a window opened onto the future.

I come equipped with strong skills and a determination that has been steeled in a tough work environment. As well, I have drawn on my French experience (mostly theoretical) to acquire the necessary keys that will help open the doors of a new world, and also what I believe to be a new beginning, more practical oriented. Some people have a vision, others have a dream. I do have my feel solidly planted in the ground, but that excludes neither the vision, nor the dream, let alone the ambition.

My motivation to come to your university is as great as my passion for physics, that is to say boundless. I can bring my enthusiasm, some outstanding skills in science and above all an inexhaustible ocean of questioning. My purpose is to learn a lot but also give a lot back by participating actively in the research, and involving myself in every activity of the department. And what a better year than this "World Year of Physics" to begin working on it.

```
In a variety of disciplines at college, my curiosity and enthusiasm have risen every time we have taken another step into deeper and more complex scientific knowledge. Working at the threshold of what is unknown in the subject which fascinates me the most, nanomaterials and their environmental applications, is what I want to be doing for my life's work.
```

```
I come from a modest background in which effort has been a standard my family has held high. My grandparents' impoverished immigrant roots go back to Sicily. My parents struggled to breach the middle class. It is my turn now to strive and access other horizons, not so much because I want to be better than those who came before me, but because I want to be better than myself. Education is to me the straight but unique path upward to achieve that ambition.
```

At this point, and wrapping up the statement, you might be tempted to bring to light some references that are dear to you, such as the people who may have **inspired you** (not your sister or cousin that attended the program before you), events that you need to contribute to, challenges in present society you are eager to take up. For example, explorers, scientists, captains of industry, creators, inventors but also those who brought about a revolution in the field of your choice.

Typically, when mentioning disruptive technologies, a comparison with a revolution – any revolution – might be welcome. You will want to be an actor and participant in it, play the role of a trailblazer or pioneer, two words that echo American history, for example.

```
Because of its dedication to applied research, UC Berkeley will help me bring disruptive ideas to life and, hopefully, be an actor in contributing to the next breakthroughs of our century.
```

In the same way, should you apply for a transportation program, projects such as the *Grand Paris* and the issues around mobility will point out to concrete projects that your science will contribute to.

10. The final sentence

The last sentence should be **short** and **strong**. Here are a few examples:

```
In return for Harvard's commitment to provide an environment conducive to higher learning, I offer a confidence in my ability to take advantage of the quality program you propose.
```

```
Princeton is therefore the next stop on my academic road, and a decisive one at that for someone like me who is eager to carve out a name in research. My strengths and experience at the top are what I bring along, thus contributing
```

to upholding the standards of excellence that are the key signatures of a University that has always sought to advance the frontiers of knowledge.

My solid scientific background and my well-rounded training will definitely be assets for the MIT's PhD program in Economics. Should I be given the opportunity, I will do my utmost to match the sterling criteria of excellence set by the Massachusetts Institute of Technology.

To become the mechanical scientist I aim to be, I will need to add professional specialization to the general and theoretical knowledge that I already have. I would like to work on the unsolved problems of tomorrow, and apply my results on hi-tech industrial breakthroughs. The close links between Stanford and the Silicon Valley will surely sustain my life project of becoming an eco-friendly industrial manager. Stanford's tuition, enhanced by unique infrastructures, will give me the key bricks to bring real added-value to Mechanics.

This degree from Cornell would be the ideal first step down that road, and I know that, if given the chance, I will make the most out of that opportunity.

I am fully committed to my long-term goal, and the University of Chicago's MS in Transportation is the natural next step.

For all these reasons, your program is perfect for me: not only does it meet my expectations of a graduate program, but I feel it will challenge my views, helping me to become the scientist I yearn to be, finding breakthroughs that will improve society.

I can only hope that my work and skills will find a home in the Yale community: it is my goal to enrich it as much as I expect it will enrich me.

Given the breadth of your program – along with the depth of my ambition - I believe that I am a perfect match for NYU's master's program. If accepted, I will contribute my boundless energy and determination so as to turn my experience into a rewarding one while continuing and building upon NYU's tradition of excellence.

I can offer to U of Illinois Urbana-Champaign my eagerness to take part in the aforementioned projects, besides my multicultural scientific experiences; the knowledge aggregation I shall benefit from, and put into use, is, however, more substantial than my modest contribution. Hence, I am entirely conscious that, once more, this one is not an undemanding step; nevertheless, I can say I am willing to further nurture my ideals, and that is something one can rely upon, for sure.

Everything I have read and heard about UCLA's Department of Physics leads me to believe that this is the place where I would grow the most, becoming an excellent experimental researcher in condensed matter, and later even a leader of a team, searching out creative solutions that are still unsuspected.

Thus, the program of Mathematics in Finance at NYU would allow me to develop the finesse and competence I need to become a professional who can make a difference in the future.

If accepted into your program, I would take advantage of all that you offer to attain my dream: becoming that competent, international engineer who will play a decisive part in tomorrow's decisions for innovative and efficient transportation, not just on paper, but on the roads.

With strong foundations in mathematics, economics, management and mechanics, I am now looking for a graduate program that will allow me to build on this interdisciplinary knowledge and at the same time give me wider international perspectives. I believe the Master's Program in Management, Science and Engineering at Columbia University meets all of these goals brilliantly.

I am convinced that the Atmosphere and Energy program is where I need to be next year if I am going to make a difference to society. In return, I would bring my theoretical training, adaptability and dedication to enhance my class.

My career goal is to work as a consultant for energy agencies, perhaps through France's Atomic Energy Agency to encourage environmental choices that will help the field of nuclear energy regain prestige in public opinion. With your program and my motivation, I would help establish those gateways between the scientific world and energy suppliers that will make a global difference.

The MS&E program would fill my gaps in economic analysis, decision analysis and management science theory and, ultimately, give me the final competence to make a difference.

I am strongly determined to be involved in the development of nuclear energy in the United States and throughout the world. I hope to take part in an international cooperation which will bring fusion as a relevant energy source to France and the United States and thus, help to provide a sustainable source of energy to the world. My experience at the University of Washington would be a significant step towards this goal.

I should love to become a tireless and valuable contributor to your program.

Science may be my first love, but the cultural richness also motivates me to choose Harvard.

11. Remember

- The admissions committee needs to get a feel for the whole person. They do not want to know just what the applicants think they want to know. Such ploys are highly obvious to admissions people and can be detrimental to your cause. Therefore, do not try to **second guess** what the admissions committee is looking for. Every sentence should come from your heart and mind. Use straightforward language. Admissions officers already know about the charms of their university, the evils of terrorism and the personal commitment involved in being a good doctor. Bring something new, and personal to the table, not just what you think they want to hear.
- **You are what you have done**. Therefore, no need to say, for example, I am hard working, since that shows through the competitive program you went through and the university you are applying to. The proof is in the pudding (bis).
- Do not be satisfied with your SOP unless **it looks like you and you look like it**. It is not rare to go through a dozen versions before you are satisfied. Hence the need to start early. The writing process goes something like this: think about it carefully, write it down, then walk away for a few hours or days, let it rest. Come back and see if you feel the same way, change whatever you need to change. You will be satisfied only when you have written who you are and who you are is what you have written.
- Do not underestimate yourself. You are worth more than the sum of a few grades. **Be bold**, and do not be held back by that C on your first-year transcript, or your B in your second-year project. What matters is your **determination** to succeed. In that respect, do not be afraid of failure. Failure is part of one's journey. Even more, failure is necessary for success. So, persist. Hang on in there. As Temiloluwa O. Prioleau – the first Black woman tenure-track faculty in CS in an Ivy League university – said, "All mountains are surmountable simply by taking one step at a time." And do not shun at asking for help when help is needed. What matters is to learn even if that takes many tries.
- Due to high volume, submitting **on the deadline day** is **NOT** recommended, and applications received late (even due to network latency issues or last-minute emergencies) will not be accepted. So, make sure you submit ahead of the deadline.
- You can attract attention in your statement with simple and clear organization, and by **bolding the major points** that you want to make. Think of the statement more like a sales pitch. Make the argument simple.
- **Do not give up** if your application does not come through. It is not the end of the world. Neither is it a reflection on your background, qualities and talent but evidence of a competitive and broad field.
- Some will recommend that you should not go through the application process on your own. I am of two minds about this: on the one hand you might want to team up, show your SOP and share thoughts with classmates, or professors and therefore make the whole process more gratifying. On the other end, the application process being an international competition, vying for the same spots with others might give away more about your intentions and application content than you would want. In the end, I believe each and everyone might seek the help of a coach, and keep themselves to themselves, friend-wise or schoolmate-wise.

IX. Formatting the SOP

There are some strictures to follow when formatting the SOP. The first thing is to **check the guidelines** of each program and make sure you **comply with their recommendations**. No matter what, the SOP ought to be edited with particular care.

- **Length**. Unless there are special instructions about the **length or format of the essay**, the SOP is usually **1,000-1,100 words** long (1-1½ pages) single-spaced, typed, 12pt. font size. Definitely not more than 2 pages (some programs say 2-3 pages, but this is a rare occurrence! Who has time to read more than that?). The trend is now to reduce the length of the essay. For example, Columbia's MS&E essay is between 250 and 500 words, others between 250 and 1,000 words (this is a recommendation as "Your application will not be negatively impacted should exceed this recommendation"). MIT's Mban is 500 words long. Princeton's ORFE essay is no more than 1,000 words. Some programs at Yale have questions that should not exceed 200 words. Even UCB has recommended to limit the essay to one page. As for British programs, the number of words is limited for each question.

  Pay attention to the requirements of each program: some programs will use **characters** (and not **words**) to limit the length of the essay. Typically, Stanford's diversity statement is no more than 1,000 characters long. 800 characters is about 10 lines.

  Adhere to stated word limits. If one of your program choices asks for only 500 words, write the 1,500-word version first, then cut back to the barebones to meet their criteria. On the other hand, be it word or character limit, it is useless to cram as much as you can to reach the magic figure. Strong statements are short. What matters is quality, not quantity. If possible, use Times New Roman. Try not to cheat by reducing the font or narrowing the margins. An essay that is too long shows lack of rigor and discipline. If you write overlong, and you copy and paste it into the submission window, the bottom part of your essay may simply disappear.

- Make sure the recommendations include either **single-spaced** or **double-spaced** as it makes a world of a difference.

- Clear **delineation** of paragraphs (one blank line between each paragraph). There is no **indent** at the beginning of each paragraph, except in the paragraph that details your formation and which is divided into three sub parts (courses, project work, internship experience), two of which will start with an indent.

- At the top of the statement, this is what you should write. Put it in the middle. Use bold letters.

Stanford University – Department of Mechanics – MS program
Statement of purpose
First name/Last name

- Your name should appear in the **Header** or **Footer** of every page.

- Do not sign your name at the bottom of your statement. Avoid the `yours sincerely, yours cordially`, etc. or even:

```
*I thank you for your consideration, and I eagerly look forward to your response.
```

You may add one line of conclusion, though:

```
In advance, I thank the admissions committee for reading my letter.
```

- A good story is linked with **continuity** and **focus**. Linguistic links are helpful, but not always necessary. An example of links between coursework and project work could run like this:

```
Studying various scientific areas and specializing in statistics and data science
have given me an overall view of theoretical solutions to scientific problems
reinforced by group projects and internships.
```

You can have separate points which need separate paragraphs (the choice of five is a guideline, not a rule). However, your thought process must always be coherent. Do not describe your third-year specialization and then talk about your second-year introductory class. Some will choose to write in a chronological order, others will choose to write by theme. The key in all cases is: **coherence** – do not lose your readers in a confusion of details. The thread of connection should reappear at the right moment: a growing understanding, an evolving competence towards the same goal.

- Make sure you have the **right spelling** for the **proper names**. That includes the names of your professors and the names of the faculty of the university you are applying to. Always use **first name/last name** the first time you mention a professor:
  Professor Jane Doe (then Professor Doe). Avoid writing Prof. as some may object to it. **Plural**: Professors Ted Jones and John Rey (then, Professors Jones and Rey). Indicate the first name of the professor or researcher the first time you mention them. If she/he is a researcher, you may use Dr. Pay attention to the **gender** of the professors, especially if you are not familiar with the language and nationality. For example, Xin Guo is a woman. So is Jean Gough or Angjoo Kanazawa. To check, go to the web page of the Department or the professor's / researcher's website. They usually post a photo.

- **Coursework**. Indicate the names of the courses in **English**. The same applies to your research project. All course titles are in italics and have capital letters on first letters. No capital on "of", "and", "for", "in". Thus:

```
I attended a class/course on Stochastic Calculus and Probabilities, taught by Amir Dembo.
```

No capital when you write about subject matters in general (I've always been fond of **physics** and **math**/I look forward to exploring how **operations research** and **machine learning** can be used). Note that **math** in US English does not take an -s whereas it does in British English.

When mentioning the courses of the program you are applying for, you can very well include the course **code**: ENME E6220 *Random Processes in Mechanics,* COMS W4776 *Machine Learning for Data Science.*

X. The Writing Process

Admissions committees will be looking at your statement of purpose (and any other writing you submit with your application) to make sure you have the writing skills necessarily to succeed in a graduate program. So, you need your statement to be well-organized and clearly communicate your ideas. A statement of purpose will be descriptive but concise. You also want your writing style to stand out. While you should not use an overly familiar tone, you also do not want to be too staid and buttoned-up. You definitely do not want to bore anyone reading your essay.

- One prerequisite is that you should **think in English** when drafting the statement. Do not write in French first and then translate into English.

- The writing process is following: first pre-write, then draft, and finally, edit.

- To begin, you must first collect and organize potential ideas for your essay's focus.

- When you have a solid draft, it is time to make final improvements, find and correct typos and errors. Remember, you are your best editor. No one can speak for you; your own words and ideas are your best bet.

- Once you have come up with a consistent piece of work, take a break and come back to it in a few days. Ask yourself: Do your main ideas come across clearly? Do you prove your points with specific details? Is your essay easy to read?

- **Feedback time**. Get someone else to give you feedback if necessary. Have someone you like and trust (someone likely to tell you the truth) read your essay. Ask them to tell you what they think you're trying to convey. Did they get it right?

- **Proofread** your personal statement by reading it out loud or reading it into a tape recorder and playing back the tape. Check for repetitions, redundancies or inconsistencies. Also, print out your essay and read the printed copy. Since it is easy to miss errors in your own writing, I recommend editing your essay from back to front (*i.e.*, from the last sentence to the first sentence). Doing this prevents you from glossing over words and lets you pinpoint punctuation, spelling, and grammatical errors more easily.

XI. The Fate of your Application

Once your application has been submitted (by hitting the submit button), you can't change anything in the application. Game over. You will no longer be able to update uploaded materials. The waiting begins. In general, do not send any materials, additional or not, before the fee has been paid and the submit button hit (see below).

Forms are filled online, documents are sent online as well, including essays and letters of recommendation. The online process has a check-off system which is reliable and resistant to human error. If the application is not complete, it will not be passed on to the reviewers. It is essential you verify the online check-off system to make sure your file has been received and logged. If you would like to check your application status, or see exactly which documents have been processed, please log on to your application. Many programs will notify you when your file is complete or if some document is missing. It is always wise to ask for confirmation and make sure that your file is complete.

University programs do **NOT** accept late applications. So, do not bother applying after the deadline. Similarly, all supplemental materials or supporting documents (3 letters of recommendation, GRE, TOEFL scores) **are due the same day the application is due**. Programs cannot guarantee that documents received after the deadline will be reviewed with your application.

If you send paper-based materials, it is preferable to do it by courier such as FedEx, DHL, or UPS. Schools are reluctant to receive registered mail as it forces them to go to the post office and pick up the delivery.

Once you have paid for and submitted your application, the recommenders will be notified personally of the need to upload their letter. A code will be sent with instructions to log in.

After all is said and done, should you want to submit **additional material**, do it by snail mail and electronically (to the admissions coordinator, for example). Such material might be your current year grades that you have obtained after the application deadline. If those grades are outstanding, no need to be shy about them. Attach a note to it such as:

```
Name/Additional material to my application for MSc/PhD program that might help
you while you review my candidacy.
```

When you apply, your file will be reviewed by the graduate school **and** the department you are applying to. They are distinct entities. When a system has a strong department, the graduate school serves as a processing center and leaves the admission decision to the department. Conversely, if the graduate school is strong, it will make the decision. In case of conflict, the graduate school has the final say.

Admissions decisions usually come around mid-March. Yet, it is not rare that stellar candidates should be contacted before that date, either by a professor you will have mentioned in the SOP through a paper you have read and commented on. When you are made an offer, including a scholarship, hedge your bets and wait until all admissions results are in.

No news is not bad news. You may have been **wait-listed**. If you have been wait-listed, the decision may come way past April 15. Sometimes, you will be informed by the program that you are on the wait list, asking you to confirm your interest for the program mentioned. Now is the time to re-assert your interest in the program, reiterating your desire to join, or sending your most recent grades.

Following the decision of the Council of Graduate Schools, some 400 graduate schools have agreed not to make you declare your final decision before April 15. Yet, your admission may depend on **yield**, that is the number of students who actually accept the admission offer and the **funding** schools have. Some programs may call you to make sure you are firmly committed to their program. If you are waiting for answers from other programs, be straightforward and indicate that, in the absence of answers and at this stage of the game, even though you are fiercely interested in their program, you need to have all the results in before you give a final answer.

Be diplomatic and professional in **declining** answers. Think about later when you may be seeking a post-doc or faculty position, or be on a research project that involves researchers from that institution. Academia is a small world with long memories.

If the final decision is a unanimous "No", you might send an email asking for the reasons why—yet expect an automatic answer that will not detail the rationale that led to the decision. The admissions answer will call up the high number of quality applicants and the tough competition that ensues to justify their decision. You may also call the admissions officers but chances are that getting some feedback will be a tall order. Committees do not have the capacity to give one-on-one feedback. Tough luck! Grin and bear it, after all you will have another chance to re-apply the following year.

Which should not prevent you from mulling the reasons that might have played against your admission: weak LORs, disorganized and unfocused SOP, lackluster resumé, lack of originality, shallowness of knowledge, lack of conviction, lack of purpose and vision, low GPA... In that case, be careful about the materials you will be sending (especially the LORs) as programs will compare both last year's and this year's documents.

XII. About Vocabulary and Grammar

1. General

Drafting an SOP is a litmus test of your language skills in many respects: first, the scientific vocabulary requires precision and a solid grasp of the technical terms. Second, it is a test of the variety and command of your English. Too often, you will hark back on to the 100 words of so that are in your possession, seeking in convoluted, cryptic, ponderous or recondite expressions a way to sound scientific while you only sound pedantic. Three, the statement must make for clear reading and therefore grammar matters.

You will need a certain number of **drafts** before coming up with an acceptable, if not tip-top version of your statement.

Be **thorough**: type and proofread your essay carefully. Get the **grammar** and **spelling right**. Spelling or grammatical errors, awkward language, or fuzzy logic will make your essay memorable - in a wrong way. Do not rely on your computer to check your spelling. Typos and spelling/grammatical errors can be, and will be, interpreted as carelessness, or just bad writing. Computer spell checks miss a multitude of problems. The best insurance is to have your essay proofread or road-tested by someone you trust. Your most important desk reference is a paper and acknowledged dictionary rather than untrustworthy websites.

2. Vocabulary

Your vocabulary is severely tested in a statement. Do not try to impress your reader by using over erudite words to pass off as an expert in the field. Ignorance of the proper terms will pass you off as ignorant. So, be simple, without being simplistic.

Yet, do not hesitate to be as **scientific as possible** when describing an experiment, a project, the content of a course. You are supposed to be a scientist, so, write as one, use the right words and **do not second guess** the officers on the adcom: they will understand what you write and the science behind. Here are some examples of unadulterated descriptions:

I also conducted an experimental project in molecular biology and enzymatic catalysis. It consisted in cloning the DHFR gene from Saccharomyces yeast into E. Coli bacteria, using an expression plasmid vector. After producing and purifying the protein, I made a series of biochemical and kinetic analyses to measure and discuss the Michaelian nature of the enzyme (DHFR).

I led a year-long team-based project which consisted in modeling and simulating chemical, radiative and dynamical phenomena that drive stratospheric ozone depletion. I was particularly involved in the kinetics of chlorine activation at the surface of polar stratospheric clouds, where heterogeneous catalysis plays a major role.

The course on *Information Theory* is bringing me in-depth knowledge about compression algorithms (such as Shannon-Fano-Elias coding and Lempel-Ziv based algorithms) and error-correcting codes (such as convolutional codes and the Viterbi algorithm).

Several classes have helped me build up my knowledge in Applied Mathematics. First, with *Statistical Methods* lectured by Professor Marc H., I acquired the mathematical instruments to analyze a concrete phenomenon, from the choice of the probabilistic model to its estimation and evaluation. I was particularly interested in the least squares estimator, the M-estimator and the Fisher information, which I used for a computational project on the Levy Distribution. This type of distribution is relevant to the financial modeling community due to its empirical similarity to the returns of securities. This approach to understanding a random phenomenon appealed to me and thus I decided to explore the subject further by following a *Statistical Learning and Nonparametric Estimation* course. There, I discovered, for example, how to estimate the density function of a nonparametric random variable through various methods. The *Quantum and Statistical Physics* course provided the opportunity to apply some of these tools in practical situations and to better assess their meaning and impact.

You should endeavor to **translate French titles** as much as possible, or explain them in few words. Thus, if some titles are easy to translate (*Microfinance* = Microfinance Institute), *La Main à la pâte*, for example, cannot be translated literally, but is best described as:

a "Foundation whose goal is to get primary and junior high school students interested in sciences thanks to hands-on experiments."

Also note:

I worked for *Asphalte*, a non-profit association committed to helping immigrants and their children integrate French society.

Une Grande École, pourquoi pas moi? (*GEPPM*) can be translated by a "non-profit organization aimed at raising the academic ambitions of underprivileged students". Les *Cordées de la réussite* should not be translated by "The ropes of success" but some expression such as "a non-profit equal opportunity organization meant to promote academic success for all."

On the other hand, the **GIGN** (*Groupe d'intervention de la Gendarmerie nationale*) might be translated by National Gendarmerie Intervention Group (*wiki*) or, better, Tactical unit of the French Gendarmerie.

Multi-syllabic words sound pedantic. So, keep it simple and make sure you check out the vocabulary you use. Using a thesaurus is fine but not all synonyms have the same meaning. An inappropriate synonym will make you sound like you do not know what you are talking about or, worse yet, give the impression that you are plagiarizing from a source you do not understand.

Pay attention to proper names. People applying to *__John Hopkins__ and *__Colombia__ will never make it (it is **Johns Hopkins** and **Columbia University in the City of New York**); do not confuse Esther **Duflo** (Professor of Economics at MIT) with Cécile **Duflot** (French politician).

French students always fear to be repetitive. They should not, for sometimes it is necessary to repeat a word for clarity's sake, especially where scientific words are concerned.

Enrich your vocabulary. In particular, there are many words and expressions that ought to be avoided: "really", "very", "bad", "good", "important", "interesting", "had to", "enable me to", "be an opportunity to"… Here is a list of possible alternates.

DON'T SAY	BUT SAY
creative	fecund, formative (event), productive, fertile, fruitful, high-yielding, inventive, thriving,
good	advantageous, appropriate, attractive, a boon, convenient, dependable, desirable, efficient, fair (weather), favorable, fine, first class, first-rate, fit, fitting, genuine, a godsend, positive, proper, reliable, satisfactory, sound, suitable, workable
bad	absurd, appalling, awkward, criminal, damaging, dangerous, defective, detrimental, evil, false, foolish, groundless, harmful, inhuman, inacceptable, rotten, scandalous, second class, second-rate, serious, undesirable, unfavorable, unfortunate, ungrounded, unreliable, unsuitable, useless
important	capital, consequential, crucial, decisive, essential, impressive, indispensable, major, of substance, paramount, portentous, requiring immediate attention, significant, of vital importance, worthwhile
interesting	absorbing, captivating, curious, entertaining, exciting, fascinating, gripping, provocative, spell-binding, stimulating, tantalizing, tempting, thought-provoking, thrilling
big	awesome, enormous, extensive, foremost, influential, huge, large, noteworthy, outstanding, salient, prominent, significant, tremendous, weighty
small	found wanting, inadequate, inconsequential, insignificant, insufficient, limited, minor, negligible, secondary, trifling, unsatisfactory, weak (argument)

DON'T SAY	BUT SAY
necessary	a matter of life and death, basic, binding, called-for, compulsory, essential, for certain, for sure, fundamental, high priority, imperative, indispensable, mandatory, required, requisite, unavoidable, urgent, vital
problem	bone of contention, critical situation, difficulty, dilemma, hornet's nest, issue, moot point, plight, point at issue, poser, predicament, puzzle, quandary, question, riddle, topic
idea	aim, assumption, belief, conviction, feeling, goal, guess, impression, inkling, insight, notion, objective, opinion, outlook, plan, principles, scheme, viewpoint
stop	ban, bar, cease, complete, clamp down on, crack down on, crush, curb, desist from, destroy, discontinue, exclude, forbid, give up, have done with, lay to rest, muzzle, nip in the bud, put an end to, quit, terminate, throttle
make	come up with a plan, cobble together (a plan), contrive, create, develop, devise, establish, hammer, organize, set up, work out
think	acknowledge, analyze, assume, believe, conceive, consider, contemplate (a problem), examine, feel, focus on, imagine, look upon, mull over, picture, ponder, presume, reckon, suppose, take it for granted (that), think over, toy with an idea, turn over (in one's mind), zero in on
succeed	carry out, carry through, come through with flying colors, find a workable solution, get ahead, get off the ground, make a hit, make a splash, make headway, pass muster, prevail over, turn out well, work out
successful	affluent, booming, fruitful, money-making, on top of the world, opulent, profitable, prospering, rewarding, thriving, up-and-coming, well-to-do, well off
like	appreciate, be eager to, be fond of, be inclined to, be partial to, be prone to, can't do without, enjoy, delight in, have a tendency to, have a weakness for, hold dear, relish the idea of, take kindly to, take pleasure in, take to, think highly of, think well of

because of	"Due to" and "owing to" are similar in meaning to "on account of" and "because of". They are all prepositions used with noun phrases and are often used interchangeably. They indicate that something happened as a result of something or introduce the reason for something happening.

Collocations are one major stumbling block for French-speaking students. A collocation is made up of two or more words that are commonly used together in English. Collocations are about using the right adjective, adverb or verb with a noun.

Adjective + noun: you cannot write a ~~quick~~ train/a ~~fast~~ meal, a ~~fast~~ reply, but a **fast** train/a **quick** meal/a **quick** reply. When you describe physical objects, you can use a wide variety of adjectives such as "large", "big", "tiny", "minuscule", "small", etc. However, when describing nouns that reflect emotions or other abstract concepts (*e.g.* "joy", "anger", "wealth") you need to pay careful attention to the choice of intensifying adjectives. "**Absolute**", "**complete**", "**total**" and "**utter**" are used to express strong feelings, extreme situations, or negative experiences. One favorite adjective, "**great**", is used in a limited number of cases: great admiration/in great detail/great disappointment/great enjoyment/

great excitement/great failure/at great length/a great number (of)/great pride/a great quantity (of)/ great skill, etc. Similarly, you will write: a large number of scientists/experts (+ countable noun) ≠ a large proportion (+ uncountable noun)/a large quantity (+ uncountable noun).

Among other examples: alternative/clean energy – the bare essentials – bright future – detailed description – ethical standards – joint efforts – key issue – rough idea – tight schedule – yawning gap – beta test – scientific paper

Verb + noun: you cannot write *to ~~realize~~ a project, but to carry out/to do a project – to give a presentation – to accept a challenge – to achieve a goal – to bring about change – to change course – to close the gap – to come to a realization – to conduct research – to do work – to exceed expectations – to face a challenge – to give rise to – to join a club – to lay the groundwork – to make a decision/a mistake/an effort/an offer/progress – to meet a need/a standard/a target/with approval – to miss a goal/an opportunity – to play a part – to play music – to take a risk – to take pride (in)

Verb + adverb: to progress smoothly – to remember vividly – to fail miserably – to vary widely

Adverb + verb: deeply rooted (in) – fully understand – fully justify

Adverb + adverb: fairly often – quite often – well after – well ahead

Adverb + adjective/PP: extremely/totally/sufficiently + satisfied – fully + aware – actively involved – bitterly disappointed – highly unlikely – quite sure – readily available – well aware (of) – widely used – staunchly opposed – thoroughly investigated

Noun + noun: a round of applause - piece of advice/of information – string theory – life science – research project

I strongly / highly recommend using a collocation dictionary such as the **Oxford Collocations Dictionary** (https://www.oxfordlearnersdictionaries.com/us/definition/collocations). There are online resources as well: https://ozdic.com is one.

Pay attention to the differences in spelling between **American English and British English**. So, depending on which program(me) you choose to apply (US / UK), abide by common spelling rules. Here are some common differences:

British English (UK)	American English (US)
aluminium	aluminum
autumn	fall
careers fair	career fair
centre	center
colour	color
day/month (eg 11/9)	month/day (eg 9/11)

defence	defense
favourable/favourably	favorable/favorably
endeavour	endeavor
mark, grade	grade
maths	math
programme	program
realise	realize

- *British English uses "-tre" whereas American English uses "-er."*

☞ theatre ≠ theater/centre ≠ center/litre ≠ liter

- *British English uses "-s" whereas American English uses "-z."*

☞ realise (UK) ≠ realize (US)

- *British English uses "-our" whereas American English uses "-or."*

☞ labour (UK) ≠ labor (US)

- *British English uses "-ll" whereas American English uses "-l."*

☞ modelled ≠ modeled/gruelling ≠ grueling/to instill ≠ to instil/to enroll ≠ to enrol but in American English, it is "enrollment" and to "fulfill." Note that the **single l** spelling is more common in the United States; the **double l** spelling is more common in the UK, Australia, South Africa and New Zealand. (traveling ≠ travelling)

- *Verbs whose past participle is spelled with a final "t" are usually spelled with "ed" in American English*: dreamed, spilled, learned, burned, spelled. *Exceptions*: wept, crept, slept.

- *Hyphenated words tend to be closed up in American English:* cooperate, nontoxic, halftime, anymore, forever.

- Avoid **barbarisms**:
  – Verbs ending with **-ate: appreciate** – **dominate** – **eliminate** – **evaluate** – **interrogate** – **invigorate** – **penetrate** – **authenticate** (but authentication **OR** authentification) and other words: **theoretical** (~~theorical~~)
  – Some verbs do not end with -ate in English: adapt (and not ~~adaptate~~) – apply (and not ~~applicate~~) – determine (and not ~~determinate~~) – evolve (and not ~~evoluate~~) – incite (and not ~~incitate~~) – inform (and not ~~informate~~) – function (and not ~~functionate~~) – interpret (and not ~~interpretate~~)
  – ***sensibiliser***: to make people aware/to heighten/to raise awareness – ***favoriser***: to encourage – ***faire pression sur***: to press sb to (and not pressurize). "Pressure" is a noun as in "to work under pressure" – ***passionner***: a subject ~~that passionate me~~ (= an exciting subject) – to be passionate about sth
  subsidy (~~subvention~~) – explorer (~~explorator~~) – competitor (~~concurrent~~) – competition (~~concurrence~~) – train (~~people~~) *(former des personnes)* – save (time, money) – founder (*fondateur*) – underprivileged (~~unfavored~~)

– a **scientist** (*un scientifique*) but **scientific** knowledge – an experiment ≠ experience: an **experiment** is a test to see what the result will be, or to prove something whereas an **experience** is something that you live through; something that happens to you in life.

– an engineer - a civil engineer - an engineering school - engineering sciences

• Pay attention to **false cognates** (*faux amis*):
actual: *vrai, réel* (≠ *actuel*: current)
college: *la fac* (≠ *collège:* middle school, junior high school)
eventually: *finalement* (≠ *éventuellement*: possibly)
lecture: *conférence, cours magistral* (≠ *la lecture*: reading)
library: *bibliothèque* (≠ *librairie*: bookstore)
pass an exam: *réussir un examen* (≠ *passer*: to take, to sit)
possibly, potentially: *éventuellement*
presently: *bientôt* (≠ *présentement*: nowadays)
to attend a class: *assister à un cours* (≠ to assist = to help)
to demand: *exiger* (≠ *demander*: to ask)
to regard: *considérer, estimer* (≠ *regarder*: to watch)
to resume: *reprendre, recommencer* (≠ *résumer*: to summarize)
virtually: *quasiment, presque* (≠ *virtuellement*: to all intents and purposes, potentially)

– Avoid **French-sounding words** when possible:
~~*I am a piano, ukulele and guitar autodidact*~~: **I taught myself** the piano, the ukulele and the guitar.
~~*I am a passionate of the environment*~~: I am **passionate about** the environment
Her remarks and observations were always ~~*pertinent*~~: **relevant**

• **Spelling**: develop, develo**p**ed, develo**p**ing – depend**e**nt – refer, refe**rr**ed, refe**rr**ing – perso**n**ality – perso**n**al – to co**mm**it, commi**tt**ed

• **Capital letters or not?** All proper nouns should be capitalized. When you mention the title of a course, capitalize the first letter of each word and put it in italics (*Stochastic Calculus*). In the same way, when you mention a specialization, capitalize each first letter (*Energies of the Twenty-first Century*). All words in a title are to be capitalized except definite and indefinite articles ("the" and "a"/"an"), prepositions of all kind and coordinating conjunctions ("but", "and", "or", "for", "nor"). Do not add bracket signs.

Capitalize the names of institutions (typically they are proper nouns): the École Polytechnique, Columbia University in New York City, *Ecole Normale Supérieure* (Paris Program).

When you are talking about a **school subject** in a general way, you do not need to capitalize it unless it is the name of a language. Fields of study such as physics, mathematics, computer science, biology, chemistry are not proper nouns although they are regularly capitalized in an academic setting but French and Spanish do need to be capitalized. Capitalize the subjects in the title of the program you are attending: the **Operations Research program**. Note that "program" is not capitalized.

Academic degrees are capitalized only when the full name of the degree is used, such as "**Bachelor of Arts**" or "**Master of Science**". General references, such as "bachelor's," "master's" or "doctoral degree", are not capitalized.

Honorary titles are to be capitalized too: Captain, Ecole CentraleSupélec Rugby Club/Treasurer, Junior Enterprise. Same for titles of papers or theses you have read or published.
Also note that **seasons**, in English, should be capitalized: Spring, Fall, Winter, Summer. So must **professor** when you add a proper name (Professor Jones).

- Do not talk about **articles** (written by researchers) but about **papers**. A **journal** is different from a **newspaper** and refers to a serious magazine published regularly about a particular subject: a medical journal, for example.

- **Do not confuse**: hearth ≠ at the heart of/affect ≠ effect/its ≠ it's/trough ≠ through
  their ≠ there ≠ they're (=they are): *All parents want **their** children to be successful/**They're** thinking of studying in the U.S./**There** is no way I will accept their proposal.*
  farther ≠ further: "farther" describes literal distance; "further" describes abstract distance. *I'm **further** from accomplishing my goals now than I was five years ago ≠ If you walk a little **farther** down the road, you will find the station.*
  insure ≠ ensure: **insure** means "to cover something with an insurance policy"; **ensure** means "to guarantee".
  to **model**: "to modelize" is obsolete.
  They modelled the data with a computer to analyze the experiment's results.
  economic (related to economics or the economy) ≠ **economical** (that does not waste money, resources, etc.) – the French Ministry for the **Economy** and Finance
  ancient (belonging to the very distant past and no longer in existence) ≠ **obsolete**, **obsolescent**
  to **realise** (**UK**)/to **realize** (**US**) = to grow aware (of) ≠ to make, to create, to achieve, to complete… (≠ to fulfil a dream)
  to **complete** (=to achieve, to cap, to round off) (*achever, finir*) ≠ to **complement** (=to be complementary to) (*être complémentaire de*)
  entry (*candidature, inscription, participation, entrée*) ≠ **entrance** (*admission*)
  to be responsible for ≠ **to be in charge of** (*être responsable de*)

- Pay attention to **indefinite articles** in front of abbreviations or **vowels**: **an** MPhil/**an** LED lamp/**a** university/**an** MSc/**an** MA/**an** MBA/**an** NGO/**a** once-in-a-lifetime experience/**a** unique experience/**an** ML class/**a** user/**a** European policy

- Refrain from using **indeed**, as most French students do. **Indeed** is used to **emphasize a statement** or **response** confirming something already suggested.
  *The pandemic was expected to last long, and **indeed** it took more than five years to peter out.*
  "Indeed" is also used to introduce a further and stronger or more surprising point.
  *The idea of teleworking soon became attractive to many firm managers and **indeed** to many employees.*
  "Indeed" is used to express that something is correct.
  *"Is it your coat?" "It is **indeed**."*
  *"That's very strange, isn't it?" "Yes, **indeed** – I can't explain it."*
  "Indeed" is equivalent to "really", "certainly", and can roughly be translated into French by "*effectivement*."

- **The former/the latter**: "the former" refers to a first term in a series of two, whereas "the latter" refers to the second term in the series. Both are pronouns.

I have visited Georgetown and UCSD and prefer the former to the latter.
Note that former / latter never take an -s when referring to plural.

- The **past** ≠ the **last** ≠ the **recent** ≠ **final**: *Over the **past** three months* (It means that several months have gone past) – *my **recent** project on nanotechnologies – It was the **last** experiment he carried out before he died – currently in my third and **final** year.*

- **The hyphen**. The hyphen may be an endangered species as it is less and less used, yet it is mandated in the following cases:
  - a **compound adjective**: a 17-year-old man, an eight-month leadership training – a short-term ambition – a year-long project – a last-minute update – a drought-free decade – the ever-evolving world of finance – a time-consuming project – a real-life experiment – high-level studies – data-oriented – wide-ranging – a long-standing commitment – a run-down district – a nineteenth-century discovery – a medium-term goal
  - **Numbers** from twenty-one to ninety-nine take a hyphen, as well as **fractions**: two-fifths, one-third.
  - A compound adjective usually gets a hyphen when it comes before a noun, like in "a **well-honed** piece of writing", an "**up-to-date** document" (but the document is up to date).
  - If you're adding a **prefix** like "pre", "un", "non" or "anti" to a proper adjective (that's an adjective made from a proper noun like American), use a hyphen: **anti-nuclear** protesters, **non-academic** projects, **un-scientific**, **non-EU** countries.
  - Hyphenate words that are spelt the same but can have very different meanings or different pronunciations (called homographs) like "**recreation**" (fun) and "**re-creation**" (creating again).
  - There are some cases where hyphens preserve written clarity such as where there are letter collisions, where a prefix is added: "co-operate." Yet, many words that have been hyphenated in the past have since dropped the hyphen and become a single word ("email", "nowadays").

  Do not confuse the hyphen and the **dash**: dashes can be used to add parenthetical statements or comments in much the same way as you would use brackets. In formal writing you should use the bracket rather than the dash as a dash is considered less formal. Dashes can be used to create emphasis in a sentence: *He may be the next Einstein – you never know.*

  - **Writing numbers**. A simple rule for using numbers in writing is that small numbers ranging from **one to ten** should be spelled out: "a three-month internship". Larger numbers (*i.e.,* above ten) are written as numerals. Writing out large numbers wastes space and can be a major distraction to the readers.

  Always spell out numbers when they begin a sentence, no matter how large or small they may be: "*Two years ago, I chose to take a gap year.*"

  When two numbers come next to each other in a sentence, spell out one of these numbers: *I taught math to **25 thirty-year old** recruits.*

  Decades or **centuries** are usually spelled out, especially if the writing is formal: *The laboratory was built in the seventies* (~~*'70s*~~).

  When a **percentage** is written as a word, it should be followed by "percent" (or "per cent") whereas when it is written as a numeral, it should be followed by the "%" sign: "ten percent" or "10%".

3. Punctuation

- **Quotation marks.** Make a difference between: British/US bracket signs: "/" and French bracket signs: « ». In US English you put the bracket signs within the sentence. It is the opposite in British English (." *vs* ".). Use quotation marks for the papers you mention.
  In the U.S. and Canada, the comma (,) or period (.) is on the inside of the bracket sign ("science,") whereas in the UK it is the opposite ("science",).
  As a rule, the title of a whole publication is italicized whereas the titles of minor works within a subset of a larger publication (poems, short stories, chapters, journal papers, newspaper articles, TV show episodes, video game levels, editorial sections of websites, etc.) are written with quotation marks.
- **Bracket signs.** Use round brackets () in English (also called parenthesis/-es in the plural), and not square ones []. [] (crotchets or simply brackets (US)) – are used to insert explanatory material or to mark where a [word or] passage was omitted from an original material by someone other than the original author, or to mark modifications in quotations.
- **Commas.** Use a comma before any coordinating conjunction (and/but/for/or/nor/so/yet) that links two independent clauses. Use a comma after introductory adverbs such as finally/eventually/historically/scientifically: *Surprisingly, the experiment worked and we were able to publish the early results.*
  Use a comma to separate the elements in a **full date** (weekday/month + day + year). Also separate a combination of those elements from the rest of the sentence with commas: *Sunday, December 7, 1941, was a day that would live in infamy for the USA.*
  Compare the two sentences: *The scientists, who had developed the new vaccine, were awarded the Nobel Prize for Medicine* ≠ *The scientists who had developed the new vaccine were awarded the Nobel Prize for Medicine.* The sentence without comma means that only those scientists who developed the vaccine were awarded the Nobel prize whereas the sentence with commas means that all scientists were awarded the Prize.
  Use commas in a **series** of three or more items: *The new regulations concern graduate students, research fellows, and post-doctoral researchers.*
  Use commas before every sequence of three numbers when writing a number larger than 999. (Two exceptions are: writing years and house numbers): *10,000 people/100,000 dollars*
  – **etc.** always comes after a comma and is followed by a period (physics, chemistry, etc.)
  – **however** is always followed by a comma when it starts a sentence; no comma when however is adverbial (*However short my stay was, spending two months at MIT was a great experience*). Note that starting a sentence with "however," is discouraged by many careful writers. A better method would be to use "however" within a sentence after the phrase you want to negate: *She never expected to obtain such sterling results, however.*
  – Introductory words such as **in addition/on the other hand/hence/thus/furthermore/nevertheless/of course/for instance/therefore/next year, next Spring/all in all** are followed by a comma:
  Nevertheless, the experiment was cut short for lack of funding.
  – Use a comma after a **participial phrase** (using the *-ING* form of the verb): *Having failed in delivering convincing results, the students decided to start the experiment all over again.*
  – Use a comma to separate **independent clauses** introduced by **and/or/nor/but/yet/for/so** (in the sense of "as a result"), **as** (in the sense of "because"), and **while** (in the sense of "at the same time"): *We came up with interesting results, but we were far from being satisfied.*
  – Finally, note that there is **no space** before the following punctuation marks: ?/!/,/:/;

4. Grammar

- **École or the École?** One recurrent and nagging question is that of the presence of the definite article with **École** (École Polytechnique/CentraleSupélec/École des Mines/École des Ponts…). There is no hard-and-fast rule that can be applied across the board here. Nevertheless, I would suggest putting the **article** with École: *The École Polytechnique is one of France's top schools.* (Don't we say The École polytechnique fédérale de Lausanne (EPFL)?). Yet, contrarian examples abound of institutions with no article: MIT, Caltech, Oxford, Duke, Imperial College… I suggest you **be consistent** in using or not the article: either you write "the + École" throughout or you don't. On the other hand, if you just write **Polytechnique** or **Centrale**, **Ponts**: no article. And no article with acronyms: ENSAM, ECP, ESPCI. As for **University**, you need to put an article when followed by **of**: the Paris-Saclay University, the University of California and **no article** when starting with the proper name: Michigan University, Boston College, Columbia University in the City of New York, Georgia Tech, for example.
- **Tenses**. First, avoid **contracting verb forms**. Thus, do not write **I'm/aren't/I've/I'd/I'll**, but prefer the **I am/are not/I have/I had**, **I would/I will** full forms. The same goes with negative forms. Pay attention to the **order of subjects**: *A classmate and I have decided to start a business* (~~I and a classmate have decided…~~)
  Simple present is for a general statement and with some verbs (to want, to wish, to like…).

> Transport **is** a field which **links** energy, environment and modern economy.

> I believe that one of the major powers of science **lies** in the strength and impetus it **gives** you to innovate. Creativity, correlated with scientific expertise, **can** lead to trailblazing ideas to resolve existing problems.

- Past action requires **past tense**:

> I spent my early education in Lebanon/I moved to France at the age of 11/I was admitted to Brown in 2019/I carried out an internship with Siemens in the Summer 2018/last year, I did a project with…/Last summer and for two months, I interned with Jane Street, a quantitative trading firm/in my third year, I started to explore energy-related issues in depth/My two-year intensive undergraduate program provided the fundamentals in physics, mathematics and chemistry

Past tense of some verbs: to lead, **led** – to run, **ran** – to strive, **strove** – to uphold, **upheld** – to choose, **chose**.

A past event that has consequences in the present time is expressed with the **present perfect** (**have + ED/have + been + ING**). In particular, it is used with **always, this year** (except when you use the present tense, such as in *This year, I am focusing on…*), **for/since**, **this year/semester**, **this/these**, **already**, **not yet**, **always**.

> - This year, I **have followed** a course on Nuclear Physics, and learned much about nuclear fission and fusion.

- My passion for transportation issues and my interest in sciences in general, **have led** me to the door of UCB.
- This year, I **have** also **been attending** an exciting course on *Groups and Representations.*
- Although I am an American citizen, I **have** always **lived** in France.

Use the present perfect when you take stock of your training in the conclusion, for example:

- At Paris-Dauphine I **have acquired** some strong quantitative tools which I will keep on sharpening at Berkeley's Haas School.
- My studies and research experience in various domains, which included biophysics, operation research, mathematical physics, high energy physics, observational astrophysics, **have shown** that I am able to work autonomously without balking at venturing into new scientific fields.
- I **have acquired** strong skills, which I **have honed** along a multi-faceted academic program and **sharpened** through several enriching research experiences.
- My extra-curricular activities and two training internships **have helped** me to know more about myself, to enhance my personal qualities as well as to develop new ones.

If you are in the process of publishing:

Our paper **has been submitted** to *Nature* for peer review.

Use present perfect with **recent past**:

Over the past two years, I have focused on several subjects that helped me acquire a solid knowledge base.

With **since/for**:

- Since last year, I **have been following** a graduate-level program in Energy.

*Since the beginning of the academic year, I **have been working** as a research assistant to Prof. Eric W. at the Irradiated Solid Laboratory.

- Since my admission to Ecole XXX, I **have developed** a marked interest for Physics.

- `Mathematics **has for long been** at the core of my studies.`
- `I **have been playing** tennis since the age of five.`

Other examples:

I **have always loved** the outdoors/Math **has been** a lifelong passion for me/ Willing to pursue down that line of research and study, I **have resolved** to apply to Imperial College London for an MSc in *Sustainable Energy Futures*/ Currently in my final year, I am enrolled in a Master's level program called Technological Innovation. We **have been exploring** various forefront domains of science – such as *Soft Surfaces, Optoelectronics* or *Photovoltaic Solar Energy*/ Subsequent journeys in China—where I **choked** over the car exhaust fumes and from asthma caused by the smoke of coal-burning industries-**have strengthened** my determination to help respond to these changes as an engineer/In my current studies at the Ecole XXX, I **have started** investigating environmental-related problems/I **have grown** aware that hands-on projects and freedom of initiative are more likely to produce results/All these classes **have prepared** me well for your program/Experiences outside the lab or the classroom **have helped** define the person I am today

- Avoid **negative** sentences in a statement. Emphasize everything from a **positive perspective**. In that way, use adjectives that will show you as an energetic, enthusiastic, resourceful, dynamic and determined person.
  ~~It is a field I have not studied~~ and that explains why I'm applying ☞ It is a field I still have to explore further, hence my decision to apply.

- **Do not abuse modals when a simple verb suffices**:
  In particular, avoid the "had to/have to" burden-like science that befell your frail shoulders and gives the impression you are a victim rather than a free agent.
  Additionally, during the second year, we ~~have to conduct~~ a scientific collective project ☞ We conducted a second-year team science project.
  At the end of the second year ~~we have to do~~ a four-week training course on the shop floor ☞ The second year is **capped** by…
  I ~~had to work~~ extra hours to complete the job ☞ *I* ***worked*** extra hours
  I ~~was able to~~ work with highly technical tools ☞ I **worked** with highly technical tools
  I ~~had a chance~~ to focus on a project with two classmates ☞ *I* ***focused***
  This track ~~allowed me to~~ be introduced to the several best practices when designing an algorithm ☞ This track **introduced** me to…
  Attending her course Network Flows and Graphs *~~would allow me to~~ complement my knowledge of the main optimization algorithms* ☞ would **complement**…
  In the same way, avoid the "manage to" when a simple verb suffices.
  In her paper, she ~~manages to highlight~~ how the flexibility of certain agents in a system can significantly reduce its cost and enhance its performance ☞ she **highlights**…

Same with **I had the chance of**:
~~*I had the chance to*~~ *do an internship with Dassault Systems during which* ☞ I **did** an internship…

- **This ≠ the**: "the" is deictic enough and should be a convenient substitute for "this."
- **Which ≠ whose**: a project **whose** goal was to…
- **Who ≠ which**: a company **which**/France, a country **which**/HEC, a school **which**
- **Having + ed ≠ ING**: *After* ~~*having selected*~~ *four parameters of interest and made our data stationary*: after **selecting**/*After* ~~*having passed*~~ *the baccalaureat* ☞ after **passing** the *baccalaureat*
- ~~the modern~~ **society** ☞ *our society*
- **prepositions**: insight + **into** – to consist + **in** – to blame sb + **for**
- a paper + **by**, not ~~**from**~~ – **a paper (written) by** – to participate **+ in**
- **One of** is always followed by a plural: *One of the* ***achievements*** *I am most proud of is/one of the top science* ***schools****/one of the current* ***problems***
- Use the **possessive form.** Do not say:

> - the ~~course of Dr. Doshi-Velez~~, *Topics* in *Machine Learning: Batch Reinforcement Learning* … **but** Dr. Doshi-Velez's *Topics in Machine Learning: Batch Reinforcement Learning* course
> - to train a platoon of ~~new students from the École Polytechnique~~ **but** to train a platoon of new Polytechnique students
> - ~~the top professional soccer team in~~ France **but** France's top professional soccer team
> - a ~~plan of career~~ **but** a career plan
> - ~~Louise Michel's middle school~~ **but** the Louise Michel middle school
> - a ~~project of two~~ **but** a paired project
> - ~~the Princeton's MPA program~~ **but** Princeton's MPA program
> - ~~the Higg's boson~~ **but** the Higgs boson

- **Uncountable names**: research/coursework/progress/advice/knowledge; they must use quantifiers such as **much, little, some** – **Work** is uncountable. Works: *les œuvres* – **data** is uncountable. Usually plural (*The data are still coming in* but also in the singular: *the data indicates the president remains healthy*).

- **Something that = what**

> And this is ~~something that~~ ☞ what motivates me to pursue my career in the health tech industry

Pay attention to the **use of prepositions** with verbs. For example, **to echo** does not take a preposition (~~echo with~~). **To fit**: *The theory fits all the facts* but *My parents arrived in France eager to **fit in** with the customs of their new country. Your program best **fits my goal** to launch a career in consultancy.* Here are some verbs taking "***à***" in French that have a different construction in English.

se décider à	to make up one's mind to
croire à qch	to believe **in** sth
s'intéresser à qch	to be interested **in** sth
jouer au tennis/football/aux échecs	to play tennis/soccer/chess
répondre à qch	to answer sb
conseiller à qn (de faire qch)	to advise sb to do sth
emprunter à qn	to borrow **from** sb
apprendre à faire	to learn **how to** do
convenir à	to be suitable **for**/to be fit for
travailler dans une équipe	to work **on** a team
participer à	to take part **in**/to participate in

Also note:

approuver	to approve **of**
se concentrer sur	to focus **on**

Plaire followed by ***à*** is a common way of saying you like something.

plaire au jury	to **please** the jury
Étudier la science me plaît beaucoup.	I **enjoy** studying science.
Cette technologie plaît aux jeunes.	This technology is **popular with** young people.
Le programme me plait.	The program **appeals to** me.

Here are some verbs taking "***de***" in French that have a different construction in English.

dépendre de	to depend **on**
parler de qch	to talk **about** sth
se servir de qch	to use sth
se souvenir de qch	to remember sth
avoir besoin de qch	to need sth
remercier qn de qch	to thank sb **for** sth
accepter de faire qch	to agree/to accept to do sth
proposer de	to suggest + ING
rêver de	to dream **of**

XIII. About Style

The personal statement should be the reflection and expression of your **voice**. The narrative should reflect your experiences, perspectives, viewpoints, worldviews, thoughts, and emotions. Focusing on events or ideas may give your audience an indirect idea of how these things became important in shaping your outlook, but many others have had equally compelling experiences. By simply talking about those events in your own voice, you put the emphasis on yourself rather than the event or idea. The voice you use must be neither pompous, nor arrogant. It is not the place to use GRE words or complicated and rarely used expressions.

Avoid using 30 words in the same sentence. Eliminate unnecessary words. Do not use 50 words when five will do, as the following examples show:

*The research and study of the deep and profound motivation behind my insights into the field of AI contains many pitfalls and disappointments but even more joy and enlightenment that I expect to find while doing my own research at your university which is to me the perfect place to do so.

*I realized I wanted to select projects aligned with my career plan to work in the Biomedical field which allowed me to mature first as a person as well as a scientific searcher anxious to leave a mark on progress in the coming years.

*Broadening my insight of the engineering work/researcher work in the Mechanical field according to the structure and nature of the working place (private companies instead of academic laboratory) was essential for me, in order to grasp all of the facets of the work and be in an interesting position professionally speaking.

*The burning fire in me coupled with calibrated motivation and relentless hard work were rewarded with an internship at T. (under the guidance of Dr Maria P.), the company founded by Professor K., which develops a polymer for nerve reconstruction in order to heal tissues of people victims of burns.

*In the laboratory where I also worked on manufactured silicon applicators, tractions testing gained me great practical skills, and a total understanding of the ins and outs of what medical device conception involves, which are key abilities, I think for a MSc and PhD student in Bioengineering.

> *Indeed, the in-depth research offered by your program is essential for my future career because it will allow me to develop further perseverance, creativity and open-mindedness, indispensable qualities in a scientific job, even if French firms do not seem to realize this yet but will soon do, I hope, given the present trends and circumstances.

Avoid **repetitions** (in words or content):

> - Working on this problem tested my **ability** to work efficiently within a group, but also my ~~ability~~ capacity to deal with new models in an advanced field of probabilities.
>
> - Apart from my scientific ~~interest~~, curiosity/passion for science, I have been highly interested in languages.

If, in the intro, you write that…

> To have this positive impact on society I need to acquire the adequate technical background which justifies that I apply to the Master of Science in Data Science of Columbia University.

…and two lines below, to introduce the next paragraph:

> I wish to strengthen my knowledge and my skills in statistics and computer science to be able to have an impact on contemporary matters…

It is just too much and redundant.

Cut the crap and do not tell them what they already know:

> For my dissertation project, I would be eager to work with the Statistical and Population Genetics and Genomics Research group ~~where Profs. Pier Francesco Palamara and Simon Myers are both members~~ to further understand the close connections between genetic mutations and recombination and genetic diseases.

> ~~The MSc in Statistical Science is a challenging program~~ but I strongly believe that my academic background fully prepared me to master the classes.
> In the *Stochastic Models in Mathematical Genetics* optional course taught by Simon M. I will learn ~~about his passionate research~~ how we can use stochastics models to understand genetic variations.

Fillers: Do not waste words: for example, filler words and phrases, such as "I do believe that", "I think that", "the truth is", "I have no doubt that", "It is quite obvious that", or "it's my personal belief that," take up valuable space. **Be concise, and precise**.

~~I personally believe that~~ Columbia offers what I am seeking for in a Master program.

~~I think that~~ what I enjoy most when committing myself to people…

~~It is my personal opinion that~~ my research interest will thrive in the fecund environment the university offers.

The program would be ~~the~~ ideal ~~steppingstone~~ to deepen my expertise and achieve my professional ambitions.

~~The different courses offered at Stanford will ideally further my formation at Polytechnique~~ ☞ *The Stanford curriculum will ideally further my Polytechnique formation*

~~I am also interested in~~ Computational Optimization ~~as it~~ would allow me to apply my current knowledge in theory of optimization to applied problems

I~~'m convinced that I could~~ bring a mix between technical, human and soft skills in to the Baruch program

Avoid abusing periphrases:

I also ~~had the opportunity to~~ attend Deep Learning in Computer Vision *taught by* ☞ I also attended Deep Learning

It ~~gave me the opportunity to gain~~ some insights into this field by implementing ☞ I gained much more insights into this field…

I ~~was lucky to work~~ with her ☞ I worked with her/it was a privilege to collaborate with her

I ~~feel certain~~ that my undergraduate studies have provided me with a solid and multidisciplinary scientific grounding which will allow me to succeed in this kind of top-level engineering program ☞ My undergraduate studies have provided me with…

This discussion ~~made me realize~~ to what extent mathematics can have a real market-impact ☞ I realized to what extent…

Individual sports are a way to ~~make me know~~ more about myself ☞ to know more about myself

In the second year, I ~~chose to broaden~~ my horizons about a variety of fields related to the environment ☞ I broadened…

My interest in the field naturally ~~led me to subsequently investigate~~ how ☞ I subsequently investigated how…

~~I decided~~ to apply this algorithmic knowledge into a competitive programming research project ☞ I applied this…

I ~~decided to~~ undertake an American Red Cross Lifeguard certification training course to learn how to rescue endangered people ☞ I undertook…

Fascinated by Dr P's research in the Machine Learning *module I ~~decided to~~ join his Adaptative & Intelligent Robotics Lab for my final year project* ☞ I joined…

~~It seems to me that/it appears to me that~~: do not be vague; be assertive; those two expressions give the impression that you question either the professor, the research or the course content.

> ~~It seems to me that~~ "Bayes Methods" as well as "Foundations of Statistical Inference" – in particular its lecture on Bayesian Hypothesis Testing, Bayes Risk and Bayes Rules – will help me get a more thorough understanding of these problematics.

Avoid cliches:
Avoid such literary devices. Some terms, phrases, or ideas, upon their inception, may have been striking and thought-provoking but became stale, trite, platitudinous and unoriginal through repetition and overuse. As the French poet **Gérard de Nerval** (1808-1855) said, "The first man who compared a woman to a rose was a poet, the second, an imbecile."

Examples of cliches: "read between the lines", "only time will tell", "to last an eternity", "at the speed of light", "a diamond in the rough" (to describe sb), "to have nerves of steel", "a win-win situation", "the calm before the storm", "an uphill battle", "to bring to the table", "a rule of thumb", "a riddle wrapped in an enigma", "a safe pair of hands", "a sea change", "a shot in the dark", "a winning streak", "to have direct impact", "to make a difference", "to make an impact", "the improvement of educational systems around the world", "to leave the world a better place than I found", "In sum, there are three reasons why you should admit me...", etc. How inane, birdbrained, airheaded, shallow, superfluous and vacuous!

Avoid abusing **quantifiers** among which: **very/often/practically/basically/really/mostly/always**. Those words are known as **padding** or **filler words** and generally add little to your writing.

Example: *I ~~have really experienced serving~~ my country while commanding 30 sailors* ☞ I served my country when, with 30 sailors under my command, I…

According to the *Collins Dictionary*: "Padding is unnecessary words or information used to make a piece of writing or a speech longer. Synonyms include: waffle, hot air, verbiage, wordiness." For example, avoid using **very** with the following:

Avoid saying *very+*:	**Rather say**:
bad	atrocious
big	immense
clever	brilliant
eager	keen
good	superb
risky	perilous
small	tiny
valuable	precious

The same goes for **always**. Consider the following examples:

Assisting people in need has ~~always~~ been one my priorities. This is unadulterated BS. At the age of five, for example, you were playing Lego or learning how to ride a bike or a pony. Your priority was NOT assisting people.

I have ~~always~~ sought unconventional tracks that have challenged my resilience and adaptability. Again, this is not true. I'm sure that at ten, your only concern was to get some bonus points and succeed at primary school. Not seeking unconventional track and all this blah blah.

I have ~~always~~ been fascinated by bioengineers designing novel research to treat Alzheimer disease. Always? Even in primary school?

Avoid overuse of **prepositional phrases**: in/over/of/for/at, etc.
*The reason **for** the failure **of** the economic system **of** the island*

Do not be **verbose. Verbosity** or **verboseness** (also called "fluff" or "fuzz") is speech or writing that uses more words than necessary, for example *~~in spite of the fact that~~* rather than ***although***.

Do not say	**Prefer**
as a matter of fact	actually
as far as I am concerned/in my opinion	for me
at the present time	today
due to the fact that	owing to/due to
for the purpose of/with the aim of	so as to
in respect of	as to
in the final analysis/when all is said and done	finally
in view of	as regards/regarding
on the grounds that	because/since
owing to the fact that/on account of the fact that	because/due to
under the supervision of	supervised by
with the result that	so that/therefore/as to

As **Mark Twain** (1835-1910) puts it: "I notice that you use plain, simple language, short words and brief sentences. That is the way to write English-it is the modern way and the best way. Stick to it; don't let fluff and flowers and verbosity creep in. When you catch an adjective, kill it. No, I don't mean utterly, but kill most of them – then the rest will be valuable." (Letter to D. W. Bowser, March 1880)

Use **active verbs**: instead of writing *~~The research proposals were reviewed by the committee~~* ☞ The committee reviewed the research proposals.

Avoid using noun forms of verbs: *~~The presentation of the arguments by the lecturer was convincing~~* ☞ The lecturer presented the arguments/argued convincingly – *~~the understanding of finance requires the analysis of macroeconomic trends~~* ☞ understanding finance requires analyzing... – *We also ~~made the hypothesis~~ that a weak signal could ~~potentially~~ be "noisy"* ☞ We also hypothesize that a weak signal could be "noisy"

Avoid unnecessary repetitions. Redundant words, statements, ideas and phrases make your sentences sound repetitive, so do your best to avoid using them. Trim your writing by cutting extra information, or even extra words, to make it more interesting for readers.

~~Among the economics courses I have attended~~, I developed an understanding of modern economic ideas: the first part of the sentence is useless.

The ~~Mathematics, Physics and Computer Science~~ preparatory program ~~I took~~ equipped me with strong knowledge in Mathematics, Physics and Computer Science.

We are ~~now~~ planning a trip to Israel this summer: *now* is implicit in *are planning.*

Apart from ~~scientific~~ classes such as fluid mechanics or data analysis, I followed… You would never guess that fluid mechanics and data analysis could be poetry classes…

~~Some people claim that~~ the internet, ~~a widely used online source of information~~, can have a positive or negative influence on students.

The study of valuation techniques, and how firms make investment and financings decisions will be important ~~for my beginning~~ in investment banking, a sector in which I envision working upon completion of NYU Stern's MSc in Quantitative Finance. "Upon completion" indicates investment banking will be your first job.

Furthermore, the case studies covering investment strategies ~~will be a big help for me as they~~ will help me have a first view of investment that I will need in my professional life ~~in investment banking~~ as a banker.

I have come to develop a strong attachment to each school I have attended: I have developed

~~I am thus convinced that~~ a major part of the future of companies lies within their ability to adapt to the new climate regulations. They care little about your convictions… so go straight to the point. And reformulate: *The future of a majority of companies lies…*

I have ~~already~~ delved into papers on online stochastic bipartite matching problems: *"already"* is superfluous, as you have a present perfect.

~~I truly believe that~~ we are only at the beginning of the use of data science to enhance sport performances: do we need *I truly believe*? No. Do they care about your beliefs? No.

Being part of an orchestra also unveiled the importance of team working and sharing ~~with others~~. "Sharing" is obviously with other people.

At HEC Paris, I ~~wanted to~~ contributed actively to the students' community. No, either you contributed or you did not. In that latter case, no need to mention it. So, I contributed actively to…

~~To bring my contribution to the problem of education~~, I volunteered to teach French for Vietnamese children in an orphanage: do we need this awkward first part? No.

One of my missions was to carry out a ~~data~~ analysis project of France's 2018 car accident data. Do we need data twice? No.

Avoid **tautologies**, *i.e.* saying the same thing twice. Examples: "a beginner *~~who has just started~~*", "I saw him *~~personally~~*", "my *~~individual~~* report", "*~~in my opinion~~*, I think", "an *~~absolute~~* priority", "my ambition *~~for the future~~*", the program was *~~then~~* complemented", "my ~~projected~~ professional future"

A team project ~~with four other~~ ~~students~~: a team project is enough (they know how to count and to oppose it to a paired project).

Working on case studies is an efficient and stimulating way of learning about this topic ~~thanks to real world examples~~.

I gained ~~much more insights~~ ☞ insight is already much + more.

During my second year at school, I was particularly interested in the ~~applied mathematics course Modelling Random Phenomena~~ ☞ in the *Modelling Random Phenomena* course.

~~In my opinion, personally~~, I think he is wrong.
Actually, the trend away from fossil fuels is bound to accelerate ~~in the near future~~
Sailing is challenging sport that requires technicity and a strategic mind to win ~~over the rivals~~.
I was ~~first~~ introduced to...
The use of machine learning when designing algorithm is a ~~new~~ innovation.
My Sorbonne education has grounded my knowledge in three ~~different~~ fields: applied mathematics, computer science and economics. It goes without saying they are different. Be economical with words and eliminate the verbiage!

Avoid **redundant phrases** (a **redundancy** is a needless repetition of words) or **pleonasms**. When it comes to writing, less is more. A message should be conveyed in its simplest form.

a ~~constant~~ work in progress	*a ~~short~~ summary*
a ~~new~~ innovation	*~~actual~~ fact*
~~basic~~ fundamentals	*collaborate/join/combine ~~together~~*
compete ~~with one another~~	*~~on a daily basis~~ (=daily)*
~~different~~ kinds	*~~end~~ result*
~~exactly~~ the same	*four ~~different~~ species*
it ~~may be~~ possible	*mix ~~between~~*
my ambitions ~~for the future~~	*~~past~~ experience*
~~past~~ history	*the ~~necessary~~ skills required*
the reason ~~why~~	*to ~~begin~~ creating*
to offer a ~~first~~ introduction	*~~true~~ facts*
~~unexpected~~ surprise	*two ~~other~~ classmates*

Avoid **overabusing adverbs**.

finished (the experiment) ~~completely~~
jumped ~~quickly~~ (to conclusions)
an ~~extremely~~ rigorous formation
~~deeply~~ / ~~specifically~~ interested
summarize ~~briefly~~
~~particularly~~ attracted
Most people ~~usually~~ think that
~~Additionally~~, another task included collecting goods, redistributing them to families in need.
Columbia offers ~~precisely~~ what I am seeking for in a Master program, ~~especially~~ its Data Science Master that will allow me ~~undoubtedly~~ to reach my goals.
In ECN334, I will ~~quickly~~ gain expertise in recursive neural networks.

"The road to hell is paved with adverbs." (Stephen King). You can also do without the adverb by **choosing a better word**. Weak words usually depend on adverbs... Be concise. The more adverbs you can eliminate, the stronger your statement will be. Adverbs are the tools of the lazy student.

~~I looked closely at~~ = *I* ***examined***
~~the models currently used~~ = *the* ***present*** *models*
~~to adjust precisely~~ = *to* ***fine tune***
~~to develop successfully~~ = *to* ***bear fruit***
~~strongly encourage~~ = *to* ***urge***
~~manage successfully~~ = *to* ***bring off***
~~to make great effort to achieve~~ – *to* ***strive***
~~to apply oneself to a task~~ = *to* ***knuckle down***
~~to become fully engaged~~ = *to* ***sink one's teeth into***
~~to change completely~~ = *to* ***switch over (to)***
~~the task was extraordinarily difficult~~ = ***it was no easy task***

(Check https://www.powerthesaurus.org)

Avoid **for me/with me** as in the following examples:

I worked towards bringing musical disciplines to the forefront of campus life, which was an opportunity ~~for me~~ to develop my sense of organization and leadership.
This course would help ~~me~~ familiarize myself with data analysis: don't overdo it!
This internship was also an opportunity ~~for me~~ to hold my own as a young female officer cadet: for who else than you?
Pursuing a graduate degree of industrial engineering is the logic outcome of my previous curriculum and will provide the necessary skills ~~for me~~ to be a successful engineer.
In line with my ambition to drive access to both clean energy and green mobility in emerging countries, the course on Firms & Markets in Emerging Countries *taught by XXX is particularly appealing ~~to me~~.* ☞ It goes without saying that it is for you (and nobody else).
My multidisciplinary background, intellectual curiosity and commitment to excellence are strengths I bring ~~with me~~ to Princeton University. Who else?

Avoid writing **Professor** (or **Prof.**) when you mention a class. Thus, do not say "*In an exciting class ~~taught by Professor John Alexander...~~*" but "*In an exciting class taught by John Alexander...*" (a class is usually taught by a professor, is it not?). And **do not discriminate between the academic ranks**: do not write Assistant-Professor/Adjunct Professor, etc., but just Professor. If in doubt whether the author teaches or not, when quoting a research paper, write Dr John Alexander.

Avoid piling up **adjectives**: *I had the ~~great~~ opportunity/It was a ~~splendid~~ opportunity/ We performed in ~~great French~~ churches.* Be concise, and to the point.

Avoid adding the **titles of the people** whose work you are interested in as in this example: *I look forward to working with S. K., ~~Senior Vice Dean of Columbia Engineering~~.* I am confident the committee officers know who those people are.

Use **to** instead of **in order to** for reading fluency:
The Bay Area is the ideal location ~~in order to begin to create~~ one's own company ☞ to create

Pay attention to **and** which often has the same value as **to** (=in order to):

My ambition is to join a consulting firm as a data scientist ~~to~~ contribute to the changes in industries through applied science ☞ **and** contribute...

My long-term ambition is to return to Morocco ~~to~~ participate in the development of the country's economy ☞ **and** participate...

Avoid stock phrases. In particular, do not shy away from using modals. Thus, instead of "be able to", "be in a position to", "have the opportunity to", "have the capacity for", "have the ability to" use **can/could**. Instead of "it is possible that", "there is a chance that", "the possibility exists that", use **may/might**.

- *the reason for/due to the fact that/owing to the fact that/considering the fact that/on the grounds that* = ***because*, *since*, *why***
- *despite the fact that/regardless of the fact that* = ***even though***
- *in the event that/under circumstances in which* = ***if***
- *on the occasion of/in a situation in which* = ***when***
- *as regards/in reference to/concerning the matter of/where ... is concerned* = ***about***
- *it is crucial that/it is necessary that/it is important that* + ***should***
- *prior to/subsequent to/simultaneously with* = ***before/after/as***
- *not different* = ***similar***
- *not many* = ***few***
- *not have* = ***lack***
- *not consider* = ***ignore***
- *not the same* = ***different***
- *not allow* = ***prevent***
- *not admit* = ***deny***
- *not accept* = ***reject***

Do not be maudlin. Be rigorous, and adopt a sensible style, not one that tears hearts apart.

> During my service months, I volunteered to teach English to NCOs on the base who were preparing for exams to become officers. They were most of the time young adults ~~with sorry and sad backgrounds who took from their free time for these sessions and they really showed me how strongly they persevered and how what courage they had to do extra work~~ ☞ who came from deprived backgrounds and made the most of their free time working hard and proving how much can be achieved with determination and courage.

Platitudes and blah blah: go straight to the point, avoid dilly dallying. Do not provide a collection of vague generic statements and platitudes ("I'm a people person", "I love hiking", "doctors save lives", "I want to have an impact", "I contributed actively"). Be specific or do not talk about it. Avoid long winded sentences.

> *This very diversified year was highly stimulating and flourishing.
>
> *I felt the need to adapt and contribute actively to the students' life.

*The United States is one of the rare countries where computing is considered as a science in itself. Most past and present key advances in computer science have taken place in the USA, and this trend is likely to continue, as the most innovative companies and research laboratories are located there.

*Indeed, these fields enable me to apply mathematics concepts I loved studying for years, to a wide range of matters which will surely shape the future of our modern societies.

*This thriving experience made me all the more motivated to strengthen my skills in data science to be able to solve more impactful problems like this one.

*Our discoveries are at the forefront of human life. They will tremendously impact the society, and lead to major shift in the way we, as human are defining ourselves and perceiving ourselves.

*Besides, I am convinced that teamwork can sublimate each member's abilities, I pay great attention to the development of my communication skills and my leadership.

*Moreover, this internship also made me realize that I wanted sciences to be at the heart of my work and that I wanted to have a more concrete and direct impact on society.

*In parallel of these academic and professional activities I committed myself for causes beyond me.

*Sharing cultural habits, discussing new opinions, or discovering ways of thinking that are completely new to me are elevating opportunities that I always seized.

*The scientific community will more than ever need to evaluate the purpose of its discoveries as well as delineate its boundaries, imposing limitations and strong control on both a social and political scale.

*I am always grateful to have these opportunities and be aware of the conditions that some people have to live in.

*I love the creative power of innovations, exploiting a new technology, imagining new applications for it and trying to see what could make it a success. I also like being part of the energy challenges and using this creativity to maybe discover a new solution.

*Years from now, I would like to look back on my career and find that I have made a substantial contribution to new generations of reactors which have exceeded expectations, that my efforts in construction include the implantation of safe and efficient power plants in less developed countries, and that my achievements include a major breakthrough in energy collecting on the ITER project that will then be built and operational.

Avoid being **chatty** and **writing** as if you were talking to your classmates at lunch.

*But ~~as you may have understood~~, my ambition and curiosity could only be fulfilled by undertaking various projects

*It ~~will be clear to you now, or so I hope~~, that my plans are to study cosmology, and more precisely interstellar gases.

*~~Let me introduce~~ Peter D's book on Neurosciences…

*The ~~ball is on your court now~~ and I ardently hope you see fit to let me study at Boston College.

Do not be a **clown**, do not be a **card** or a **raconteur**, avoid being perceived as a wit. Gentle **humor** might be OK, yet I discourage it for two reasons: American and French humor are not exactly aligned and, on the other hand, the language level required to get a humorous message across is way too high for French speaking people. Besides, it will not impress a jury.

Reducing the word/character count. You have penned a hard-won draft of SOP whose word count is above the 1,000-word or character limit. The question is how to tighten the text to meet the limit. The first rule is to **cut the clutter**. Words must add meaning and those which do not must be deleted. So, slash repetitions, reduce redundancies, remove filler words and unnecessary content. In particular:

- Remove unnecessary **adverbs** and **adjectives**: *to be ~~really~~ passionate about a subject* ☞ *to be passionate* is enough – *whose results ~~overwhelmingly~~ exceeded our expectations* – *will ~~significantly~~ enhance my skillset* – *the ~~complex~~ problem of digital inequality* – *a ~~solid~~ bedrock* – *an ~~entirely~~ new point of view on climate* – *an ~~efficient~~ and ~~stimulating~~ way of learning*
- **That** can be deleted with ease: *the results ~~that~~ we achieved*
- Use **shorter words** or synonyms.

Instead of	Use	Instead of	Use
accordingly	so	consequently/for this reason	so
at this point in time/at the present time	now/currently	due to several reasons/due to these reasons	because
compared with	*vs*	have the ability to	be able to

facilitate	help	as a matter of fact	in fact
indispensable	key	at the end of the day	finally
investigate	study	because of the fact that	because
point of view	viewpoint	in spite of the fact that	because
the majority of	most	in the final analysis	finally
use to maximum advantage	leverage	utilize	use
in terms of	in/for	in the event that	if
with regard to	about	prior to	before
more than two years	**over** two years	**all that** (I have learned)	**what** (I have learned)

- Shorten lengthy sentences and remove needless words: *During the ~~course of the~~ project*
- Remove needless **transitions** such as "indeed", "then", "furthermore", "moreover": they can be deleted with ease without compromising the content.
- Eliminate conjunctions: "*e.g.*", "and", "or", "as", "but" that connect two independent statements and write **two sentences:** *I would be interested in Quantitative Trading: Algorithms, Data, and Optimization* and *Big Financial Data and Algorithmic Trading ~~as~~/The classes would provide me with different techniques of active portfolio management. – I would be keen on discovering the theoretical foundations of deep neural networks through attendance in Dr Tanner's Theories of Deep Learning class ~~as~~/It would be a great continuation to courses and projects I have undertaken before.*
- Eliminate **phrases** such as "there are," "it is," and "the fact that." These phrases can be rewritten to shorten your text and make your writing more concise: *~~It has been reported that~~ algorithms about gradient descent work better with...*
- Use **possessives** and eliminate the "of" "at" or "from". *~~Students from the Marc Bloch University~~* ☞ Marc Bloch University students – *My formation ~~at~~ Ecole des Ponts* ☞ My Ecole des Ponts formation
- **Pluralize**. In some cases, you can transform the singular form of a word into the plural form to reduce the word count. *~~An Algorithm is a sequence~~ of steps that describe how a problem can be solved* ☞ Algorithms are sequences of steps that describe how a problem can be solved – *The program focuses more on quantitative areas of ~~a modern investment bank~~* ☞ of modern investment banks

When all is said and done, consider that there is no ideal version of a statement. You may eventually show your final version to some people you trust, and get as many dissenting opinions as to its content and form. Listen to their opinions, but at the end you are the one making the final "submit" decision. And that decision relies on one and only one criterion: be satisfied when you look like your statement and when your statement looks like you.

XIV. The Video Essay

Increasingly, competitive programs are using "video essays" or "timed video assessments" as a way to get to know their future students. You need to make a difference between:

- a **video question** (a simple question and 60 seconds to answer and upload, one take only (you can only record once), no editing, selfie-style is OK
- a **self-introductory video** (60 seconds to introduce yourself to the class)
- an **interview**
- MIT's MBan program **interview**

The programs will be evaluating an applicant's language abilities in addition to finding out what is important to her/him. Interviewers will seek to know more about who you are and how you would introduce yourself.

1. Video questions

The video is used in graduate programs such as MIT's MFin/MBan, Columbia's MSFE, Princeton, Berkeley's IEOR, the Haas School (among others). For a timed video response, you will need to answer one to three questions using your microphone and webcam in a given time limit, usually one to three minutes (the format can be different from one school to another). The most striking aspect of this is the 'asynchronous' nature of it; there will not be someone to converse with like a live interview. You will be speaking directly to the camera, responding to the question. It is a general interest question, an open-ended question, a randomly generated question, not something that you will prepare in advance. No preparation is needed. There is nothing technical in it. But it does happen that, for some programs, Imperial College, in statistics for example, you will be requested to answer math questions and brain teasers. Furthermore, they may ask you to reflect aloud on the way you would solve the questions.

Schools will likely give you a short prep time after hearing a question before starting to record, but you won't be able to go back to perfect your wording or change your answer. It is a one-shot take. Therefore, beforehand, record yourself taking a few common questions with your webcam and review your responses. Common questions include "Tell us about yourself", "Walk me through your resume", "Why do you want to attend the program?", "What is your favorite hobby and why?", etc.

MIT:

> Please upload a one-minute (60 second) video introducing yourself to your future classmates and letting us know why you are interested in the field of analytics and data science. The video should be a single take (no editing) and lasting no more than one minute, consisting of you speaking directly to the camera. We recommend using an application such as QuickTime or iMovie to record yourself.
>
> All MBAn applicants must submit a brief video statement in response to a simple, open-ended general interest question. The question is designed to help us get to know you better; to see how you express yourself and to assess fit with the MIT Sloan culture. It <u>does not</u> require prior preparation and will not be a technical question. The Video Question 2 is a part of your required application materials and will appear as a page within the application, once the other parts of your application are completed.
>
> Applicant receives a randomly generated question and has one minute to prepare a 60 second response.

Columbia University in the City of New York:

> After submitting the application, applicants will have the access to submit the video interview in the application. You will be asked three random questions, and will have three minutes to answer. Please answer as if we were having a face-to-face conversation, you should not stress about the interview - it's just a way for us to get to know you better. Please submit your interview by the deadline listed in your interview link email.

The questions can be on **anything**. They are randomly selected from hundreds of questions. Which means the likelihood that you will prepare for exactly the right question is zero. Yet, do not be flustered. Instead, make it your priority to practice the act of answering questions, rather than to memorize responses to specific questions. Columbia advises students to remember the **7-38-55 Rule**. "Pioneered by psychology professor Albert Mehrabian at UCLA and popularized through books such as *Never Split the Difference* by FBI Hostage Negotiator Chris Voss, that 55% of meaning in conversation is communicated by **body language**, 38% by the **tone** of your voice, and just 7% through the **actual words** that come out of your mouth! There is a reason why many politicians including Donald Trump replay their TV appearances on mute – that's how people get most of the meaning. If you just practice the words to say, you are missing out on 93% of the meaning! Instead, practice looking and sounding excited, open, and friendly by rehearsing answers to questions in front of a mirror or by video recording yourself."

This aspect of the assessment gives admissions teams a chance to see how applicants think on their feet and communicate unscripted, without having to fly them to campus to meet them in person. This is a chance for you to pitch your application, it is a brief advertisement for yourself.

There might be more specific questions such as the following (**UCB, IEOR Meng**):

> Please upload a 1-2-minute video or audio fine on the Audio/Visual page explaining how you have solved an engineering problem.

An "engineering problem" is any type of disturbance from normality that is hindering progress, that is time consuming or energy wasting. If there are any hiccups in a process, everything can easily go awry. Even though content matters, I would focus more on the method you used to solve the problems. Actually, how you think as an engineer would, trumps the problem itself. Several steps can be found to problem-solving:

Define/identify the problem or the root of the issue (the five W's technique: **Who** (=the user), **What** (=the need), **When**, **Why** (=insight), and **Where** to identify where the problem comes from). Draft the problem statement, by reducing it into the simplest of terms and put it on paper.
List possible solutions. This can be done by brainstorming, possibly in a group setting. The more input, the better. Different perspectives lead to different solutions. Just like brainstorming, as choosing a solution doesn't have to be done alone.
Evaluate and rank the possible solutions.
Develop a detailed plan for the most attractive solution(s). To do so, analyze every possible resolution and decide which is best for the situation you are in. You might want to consider many elements before choosing one solution. These elements include efficacy, practicality, timeliness, resources, and cost. The process of elimination is another good way to narrow your choices down.
Re-evaluate the plan to check desirability.
Implement the solution you have chosen.
Check and **evaluate** the results.

The reasoning about the problem is more in line with what they might expect than the problem itself.

2. The self-introductory video

It is a video introducing yourself to the class such as the following (MIT MFin program):

> *Introduce yourself to your future classmates. Here's your chance to put a face with a name, let your personality shine through, be conversational, and be yourself. We can't wait to meet you!*

There is no set template to make the perfect one-minute video. There is basically no right or wrong, but what matters is that you feel comfortable and the video represents you.

A few tips might be helpful, though. When recording a self-introductory video, think about the techniques used for writing the SOP. In other words, no need to start with your name, they already have this information in your application. Begin your script with a short sentence that captures your viewer's attention. The ideal hook is a concise introduction that suggests a **larger story**. Also, explain why you chose this school and how it will help you achieve your goals.

You might also use the video as an opportunity to show your true colors, your true passions, your motivations and what matters to you. State your goals in a clear fashion. Be convincing. Be genuine. Be you on screen.

Organize the video around two or three themes/principles/activities that say something about you while not losing focus on what you will add to the cohort. For example, if you are an accomplished high-level athlete, say to what extent it has shaped your character and personality. In that case, the video will add something extra to your application. It is another way of showcasing your application.

Do not make the video a summary of your CV, but organize it according to your **strengths**. For example: competitive spirit around the sailing world championships you took part in; solidarity and attention to others around the humanitarian trip you took to India helping build a school, or bringing school supplies to the Atlas Mountains; quest for excellence when you left your home country to study mathematics in France, for example.

What matters is to **stand out** while highlighting your skills, competencies and achievements that will turn you into a shining star. Authenticity matters.

The script you prepare will be your guide to the video you ultimately create. Be well prepared: a minute is a short time. However, when you are filming, it is imperative that you do not read from a script or you will come off as a robot. Being on camera may be intimidating, and your own worst critic is often yourself. Nevertheless, I would encourage you to slow down your speech rate and remember to smile. If you can make the viewer feel comfortable and smile, you have done a good job. You may show your performance to friends and family too, therefore you might get interesting feedback on content, flow, consistency and how you come across on camera: they will tell you whether you were convincing or whether the message was clear enough.

XV. The Interview

1. General

Once all the **MSc** applications have been processed, candidates are shortlisted and graduate programs (in the U.S. **and** the UK) schedule one-on-one interviews, conducted either in-person, by phone or through Zoom or Skype. Some programs run math assessment tests whose technicality spans 12th grade knowledge to complex questions tackled in undergraduate studies. Other programs, in the UK, for example, give students 48h to do admissions exercises to be solved prior to the interview.

There can be a written response question in the interview and therefore, you will be required to use a computer to complete it. Example: "Write a letter to a professor on the charity board of a company asking for an introduction to a senior exec at that company." (Imperial College, MSc in Business Analytics). Also, expect some quantitative and problem-solving questions, as for example for the Imperial College or MIT Business Analytics program.

Not all programs require an interview, not all applicants get an interview (the figures vary, in general 10-30% of applicants get one, and two thirds of those will eventually get in). Interviews are **by invitation only**. The interview is a required component of the application process without which you cannot be admitted. It is the **final hurdle** in the admissions process, and even more importantly, your final chance to make a good impression. An interview, however successful, does not guarantee admission, but better have an interview than none. If you have **not** been invited for an interview, your application is no longer considered.

As there might be one or two rounds of invites sent for interviews, patience is of the order if your classmate has received an invite and not you (yet). Not all invitations are sent on the same day.

After being invited to an interview, you will be given further instructions on how to schedule it, and whom you are interviewing with. Students are sent slots to schedule the interview and meanwhile can prepare.

In general, an interview lasts around 30 minutes. There is an average of 12 questions. The questions will be **technical**, **academic** and **personal**. Technical questions will be about your knowledge of the science, your experience in the lab, your research focus. Academic questions are specifically related to the studies that you have done, your interest in the field, and what you will be doing, if accepted. Personal questions are about your own attitudes and experiences, including your extracurricular activities. They are looking for well-rounded students, so don't be afraid to inject a bit of your personality– your hobbies and interests, and take the opportunity to tell them about what you enjoy doing in your spare time. This is a chance to broaden the scope of your personality beyond the academic realm, through, for example, that teaching experience in China, the piano competitions you took part in, or that chess tournament you won a few years back. Each activity will add to the picture that is being fashioned in the mind of the interviewer.

An interview should be considered not as a test – there are no trick questions – but as a **discussion**, or sometimes a **conversation**. They want to find out more about you as a **person**. They want to see the **real** you, the genuine, not feigned, passion. Try and be natural, don't just say what you think they want to hear, and be honest in your answers. They want you to be a good fit for your chosen program, but they also want their program to be a good fit for you. They want to make sure that you are **motivated** enough to join their program, that you will be the **right fit** for the class and that what you say squares with what is inside the application file. In other words, they want to make sure you have not misrepresented yourself. On the other hand, they are also looking for the somewhat indefinable quality of **likability**. For you, it is a chance to learn more about the faculty and the program.

Prepare but do not overprepare. An interview must be taken seriously. It helps you to add new depth to your brand through personal connection and gives you an opportunity to prove yourself when it comes to the intangibles you have alluded to in your application documents. On the other hand, it is a chance to connect and compare what the admissions officers **know about you** from your essays, transcripts, LORs and test results.

Come into the interview **informed**, **interested** and **inquisitive**. Being informed is about knowing the program requirements, the concentrations, the internship opportunities, the faculty and their research. It is also knowing about what distinguishes the program, what it offers that is distinctive and of particular interest to you. Think about what prompted you to apply to this program and why you thought it would be a good fit for your career aspirations. If you had not been interested you would not have applied in the first place. And as for inquisitive, nothing signals interest more than asking questions. During the interview you will have a chance to ask questions (see below "Do you any questions for me?").

When providing your spoken answers, you should be concise and make sure you **stick to the question being asked**. When you know a lot about a topic, it can be easy to get carried away and answer a slightly different question rather than the one being assessed. So, if you are asked about a time when you had to keep a team motivated, do not just explain why teamwork is important. There is nothing worse than getting to the end of your time and realizing you haven't started to answer the actual question yet!

Admissions representatives are looking for the key **skills** and **attitudes** that will make you a successful student in their program. The interviewer will be evaluating both the **content** and the **delivery** of your answers to her/his questions. They look for many attributes such as:

- career vision
- confidence
- general likability/charisma
- good sense of communication

– intellectual aptitude
– leadership ability
– maturity
– passion for the school
– plans for meaningful contribution
– potential to shine outside the program
– professional focus
– reasoning and analytical skills
– sense of humor

Interviewers can be program staff or managers, alums or members of the admissions committee. Their goal is to make sure they recruit qualified, high-potential candidates who fit the program and the community and will become productive alumni post-graduation. Depending upon the school's location, values and interview process, interview formats and numbers can vary.

If interviewers will not grill you, be aware that they may look for **inconsistencies** in your background: that is why you should know your CV and SOP like the back of your hand to avoid pitfalls: imagine you mentioned your interest for working in the energy sector but declare in the interview you want to launch a fitness club! So, freshen up on the topics you have introduced in your application. The interview is a chance to sell yourself, so do not be tripped by the contradictions that interviewers might find in your answers. Be consistent with your personal brand!

Interviewers are keeping an eye out for overconfidence and laziness. Be wary of the admissions officer who seems a little too casual; they might be trying to catch you off guard. Seemingly innocuous questions – questions that seem simple, and that you could answer "off the cuff" – have a deeper meaning behind them. Keep on your toes and be attentive to the fact that you are being evaluated **at all times**. But bear in mind that making it to the interview stage for a graduate program means that they are likely looking for reasons to keep you, rather than reasons to exclude you. Your application materials and SOP have piqued the review committee's attention, and they want to see if you are as awesome as you seem on paper – that is, if you are someone with promising ideas, they will be interested in bringing into their departmental community.

Your interview will be **evaluated** using a numerical system created by the program itself. These systems generally include the qualities mentioned above, but not only. Interview scoring systems are complex processes.

For each dimension, the interviewee receives a raw score and justification. For example, "4.5/5 in intellectual aptitude as she/he looks quite bright" or "2.5/5 in expected contribution to the alumni community because she/he is too individualistic". You are awarded a total raw score and a composite score out of an often much larger total (out of 100). The interviewer drafts a general summary on how she/he thinks you performed and how they feel about you as a potential student. It is based in part on how much you scored in the outlined categories and partly on personal impression you made. Recommendations are then made to admit you.

For PhD programs, you might be contacted directly by the head of department or one of the faculty members you mentioned in your statement and whose research you have quoted and/or criticized.

In that case, the professor might give you 48 hours to critique her/his work which will eventually be discussed on the phone. That is the reason why you should pay close attention to the papers you read and quote in your statement.

You need to prepare carefully, no matter what your other options are, if not because you need to uphold the standards of your school and the choice of your application. You should know the program you are applying for inside out (their courses, values, what you will add). How you will contribute and benefit from the program is also a relevant question. Do not hesitate to contact the students you know in the program for tips. You also need to prepare the questions thoroughly (there are loads of them you can find on the Internet) – in addition to the short elevator pitch which will help describe yourself and your interests. There are also tutorials galore provided by the institutions themselves. Practice with a classmate, coach or mentor as well: this will not only cure the interview jitters but help test the best angles.

If you are a non-native speaker, prepare ahead of time, test the accent and the right vocabulary in the run-up to the interview. Therefore, you will be able to put your best self forward.

2. The PowerPoint interview: MIT's Master of Business Analytics (MBAn)

A few selected applicants to MIT's MBAn program are invited to an interview. The invitation to interview signals that your application has reached an advanced stage of consideration, but does not guarantee admission. Those invited to interview will be asked to submit a response to the following question, prior to the interview:

> Shortlisted candidates will be invited to interview, which assesses you both technically and behaviorally. Prior to the interview, candidates have to submit a recent data science or analytics paper they have worked on, with three presentation slides to represent the work.
>
> Please describe a recent analytics/data science project that you have worked on and include up to three presentation slides which best represent your work. The slides may include data visualization examples, but must be uploaded as a PDF. The project presentation slides must be in English.

The data analytics slide show should include some level of technicity regarding machine learning, optimization techniques, etc. The impact of the project, especially on business, should be made clear. No typos are allowed, so double check the language carefully. The interview will be focused more on a simple but clear explanation of the project than on its technicalities, all the more so as the interviewer is generally a member of the staff and not a data expert. Yet, the project has been reviewed prior to the interview and vetted for its scientific content.

MIT favors what is called the **STAR template** (Situation/Task/Action/Results), so try to follow it to showcase your skills and experience while demonstrating your sense of organization.

S for **Situation**. Describe background and context of situation. These are the details from past work experience on specific task.
T for **Task**. Describe the tasks you had to complete in order to solve the issue at hand.
A for **Action**. Explain what steps you took to address the situation, complete the aforementioned task.
R for **Results**. Talk about the outcome and impact of your actions and lessons learned, as well as the results you can take credit for.

The STAR method is an efficient way to prepare for interviews. First, it is a way to cram maximum information on minimum space. The structural approach to answering questions shows the interviewer that the candidate is focused and that she/he can communicate competency-based experience. Moreover, it gives the impression that the applicant has the ability to make decisions under pressure. The tasks or target is analyzed by asking questions like who, why, where, what, etc. It results in delivering actions and quantifying the effects.

Slide layout design variations and be appealing. Slides may include vector-based graphics, columns, tabular, and matrix diagrams, use different color codes and clipart icons to visualize the steps of STAR method.

Also, note that not every interview response calls for a STAR framework. Some responses may be a better fit for the **CARL** (Challenge, Action, Result, Learning) or **PAR** (Problem, Action, Result) frameworks.

- The first part of the interview is about the **slideshow**, your comments about the analytics project and some basic queries to explain it.
- The second part is about **brain teasers and puzzles** to test the applicants' critical thinking skills rather than their knowledge of a precise answer, such as "How many croissants are eaten every day in Paris?", "How many windows are there in all the buildings in Manhattan?", "How many people are currently online in Germany?" What matters is the logic and rigor of the reasoning in the way an applicant deals with uncertainty, thinks analytically and communicates clearly.
  Work on analytical puzzled and brain teasers. geeksforgeeks.org
  https://www.geeksforgeeks.org/puzzle-1-how-to-measure-45-minutes-using-two-identical-wires/
  – https://www.analyticsvidhya.com/blog/2016/07/20-challenging-job-interview-puzzles-which-every-analyst-solve-atleast/
  You might also find resources at https://www.pdfdrive.com/brain-teasers-books.html
- The third part is **behavioral**, to check whether the applicant is a good fit for the program. The questions will help the committee to learn more about how applicants work with a team, make decisions, and solve problems. The number of questions is limited. At the end, they may also ask a simple question such as "which restaurant should I go to when I visit Paris?"
  For more targeted data science questions, check https://towardsdatascience.com/50-statistics-interview-questions-and-answers-for-data-scientists-for-2021-24f886221271

3. Examples of video and interview questions

We should make a difference between the **experience-based questions** and the **behavioral** and **hypothetical** ones. The former are standard questions about you (your resume), your field or subject of interest, the reason for choosing the program, career goals, academic, research and internship experience, for instance. There can be surprising questions too, such as "Which monument would you recommend I visit in Paris, and why?", "What's your favorite food/dish?", "Tell me about your home city", "What TV shows do you watch? Can you recommend one?", "What's the best concert you have ever been to?", "What have been your favorite places to visit?", "What makes a good day for you?". So, be aware.

Behavioral interview questions inquire about situations and problems you faced and help the interviewer understand how you handle them. One easy way to answer behavioral interview questions is to follow the STAR method. It is a great opportunity to showcase your skills and the results you have gotten from putting them into practice.

Situation scenario questions (also called behavioral interview question) are hypothetical situations to work through, or an imagined series of events. Situation scenarios provide insight into the interviewee's key strengths and weaknesses as well as soft skills and help interviewers better understand your thought process. Your goal is to demonstrate soft skills that would help you deal with the hypothetical workplace scenario and predict your future performance. Such skills could include: teamwork, critical thinking, leadership, adaptability, decision-making skills, problem-solving, teamwork abilities, time management, self-motivation, conflict resolution, among others.

Examples:

- Tell us about the time you did something for your community.
- How are you involved with your community outside the classroom? What impact have you made in this area?
- If you had unlimited time, to what would you devote it?
- If you were in a soccer team, what would your position be?
- If you were CFO of a company, what would keep you up at night?
- If you were to enter an academic/career path entirely unrelated to science and engineering, what would it be and why?
- Imagine a situation where you weren't satisfied with your job. What could have made it better?
- Imagine you are proposing a business innovation idea for a class project and the audience is not interested.
- Imagine you were transported to the year 1900. How would you explain a smartphone to a person from that era?
- Say you have applied to three top companies. One has given you a positive answer and you accept the offer. Two weeks later, another company makes an offer. It is your dream company and top choice. How do you handle the situation?
- Tell us about a long-running project you handled. How did you manage your time to meet your deadlines?

1. About yourself - Starting questions

- Walk me through your CV.
- Have there been any changes to your resume since you submitted it?

> Be concise: I usually recommend three parts: curriculum, research or project work, internship/professional experience, and outside experience if interesting.

- Tell me about yourself.

> This is the **elevator pitch** in which you provide context to your CV and general story, achievements, motivations. Discuss your education and work experience, highlighting your achievements and qualifications. Avoid talking for too long and do not go into detail about your social life. One of the mistakes applicants make is to drone on and on, losing the interviewer's interest and attention in the process. To make sure you open your interview strongly, memorize the key points you will cover during this common opening question. Keep your answers focused, concise and to the point.

2. Your interest for the program you are applying for

> Here they are seeking whether you will be a good fit for the program.

- Why do you want to study financial engineering/data science/robotics?/Why are you interested in this field?
- Why Princeton/MIT/specifically?/Why are you drawn to this program?/How do you justify your application?
- How did you learn about our program?
- Among the programs you have applied for, what are the qualities that you seek?

> Let your passion for the topic you are interested in shine through. Explain and describe what got you interested initially, what you have accomplished so far, and what you are hoping to do in the future. As for the qualities you are seeking, you can mention how the school fits your own mindset: competitive, problem-solving, a taste for teamworking, and the mirror qualities offered by the program such as acquiring the ability to solve complex problems, the stimulating study environment, the cosmopolitan cohort of like-minded students, the Career Center's impeccable placement record, proximity to the industry, the mix between faculty and experts in the field, the opportunity to attend classes in other departments, the various student associations, a widespread alum network…

- Why do you want to study in the United States?/Why not study in France?
- What does financial engineering mean for you?
- How do you think your interests will fit in with the program?
- What are your goals? How does MIT fit into them?
- Do you know any alumnus/ae/i/a from Princeton? MIT? Columbia?

- Which faculty members' work particularly interests you and why?/Have you read papers by some of our faculty? Which ones?
- Have you established a relationship with one or more faculty members within the program?
- What is a must-take course for you?/What coursework are you interested in? Why?
- Which concentration are you interested in? Why?
- What's an interesting thing that's been happening in the news / in your field recently?

If possible, try to call out specific **courses** you want to take, **faculty** you hope to learn from, and **opportunities** you are interested in. Highlight what makes the program unique.

- What do you expect to be challenging about graduate school? What are your plans for managing those challenges?
- What interests you about the city the institution is located in?
- What is your Plan A regarding quantitative finance? If Plan A does not work, what is your Plan B?
- How do you rank XXX among other universities you applied to?
- Who will finance your studies?/How will you finance your studies?

Here, always say you have what is necessary to pay: mention personal savings, personal loan, family loan, interest-free school loan.

- If admitted, how likely are you to attend XXX University?

What other programs have you applied for?

This is a question that is often asked, either on the application form or during the interviews. This is not an innocuous question. Will my answer harm my chances of admission and play out badly for me, or will my answer have no part in the process?

The National Association for College Admission Counseling (NACAC) advises against asking "candidates… to divulge or rank order their college preferences on applications or other documents" in their Code of Ethics and Professional Practices. The NACAC states "they may ask the question verbally only if the answer will not be used to influence an admission, scholarship, or financial aid decision." No matter what, the question pops up.

Why do universities require this information? There are several reasons:

- The information is only for internal statistics.
- Departments want this information to schedule prospective graduate visit days in ways to get the most attendance (by avoiding conflicts with other schools that the students they have admitted are applying to).
- The information may be used to learn which other institutions they are competing against, size themselves up with the competition and refine their recruitment strategies.
- Schools do data mining to see what other programs you have applied to in order to gauge your general competitiveness as a candidate in that field.
- Schools are quite protective of their "yield" (number of people enrolled as a percentage of admits) which they correlate with "prestige". If you show that you have applied to higher-ranked schools, they may think that their program is a plan B or a safety school and thus reject you… or tempt you with a hefty scholarship.

- Schools are increasingly relying on data analytics to compare whether former students from such and such universities have chosen them as their top choice. They will use the past admissions data to build a predictive model to calculate the chance of a student coming to enroll after admission. For example, if MIT realizes that a large majority of students from a top school have rejected the offer that had been made the year before and gone to Stanford instead, there are strong chances they will be reluctant to admit you this year.

  A variation of the question is "**Where have you been accepted?**" When asking this question, schools are also trying to gauge the likelihood of you attending. For example, if you have already been accepted at a higher-ranked school, the odds of you choosing them are diminished. So, the lower-ranked school may not accept you to protect their yield.

How to answer the question on the application.

You can refuse to answer it. Therefore, leave it blank on the application. Yet, who would seriously apply to one school and limit her/his opportunity? A student who writes that she/he has not applied anywhere else might be considered somewhat economical with the truth.

If asked to list the universities that you have applied to, a strategy would be to send first the application requiring this information stating that you have not applied or submit any applications to any other schools yet, which would be a true statement.

If an answer is mandatory, you need to think it through. You can be truthful and sincere and think that they want to check the coherence of your choices. Therefore, you list all programs, thinking that they want to know whether you are a good fit, whether you have done your homework regarding program content, whether you are realistic about their expectations, and whether that aligns with your career goals. The rankings of the universities a student has applied to is proportional to the level of the student. The question innocuously meets that purpose.

Presenting a long list of programs is likely to disqualify you, making you sound under-ambitious, unsure of yourself, or plainly desperate to get into a school at all costs. Applying to a bunch of schools makes it seem like either you do not know the field or have no focus. It does not sound like you are a serious candidate. And the more schools you apply to, the less likely you will be to accept an offer.

How to answer the question during the interview. There are several ways of answering the question in the interview.

You may give a vague answer and tell the interviewer you are applying to a few other schools without naming them.

You can talk about the shared general characteristics of the schools you are applying to, without naming specific colleges, spotlighting a particular aspect of the school that is asking you the question. ("I'm looking for a school with a strong program in market finance/a school with project-based classes that provide real-world experience in the field," for example).

If you are hard pressed for a direct response, the best strategy is to redirect the question and say that you'd rather talk about their school and **not** other schools. This is often a great chance to talk about the aspects of the school that are particularly attractive to you.

Obviously, the **cons exceed the pros** when answering the question. I would therefore recommend you list **2-3 schools** (top schools preferably) and not the 5-12 you have applied to. Leave it at that. Chances are no one will ever ask you afterwards. Now, if you believe universities across the U.S. keep a large database with the names of all the applicants and the programs they have applied to… dream on. In the end, answering the question may not make any difference: what matters is the strength of your applications and nothing else.

Which university will you choose? is the next logical question. Just say that at this point you haven't got all the answers from all the programs you have applied for and therefore cannot give an informed answer, but surely your program is top of the list or close to.

3. Interest for the field

Here, they want to check your knowledge in the field you are interested in. Be ready to answer questions such as: How do you keep informed (about your field?). Mention blogs, books, magazines, papers, for example.

- What field of industry are you interested in? Why are you interested in this field and how did you develop that interest?
- How do you think that you studying this subject can affect society or add to it?
- What are the main stakes of the industry today (meaning the financial industry/big data/the power of analytics)?
- How have developments in technology shaped the finance industry in recent years?
- Where do you see your field going in the next ten years?
- What is an issue in the news you always follow?
- How do you keep up-to-date with financial markets?
- What do you see as the major trends in your field of study?
- What are the major trends in financial markets today?
- What financial articles have you read recently?
- What financial paper / magazines do you read on a regular basis?
- If you could only pick one stock today, which one would it be and why?
- What problems are you interested in in ML? in supervised learning? in NLP?

Depending on your field, there might be questions such as: What can you say about the financial situation in Greece/Italy/France/USA-China economic relations? – What do you know about the development of autonomous driving? - Are driverless cars dangerous? – What do you know about the Federal Reserve and the way finance works in the U.S.? And in Europe? – What has been the impact of Brexit on the finance industry?

- If you could travel across the United States in a car with anyone, whom would you choose to travel with and why?
- If you were given a chance to meet anyone, current or historical, who would you meet and why?

These two questions are meant to test the depth of your interest for a science or a field through a personality. At the same time, they will reveal how creative you are. Everybody has their own opinion, which makes it difficult to answer. Even if you are just having a conversation with yourself, the answer will be different each day. However, since the questions focus on your personal opinion, the criteria can be narrowed down based on a few key factors that can be considered relevant: impact on culture, science, arts, society. What matters is that their deeds, values and principles find an echo in your heart and mind.

4. About uniqueness

The question gives you an opportunity to set yourself apart by focusing on the unique skills and experiences you bring to the table. Whenever possible, be specific about the ways you want to get involved on campus.

- As you know, I am seeing a hundred candidates for the second round, why you?/What makes you unique?/What makes you stand out from other candidates?/Why do you stand out compared with other candidates?/How will you contribute to the program?/What are the top three skills you can bring to the program?/What can you bring to this program that you are certain other applicants can't?/Why should we admit you?
- Tell us about something about yourself that isn't in your application/on your CV/What is the most interesting thing about you that we would not learn from your resume alone?/Tell me something about you that would surprise me.

Proceed with caution. You are comparing yourself with other candidates and trying to set yourself apart, yet without sounding like an overconfident show-off. Think of a few skills that make you uniquely qualified for the program. Of course, avoid generic answers such as "I'm smart, qualified and I want this program." If there is no canonical answer, you may bounce back by mentioning **situations** that revealed some of your strengths (leadership, team management, tasks for which you exceeded goals…).
"What makes you unique" actually means, "What makes you an exceptionally good candidate?" So, do not let the word "unique" confuse or intimidate you. The interviewer seeks to identify the qualities and skills that make you a good fit and understand what you value about yourself.
A tip to answer the question would be to start with "I was the only one who…" or "I was the first to…" and fill in the blank with what you have accomplished. Take examples from past experiences or events.
Do not use generic phrases like "I'm a hard worker", "I will make the University famous", or "I'm a people person."
Think about what you bring: diversity, experience, involvement in campus life, strong quantitative skills, cross-cultural background…

5. Self-portrait

- What would you like to tell your future classmates?
- How have you changed in the past five years?
- What word describes you best and why?
- What do you feel passionate about?

You don't choose your passions; your passions choose you." (Jeff Bezos)

- What would co-interns and managers say about you?/How would a classmate describe you?/How would your best friend describe you in two words?

- Can you give me an example of a time when people's first impression of you turned out to be wrong?
- Describe an academic or extra-curricular activity that helped you shape your personality. What did you learn?
- What do you do when you have a real bad day?
- What are your greatest strengths and weaknesses? Name three of each.

Interviewers are interested to know if you know your own strengths, if you are realistic about them, and if those strengths are relevant to the program. Justify your strengths through relevant examples or stories of the strength in action, how successful you were and the impact you had. The more specific the example, the better. Make sure you also give some background and context if necessary. And remain humble when you talk about your strengths.
Rather than dropping in your sporting prowess or musical ability, try to choose examples from different parts of your life (leadership experience, community work, extracurriculars, personal obstacles you faced…). Mention what will help you in the program, such as your creativity (As Albert Einstein said "Logic will get you from A to B. Imagination will take you everywhere"), determination, open-mindedness, thinking on one's feet, working under pressure (with a limited time-frame), timekeeping or time-management skill, ability to think for oneself, investment, communication and people skills, attention to detail, commitment (to gain knowledge, to complete work or to do well), dedication, perseverance, tenacity, resilience, ability to overcome obstacles, cross-cultural background, being diplomatic, learning new things, being good at multitasking **and** prioritizing responsibilities, problem-solving, scientific and intellectual curiosity, enthusiasm, passion for the field, strong work ethics…
Amongst **weaknesses:** reluctance to delegate (which puts more pressure on yourself), shy when speaking in public ("but I'm working on it thanks to the debating class I'm taking" or "the drama club which I have signed up for"), being too much hands-on, multitasking, being too detail-oriented and missing the big picture, being impatient with others, too harsh on myself or self-critical, and taking negative feedback too much to heart, having difficulty maintaining work/life balance, taking too many risks… Also explain your plan of action to overcome a weakness. Or rather, choose a weakness that you're currently succeeding in overcoming.

- Are you the smartest person you know?

This question begs an explanation. There is no correct answer, yet answering "Yes" would smack of arrogance if you are smarter than anyone you know. So, be nuanced. How do you define smartness? Actually, it is measured in different ways. Do they mean the person with the best grades or highest education? Does it mean highest IQ test results? There is more than just being good at math: emotional, cultural and artistic intelligence, business savvy matter too. So, take a step back when answering such a question.

- Identify an influential figure in your life, and why/Who has influenced you the most?/Who is a role model for you?/Tell me about an inspirational figure of yours.

The interviewer asks you to describe someone you admire. Be honest and thoughtful. Family members, fathers or grandmothers, and friends (but not a pet) are all appropriate answers. Teachers and coaches are fine, especially if they got you excited about learning or a subject area. Community members who teach us to think outside of the narrow sphere of our families are relevant examples, too. There is no right answer other than a sincere answer.
Do not try to impress your interviewer with historical figures like Abraham Lincoln, Gandhi, Mother Teresa or scientific luminaries like Elon Musk, Steve Jobs or Mark Zuckerberg. Entertainers, movie actors and actresses are no-brainers.
Be careful with polarizing political figures since it can a challenge for your interviewer to be entirely unbiased. Avoid mentioning "Me" or "God".
I would suggest looking for a figure that possesses the qualities that you value most. It will make the explanation easier as well and avoid vague generalities.

- What do you want your legacy to be?

"If you would not be forgotten, as soon as you are dead and rotten, either write things worth reading, or do things worth writing." (Benjamin Franklin, 1706-1790, writer, scientist, inventor, statesman, diplomat, printer, publisher and political philosopher)

- What drives you as a scientist?
- What is something you want to start doing, stop doing, and continue doing?
- What is your favorite motto or quote, and why?
- What is your favorite place of vacation and why?
- What is your take on a meaningful life?

"But what is life without a passion?" (Avijeet Das)

- What matters to you, and why?
- What motivates you (to work hard every day)?
- What superpower would you want and why?
- Tell me why you think people should go to university/graduate school.

6. Cultural background

- What books do you read?/What have you been reading (outside the curriculum)?/What is the most recent book/fiction book you have read?/What is the best book you have ever read/What is the best film you have ever seen and why?
- Tell me about a book or a movie you read or watched recently.
- What is the latest book you have read about the science?
- What is your favorite song/artist/album?
- What does sport/music represent for you?
- If you were an instrument, what would it be?
- If you could witness any event, past present or future-what would it be?

However surprising, there are many reasons why outside reading matters. Officers are looking for applicants who are curious, academically engaged, and eager to take their knowledge to the next level. Make sure you can name a few books and discuss them in detail. As Descartes wrote, "The reading of all good books is like conversation with the finest minds of the past centuries."

7. Outside interests

- Tell me about something you're interested in outside of work/Outside of family and work, what is something that you are passionate about and why?
- What's most important to do that you do outside of work?/What do you do outside of work?/ What do you do for fun?

8. Accomplishments

- Tell me about a time you went above and beyond for work.
- Tell us about a time when you made an impact.
- Tell me about a time when you set a goal and achieved it.

The interviewer wants to see how self-motivated you are and what steps you took to meet your goal. Goal setting is a motivation to turn an idea or a vision into reality. "A goal properly set is halfway reached." (Zig Ziglar, 1926-2012, US motivational speaker)

- What is something you're good at?
- Do you have any recent accomplishments you want to share?
- What is your most significant/proudest accomplishment?/What accomplishment in the past year at work/at school are you proudest of?

For this question, I would stretch myself outside the curriculum and not mention when you got accepted to a prestigious school. Think about that piano competition you won, a mountain you climbed, a book you have published, a student you helped succeed in his studies, a community center you helped to build in an emerging country...

- What is the biggest risk you have taken so far?

9. Career plans

- Where do you see yourself in five years? ten years?/What career do you envision after your degree?
- What is a personal goal that you have set for yourself recently?
- What is your dream job?/What is your dream company?
- What is the biggest risk you have taken so far?

Admissions staff are trying to see if you have logically thought through your future plans and how the program and degree fit in with these. A disconnect doesn't reflect well, so your career trajectory must look like a sensible, relevant choice. You should demonstrate that you have knowledge of the prospective industries and the job market.

- Which geography would you like to work in?/Would you rather work in the U.S. or in Europe? Why?
- Would you rather work for a large company or a small- or medium-sized one?
- You mentioned starting your own company, which sector would you like to invest time in?

Programs are keen to produce high-achieving students, so when answering a question about your future, try to show that you have the potential to do something that will benefit society. Set your sights high. Show your ambition. Try to think and dream big. Be it as it may, no one is going to track you down in five years and make sure you have fulfilled your prediction, so your answer doesn't have to be set in stone. Yet an answer such as "get a job so I can earn some money" isn't going to make you seem very forward-thinking or driven.

10. Academic background

There will be questions on coursework. They want to check the fundamentals of the courses, the basic knowledge, for example Brownian motion, Black Scholes, martingales (for a finance program). There are also questions concerning the algorithms you have studied as well as the basic in programming languages, ML, Data Science, Computer Science, Programming (what languages do you now?), lab work, experiments you have carried out…

- How do you deal with the stress of academia?
- If you could teach a class on any topic, what would it be and why?
- Talk about a work or research project you have done. Was it successful? Why? Why not? What did you learn? Were you satisfied? In what way did it broaden your knowledge?
- What was the worst/best class you had in college?
- In which coding environment do you feel more comfortable and why?
- Do you think that your undergraduate record accurately reflects your effort and ability?

This question gives you the opportunity to explain a poor grade or an off-color semester. Tread carefully: don't come across as a moaner by blaming others. This might also be an opportunity to let the interviewer know if you did have extenuating circumstances: an out-of-line mark that you feel doesn't reflect your knowledge and ability could be highlighted.

11. Previous research

- Do you expect to publish before starting graduate school?
- How did you manage your research project?
- How has your research experience prepared you for graduate school?
- How many total years of research experience do you have?
- If you were starting your project again today, what would you do differently?
- Please, list the different research experiences you have had.
- What do you consider to be your best paper/work and why?
- What do you think are your most significant research accomplishments?
- What has been the impact of your research?
- What questions did your research help answer?

- What was innovative about your research?
- What was the biggest challenge you encountered in your undergraduate research, and how did you deal with it?
- What was your favorite technique that you used in your undergraduate research?
- What was your role in developing research ideas?

12. Current/future research

- How do you see your research work impacting the field?
- How does the work you propose follow on from what you are already doing?
- How would you convince a funding body that they should fund your research?
- How would you fit with the existing activities in the department?
- What are the big picture questions you want to investigate?
- What are the biggest challenges/questions in your field of research?
- What are your research interests?
- What is an interesting paper you have read lately?
- Who do you expect to collaborate with in the institution?
- Why do you want to collaborate with them?

13. Teamwork

- Do you prefer individual or group projects? Why?
- Do you prefer teamwork or individual work? Why?

> *"Alone we can do so little; together we can do so much." (Helen Keller)*

- Explain a situation when you had to change your communication style. What was the outcome and what did you learn?
- Give me an example of a time when you and your team had opposing views on an issue. How did you persuade them to go with your decision?
- Have you ever had trouble while working in team?
- How do you build trust on a team?
- How do you react to feedback?
- How would you lead a dysfunctional team?
- Tell us about a time when you were part of a team that didn't get along well. How did you help solve the issue?/Tell us about a time you couldn't get along with a person at work/Tell us about a time you had to manage conflict at work/in your team/Tell us about a situation where you had to work with someone you found to be difficult.

> Interviewers ask this question to see how you deal with conflict and work with others. Be sure to include the end result of your efforts in your answer.

- Tell us about a time you were overloaded with work, how did you handle it?
- What is your definition of teamwork?

- What makes a group successful?
- Would you rather work on a team you know or a team you do not know?
- Would you rather be captain of a losing team or a random member of a winning team?

"If you want to go fast, go alone. If you want to go far, go together." (African proverb)

14. Interpersonal relations

The interviewer wants to know that you will work to overcome challenges instead of running from them.

- If you had to collaborate with a coworker who was tough to please, what steps would you take to address the issue?
- Talk about a time when you had to work closely with someone whose personality was very different from yours.
- You have had to work with another data scientist who complained a lot about your projects. How did you react?
- Tell us about a time you needed to get information from someone who wasn't very responsive. What did you do?/Describe a situation where you needed information from a coworker who was slow to respond. What would you do?
- Tell us about a time you encountered an individual who was resistant to change, how did you deal with it and what was the outcome?
- Tell us about a time you had to persuade someone to see your side of things.
- Tell us about a time when you handled conflict well.
- Tell us about a time when you had to hold someone accountable for their work.
- Tell us about a time when you had to persuade/convince others.
- Tell us about a time you had a challenging interaction with someone. How did you handle the situation?

15. Leadership experience

"If your actions inspire others to dream more, learn more, do more and become more, you are a leader." (John Quincy Adams, 1767-1848, sixth president of the United States, 1825-1829)

- What is your approach to/definition of leadership?
- What is your definition of a leader? Can you give some examples?
- Provide a situation in which you performed as a leader/Tell me about a leadership experience/Tell us a time when you led a project and how you managed.

"Do not follow where the path may lead. Go instead where there is no path and leave a trail." (Ralph Waldo Emerson, 1803-1882, American essayist, lecturer, philosopher, abolitionist, poet and champion of individualism)

- Tell me about the leadership positions you have worked in.
- Tell us about a time when you led a meeting, what were the consequences of your actions?

> *"I believe leaders are not just born, they are made." (Bill Clinton, 1945-present, 42nd president of the United States, 1993-2001)*

16. Internship experience

- What was your internship experience about? What did you learn? How did it contribute to consolidate your knowledge? Why choose a startup/bank/fund?
- Describe your typical day at your internship or your current job if you are graduated.
- What were your last internship positive and negative feedbacks?

17. Coping with challenges

- Tell us about a tough challenge you faced. How did you solve it?
- Tell me about a time you faced a challenging task and how you faced it.

> Challenges make you discover things about yourself that you never really suspected. This is a chance to show the interviewer that you do not shy away from them but rather that you embrace them. Challenges are motivating, and meeting, taking on and overcoming them will show your resilience and your ability to go through life's ups and downs thanks to patience, passion and persistence. It is a measure and test of your character.

- Can you tell me about an ethical dilemma you faced?
- Describe a situation where you saw a problem and took steps to fix it/Give me an example about a problem you observed and how you solved it.

> Both questions address your creativity, sense of initiative and problem-solving skills. You need to show that you made a valuable contribution without being asked.

- Describe a situation where you were expert in your field and solved a problem.
- Describe a time that you encountered a significant personal obstacle? How did you handle it?
- Describe a time when you showed great resilience and tenacity and it paid off. What were the results?
- Give me an example of a situation when you showed initiative and took charge of a situation.
- How do you deal with failure/disappointment?
- Suppose you worked for a company and you learnt that your team had made a serious mistake likely to impact the client, how would you react?/Assume you have worked for a long time for a client. Just before a meeting, you realize there's a huge mistake and it's your fault. What do you do?

> Interviewers seek to assess your integrity and determine whether your ethics and beliefs align with the program's values. Your response is an opportunity to share your commitment to honesty and quality work.

- Talk about the time when you made a wrong decision, what was the setback and how did you handle it?
- Tell me about a time when you had the liberty to be creative with your work. Was it exciting or difficult for you?/Tell us about a situation when you implemented a creative solution.

> *"Everything you can imagine is real." (Pablo Picasso, 1881-1973)*

- Tell me about a time when you were given unreasonable responsibility.
- Tell me about when you had a difficult time with a project/a job.
- Tell us about a time when you had to ask for help.
- Tell us about a time when you had to step outside your comfort zone.
- When was the last time you did something for the first time?

> *"A ship is always safe at the shore-but that is not what it is built for." (Albert Einstein, 1879-1955)*

- Tell us about a time when you handled a task on which you had zero information. What were the steps you took to begin with, what were the strategies and what were the end results?
- Tell us about a time you took an initiative.
- Give me an example of a difficult decision you had to make. What steps did you take to make it?

> The intent behind this question is straightforward: interviewers want to see your decision-making process, reasoning ability, problem-solving skills and judgement. Talk through your logic as you explain how you solved the problem and outline the steps you took to make the decision. Do not be afraid to laugh at yourself or criticize yourself as you talk through it too.

- Tell us of a time when you took a risk. What lesson did you learn from it?
- What hurdles or obstacles have you overcome in your life/at school?
- What would you do if you made a mistake that no one else noticed? Would you address the error and risk slowing things down or ignore it to keep the project or task moving forward?
- What would you do if you were asked to perform a task you've never done before?

> The interviewer wants to know whether you are willing to take on new challenges independently. The answer to this question will also provide some insight into your problem-solving skills.

- Tell me about a time you were in a high-pressure situation. How did you get through it?
- Tell me about a situation when you had an especially heavy workload. What did you do?

> The interviewer is curious about the different steps you took to make sure to deliver, along with your organizational and time management skills.

- Describe a time when you had to make an immediate decision/What's a spontaneous decision you have made?

> *"Do one thing every day that scares you." (Eleanor Roosevelt, 1884-1962)*

18. Coping with failure

> *"Success is not final, failure is not fatal: it is the courage to continue that counts." (Winston S. Churchill, 1874-1965)*

- Tell us about a time when you faced rejection.
- Tell us about a time when your expectations were not met.
- Tell me about a time when somebody failed you.
- Tell us about a time when you failed somebody.
- Tell me about a time when you failed.

> However uncomfortable you might be to talk about a time you did not succeed right away, the question gives you a chance to show how you learnt from your mistakes, how you overcame adversity, recovered from defeat and whether you took responsibility for your action. Encountering defeat does not mean that you are defeated. Rise from defeat, show that you do not fear failure but rather fear not trying. However hard it is to fail, it is worse never having tried to succeed. Instead of dwelling on what went wrong, focus on how you have grown from this challenge and what you plan on doing differently going forward. "Fall down seven times, get up eight" (Japanese proverb): No matter how many times you get knocked down, you get up again.

19. Miscellaneous

- Do you see AI as a boon or a plague?
- Explain financial modeling.
- How do you explain quantitative finance to a grandma?
- How can (financial) engineering bring positive change?
- If you were admitted to the MFin, which element would please you the most?
- What is quantitative easing? How does it work?
- Tell me about the financial markets of your choice.
- What does negative working capital mean?
- Which concentration would you be interested in? Corporate finance, capital markets or financial engineering?
- Why would two companies merge?
- Have you ever faced discrimination? How did you react?
- How can finance contribute to progress?
- How do you celebrate success?
- If money was not a concern, what would you do?
- If you could live anywhere in the world, where would it be and why?

- If you could travel anywhere for a month, where would you go and why?
- If you had an extra hour every day, what would you do with it?
- Talk about your last speech or presentation. How did you prepare it? How was it received?
- Tell us about the most interesting place you've traveled to. What did you enjoy most about it?
- What are the qualities to be a successful startup creator?/What are three key successful factors to be an entrepreneur?/What skills do you think are necessary for an entrepreneur?
- What do you think of New York City?
- What invention during your lifetime has had the biggest impact on you and why?
- What is the best advice you have received and how have you used it in your life or career?
- What are the qualities necessary to make a successful student?
- What makes a good financier? a good data scientist? a good engineer?
- What piece of technology could you not live without and why?
- What possession or memento do you treasure most and why?
- What process/method do you use to ensure accuracy?

20. Social/Economic issues

- Is what we do today enough to solve climate change? Why or why not?
- How do you see emerging countries growing in the next 10 years? What impact will they have on global economy?
- How would you describe your current thinking about diversity, and how has your thinking changed over time?
- What does it mean for you to have a commitment to diversity? How have you demonstrated that commitment?
- What do you feel is the biggest challenge when dealing with people from another culture?

21. Closing questions

- Any questions for me?
- What question do you wish I had (not) asked you? [my question] Could you answer that?

4. Be an interview star

Taking an interview is central to admission. I suggest you do **mock interviews** with a classmate or a coach, focusing on each of the categories mentioned above.

Technicalities

Make sure you have a **strong and secure Internet connection,** a functioning webcam and that your software is up-to-date before you prepare for the questions or the interview. Check to see if you have at least an hour of battery life or, better yet, plug into a power source. All too often, you will have only **ONE** chance at responding. There won't be any second chance.

Before you start recording or doing the interview, turn off **ALL notifications** on your machine (email, MSM, etc.). It is advised that you temporarily disable browser extensions whilst conducting an interview. Close any programs that might prompt you with push notifications or pop-ups. It will prevent all distractions from the outside and allow you to laser focus on the questions asked and the answers you have to give.

Find **a well-lit setting**, turn on your webcam and adjust your location to ensure you have a clear backdrop behind you. Do not have a **bright light** behind you that may blind the interviewer during the exercise. Adjust your lighting and position to find an arrangement that shines light on your face, rather than backlighting you.

You may use a pen, paper and calculator but not a mobile phone or other computer device. Smart phones are not supported for an interview. Have your government-issued ID ready.

Windows, pictures, postcards, mirrors, or cluttered shelves are best avoided if possible. Also, take down that Lady Gaga or Brad Pitt poster on the wall behind you.

Avoid any **distractions around**. There should be no people walking around. Make sure your family, friends, classmates know you are going to take the interview. Put a 'do not disturb' sign on your door if you must!

The camera

Avoid any camera movement. The camera should be **static** so as to avoid any interferences with your environment that might take the viewer's attention off the message you are trying to get across while filming or being filmed. Prefer a **close-up shot**. With a close shot, the subject's head/face takes up the majority of the frame. The subject becomes the prominent focus and helps the audience build a personal connection, without being distracted by background interferences. You can also film yourself from the waist/neck up but avoid the full shot (the entire body of the subject from head to toe). This latter shot tends to focus more on movement and gestures, rather than message content. Similarly, avoid the medium shot that shows the subject from the knees up. It allows the viewer to see the background environment and the character's gestures and distracts the viewer's attention.

Language

The **quality** of English is essential. Checking your linguistic abilities is actually one of the reasons why you are being interviewed. Therefore, before you commit to the interview, practice the language by **reading aloud in English** every day and for five-ten minutes prior to the call or video.

Speak slowly and be clear in your elocution and pronunciation.

Take time to ponder the question. Do not rush it before you start rambling. For the most part, you can follow your interviewer's lead regarding the length of your answers. Researching your interviewer ahead of time will help you. If the interviewer shuts you down (*e.g.,* "Okay, great."), move on. If she/he is asking you to elaborate, keep going!

As a general rule, you should never spend more than **two minutes** answering a single question. Do not try to feed the interviewer all the info in one go or you may dig yourself into a hole. Let the interviewer follow up with another question, if necessary.

Make sure to provide **examples**. If you say that tenacity is one of your qualities, then make sure you have some proven experience to back it up.

Build your answer. Every answer you give should begin with two to three main points, so that your interviewer doesn't miss half your answer if they cut you off. So, use link words such as "first of all", "then", "finally", "There are two reasons for this", "I see two advantages to this…". Structuring your thought process will show that you have solid reasoning skills.

Do not be **robotic** in your answers. Your verbal and nonverbal behavior will be on display during the interview, but do not try to impress the interviewer with lofty language and vague sounding statements. Try to remain conversational and personable using language that is clear, concise, and compelling. Do not look bored but come across as engaged.

Have a positive attitude. Look confident and smile. After all, you deserve admission and there is ample reason to look forward to a bright future. On the other hand, be yourself: they will admit you or not, and this is not the end of the world. This is a learning experience.

Do not be **destabilized** by the questions you have not prepared. Take a deep breath, regroup and stay calm. Answer the question directly, find an example to support your answer. If you cannot tap into your own personal or professional experience, use a hypothetical answer about how you would react in a given situation.

Never panic. If you feel you have not answered one question as well as you wanted to, don't panic. They will assess your interview as a whole and will take each of your answers into consideration, so do not worry too much if one question does not quite go to plan. Just try to gather yourself together, move on and refocus your energy for the next question. Remember that the interview is only one component of your overall application and will be reviewed alongside your written form. Do not be thrown off balance if questions have no relevance with each other.

If you have not understood the question, ask them to repeat: "*Could you repeat your question, please?*"/"*Would you mind repeating the question, please?*" If you do not have all the answers to the questions, say so. It is no sin to still have to learn. It is a sin to try to waffle a question.

Do not be afraid of **silence** in between questions.

If you need some time to reflect, have a sip of water. If you need a few seconds to think about the answers, use **gap fillers**, such as *hum… well…, I mean…* or just say "*that's an interesting question, let me think about it…*"

Writing and **memorizing** page-long scripts/questions gets in the way of building empathy and relating to people. You need to establish eye contact with the interviewers so reading a prepared and rehearsed script as if you were reading lines in a Shakespeare tragedy will not play in Peoria. You should be able to pick up on subtle body language cues that prompt you to adapt your answer and build a rapport with your interviewer. Besides, if you decided to memorize your lines, you would run the risk of not being able to remember it all especially in such a stressful situation. So, instead of writing out entire answers, write out 1-3-word bullet points that correspond to the key points of your argument.

Do not stress out if the interview is not as long as expected or is longer than expected.

Dress code

It is essential to be **well-groomed**, clean-shaven (avoid that 6 o'clock shadow), that your clothes fit well and are clean. White or light blue shirt. A jacket is fine. No tie is necessary unless you want to. **Dress decently** in clean, and simple attire. Play it safe with solid colors and comfortable materials so you can focus on the content of your responses. Even though it is not a fashion show, you need to look polished and put together so as to leave an impression.

Position

Sit on the edge of your seat, as it forces you to sit up straight. Use a chair without arms, not an armchair. No hand movement: do not speak with your hands and keep your arms crossed.
Look the interviewer **straight in the eye** and maintain eye contact. It will reinforce the trust between the interviewer and you. No staring but no wandering eye or looking right and left: avoiding eye contact for extended periods of time can make it look like you have something to hide and make you less trustworthy to others. If you look away, it may appear as though you are inattentive or uninterested. So, match your attentive eye contact with an appropriate facial expression. Convey interested attention with an open, positive expression.

"Do you have any questions for me?"

It is common for the interviewer to ask interviewees whether they have questions, especially at the end of the interview. "**Do you have any questions for me?**" is the standard query. Do not say "Thanks, none come to mind!" So, make sure to ask a few thoughtful questions at the end of your conversation. This is your time to create a connection, show your knowledge of the program, get advice, understand the interviewer's career and impress them as a curious and thoughtful candidate. When considering interview questions to ask, keep these rules in mind:

- If your question can be answered by reading their website or a Google search or it is not critical to your interest in the program, do not ask it.
- Look for questions that are open-ended and will lead to more than a "yes" or "no" answer.
- Avoid questions like "Which classes do you think I should take?" since you should already know your answer to this.
- **Avoid asking questions** such as: "How much does the rent cost on campus?", "What was your GMAT score?", "Is there a swimming club at MIT?", "Why did you decide to work for Yale?", "What are the parties like on campus?", "How often do students fail out of the program?"
- Try to have **two questions** ready for them (their time is limited), such as:
- "What internship perspectives does the program offer?"
- "What are the classes you recommend I should prioritize regarding my career plans?"
- "What are the alumni group connections in my home country?"
- "What do your most successful alumni have in common?"
- "What did you gain from the program and how it helped you achieve your goals?"
- "What advice do you have for admitted students looking to maximize their success?"

If necessary, background the interviewer if you have her/his name, that is. The questions will help build a connection with the interviewer, for example if you have a goal similar to the interviewer's path it might be the time to ask for advice.

Once the interview wraps up, get the interviewer's contact information if you do not have it already. Make sure you are up to date on interview etiquette. Seemingly small gestures like writing a thank you note and a follow-up email can have a big impact and showcase a student in the best light possible. Thus, courtesy dictates that, within the next 12 hours, you send a polite thank-you note to the interviewer along the following lines. It gives applicants an opportunity to reinforce their interest and enthusiasm for the program. So, be short, keep it professional and spell-check before sending.

```
Dear Ms/M… Thank you for taking time to interview me [state when the interview took place].

It was quite interesting/stimulating/exciting to talk to you/It was a pleasure speaking with you and learning more about the program.

Our discussion has strengthened my aspiration to join the program ever more.

I look forward to hearing from you.

Cordially/Best regards/Sincerely/Respectfully
```

If you already have been in email contact with the person responsible for the interview, it is easier to continue the email thread by replying to the last email between the two of you. If you are drafting a new message, the subject line should be relevant to the recipient and make them want to open it. This might include an expression of thanks and a reference to the interview. Pay attention to the appropriate salutation. Add a signature. Sign off with a formal or semi-formal closing phrase, depending on the degree of formality established in your previous exchange with the recipient, along with your name and contact details.

You may also send the interviewer a LinkedIn connection request so they might be tempted to look further into your profile and perhaps find additional points of commonality with you.

Interview don'ts

- Don't be chatty
- Don't be rude
- Don't be too loud
- Don't give unorganized answers
- Don't give vague answers
- Don't look scared like a rabbit caught in the headlights
- Don't make jokes
- Don't speak too fast
- Don't speak too slow
- Don't sweat
- Don't talk with your hands
- Don't use an unprofessional tone
- Don't use verbal junk (umm, uh…)
- Don't whisper

5. Admissions results

Now that you have completed the interview process, there is only one thing left: wait for the final decision. It is rather swift, and can be as short as one week once all the candidates have been auditioned.

Do not rush before making a decision and accepting a first offer, however enticing it might be. Wait until all the admissions results are in. If you have two offers, one with funding and the other without, you might explain this to your contact in admissions and hope for a better offer.

On the other hand, a program (which is not your top choice) may ask for an early answer (by the end of February or even before according to their listed deadlines), when all admissions results are not in. This is a school's way of getting you to commit to them early and not accept any other offers from other schools. In addition, the program you have been admitted to requires a non-refundable $4,000 deposit.

This is **unacceptable**. It **goes against the grain of ethics**. An early decision is non-binding. You can decline a graduate admission offer after accepting it. Technically speaking you are allowed to change your decision any time before April 15th, the universal deadline.

Yet, you need to weigh all offers before making a decision. If you hear back positively from your first choice before that acceptance expires, all the better. If you don't, then you are caught between a rock and a hard place. You can naturally accept the offer, pay and if you later decide not to enroll, you can retract the offer and lose your deposit. My advice would be, upon receiving an offer, to immediately contact all other programs that you have applied to and that you would prefer, to let them know that you have another offer – so that they can either also offer you admission, or confirm that they were going to reject you. You can then accept your best offer with the peace of mind that no better offer will come along later. Alternately, you can:

- Ask grad school A (your second choice) to hold off until you have all offers in your hand.
- Ask grad school B (your first choice) for an early release of the admissions and tell them you would rather go to their school instead.

Decision-making means **choosing among graduate programs**, usually the top two you favor if you have been admitted to both. Weigh the pros and cons. There are several factors that you might consider: funding, academics, reputation, your gut intuition. Also consider your personal life, your own desires, and your quality of life. Do not just look within. Talk to other people. Close friends and family can offer a fresh perspective. Professors can discuss the decision from an academic and career development perspective. Ultimately, the decision is yours. Once you have reached a decision, do not look back.

Once you have received all the answers and reached a decision of which program you will choose to attend, **inform each university** you have applied to of your decision, especially the programs whose offer you are declining or the faculty that went to bat for you. Once they receive word that you are declining their offer of admission, they are free to inform applicants on the wait list of their admission. Email is an entirely appropriate means of communicating your decision. Remember to be professional. Use proper forms of address and a polite, formal writing style thanking the admissions committee.

If you **decline admission to a PhD program**, for example, and they request some explanation, keep it short and sweet: thank them for their time and do not apologize. Do not say that the faculty at A is stronger than at B, for example. You might say either that B is a better match to your current interests at the other university even though both are great, that you have significantly better financial aid elsewhere. You can also mention locational or partner preference.

```
I regret to inform you that after much consideration I have decided not to join
your university. I have accepted another PhD offer that more closely aligns with
my research aspirations and longer-term career ambitions.
Thank you for your time and consideration
```

Also, do not forget to send thank-you notes to all those who helped you in the process, especially your recommenders.

Read thoroughly any admitted student information you are sent (instructions about your enrollment deposit, financial aid, housing, admitted student campus visit programs, academic advising, course scheduling, new student orientation, student life, etc.). Many institutions offer admitted student the means to visit, which provides an opportunity for you to meet fellow students, faculty, and staff.

6. Waitlisted

A few candidates will receive an offer, many will be denied admission after the interview and the rest will be put on a waitlist. The number of waitlisted candidates vary from one program to another, and can be as high as two thirds of the applicants having been offered a slot.

The reasons for being waitlisted are never given (nor are those given for a rejection, the standard explanation being that the program had stellar applications this year and they had to make difficult choices). There are some simple reasons for that: providing explanations or reasons would be just begging for lawsuits. On the other hand, admissions offices have to process a huge amount of application materials. Going through and assigning reasons for rejection is additional work that there is no time for. So, do not waste the admissions officers' time by enquiring why you have been rejected.

Some online resources provide information on the admission process and results, be they painful or joyful or checking whether you have made the grade or not. (https://www.reddit.com/r/gradadmissions, https://www.thegradcafe.com) or https://www.thestudentroom.co.uk

However, we must consider the following reasons if you have been waitlisted or rejected:
- Not the right fit. Admissions officers may decide that however solid your application may be, the program you chose does not match your aspirations. Conversely, you may not be the right fit either because you appear be overqualified for an MEng program whereas you are PhD timber, for example.
- The application is incomplete.

- Too many errors. Do not put Harvard University when you are applying to Princeton. Admissions officers may be willing to overlook a minor mistake, but submitting applications filled with typos and errors shows admissions counselors that the applicant is not serious about their institution, or that the applicant does not have sufficient writing skills to succeed at the college. That is why penning a pristine SOP matters...
- A weak GPA (3.60 might be considered a high according to some schools, whereas other schools consider it far too weak). Simply put, the applicant does not meet the academic threshold.
- A lack of passion, motivation, ambition... and a weak record in terms of experience, academic, professional or extracurricular.
- A lack of practical or work experience (especially in applied programs).
- Weak letters of recommendation (hence it is recommended that applicants check with previous admits to see who supported their successful applications).
- A weak professional project that is no match for the program you are applying for. In that regard, some "lucky" students might be offered a spot in another program, the school reserving the right to propose another program if they deem that it is more suitable.
- Too many deferrals from the year before have limited the number of slots available for the present year.
- The decision of former applicants who, having been offered a slot, decided to decline admission. The desirability score is calculated on the basis of actual student decisions. Schools look closely at their desirability statistics, and therefore when a number of cross-admits from a same college turn down an offer, it is sure to reflect on the next cohorts. Make sure that your school has a coherent application policy then.

However disappointed you might be, do not lose heart if you have been waitlisted. What you can do is simple:

- Reiterate your **strong desire** to join the program in a short email, pointing out that it is and has always been your number 1 choice. Here is an example:

```
First, let me reiterate my strong motivation for joining your Master of Science in XXX. Being part of this program has been one of my dreams since I started studying at college: I have grown convinced your program is the ideal fit to fulfill my career plan and that I will blossom/thrive in XXX's academic environment and work atmosphere.

I bring to Stanford my academic experience in both engineering and business but also my extra-curriculum experience along my interpersonal skills and my great creativity.

Even though I was sadly disappointed by your decision, I hope I can still have a chance to be accepted. I will make sure to keep you updated of the future development in my studies and experience.
Cordially,
```

- Send your latest grades (provided they are strong, of course) as additional material to your application.

- Keep sending updates to the program on your experience, be it academic or internship. The process can be rather long before a final decision is made (sometimes end of May, or even July, according to what some programs claim).

What happens if you are admitted to a PhD program before April 15th and then **get accepted to a far better program** after April 15th? Can you go to the other program instead? Such a decision ought to be weighed carefully: is the second program a better fit, do they offer a better financial package, better research facilities, better housing, do they have a better placement record, will the professors be able to advise you five years down the line and not retiring soon…? Then, choose carefully the reasons why you have changed course and explain them in polite terms.

If you decide to accept the offer from the second program, contact them and tell them you have already accepted an offer, but you like their program better and that you would be willing to renege to accept their offer. Ask them explicitly if they agree with this. If they are, accept their offer, make sure it is a done deal and then tell the first program (they won't sue you for breach of contract). Obviously if you don't want to be here, they do not want you here either.

Do not contact the first program before the second program: they might be annoyed, withdraw their offer, contact the second program and use the Council of Graduate Schools resolution to complain. In that case, the second program may also withdraw their offer and you might be left high and dry.

On the other hand, if you renege on the first offer, chances are that they will release you. They do not want to run the risk of you dropping out after a year. They will pick someone from the waitlist even though the professor that counted on you to advance her/his research might be unhappy. Conversely, you might feel bad about getting their hopes up and walking away. Yet, if you know in your heart that the first school is not a good fit, do not feel bad about backing out.

Ultimately it is about you and your life. You are going to be devoting 5+ years of your life to research, and potentially have the rest of your career/life shaped by it. So, choose the program that will be better for you, regardless of the earlier commitment. In the best-case scenario, the people in the first program will be understanding; in the worst-case scenario, you will have made an enemy and someone will hold grudges. You will probably be burning bridges with the first school but after all you are not a slave and it is a slight burn. You might still be living with the consequences and create bad blood if the faculty in the first program are important in your field, and might blackball the papers you submit for peer review. This is a risk to take but chances are that by the time you have a paper ready for publication, the whole episode will be water under the bridge. Also, do not fear retaliation if ever you apply for faculty positions. Five years down the road, the hatchet of your decision will have long been buried.

7. Deferment policy

Deferrals and **deferment** policy. Once all the results have been in, once you have been admitted to the program and accepted the offer, you may have cold feet and think twice about spending oodles of money on a program you are starting to have misgivings about. Or you may want to pursue other personal goals. Or your personal situation may have changed. Therefore, you decide to defer admission for a year (you cannot defer admission for longer than a year), which means you decline to enroll the coming year and request to join the program the following year. All institutions have deferral policies. This decision needs to be weighed carefully.

There are several steps you need to take, the first of which is to inform the admissions committee of your intentions. You need to have strong arguments to ask for a deferral. In most cases, deferral is granted for extenuating circumstances:

- You have experienced a major downturn in finances.
- You have experienced a personal crisis such as a medical emergency, a pregnancy, or the loss of a loved one.
- You have decided to take a gap year to build up experience and be better prepared for the program you have been selected for.
- Job changes might also be factored in, such as a recent promotion, increased responsibilities, etc.

However, these circumstances should be able to be verified: the admissions office will look closely at the reasons before making a decision to deny or grant a deferral.

Let the admissions office know as soon as you have made your decision to defer. There are other applicants still interested in this program, and some may be on a waitlist. Having the courtesy to let admissions staff members know of your decision as soon as possible provides them an opportunity to admit someone else in a timely manner.

If you accept the deferment decision, you will be asked to pay an additional enrollment deposit, which – like your initial deposit – is non-refundable. This is the institution's way of making sure you are serious about joining the student body in the future.

If your request for deferral is denied, you will be instructed to withdraw and reapply. In general, admitted students who withdrew and reapplied – and who clearly explained the reasons for that course of action – were offered readmission.

Make sure you check out the financial aid implications: If you have been awarded a scholarship or fellowship, make sure you find out if this award will still be available to you if you defer. In just about every case, the award is not held if you withdraw.

Can an **admission offer be rescinded**? If an admitted candidate has made misleading, incomplete, or inaccurate statements, submitted false material in connection with the application, or has been found to have engaged in reprehensible academic or personal conduct the programs can take appropriate action, which could include rescinding an offer of admission or revoking a degree. Newly admitted candidates are expected to inform the Office of Admissions of any past or present conduct that is inconsistent with these standards.

Whatever the outcome of your applications, do not be disappointed if you are denied admission. Always have a plan B or even a Plan C, just in case. Whatever the outcome, there are several hidden benefits to applying, even if it looks like it cost you. The whole application process will have helped you define and clarify your goals. It will have provided some useful clues as to which direction your future path will take you and help you know yourself better.

PART II
THE ACADEMIC CV

1. The basics

The CV is a component of any graduate application file. It is the right place to fit in all the details that cannot be covered in the balance of the application.

A CV is designed to give admissions committees insight into your academic potential, background in the field, and extensiveness of that background. Your purpose as an applicant is to create a document that best showcases your talent, accomplishments and experiences. Admissions committees and faculty members will seek how your skills, experiences, and qualifications make you a right fit for their program and university. So, before you even begin to compose your CV, consider that your readers will have seen hundreds if not thousands of applicant profiles. Keep these considerations in mind to make your CV stand out.

A CV should be well-organized, to the point, and easy to read while accurately representing your highest accomplishments. Applicants will mention details about their courses, projects, work experience, publications, extra-curricular activities and other achievements including honors.

However, applicants should not rely on the committee members reading all the details in the CV or even going through the CV at all. Key information that applicants definitely want the committee to know should already get mentioned in one of the application components mentioned so far.

Typically, the CV is one page long, yet, it can go longer depending on an applicant's research experience, publications, conferences, fellowships... Members on the committee will spend 30 seconds at most to peruse the CV, so it has to be concise, clear and readable at first sight.

- Find a template that is picture perfect, stylish and classic.
- A CV should be written in a readable font. Tried-and-true classics like Times New Roman, Arial, Helvetica, Calibri and Georgia are still among the best font options for your résumé (typically **12)** but check with the requirements for each program: sometimes it can be 10); use **14 to 16pt** for your name at the top and **bold** section headings.
- Margins on each of the four sides (1 inch or 2.5cm).
- Dates either to the right (preferably) or to the left (Nov. 2021-Jan. 2022, or for work in progress: March 2021-present).
- A resumé will consist in several **headings** that you may put in small capital letters for clarity's sake.
- List content in **reverse chronological order**, starting from the more recent to the less recent.
- You may indicate an incoming internship, mentioning the date, the place, the goal and the supervisor's name(s).
- Include **bullet points** in some sections. If you do use them, try to limit the number of bullet points to five per section, and order them so the most relevant point is at the top.
- For projects or internships, the number of bullet points should be in relation with their **importance**. A major project may have 4 bullet points, a minor one 1 or 2.
- Put a double blank line before all headings and one blank line after them. White space is good for readers as it guides the eyes to the important parts.
- **Punctuation**: in general, no full stop (UK)/period (US) at the end of a line without a verb in tense form.

Pay attention: the program you're applying to may have **specific guidelines** for how to structure your CV. Perhaps they do not want you to include any references, or they are not interested in community work. The program guidelines take precedence over anything included in this guide so make sure you check to see if there is anything listed you need to follow.

If being creative is a good thing, when it comes to CV's it is vital to **stick to the basics**. Do not try coloring your entire CV baby blue or try that new cursive font that is impossible to read. The admissions committee is interested in finding your information where they expect it while making sure the format is consistent and it comes across as professional.

2. The CV and the résumé

There are three major differences between **a CV** and **a resume**: length, purpose and layout. A résumé and a CV are not always interchangeable.

A **CV** emphasizes academic accomplishments, and always begins with education. A CV is **credential-based**. It is **detailed** and can stretch well beyond two pages although two pages is a stretch. It is often used in the academic field as it encapsulates your education and academic background. The CV provides a comprehensive (and often lengthy) listing of one's education, certifications, research experience, and professional affiliations and memberships.

A **curriculum vitae summary** is a one-to-two-page, condensed version of a full curriculum vitae. A CV summary is a way to quickly and concisely convey one's skills and qualifications. Sometimes large organizations will initially ask for a one-page CV summary when they expect a large pool of applicants.

A **résumé** emphasizes skills, notable achievements and work experience. It leads with work experience and places education section at or near the end. A résumé is **competency-based**. It is a summary of your skills and experience over one page usually, two at most. It is a marketing document intended to showcase a candidate's skills, notable achievements, and work experience to the greatest advantage. Resumes are often used in the professional field and are designed to give potential employers a "snapshot" into your relevant background. The resume will be tailored to each position (academic, industrial, private, public). It is a short, straight-to-the-point, document created for the purpose of applying for a specific job. The resume is usually accompanied by a cover letter which states your intent for applying for the job. The cover letter builds upon the skills and experience you have touched upon in your resume, explaining how they're going to help you excel at the job you're applying for.

The analytical/quantitative resume. The CV can sometimes be different from the **résumé** (spelling closest to French), **resumé** (to differentiate the noun from the verb "to resume") or **resume** (the most common spelling). Some programs will require an **analytical/quantitative/language** resume that will provide the committee with additional information on your quantitative and language knowledge and proficiency. A quantitative resume gives the admissions committee a sense of an applicant's quantitative ability and potential. This is especially the case for MPA, MPP programs, for example. The special quantitative/language résume **should elaborate upon the skills you have developed related to quantitative methods** and language learning. It is acceptable if some of the information included in this résume **overlaps with your standard/traditional** résume. The program officers want to make sure applicants provide as much information as possible about their quantitative aptitude, experience, and capabilities. This can include academic coursework in mathematics, statistics, economics, engineering, natural or computer science, etc., as well as the use of quantitative methods in a professional environment (paid, volunteer, or intern work is acceptable). Within quantitative coursework, a details column sometimes includes specific textbook titles and/or term paper titles. It should include: **Subject/Course/Grade/Details (Textbook, Major concepts covered)**. A few lines about the Details should suffice (typically, as in the example: Major concepts covered: functions, logarithms, limits, derivatives and rates of change, product and quotient rules, the chain rule, differentiation, optimization, the mean value theorem, antiderivatives, integrals and the fundamental theorem of calculus.). (https://sipa.columbia.edu/sites/default/files/Sample_Quantitative_Langauage_Resume-2015.pdf)

A Quantitative resume may also include the following:
Academic Experience
Relevant coursework including, but not limited to mathematics, statistics, economics, logic, calculus, linear algebra, information technology, data analysis, methodology course, and engineering. Include the institution, grade earned, date of course, main concepts covered.

Professional Experience
List substantive projects completed in a professional, co-curricular, volunteer, or internship setting including a brief summary of any analytical skills acquired (*e.g.* data analysis software, programming,) or quantitative work entailed in the project. There may be some overlap with your professional resume.

3. Content

While there is no golden CV template that every candidate should follow, it should be structured in an easy-to-follow format and include several elements of your life and track record. "Several" means you will have to pick and choose what is relevant. It is organized along several sections, or headings and subheadings.

- **Personal information**: on top, indicate first name/last name, and below: email academic address (ecole.edu, for example) (avoid using a personal account such as Gmail), cell phone (with country code), QR code for your LinkedIn if you have one, and GitHub address. Both LinkedIn and GitHub are optional. No need to put a mailing address. Citizenship is optional but can be mentioned if you have double citizenship, such as French and American. Warning: some programs may ask the student to **redact** (=to remove) name and contact (in other words they require an anonymous CV).
  Below the personal information add one line stating the objective: **Application for PhD program in Materials Science**, for example. It informs at a glance the admissions committee of your status.

- **Educational background/Education History:** A rule of thumb for any graduate application is to emphasize your academic achievements over your professional ones. This will inform the admissions officers of your background, which can be a helpful way to understand more about your fit for the program you are applying for. You can either inform the name of the institution, followed by that of the degree, or vice-versa.
  - List your experience in reverse order, most recent dates first. Indicate the institution (name and city/country), the degree and the date.
  - Indicate undergraduate and graduate education. For each degree, list the institution, location, the degree that you obtained, the field of study, and graduation year.
  - If you're not finished with your degree, you can still include work you've done and when you plan to graduate (to be completed in…).
  - Indicate relevant coursework or key subjects, in italics, and with capital letter on each course first word.
  - Include Erasmus exchange, semester abroad, Summer workshop at Stanford, but not the summer courses at a language institute in Cambridge when you were 15.
  - Put in your GPA (you may not want to include this if it is not above 3.4…) even though it will be on your transcripts. But a stellar GPA won't hurt your chances and likely catch the reader's eye. Check difference between GPA and CGPA.
  - An alternate model to the standard format model below will have you put the dates, degree and location first as in the following:

2018–present
- Doctor of Philosophy (expected June 2021)
- Department of Management Science & Engineering, Stanford
- Thesis: Equilibria in two-settlement markets: market power, uncertainty, and risk aversion

Supervisor: Professor Tracy Austin

2016–2018
- Master of Applied Mathematics
- Operations Research Center, MIT
- Thesis: Applying selected ML technique to query optimization

Supervisors: Professors Hans Kohlberg and Gertrud Ginzburger

2012–2016
- Bachelor of Applied Science (first class honours)
- Ecole/University XXX's, City, Country
- Sir Alfred Guyard Foundation Medal winner for Highest Academic Standing in Physics Program

- **Project/Research work.** As with teaching experience, research experience may be rare for first-time grad school applicants. But if you have any assistantships, practica (sg practicum: a practical section of a course of study), or other research experiences, list them here.

– name of lab, department or institution,

– short title of the work,

– supervised by/under the supervision of (essential if that person is writing you a letter of recommendation).
– Even the *prepa* projects (called *TIPE*) you carried out do matter. So, put them in.

• **Publications** are to be mentioned here if you have some under your belt. Put your name in bold letters if there are co-authors. If you have filed patents, this is the place to provide information.

```
Martin, B., additional authors. (in press). Title. Journal, Volume (Issue), page
numbers.
```

There are several kinds of publications: peer-reviewed, *i.e.* reviewed by a community of experts in a given field prior to the work being submitted for publication, non-peer reviewed, works submitted and works in progress (demonstrate your engagement with your field, the currency of your research, and your desire to publish). If you have submitted a work but it has not yet been accepted, list the title and the journal or press; if you are currently completing a work that you intend to publish, cite it as a work in progress. Scholarly reports can also be included in the publications section of your CV as a way of illustrating your written work.

Conference presentations/poster presentations, conference papers, posters, presentations and proceedings are to be mentioned here as well. Include title of presentation, conference name, location of conference, date of conference and a brief description of the content you contributed.

• **Internship/Professional experience/Work experience/Work record** (volunteer work, blue-collar work experience, work placement, traineeship, part-time job, summer job, teaching, responsibility in a club, leadership training…)

• **Skills**
– List here **IT skills**, or computer literacy; mention only those programming languages you are proficient in, the operating systems you have worked with, the networks you are familiar with. Do not mention Word or Excel, or MS-DOS. But if you contributed to the school magazine using QuarkXpress and Photoshop, mention it.
– **Language skills**: mention the languages you speak and the level of proficiency (basic, working knowledge, business proficient, intermediate, fluent, native/bilingual). For English, indicate TOEFL/IELTS score. Mention your native language as well. But any language of which you only have some very basic understanding is to be left off. Do not mention the Common European Framework of Reference for Languages (CEFR) (*Cadre européen commun de référence pour les langues (CECRL)* as it means nothing to the Americans.

• **Outside experience** (other names for this section: **Personal interests**, **Interests**, **Extracurricular**, **Additional information**). This section is meant to showcase the following skills: team work, time management, organizational skills, involvement in student life, competitive spirit, team spirit, creativity, motivation, caring, trustworthiness, leadership qualities, community work.
Mention team sports as well as individual sports (especially if you are at a competitive level), volunteer or community work, membership of clubs or organizations.

What also matters in this section is to prove your resilience, well-roundedness, open-mindedness and commitment.
It is equally important to mention your experience of different cultures, travelling abroad and artistic competency or appreciation. Blood-giving or training a blind dog is to be mentioned as well.

- **Awards and honors** (optional). Indicate (in reverse chronological order) any prizes, awards, honors or other recognitions for your work with the year it occurred and the organization that granted the award. This may include participation in the Olympiads, prizes at the *Concours general* or any awards bestowed by Ecole/University XXX. This section should also include excellence fellowships awarded by government or public/private institutions.

At this stage in your academic career, it is not vital to put in any references at the end of the CV. On the other hand, when being recommended by a researcher or professional (in bold letters), you should bold her/his name next to project or internship.

4. Do's and don'ts

A few basics for a CV which is to be sent to **academic** institutions:

- Do not replace undergraduate qualifications by Anglo-Saxon equivalents. A bac is a bac or *baccalaureat*(e).
- Your CV should be error-free. Read through and **proofread** it for any spelling or grammar errors.
- Be consistent: use only one font type.
- Make your CV airy.
- Highlight places of education or employment.
- Quantify wherever possible. "Managed a team of five that increased sales by 40% over two years" works better than "Managed a team that significantly increased sales."
- Fancy formatting like **columns** or added **images** can be less readable if the system is scanning left to right.
- Make smart but sparing use of **bold** and *italics*. Avoid underlining for emphasis.
- Use a footer with **page numbers** and your last name, in case pages get separated.
- Label the bottom of every page of your CV (header and footer). This should include your first name, last name and the page number. This way your CV can be put back together.
- For the length of an internship project, at the beginning of the sentence, write it in letters, not figures. Example: `Six-month (* not ~~6-month~~) mission for XXX's Junior enterprise on behalf of a major cosmetics company`
- Save your CV as "BillMartinCV", which makes it easy for the reviewer to find your document instead of a file named "myCV" which could be any student and frustrating to navigate.
- Do not invent or self-aggrandize your skills. If your command of Spanish is basic, do not write that you are bilingual.
- Never put your **photo** on a US or UK CV.
- Do not put your **date of birth**.
- You may use **ONE color** for the headings (dark blue is preferred) as the CV might probably be photocopied. Don't try to trick a software with keywords in white text.

– Do not mention your nationality, race, religion, sex, age (US laws forbids to discriminate on those grounds).
– Do not include adjectives that characterize your studies, research, internships, activities, etc. (`*Did a great internship/fabulous research/an exciting project on...`)
– Do not **go overboard with your descriptions**. Each entry (even those that are highly relevant to your field) should only contain as much detail as is necessary without devolving into verbosity. Generally, anywhere from two to four bullet points per entry should suffice.
– Above all, **never lie** on a CV.

5. Power verbs

There are a certain number of **verbs that you should avoid** on a resume such as do/make/use/get/look/take/keep/have/say/talk/tell/change/start/finish. On the other hand, you should use **dynamic verbs** or **power action verbs** to describe past and present experience. It will grab and keep the readers' attention and give the impression you are a doer. Here are some examples:

Attaining a goal and getting results	to accomplish/to aim at/to attain/to award/to achieve/to advance/to complete/to demonstrate/to earn/to eliminate/to exceed (expectations)/to expedite/to finalize/to fulfill/to generate/to grow/to hasten/to invent/to launch/to optimize/to outperform/to reach/to showcase/to succeed/to surpass/to target/to transform/to uncover
Being creative	to backtrack/to brainstorm/to compose/to conceptualize/to craft/to create/to customize/to design/to develop (*mettre au point*)/to disrupt/to draft/to envision/to fashion/to generate/to imagine/to improvise/to initiate/to innovate/to intuit/to invent/to model/to perform/to problem-solve/to research/to shape/to strategize/to storyboard/to synthesize/to test/to upgrade/to visualize
Being in charge	to be in the driving seat/to be at the wheel/to be at the helm/to be in command/to chair/to coordinate/to delegate/to distribute (tasks)/to ensure/to guide/to handle/to look after/to orchestrate/to oversee/to make sure/to preside over/to resolve/to supervise
Being successful	to achieve (success)/to achieve first place (in an exam)/to bear fruit (*porter ses fruits*)/to boost/to come out on top/to come in first/to come through with flying colors/to bring to fruition (*mener à bien*)/to come to fruition (*se réaliser*)/to deliver/to earn accolades/to earn kudos (for)/to enhance/to expand/to expedite/to face a steep challenge/to further/to gain/to generate/to hit the mark/to implement (*mettre en œuvre*)/to improve/to measure up to expectation/to meet the standards/to optimize/to overcome a challenge/to prevail/to pull it off/to score a success/to secure/to see daylight (*voir le bout du tunnel, voir le jour, aboutir*)/to rest on one's laurels/to roll out (*déployer, lancer*)/to win acclaim/kudos (for)

Being supportive	to advise/to coach/to educate/to guide/to lend a hand to/to mentor/to sponsor/to support
Bringing a project to life	to build/to chart/to create/to design/to develop/to devise/to engineer/to establish/to found/to formalize/to form/to implement/to initiate/to introduce/to launch/to pioneer/to spearhead
Changing/improving	to clarify/to expand/to influence/to integrate/to modify/to overhaul/to redesign/to refine/to refocus/to remodel/to reorganize/to restructure/to revamp/to streamline/to strengthen/to upgrade/to transform
Doing research	to analyze/to assess/to bring to light/to calculate/to compile/to compute/to correlate/to critique/to diagnose/to discover/to evaluate/to examine/to experiment/to explore/to extrapolate/to formulate/to gather (together) /to identify/to inspect/to interpret/to investigate/to map/to measure/to monitor/to observe/to organize/to prove/to publish/to qualify/to quantify/to review/to share/to survey/to test/to track/to uncover
Doing things (**avoid DO**)	to act/to activate/to administer/to apply/to arrange/to carry out/to conduct/to execute/to facilitate/to handle/to perform
Fixing things	to debug/to detect/to diagnose/to fine-tune/to investigate/to probe/to remedy/to repair/to solve/to streamline
Helping (**avoid HELP**)	to aid/to assist/to bolster/to enhance/to enrich/to provide
Leading a project	to chair/to conduct/to coordinate/to head/to operate/to organize/to oversee/to plan/to produce/to program/to schedule
Making things (**avoid MAKE**)	to assemble/to compose/to create/to design/to develop/to devise/to engineer/to establish/to fashion/to formulate/to generate/to produce/to synthesize
Managing a team	to be in charge (of)/to bring together/to champion/to direct/to empower/to enable/to facilitate/to foster/to guide/to inspire/to mentor/to mobilize/to motivate/to program/to schedule/to shape/to supervise/to teach/to train
Meeting with approval	to bring oneself up to standard/to bring oneself up to speed/to come up to scratch/to get oneself up to scratch/to do credit to/to fit the bill/to find favor with/to make the grade/to measure up/to rise to the challenge/to satisfy requirements/to stand the test/to stand up to (the conditions, requirements)
Overseeing/supervising	to apportion/to authorize/to correct/to delegate/to dispatch/to enforce/to ensure/to inspect/to itemize/to modify/to monitor/to overhaul/to screen/to scrutinize/to trace/to verify
Planning	to anticipate/to commission/to determine/to develop/to evaluate/to forecast/to formulate/to identify/to observe/to prepare/to prioritize/to research/to reserve/to strategize/to tailor

Problem solving	to alleviate/to analyze/to brainstorm/to conceive/to conceptualize/to create/to debug/to decipher/to detect/to diagnose/to elucidate/to construe/to engineer/ to fathom (*comprendre, percer un mystère*) /to figure out/to find an answer to/ to formulate/to get a grip on/to get the better of/to get to the bottom of/to hit upon (an idea) /to investigate/to piece together (*reconstituer*) /to put one's heads together/to puzzle out/to put two and two together/to recommend/to remedy/ to remodel/to repair/to revamp/to revive/to solve/to sort out/to surmise (*conjecturer*) /to suss out that (*comprendre que*) /to synthesize/to theorize/to untangle/ to unlock/to weigh the pros and cons/to work on
Teaching/advising	to adapt/to advise/to assist/to clarify/to coach/to coordinate/to encourage/to evaluate/to explain/to foster/to educate/to empower/to encourage/to explain/ to guide/to highlight/to inform/to instruct/to mentor/to present/to promote/ to serve/to supplement/to teach/to train
Writing/ communicating	to address/to advise/to author/to clarify/to co-author/to collaborate/to consult/ to challenge (sb's findings) /to convey/to convince/to contribute/to coordinate/ to counsel/to critique/to debate/to define/to document/to draft/to edit/to enlist/to explain/to formulate/to highlight/to illustrate/to influence/to inform/ to inspire/to interact/to lecture/to mediate/to moderate/to motivate/to persuade/to present/to promote/to question/to review/to submit/to summarize/to supervise/to supplement/to transmit/to update/to welcome

6. Standard format example

BILL MARTIN
Cellphone
Email/LinkedIn QR code (if justified)/Github (optional)

Objective: Application for Graduate Program in Operations Research

Education

ECOLE XXX / University, city (country) **2022-Present**

- One of France's top(-ranking)/leading/premier universities for science and engineering/Business and Management/Education and Research/France's leading science and technology university
- Third-year student specializing in a Master's level program in Operations Research/Applied Math/Biology/Economics/Statistics (with a minor in… see *infra*)
- Double degree program (XXX and XXX)
- BSc with a major in … and a minor in … **2020**

→ *This line is meant for grandes écoles students, to show the difference between the students from the Cycle ingénieur via the University track and those who have enrolled in a Master's degree program only. Note that the diplôme d'ingénieur is recognized as Master of Science in Engineering in the United States and in the countries of the European Union (including France). Since 1999, the*

European Master's Degree is also conferred by the state to the holder of a diplôme d'ingénieur. This is to be differentiated from BS and MS degrees in engineering issued by public universities.

(for bachelor students):
- BSc in Applied Mathematics/Computer science with a minor in… – Final year student

- Relevant coursework includes *The Power of Regression, Simulation and Optimization, Statistics in Action* (do not list all your courses, as the adcom has your transcripts).
- Minor in…

→ *Put course titles in italics and capitalize each first letter except of/in/at*

GPA: 3,97/4.0 (Ranked 1st/2nd in/at the top/in the top 4% of the 2020 class/cohort)

LYCÉE XXX, PREPARATORY PROGRAM, city (country) **2019-2020**

- A **post-secondary** (two-year/three-year depending whether you were 3/5 or 5/2 in a scientific program, or *cube* in a **literary program** or *carré* in a **business program**) **program** in advanced math and physics/math and economics/**leading to nationwide entrance examinations to the *Grandes Ecoles* for scientific studies/business/literary studies/*Ecole Normale Supérieure*[1]**
- Undergraduate coursework includes *Topology, Linear Algebra, Thermodynamics / Literature / the Humanities/Micro/Macro-economics*
- Ranked in the top 5% of admitted students to Ecole XXX (if relevant)

GPA: 4.0/4.0

LYCÉE XXX, CITY (COUNTRY) **June 2019**

Baccalaureat in sciences (=A-levels) awarded with highest honors/high honors
International track in Mandarin (9 hour/week Mandarin classes)
Sports study program (*sport-études*) – High level competitive tennis/rugby/soccer…

Selected research/Project work

TEAM RESEARCH PROJECT **2019-2020**

→ Project subject – Department of – Under the supervision/guidance of Dr/Prof *(if recommended by her/him)* – Brief summary of (current) research

→ *Use dynamic and past verbs. If this is an ongoing project, use the -ING or noun form (developing, devising, designing, development/design of…). If it is a major project, put three bullet points if possible, if less important two or one bullet points.*

- Developed…
- Devised/Designed…
- Evaluated/Selected…
- Built/Structured…
- Used techniques/methodologies…
- Working paper/to be published in/when (if relevant)

1. ENS is an institution training researchers, professors, high-level civil servants, as well as business and political leaders. It focuses on the association of training and research. Make a difference between ENS Paris ULM program and the other ENSs.

- Researched and wrote a term paper analyzing NLP techniques.

→ *Include any publications, such as books, book chapters, articles, book reviews, and more. Include all of the information about each publication (title, journal title, date of publication, and, if applicable, page numbers). Include invited talks and conference participation as well.*

RESEARCH ASSISTANT **2021-PRÉSENT**

– Ecole XXX / University, Department of XXX

- Assistant to Professor **John Warren**, conducting primary and secondary source research.
- Carried out experiments and research according to protocols laid out by Prof. Warren.
- Collected and logged experimental data.
- Assisted in the development and preparation of experiments.
- Conducted statistical analyses of data sets.
- Checked facts, proofread, and edited research documents to ensure accuracy.
- Maintained laboratory equipment and inventory.

EXPERIMENTAL PROJECT *(Modal)* **JAN-JUNE 2021**

– Department of/Laboratory of Optics – Dr/Prof. (first name/last name)

- Research project on risk-return measures and LDI (liability-driven investment) strategies
- Assisted team members in coding (C++ and VBA).
- Enhanced the accuracy in modeling results.

EXPERIMENTAL PROJECT (*TIPE*), Lycée XXX, city (country) **JAN-JUNE 2020**

- Undergraduate research project on…/under the supervision of…

Publications

- Martin, B., other authors. (in press). Title. *Journal*, Volume (Issue), page numbers.
- Martin, B., other authors. (Year produced). Title. Manuscript submitted for publication.
- Martin, B., other authors. (Year draft produced). Title. Manuscript in preparation.

Conference presentations

- Martin, B., other authors. (in press). Title of conference – Place – Paper on… **JUNE 2021**
- Poster presentations
  - Martin, B., Poster session presented at Seattle, WA, USA **FEB 2021**
  - Martin, B., Poster session presented at Sydney, Australia **OCT 2021**

Internship/Work/Leadership + experience *(choose one)*

NAME/PLACE OF INTERNSHIP **2020-2021**

- Name of Company – Desk/Officer – Team under the supervision of (if recommended by the tutor)
- Subject/Topic

- Missions/Tasks/Assignments/Goals
  - Developed a user-friendly budgeting software using JavaScript and Python.
  - Coordinated data mining team and presentations to management.
  - Created a training program for new hires.
  - Was put in charge of designing new web interface.
- Findings/Results
  - Achieved 98% improvement in data accuracy.
- Processes (tools, methods, skills)
- The human factor
  - In charge of the Python coding team
  - Led the development of new programming tools
  - → *Bullet points for accomplishments (use verbs in the past) (put two or three bullet points depending on relevance)*

French Navy – Leadership training, Officer cadet **2020-2021**

- Part of Ecole XXX's first-year curriculum
  - Officer on/of the watch (OOW) on board the *Jane Eyre* frigate/aircraft carrier *Charles de Gaulle*
  - Deployed to Indian Ocean.
  - In charge of the bridge team
  - In charge of smooth and safe navigation of the ship
  - In charge of surveillance missions and anti-pirate operations off Somalia
  - Monitored and arrested smuggling gangs off Libya.
  - Boarded and searched (*arraisonner*) vessels suspected of human trafficking.
  - Carried out fishing inspections in France's territorial waters.
  - Taught math and physics for servicemen/enlisted men/enlisted personnel/new recruits/NCOs (non-commissioned officers) preparing internal examinations/to advance through the ranks/ to advance their careers.

Paris Fire Brigade (BSPP)/Marseille Naval Fire Battalion (BMPM) **2020-2021**

- Emergency Medical Services vehicle crew leader. Commanded a rescue and rapid response vehicle comprising a crew and emergency material equipment for firefighting operations, first aid and rescue service, property and environment protection.
- Part of Ecole/University XXX's first-year curriculum
  - Served on a first aid and emergency vehicle.
  - Rotated between night and day shifts.
  - Assisted medical first responders in traffic fatalities, suicide attempts, apartment fires.
  - Taught first aid.
  - Field operations combatting wildlife fires
  - Rescued people from road traffic accidents.
  - Led investigations in possible cases of arson.
  - Delivered basic life support for cardiac arrest victims.
  - Inspected building to ensure they were up to current building fire codes.
  - Brought first aid to car crashes victims.
  - Coaxed suicidal people out of jumping (from).

National Gendarmerie – Officer cadet **2020-2021**

– Part of Ecole/University XXX's first year curriculum
- Assisted unit commander in drawing up emergency/contingency plans for riot control and prevention.
- Took part in field operations (investigations, tracking of suspects, hot pursuit of wrongdoers, arrest of drug kingpins and traffickers).
- Dealt with cases of family abuse and battered children

Apprentis d'Auteuil, Paris (France) **2020-2021**

– A 150-year-old non-profit youth development charity/committed to helping young people in distress/providing access to quality education and training/whose mission is to help struggling youths in need and raise their academic ambitions.
- Taught math, physics and English to 11th grade students/undergrads.
- Mentorship of/mentored students seeking to strengthen their competencies.
- Created and graded course assessments to ensure students understood material and stayed on track.
- Planned lessons and assignments, led discussion sections, graded papers and exams.
- Organized and led group discussions on social and academic issues.
- Assisted troubled youths in pursuing a professional path so that they could integrate society.
- Supported young drop-outs to help them find their way back to school and to society.
- Helped young people to gain confidence in themselves, become free and responsible adults.

La main à la Pâte, Location **2020-2021**

– A non-profit educational association which aims at improving the quality of science and technology teaching in primary and middle schools
- Implemented inquired-based learning to stimulate a scientific spirit in pupils.
- Designed and conducted scientific experiments in physics.

L'enfant @ l'hôpital, Location **2020-2021**

– A non-profit association meant to help hospitalized children
- Visiting young hospitalized patients/inpatients across France
- Set up workshops to initiate children to digital photography.
- Set up writing and drawing workshops.
- Established a routine of play-based activities to help physically or mentally handicapped children develop social skills.
- Updated content for the association's website.

High School Instructor, Location **2020-2021**

– Teaching in a priority action school (ZEP or priority action zone)

– A second chance school committed to facilitating the integration into society of drop-out youths
- Taught math and physics to middle school children from underprivileged backgrounds.
- Collaborated weekly with other tutors and professors to develop effective tutoring strategies.
- Set up activities and workshops in math and physics.
- Organized field trips to science museums.
- Invited lecturers specialized in science for all (astrophysics, nanotechnology, AI).

Skills

– **Computer/Programming/IT**

- C/C++, VBA, JavaScipt, Matlab, VHDL, LaTex, Visual Studio, Mathcad, Xilinx, HTML, CSS, Ruby
- Computer aided design/engineering: optical imaging, AutoCAD, Patran, Abaqus

→ *Do not include Microsoft Office tools (Word, Excel...)*

– **Languages**

- Mandarin (native), French (fluent), English (TOEFL/IELTS score), Japanese (basic); German (intermediate), Russian (advanced)

Awards/Honors/Citations

International Olympiads of Mathematics

- Gold medal winner (Bulgaria) **2021**
- Silver medal recipient (Ukraine) **2020**
- Bronze medal (Outer Mongolia) **2019**
- Honorable mention **2018**

France's National Academic contest for 11th and 12th grade high school students

- First Prize (Math, Physics) **2020**
- Second/Third Prize (Latin, Greek, Philosophy) **2020**
- Regional Award (Chinese, Geography, History) **2020**

Awards

- France's Defense Ministry Bronze Medal for acts of courage **2020**
- Outstanding Leadership award bestowed by XXX **2021**
- Outstanding Investment award for involvement in XXX's student community **2021**
- Flag Honor Guard member **2022**

Academic awards

- Academic Excellence award **2020**
- Morocco's Ministry of Education, Academic scholarship **2019**
- Summer Research Grant, Center for Summer Studies, Palo Alto, CA
- Recipient of the McArthur grant **2022**
- Fulbright Scholarship to pursue an MS at Harvard **2022**
- Graduating with honors and ranking 3rd among engineering majors at XXX (second year) **2021**

Extracurricular/Outside activities

STUDENT ASSOCIATIVE LIFE/ASSOCIATIONS/CLUBS/SOCIETIES **2020-2021**

1 – **Junior enterprise** – Treasurer/President/Officer

2 – **Career Fair** (careers fair, UK, job fair, career expo)
- In charge of public relations
- Point student for school management and the corporate world
- Prospected and pitched potential exhibitors.

3 – **Cabinet Start-up**
- A non-profit association whose mission is to promote entrepreneurship and innovation.
- Organized start-up contests/entrepreneurship competitions/business plan competitions and start-up week-ends.
- Set up conferences with innovators as lecture guests.

4 – Ecole/University XXX's **Music Festival Club**
- Chair/Vice-chair
- In charge of logistics and management of a 30k€ budget
- In charge of fund-raising/public relations/liaising with partner schools

5 – Ecole/University XXX's **Film Society**
- Organized screenings and debates with audiences and filmmakers.
- Led group discussion for students on cinematic techniques topics.
- Project producer for school documentaries
- Wrote storyboards and developed animation films.
- Screenwriting/casting/shooting/sound recording and pre-production/editing, and screening

6 – Ecole/University XXX's **Welcome Week**/Orientation Week/Frosh Week/Freshers' Week
- Planned and strategized the events calendar/orientation program.
- Organized a Welcome BBQ/Pancake breakfast.
- In charge of logistics for a ski week-end trip to the Alps
- Assisted with check-in procedures for incoming international students.
- Helped incoming international students with information on procedures and resources for their successful arrival on campus.

7 – **Editor-in-chief** of *XXX Magazine*
- The school monthly magazine
- Addresses issues of arts and sciences.
- Managed a team of 12.

8 – **Model United Nations** (MUN/Model UN)
- MUN Madrid Conference 2022 – Chair (moderator/director)/Vice-chair of a committee dais – Crisis staffer of a crisis committee
- Sharpened research, public speaking, debating, negotiation and writing skills, in addition to critical thinking, teamwork, and leadership.
- Developed a deeper understanding of current world issues as representative of (XXX).
- Formulated position papers and created policy proposals to be debated with other delegates in their committee – Drafted policy resolutions.
- Voted Outstanding Delegate/Received Best Delegate award – Awarded best position paper

9 – **Miscellaneous**
- Charity Gala Ball Association
- Cooking Club
- Drama Club
- Eventing/three-day eventing
- Ecole/University XXX's Debating Union/Debate Society/Debating Society/Debate club
- Heritage club: an association dedicated to maintaining the school's centuries-old traditions
- XXX's Improv' Group/Theater company/Performed to live audiences.
- Robotics Club
- The Fair Trade (and organic food) grocery shop
- Week of International Languages and Cultures
- Week of Sustainable Development

STUDENT REPRESENTATIVE COUNCIL/ADMINISTRATIVE COUNCIL **2020-2021**

– Ecole XXX – In charge of international affairs/International students' representative
- Was a voice for the students to ensure that they have a qualitative learning experience.
- Acted as a bridge between the college staff and the 2020 cohort/class.
- Resolved issues and shared ideas for enhancement of teaching and learning.
- Acted as a key contact between staff and the fellow class members regarding safety, facilities and student welfare needs.
- Gathered feedback to share with staff and work collaboratively.
- Communicated new ideas and concepts with XXX teams in the best interest of students.
- Coordinated with office bearers of student societies.

MICROFINANCE INSTITUTE, ECOLE/UNIVERSITY XXX **2020-2021**
- Officer in charge of fund raising
- Put together mission to distribute £300k in microloans and credit access to a hundred of families in Totonicapan and Villa Nueva.
- Allowed businesses and their owners to build or expand their small business (weaving, sewing, craftsmanship, candle making workshop, baking business), and make purchases that lie outside of their disposable income.
- Helped support Guatemalan families, improve their lives, and provide an education for their children.

TEACHING EXPERIENCE **2020-2021**

1 – **Oral examiner** in math and physics for undergraduates preparing for *Grandes Ecoles* examinations
- Set up weekly two-hour sessions to train the students for national exams.
- Held weekly sessions to answer questions on course material.
- Used instructional technology to enhance pedagogical techniques.

2 – ***Tremplin* association** – Ecole/University XXX

– A non-profit association run by students and whose mission is to promote equality of opportunity
- Helped struggling students from less privileged districts.
- Designed class material for high school students.
- Assisted 11th and 12th grade students/post-bac students in organizing their homework and work methods and raising their ambitions/to succeed in their college education/university curriculum.

- Advised, tutored and mentored two students from Syria.
- Taught math and physics to a class of 15 college freshmen.
- Counselled students experiencing difficulties in the course.
- Tutored students needing remediation in math and physics.
- Graded term papers, test papers, and student tutorial participation.
- Organized field trips to local museums.
- Put together scientific workshops in preparation for the *baccalaureat* during midterm breaks.
- Led discussions/debates on scientific topics of general interest.

Music and music appreciation

- Piano/Cello/Violin (15 years) – Numerous concerts across Europe (Berlin Philharmonic Orchestra, Paris Orchestra, guest player)
- Member and soloist of Ecole/University XXX's philharmonic orchestra
- Lead singer in Ecole/University XXX's *Romeo and Juliet* musical

Volunteer/Charity/community involvement **2020-2021**

- Member of *Cheer Up!,* a non-profit organization dedicated to teaching and entertaining young cancer patients in hospital cancer wards/organizing play-based activities for disabled students/to help them develop social skills/fund-raising activities for the association
- Red Cross: outreach missions on mobile assistance teams – Distribution of food and blankets to homeless people/assisted people in need – volunteer at a soup kitchen/food kitchen/meal center
- Promoted ethnic, gender and geographical diversity in STEM fields across France's high schools as part of the *Opération Monge.*
- Youth summer camp counselor - Counselor in training (CIT) – Organized summer camps and ran activities for 8-12-year-old children.
- Scout leader – Organized and managed several Summer camps for 12-15-year-old youths.

Arts (Photography/Drawing/Painting/Dancing)

- Numerous exhibitions in Paris - Portfolio to be accessed at [link]

Sports

- Tennis (15 years, cadet and junior national champion/world champion/Wimbledon jr. championships, semi-finalist)
- Chess (Glicko rating system, Glicko-2 rating system, Elo rating system: Class D, category 4/ Class C, category 3/Class B, category 2…)
- Marathon running (took part in the Boston, New York and Paris marathons)
- Soccer: XXX's A-team, midfielder, center (*pivot*), center forward, goalkeeper…
- Adventure racing (*raid*), sky diving (*parachutisme*), scuba diving (*plongée*)
- Judo (15 years, brown/black belt)
- Head of judo section – in charge of events and logistics
- In charge of organizing a trip to Japan for the 50-member judo team
- In charge of supplies for the sports section common room (*bar d'étage*)

EDUCATIONAL TRAVEL

- Names of countries, dates, purpose **2020-2021**
- Extensive traveling across the four continents

Miscellaneous

- First aid certificate
- Youth worker certificate/Qualified youth worker/Youth activity leader certificate/activity organizer certificate/teen leadership certificate (***BAFA***)
- Blood giver
- Trainer for assistance dogs/guide dogs/seeing eye dogs (US)
- Farm hand during harvesting season
- Pet sitter, dog walker
- Delivery driver
- Certified lifeguard at the local swimming pool (trained in CPR, AED and first aid)
- Dishwasher, server, hostess

PART III
THE LETTER OF RECOMMENDATION (LOR)

1. General

Letters of recommendation play a vital role in the admission process. They provide evaluations of the applicant by professors, advisors and/or supervisors who have monitored the applicant's work or research over a period of time.

Graduate schools seek recommendations for the same reason employers require career references. They want to know what people who have seen you in class, who have supervised your research or project work and experienced your efforts firsthand have to say about you. Nearly every other resource you provide to a school is a first-person accounting. Your résumé is your interpretation of your career achievements, your essay answers a question with your opinion or tells a story from your point of view, and your admissions interview includes questions that, again, are answered from a technical or personal point of view. A recommendation letter, on the other hand, is all about someone else's perspective on you, your potential, and your accomplishments.

The more competitive the program, the more the letters count in the final decision-making process. All the finalists in a competitive program are outstanding in many respects (such as grades, research experience, test scores) and therefore letters of recommendation help in selecting the pick of the litter. If you are a borderline candidate, the letters will count even more. A carefully thought-out letter can push you into the admit category whereas a lukewarm endorsement will doom your candidacy. A strong letter could even erase almost any blemish on your application.

A recommendation letter is an exercise in **transparency** and **honesty**. An admissions committee is shrewd enough to spot anomalies in the letters. They have faculty who have reviewed applications year after year and have read a variety of recommendation letters, besides composing them for their own students. They can thus use some helpful clues to find out whether the recommendation has been drafted in confidentiality by the person it claims to be. Even easier to figure out are cases where the recommendation writer clearly does not know the applicant well and has written the letter off a standard template. Such letters usually just praise the applicant without citing any personal experiences or facts to support their claims. Therefore, they sound too generic and could have been written by the recommender for any applicant.

A good letter is one where the recommender talks in detail about the actual work done under their supervision by the applicant, how they fared at the task and other specific instances from their interactions with the applicant. That is why graduate schools encourage you to choose a reference who knows you well enough to write about you in a detailed and persuasive manner. Do not hesitate to go and talk to the potential recommender and to make yourself known. Discuss your options. Ask for advice. For those who are shy, that can be a problem but you need to get out of your shell and spread your wings.

Make a **list** of possible recommenders prior to asking any of them. Fact is some professors will clearly not bother to answer, will be too busy to deal with the matter through a "write it yourself and I'll sign it". Some are ignorant of the application process and, being French, believe that a two-paragraph letter is enough for the bright student she/he thinks you are. Others clearly have no command of the language and either will ask you to write the letter or will pen a gargled draft that does not make head or tail of your qualities and performances.

Better have someone that knows you well and thinks highly of you than a celebrity letter writer who knows nothing about you. In the same way, a letter from your immediate supervisor will have more clout than a vague letter from someone higher up. This ensures that their letter of recommendation will actually have substance and will not simply be full of fluff or vague opinions about your work attitude and academic performance. Someone who knows you well will be able to provide well-informed opinions and concrete examples to back them up. The more **detailed** the letter, the more likely it is to tip the admissions scale in your favor. That is why you should choose the recommenders **carefully**. A letter of recommendation can easily make or break your application. That is why it matters to interact with the professor, and make sure you count in and outside class.

Now, avoid the letter by 'recommenders' that will not pen the letter themselves but will let the students do so with a flippant "Write it and I'll sign it". After a while, you can be sure that the letters coming from those recommenders (and in which the students will write `"Bill XX is the brightest student I have ever had the pleasure and privilege to teach over the past decade/in my entire career"` will soon carry no weight whatsoever. **It is the duty of a professor or researcher worthy of the name to take her/his students and mission to heart, and that means supporting personally the students' applications to graduate programs**.

Keep in mind that the admissions committee will expect letters from certain people – a project supervisor, a professor that is key to the subject matter you target in a school. A customized letter according to each program is welcome if it mentions personal ties between the recommender and the targeted school.

2. Approaching potential recommenders

Who should you approach and how? There are two basic conditions: approach someone that knows you well and someone in whose class, during whose project or internship you performed at the top. For example, a professor in whose class you had an A+, in which you did a project, and in which you were an active participant. Similarly, a professor whose research you have read about would be a good fit and a strong basis for discussion and application options.

When should you approach a potential recommender? Conditions vary, of course depending on whether you ask a faculty or someone in the industry, after an internship, for example. Approaching a professor at some point in the last few weeks of the Spring term is an ideal solution, providing you already have a general idea of the program you might apply for. By doing so, you give the recommender a heads-up way before the hectic Fall semester starts. Of course, you can always try to secure a recommendation in the Fall term. Yet, you run the risk of being turned down and having to scramble to find a suitable substitute. Also, the recommender will not have any concrete results on hand to post a strong evaluation. Any last-minute option is to be avoided.

Should that professor be aligned with the program you are applying for? Not necessarily, and perhaps it is ill advised. You need to have as different people write as many different (and positive) things about you as possible. Therefore, selecting a Mechanics professor when you apply for a data science program is not an idea that should be rejected outright. The recommender will stress the skills you have developed, the interest you have taken in the subject matter, your commitment and seriousness, etc. In the same way, you may try to think of a recommender beyond the curriculum and the internship or professional experience. Suppose you have been playing the violin at an advanced level, performing on stage across the country's top concert halls, and being part of a well-known orchestra: in that case, why not ask your former/present music teacher to pen a letter?

How you approach a professor, a researcher or a tutor for a letter of recommendation is part of a strategy to build a strong application. You must approach the letter writers at the earliest possible moment yet under the condition that they have some material to base their letters on. If you ask a recommender right from the beginning of the term, chances are that you will be spurned, and rightly so.

Also, recommenders are busy people, and you should be considerate of their time commitment. So, when you approach them, be sure to have several documents in hand so that their time will not be squandered. Plus, you will be taken seriously.

One thing **you should never do** is write a professor cold to ask him for a recommendation as in the following example:

```
*Hi, I am preparing my application to study in the United States. Could you write me a recommendation letter? Thank you very much and have a nice day.
```

But I suggest an email along those lines:

```
Dear Professor Martin,
My name is XX, I was a student in the class on… you taught last year/I was part of the project on… that you supervised last year/I was on the team you supervised at…
I am currently considering my options for graduate studies and would be much interested in having your views and advice on the subject.
Would it be possible to arrange a meeting at your convenience? I look forward to hearing from you.
Respectfully/Cordially
```

3. Help them be a good writer

You should not appear unexpectedly at the professor's door to ask him for a letter, nor should you corral her/him at the end of a long class to put in your request. Selecting a professor that knows you well means you have interacted with her/him during your undergraduate years and possibly exchanged on your academic plans at the graduate level. If that is the case, it is not rare therefore that the professor will raise the question of the LOR herself/himself.

In any case, you ought to make an appointment with your recommender to discuss your options for graduate studies. When you go in for the meeting, bring some essential elements that might be helpful for the professor to write the recommendation, such as:

- a **CV/resume**
- a copy of printed **transcripts** with the relevant classes highlighted and the corresponding grades
- a list of **targeted programs** you plan to apply for
- a **graded work sample** (paper/lab)
- a **list of professors** you intend to ask for letters
- a **draft** or **outline** of your **personal statement** or **statement of purpose** (to help the recommender tailor the letter better)
- a list of bullet points or **talking points** reminding the recommender of the class you took (content), the skills you demonstrated, detailing your ambitions by joining a graduate program. Those can only be suggestions as some recommenders resent all kinds of interference in their tasks and duties, whereas others are rather hands-off. So, handle the matter with care.
- a **list** of what you think would be most **important** for a graduate program to know about you.
- a clear **indication** of when you need the letters to be **submitted**. In that respect, **keep track** of the status of the letters. Remind the recommenders every so often to upload their letters and give them a big heads up two weeks prior to the deadline. It is your responsibility to make sure the letters are sent in time.
- Also, take some notes during the interview, ask whether she/he knows professors/researchers in the programs you are aiming at. Naturally ask her/him about the quality of the schools you plan to attend. This part of course is not necessary if your recommender's domain is not the one you are aiming at in a program abroad.
- At the end of the interview, ask her/him whether she/he would be willing to write you not just a letter but a **strong letter**:

Professor Martin, would you be comfortable making a **strong** recommendation for graduate studies in XXX?

If the answer is somewhat lukewarm, explore other options.

Always stress the **dates** when you are going to apply and the deadlines as well. Some recommenders may feel time-constrained and unable to honor their recommendation obligations. That is why it is preferable to give the recommender at least **two weeks' notice** to write the letter. So, do not hesitate to ask:

Professor Martin, I will be applying by December 15. Will you be able to have the letter ready by then?

If the recommender accepts, please send a warm-hearted message of thanks once the letter has been submitted (the university will inform you about it). And of course, if you get admitted, send your recommenders a warm thank-you note.

4. Waiving your right to see the letters

In the U.S., letters of recommendation can be reviewed by an applicant thanks to the Family Educational Right and Privacy Act (FERPA), commonly known as the Buckley Amendment (1974). It is a federal law that affords parents the right to have access to their children's educational records, the right to seek to have the records amended, and the right to have some control over the disclosure of personally identifiable information from the education records. When a student turns 18 years old, or enters a postsecondary institution at any age, the rights under FERPA transfer from the parents to the student ("eligible student").

Because it has made professors nervous and because nervous professors do not make honest letter writers, universities have come up with the idea of allowing students to **waive their right to see the recommendation letters** when they apply online. **You should waive your right**. There is no question about it. First, you trust your recommenders enough to draft strong and supportive letters, so no need to plant the seeds of doubt in their minds, especially as they will be informed of whether you have waived your right or not when uploading the material. Second, the committee looks more favorably at letters for which the right has been waived, since this ensures confidentiality of the letters and reduces the chance that the letter writer was influenced by the applicant. Graduate programs are most likely to discount the recommendations, however strong they may be, when a student retains the right to review the file. Three, recommenders generally will share the letter with you (if not why would they recommend someone they do not support?) so you have a general idea of the content.

5. Additional information for recommenders

In addition, there are fields that the recommender will have to fill in the recommendation form. They may include:

- The recommender's position/title. In general, the higher the title, the stronger the recommendation. Recommendations from the Head of the Department, a dean, a senior researcher or a senior manager also carry weight. Please, note that any recommendation will work only if it has a personal touch to it and if the recommender has indeed had a close association with the applicant.
- The recommender's relation to the applicant.
- The duration for which the recommender has known the applicant. It is highly preferable to have at least one recommender who has known the applicant for a year or more rather than during just one class or one project.
- The duration for which the recommender has been writing such recommendations for his/her students/employees. The committee is more comfortable with someone that has been writing letters for their students for a while than with someone who is writing their first letter.
- The number of such recommendations she/he has written earlier.
- The pool of students/employees she/he is comparing the applicant with, and its size. The recommendation form typically asks the recommender to rate the applicant as being in the "top 1-2%", "top 10%", "first quarter", "second quarter", etc., of an evaluation pool. The pool might be a class, a group of interns, the group of students supervised by the recommender...
- The rank of the applicant when compared to that pool.

- The strength of the recommendation. The recommender has to choose on the form whether she/he "strongly recommends", "recommends", "recommends with reservations" or "does not recommend" the applicant. This, along with the rating gives the committee a summary of the recommender's opinion, even before reading the actual recommendation letter. Each of these elements play a role in determining the overall efficacy of the recommendation.

If the recommender is not receiving an email containing a unique link to upload their letter, resend the link via your application management and ask your recommender to check their **spam** folder. If they still do not receive it, the recommender can email their letter directly to the department to upload. Please note that due to staff availability, this will also take time. If not received by the deadline via email, the letter will not be considered.

You are not supposed to update documents after the deadline. Updated documents (*e.g.* transcripts, CV/resume, statement of purpose) are not uploaded to applications after the deadline. If you have submitted your application before the deadline and have emailed an updated document on or before the deadline, they will do their best to upload it. Due to the volume of requests and limited staffing, they unfortunately cannot guarantee it, most especially the weekend prior and/or the day of the deadline.

6. The format

- Letters should indicate the candidate's full name (*i.e.* first and last name). Preferably in the 1st paragraph.
- As the letter is in English, first name is OK to characterize the recommendee.
- Letters should not reference a particular institution or program.
- Letters should be typewritten or word-processed. Handwritten letters do not scan clearly.
- Letters require the writer's signature. Please use blue or black ink as lighter colors do not scan well.
- Letters should conclude with legible identifying personal information: full name, title, institution, mailing address, telephone number and email address. If you provide an e-mail, a confirmation will be sent informing you that they have received your letter.
- Programs will require three letters of recommendation in general. Choose two professors + one professional (internship supervisor) or project tutor. Pay attention to PhD programs: usually they require three letters from academics. An 'academic' referee is someone who has taught you during your university-level studies.
- In accordance with US federal laws and university policy, authors of letters of recommendation are asked to refrain from comments regarding a candidate's race, color, gender, religion, age, physical or mental disability, marital status, sexual orientation, national origin, citizenship, medical condition, or political affiliations, beliefs or activities.

7. Don'ts

- Pay attention: the committee takes the **overly glorifying letters** with a grain of salt. The letter must present a fair and positive assessment of a candidate, without being over-enthusiastic.

Thus, sentences like `Bill Martin is undoubtedly the next Bill Gates of his generation` smacks of bombastic flatulence.

- **Don't** fall into the **trap of cliches**. Calling someone a *go-getter with a heart of gold who leaves no stone unturned and is a friend to all* may elicit a yawn or eye roll from the admissions officer.
- **Don't** accidentally communicate **something negative** about the student. For instance, a phrase like "leads by example" or "excels at working independently" could indicate that the student keeps to herself/himself and has trouble working with others.
- **Don't** feel compelled to **repeat** every grade, club, and award which is on the student's resume. A letter of recommendation is not a repeat of a student's resume. It is not a catalog of data points.
- **Don't** speak about every **quality** that makes the student great. In fact, well-rounded students aren't necessarily what the most competitive schools are looking for. While selective schools look for academic excellence in most subjects, what they really appreciate is a student's singular commitment to a specific and distinct area.
- **Don't cast too wide a net** and end up saying very little, because you tried to say too much.

8. The 3D approach

- Three letters of recommendation mean that each will contribute to giving a **holistic** portrait of who you are. Make sure your recommenders' letters do not **overlap**, in other words make sure they will add to your portrait and avoid redundancy. Make sure the letters do not repeat the same things. You need to extract as much value from each letter as possible. Ideally, they ought to cover different aspects of your personality and focus on different strengths. You can work this out by collaborating with the recommenders, and ask them to highlight certain strengths.
- Do not ask a professor that taught you high school math. This is too long ago and it conveys the message that no one since then has been in a position to support your application, for lack of results, performance, etc. It sends a wrong signal.
- A letter of recommendation should highlight the **uniqueness** of a candidate providing insights into her/his talents and personality.
- It **does not matter** whether the recommender is **well known** or not. What matters is that she/he knows you from the inside, because of specific reasons (you were in her/his class, she/he supervised your research, etc.). Of course, if a Nobel Prize winner for whom you have done research wishes to recommend you, say yes!
- A letter outside the academic realm is not necessarily to be pushed aside. For example, a student who has been playing the violin since the age of six, has performed in an orchestra and played abroad, while continuing to study with a renowned violin professor. The student also happens to be outstanding in science as well. Therefore, letters from science professors might repeat how good and proficient the student is, whereas a letter from the violin teacher will add a different touch to the portrait.
- To have as extensive a portrait as possible:
  – A professor will focus on your theoretical intelligence, analytical, reasoning skills.
  – A researcher will mention your skills at research and projects, autonomy, risk-taking.
  – The project/internship supervisor will describe your contribution in a professional context and your capacity at handling problems.

- Be enthusiastic in your recommendation, discussing both a student's academic ability and potential and her/his character and personality.
- Letters of recommendation are read with great care. Admissions officers put a lot of weight on them, be they academic skills or personal qualities. So, make no mistakes about it: LORs are key components of a successful application.

9. The key points

a. Why I am recommending Bill Martin and how I met him
b. How I recruited Bill Martin
c. Who I am and what I do
d. Coursework/Research project/Internship
e. The student's/intern's skills and personality as they could be observed
f. A personal anecdote if one
g. Why the recommender thinks you'll be a splendid addition to the program

a. Why I am recommending Bill Martin and how I met him
You can begin the letter with a **creative or catchy hook**, or a more straightforward **statement of endorsement**, as long as you include these key components in the introduction. Here are a few examples:

- I'm writing to express my wholehearted support for Bill Martin's application to graduate studies at your university. Bill was a student of mine in the class I teach on… .

- I'm writing to recommend Bill Martin. I worked with Bill for the three months at EdTech Projects in the summer 2021; for four of six missions he was my direct report.

- It is my pleasure to provide this letter of recommendation for Bill as he seeks admission to a graduate program in your university.

- It is my pleasure to offer my unreserved recommendation for Bill Martin for his application to graduate studies in your university.

- It is my honor and pleasure to provide this letter of recommendation for Bill Martin as he pursues admission to graduate studies in the U.S./UK.

- As Bill Martin's sole direct manager at EdTech, I've worked closely with him over the past three months, sharing the same open office space the majority of the time. Bill showed excellent communication skills and consistently exceeded my expectations.

- We hired Bill after graduation in part due to his outstanding performance as an intern the previous summer.
- It is my great pleasure to provide this recommendation for Bill, whom I enjoyed teaching and getting to know as his Statistics Professor.
- I have known Bill for three years in my position as Dean of Studies of the Paris VI University.
- I am delighted to write this recommendation for Bill, whom I have mentored since last year and whose research I supervised as her academic advisor.
- Please accept this letter as my enthusiastic endorsement of Bill, the top student in my Chemistry class.
- Bill Martin has asked me to recommend him for graduate studies in the United States. He was my student in the class on… I teach/an intern with the company I run…/I know him well and am happy to oblige.

b. How I recruited Bill Martin

Say something about how you recruited Bill, if you were a supervisor or a manager:

- I met Bill Martin when he was hired for the company I work for. He was put under my responsibility and for several weeks I was his direct supervisor.
- We recruited Bill amongst several high-quality candidates and following three grueling rounds of interviews. He passed them all with flying colors.
- I was in charge of interviewing Bill Martin after he had applied for an intern position in the Pricing Department I am in charge of.
- I met Bill Martin at Ecole XXX's career fair when he came up to discuss options with the company. I was immediately and pleasurably awed by his determination. He was to be invited for a round of interviews in the following weeks.
- Bill Martin was recruited through an exacting interview process during which he was duly vetted. He was given three sets of interviews—technical mostly—during which he sailed through/performed splendidly/impressed the HR/me for his knowledge and skills as well as his dynamism and ambition.
- As Bill's direct manager who worked closely with him throughout his time here, I was impressed with his work ethic, friendly personality, and ability to work well under pressure.

c. Who I am and what I do

Graduate schools are primarily interested in recommendations that come from **professors** who **know the applicant** and her/his academic work as well as from employers. They are interested in faculty members' summary estimates of the candidate's general promise as a graduate student. The more the recommendation reflects real knowledge of the applicant and her/his performance, the more useful the letter is to the graduate school admissions committees and thus to the applicant. Therefore, state who you are, your position at the school/company/laboratory, etc.

Say something about what you teach and how long you have been teaching at the institution or what is your area of research and for how long/What you specialize in…

- Who I am (Prof./Dr/Head of a Lab/member of the CNRS).
- I am head of the Pricing Division at SocGen/HSBC.
- I am CTO of a fast-growing startup located in San Francisco.
- I am Director of the Private Equity Division at Goldman Sachs.
- Our factory is a global automotive supplier. The main customers are VW, Audi, Jaguar Land Rover, BMW and Daimler.
- The quality department comprises the areas "quality projects, quality assurance customer/production, examinations, factory quality" and includes a personnel responsibility for 14 employees.
- The team Bill worked on comprises 20 employees placed under the supervision of an assistant manager and myself, the manager.

Say something about your school, college or *grande ecole*: one of the finest universities for science that selects the top XXX science students in France following a rigorous selection process through nationwide entrance examinations, for example.

d. Coursework/Research project/Internship

- Course description and various subjects tackled during the course
- Description of the research project carried out by the student:
  - project goal
  - findings
  - process (methodology)
- Description of the various missions/assignments/tasks the intern carried out at the French embassy/with a company/with the R&D department of a large business/in a research lab/in a law firm/in a medical ward/at the desk of a daily newspaper/magazine
  - mission goal
  - results
  - process (methodology)
  - performance
  - skills developed
- The student's performance (results)

- She/he consistently ranked in the top 5% of the class.
- Bill is the most talented and driven law student I have taught in my twenty years at University XXX.
- Bill is one of the top three students I have ever had the pleasure of teaching.
- Bill is by far one of the best interns I have ever been privileged to work with.
- Bill's results were among the best of the class in the finals.
- He persistently performed in the top 1% of the class in the various assignments I gave.

e. The student's/intern's skills and personality as they could be observed

We'll distinguish here Bill's **intellectual characteristics**, his **knowledge of the field of study**, his **communications skills**, his **personal characteristics**, his **interpersonal skills and leadership ability**.

- **Intellectual characteristics**:
  – ability to deal with complex or abstract matters
  – ability to grasp new ideas
  – analytical skills
  – blazing trails, exploring areas of research he is not familiar with
  – capacity to learn and retain information
  – fine attention to detail/detail-oriented
  – focused, goal-driven
  – forward looking
  – intellectual and scientific curiosity
  – not risk averse/bold
  – overall intelligence
  – pushing the borders of the science
  – reasoning skills
  – skill in analysis and logic
  – thinking outside the box
  – willingness to take intellectual risks
- **Knowledge of field of study**:
  – ability to use the methods in the field of study or experience in research
  – depth and breadth of knowledge in the field
  – has the requisite laboratory techniques
  – in-depth research through papers and books
- **Communication skills**
  – active in class, stellar class presentation
  – an effective writer
  – articulate in oral expression

– clear, well written and forceful presentations and written work
– clear, well-organized and forceful written material
– the written work submitted demonstrated a mastery of the conventions of English

- Bill was a pleasure to work with, bringing his attention to detail to every project. His communication and people skills are excellent, and he elicited some innovative ideas.

- I was impressed with Bill's writing skills, initiative, and ability to meet deadlines.

- His enthusiasm for his work and his superb communication skills made him an instant asset to the company.

- He has worked across social media, email campaigns, and other public relations outreach to effect viral engagement.

- He showed remarkable skills in communicating effectively with all via email or in person calls.

- His analytical abilities are first rate. He has designed several methodologies that are now in use throughout the company. Perhaps more importantly and harder to define, he always understands the reasoning or the goal behind any analysis that he performs. This is a rare and refreshing trait.

- Bill has his finger on the pulse of technological trends and provides content that is both useful and meaningful to clients.

- Bill has the combination of business acumen and communication skills that makes him an outstanding intern.

- Bill also impressed me with his commitment. He successfully collaborated with his mentor, took advantage of several professional development opportunities offered by the company, and took online classes on digital technology to keep up with the state of the art.

- Bill made the most of technology to provide modern solutions, and drive results.

- When I gave Bill an assignment, I knew it would be done right, on time and in excess of my specifications. If he has any flaw, it is adding enhancements to assignments, doing more than what was asked. In summary, he is a true gem to management and will rise rapidly in any organization that will employ him.

- **Personal characteristics**:
  - strong team worker
  - ability to sustain long-term focus
  - able to work independently/autonomously
  - capacity to take criticism and build on it
  - charismatic and exercises compelling charm that inspires those around him
  - possess conflict resolution skills
  - creativity, inventiveness, ability to apply knowledge creatively
  - capacity to develop a rapport with management characterized by mutual respect
  - passionate about helping
  - enjoy the trust and respect of fellow students and peers
  - fine-tuned leadership skills
  - have empathy
  - industry and self-discipline
  - lead by example
  - persistent, efficient and motivated
  - possess maturity and personal adjustment requisite for graduate study
  - rigor, enthusiasm, curiosity, energetic, thoroughness
  - sense of initiative
  - sense of responsibility
  - seek or create opportunities to make use of his native ability and how effectively he exploits it
  - well-rounded personality
  - willingness to work together toward the common good

- Allow me to point out three examples of Bill's strengths.
- Bill quickly became a valuable member of the leadership circle. He was able to sustainably improve projects through good impulses and pronounced tenacity.
- He is the perfect person to get a group project rolling, but he also knows how to sit back and let others take the lead.
- Within his department/On his team, Bill enjoyed the trust of his colleagues and teammates thanks to his respectful and correct leadership style.
- Bill also went out of his way to elicit feedback from his colleagues and invite them to share their experiences.
- Bill is cheerful in the face of daunting deadlines and always available to lend a hand to co-workers when necessary.
- Beyond his coding skills, Bill left a mark with his open, thoughtful personality. He is well-spoken and intellectual, and he lights up when talking about ideas and scientific trends.

- On a personal level, Bill is charismatic and well-spoken, both qualities that have served him well in his role as intern on the development team.
- He is hard-working, thoughtful, charismatic, and open-minded, and he has a clear commitment to cross-cultural communication.
- He performed beyond our expectations to such an extent that we have offered to prolong his contract on a weekly basis during the balance of the academic year.
- Bill has that combination of a positive attitude and the belief that he can always improve that's rare in an intern, but so essential to the learning process. I am confident that he will continue to display the same commitment and diligence in everything he does.

- **Interpersonal skills and leadership ability**:
  - – ability to accept differences
  - – ability to work well with and/or through supervisors, peers and subordinates
  - – ability to relate to others
  - – able to demonstrate willingness to work in a team environment
  - – ability to place oneself in someone else's shoes
  - – effectiveness in establishing and maintaining relationships
  - – patience with others
  - – sensitivity to those less competent
  - – splendid capacity to lead, to delegate responsibility

- He built strong relationships and ensured successful events.
- Bill's personal strengths are as impressive as his intellectual accomplishments. He is an active, outgoing presence with a great sense of humor.
- Bill was a fantastic addition to my team. He assimilated easily into our department, quickly and thoroughly learning about all of our competencies and needs, not just those he was responsible for delivering the software.
- Bill effectively scheduled and managed several team members to maintain efficient office operations.
- He was always willing to offer assistance and developed an excellent rapport with the many constituents served by our office, including clients and professional organizations.
- In addition to his professional qualifications, Bill has personal qualities that make him well-suited to leadership. He has naturally fallen into the role of "point person" that many in the class/company go to with questions.

- Bill's passionate about connecting with people across cultures, whether that means exploring new ideas through science or volunteering as a tutor to help his colleagues work through the coding handbook he wrote for the company.
- Bill proved himself to be a strong cultural fit here at EdTech. He was always ready to lend a helping hand to his teammates and contributed during brainstorming sessions and meetings between the pricing and structuring teams.
- Bill went above and beyond the call of duty to help us deliver the product on time, to the full satisfaction of the client.

Useful words: active listening skills/adaptability/ambition/at home wherever one is/capacity to synthesize information/commitment (*engagement*)/communication/competitive spirit/decision making/disciplined/flexibility/foresight (*sens de l'anticipation*) /immunity to stress/independence/ keen sense of communication/know how/leadership/managing people/managing time/meeting deadlines/negotiating skills/passion/people skills/perseverance/persuasiveness/positive attitude/ pragmatism/problem solving/pugnacity/social skills/teamwork/tolerance

Useful adjectives: adaptable/ambitious/analytical/confident/dedicated (*dévoué*)/demanding (*exigeant*)/dependable/enthusiastic/experienced/innovative/insightful/observant/open-minded/ organized/passionate (about) /reliable/resourceful/responsible/result-oriented

Useful verbs for experience: power verbs: to achieve/to coordinate/to create/to deliver/to execute/to fine-tune/to handle successfully several tasks/to implement/to improve/to manage/to maximize/to negotiate/to plan/to train/to work against deadline pressure

Useful verbs for education: graduated in the top 2% of the class/his final grade was… /his stellar work earned him the outstanding grade of 20/20/proficient/experienced/fluent (in English)

f. A personal anecdote if one

Personal anecdotes should help picture the person being recommended as a human being, endowed with qualities but also with some mild flaws. So, students should not take offence if it is mentioned in a letter, in passing. A personal anecdote can show that the student/intern is also a warm-hearted human being/a good team worker with human qualities but above all that she/he is able to learn from her/his mistakes. Such an anecdote is not mandatory nor necessarily mandated.

- You may point out to:
  - the difficulties you managed to overcome (rising from humble beginnings)
  - diligence as a student (helped classmates/teammates)
  - how you learned the methodology in record time
  - how you would stay at the office after hours to catch up on the literature
  - how you sacrificed your weekend to complete a job in time
  - how you overcame special circumstances (illness, injury…)

In the same way, a personal weakness goes a long way towards showing the student as a human being (for example a thorough attention to detail, a hands-on approach that prevents her/him from delegating responsibilities, forgetting time to relax and "smell the roses", the fact that she/he ignores all distractions…).

g. Why the recommender thinks you will be a splendid addition to the program

A solid letter will point out to the bright future of the applicant, in line with what graduate programs are seeking: outstanding students making an outstanding contribution. They will enhance the reputation of their school by the success of their careers (and later become generous benefactors of their endowment funds…).

- Potential for graduate study and potential to contribute to the program:
  - What is your prediction of the applicant's probable performance in graduate school?
  - Does the applicant have any specialized skill or studies in the field?
  - Does the applicant have an aptitude for the chosen field?
  - How does this applicant rate with other candidates who have been evaluated?
- Why the applicant will be an asset to any program she/he have chosen to apply for:
  - eagerness to go beyond the course material and investigate the field further
  - rising from a small and remote school village to one of the top universities in France
  - splendid abilities and mindset
  - strong skills, both analytical and reasoning
  - talent and abilities that have been tested and proven
  - the fact that the applicant is the first in the family to go into higher education, which speaks volumes about the courage to face long odds
  - unique personality
- Why, therefore, I strongly/wholeheartedly/warmly recommend the applicant to your attention knowing she/he will be a great asset to the program/she/he will be a great scientific fit to the program
- As a conclusion: should you need further information, do not hesitate to reach out to me.
- Cordially + signature

- We have come to appreciate Bill's personality very much.
- Bill's achievements are way beyond any other intern's I have known.
- Bill has my wholehearted and unequivocal support in his search for a graduate program where I am fully confident he will shine.
- Bill is a talented and engaging young man driven by a passion for science and programming. Please do not hesitate to contact me for any further information. Thank you for your time.
- Bill consistently impressed me and the rest of the staff with his work ethic, attention to detail, and burgeoning managerial skills.

- Clearly, this remarkable young man will be a leader in his class and leave his imprint wherever he goes.
- Wise, responsible, empathetic, these traits combined with Bill's resourcefulness and industriousness will prove a tremendous asset in his chosen field of study.
- In terms of the combination of energy, intelligence and enthusiasm, Bill has been one of the most exceptional students I have come across in years.
- Bill has my highest recommendation for… His quest for excellence, coupled with his *joie de vivre* and infectious nature make him an outstanding and charismatic personality.
- Bill has demonstrated excellence in all that he puts his mind to, whether it is designing an experiment, collaborating with others, or teaching others how to use his code.
- Bill's skills and leadership qualities will make him an invaluable addition to your graduate program.
- It is hard to overstate the meaningful contributions that Bill has made to our company and surrounding community.
- In closing, I would like to restate my strong support for Bill's application to/for…
- We appreciate the support, which was extremely helpful and valuable, especially during the critical phase of his mission.
- He is well suited to the challenges a PhD program provides.
- He will be an asset to any organization/program he cares to join. Please do not hesitate to be in touch if you have any further questions.
- I am confident that Bill will surpass the program's expectations in his new role. He is driven, self-confident, proactively helpful, and smart, and I know he will continue to find success at your university.
- Rarely do you come across someone who is talented at both big picture ideas and executing the small details – Bill is just that person.
- I believe that Bill has a tremendous amount of potential and would be an outstanding addition to your program. I would have no reservations about hiring him again and am confident in recommending him for graduate studies at your university.

10. To wrap it up

- Remember: the letter of recommendation should be **between 1 and 1,5 page long**. It should be uploaded on official letterhead paper if possible.
- Most importantly, for US programs, **always waive your right** to see the letters when you fill in the application form online!
- Before you ask your recommender, better **provide** him your CV, transcripts, draft of SOP and a list of bullet points summarizing your experience with her/him.

11. The consulting industry letter

If you are recommended by the consultancy industry, here is some of the jargon in the consultancy industry that you might want to use:

Actionable: what can be acted upon or what can be done. For example: "That recommendation is not actionable because we do not have the managerial talent to implement it."
Adding value: being productive in a positive way
AOB: any other business
Bandwidth: energy, skills and time that you can bring to bear on a project. Bandwidth is an all-encompassing term that combines each aspect and sounds more professional than, "I don't have the time nor the energy to do this.
Beach: refers to a consultant who is not actively enrolled in any project (to be on the beach). Syn. to be on the bench
Benchmark: metrics or standards of competitors in a client market
Best of breed: what is considered superior to its substitutes.
Best practices: whether you're talking about a business sector, your client company or in general, best practices are the methods and means that have the most benefit.
Blue sky thinking: thinking out of the box
Boil the ocean: describes what might occur if a consultant is not being focused enough.
Bottoms-up: developing an estimate by starting with the lowest-level assumptions and building those all the way up to an estimate.
Boutique/Niche consultancy: a specialized consultancy
Buckets: categories
Buy-in: agreement and/or consent (to have the CTO's buy-in)
C-suite: any number of executives with a capital C at the beginning of their title (the C stands for Chief. For example: COO, CFO, CEO, CIO, CMO, etc.
Campus hire: a consultant hired directly from undergraduate or business school.
Case: a consulting project
Circle back: to catch up again later, but used to indicate that now is not the right time.
Close a deal: to sign a contract
Close the loop: in meetings = finishing an item on the agenda or a topic of discussion with everyone in agreement. It can also be used to describe an item still to be done.
Consultancy: the British English term for a consulting firm
Core: the main concerns of a company or business unit

Core competencies: focusing time and resources on a company's core competencies *i.e.* core business
Crisp: thorough and compact (work)
Critical path: key tasks needed in order for a process to achieve a desired result.
Deck: a slide presentation, typically in Microsoft PPoint
Deep dive: thorough in-depth exploration of a particular topic. See the verb to deep dive. Syn. double clock.
Deliverables: any tasks to be completed.
Drill-down: to get beyond the higher-level summary into the details.
Due dil: short for due diligence
Due diligence: comprehensive study/survey of a business model with an aim to set clear expectations, risks, dependencies, etc., as part of a business proposal
Elevator test: a test of one's ability to explain concepts in a short-period of time (typically 60 seconds or less)
Engagement: a consulting project (Syn. case, study)
EOD: end of day
Exit: occurs when an investor decides to get rid of their stake in a company.
Exit strategy: contingency plan that is executed by an investor, trader, venture capitalist, or business owner to liquidate a position in a financial asset or dispose of tangible business assets once predetermined criteria for either have been met or exceeded.
Experienced hire: compare with campus hire
Facetime: meeting in person
Gain traction: to have a client or senior person engaged in an idea.
GMC: Global Management Consultancy, sometimes referring to just the Big 3 (McKinsey, Bain, BCG aka "MBB") sometimes plus the Big 4 accounting firms (Deloitte, Ernst & Young, KPMG, PricewaterhouseCoopers)
Granular: a detailed level of abstraction; often used in the context of increasing the fineness of the analysis, as in: "We need to get more granular here".
Greenfield: new opportunity for a company
Guesstimate: educated guess
Hit the ground running: the ability to add value in a project quickly, getting up to speed on the details, taking the next steps in no time.
Keep in the loop: inform
Key: critical, essential, central
KPI: key performance indicator
Legacy tech stack: nest of old and incompatible systems
Leverage: use, included in reports to give a sense of strength or careful thinking to the reassignment of resources.
Low-hanging fruit: things that can easily get done.
Managing up: helping superiors to do their job better by giving them feedback, keeping them in the loop, and anticipating problems they may have and helping them resolve them.
MECE (Mutually Exclusive, Collectively Exhaustive): a standard for developing communications that cover all of the relevant issues effectively without redundancy. Prominent concept at McKinsey.
Mission-critical: a product, concept, analysis, or service that is irreplaceable.
On-board: the status of being assigned to a case, engagement, or project. To onboard: to go through procedures to integrate (a new hire) into an organization or familiarize (a new customer or client) with one's products or services.

Paradigm: pattern, model, framework
PE: private equity
Ping: contact (verb and noun)
Pipe/Pipeline: upcoming projects (example : Hey Sir, what's in the pipe?)
Pipeline: describe progress toward a long-term goal that involves a series of discrete stages. "Acquisition pipeline" refers to a series of companies flagged as potential acquisition targets in PE.
Platform system: an ecosystem in which others can interact
POA: plan of action
Progress review: periodic review of work in progress.
Push back: to indicate to a superior consultant that something is difficult or challenging and may not be realistic (a delicate skill…).
Right-sized: downsized
Roadmap: planning (*calendrier de lancement, feuille de route*)
Rock star: a star performer
Scope: the agreed-upon list of deliverables and boundaries that underpin any client engagement.
Sea change: major shift
Smell test: to determine whether a result makes sense based on intuition and experience.
Stand-up call: a quick round table team call to update status from each team member/lead.
Study: a consulting project (also case or engagement)
Summer: short for summer intern
SWOT analysis: analyzing the Strengths, Weaknesses, Opportunities, and Threats for a company or set of companies in an industry.
Take the lead on: a clever phrase used by more experienced consultants when they wish to delegate a menial task.
Takeaway: a set of key points that the audience should understand by the end of a presentation or meeting.
Thinking out of the box: the ability to be creative or innovative in solving a difficult problem
Throw (sb) a curve/curveball: present (sb) with a difficult, confusing, unexpected (and sometimes unpleasant) problem, situation, question (baseball term: curve ball is a pitch intended to be difficult to hit due to its curving path).
Top-down: developing an estimate by starting with the highest-level assumptions and using estimates to drill down to a smaller-level estimate.
Touch base: to catch up with someone
Upward feedback: feedback provided to more senior employees
Weeds: the intricate details of an analysis
White space: an opportunity for company to generate revenue where it is not currently.
Workplan: schedule for completing a project or set of tasks for a project
Workstream: a group of tasks that make up a project.
Writing a deck: compiling a slide presentation
Zero-Defect (ZD): a mindset of double and triple-checking work before submitting

At the beginning of a project, it is often necessary to just **ballpark** the number or do a **back of the envelope calculation** to get some initial estimates.
After completing a broader analysis, it is often necessary to **do a deep dive** in specific areas. You often have to **drill down** into the data to really find out what is going on.

PART IV
VOCABULARY FOR THE STATEMENT OF PURPOSE/

LE VOCABULAIRE POUR LA LETTRE DE CANDIDATURE

I. From the Bac to College/ *Du bac à la fac*

The baccalaureat/*Le bac*

to take/to sit an exam: *passer un examen*
to pass the *baccalauréat*: *réussir le bac*
a scientific baccalaureate: *un bac scientifique*
a baccalaureate in sciences: *un bac S*
the equivalent of A-levels (UK): *l'équivalent des A-levels*
to graduate (from high school): *terminer ses études secondaires (à)*
with highest honors/highest distinctions: *avec félicitations du jury/mention très bien*
with (highest) honors: *mention (très) bien*

📖 **A-levels** are British educational qualifications which school children take when they are seventeen or eighteen years old. People usually need A-levels if they want to go to university in Britain.

high school: *le lycée*
a high school diploma: *un diplôme de fin d'études secondaires*
to skip a grade: *sauter une classe*
to obtain one's bac: *obtenir son bac*
to be awarded a bac in science: *décrocher un bac S*
upon completing high school: *à ma sortie du lycée*

The preparatory program/*Les classes préparatoires*

a competitive examination: *un concours*
to enter through a competitive exam: *être admis sur concours*
advanced post Baccalaureate courses in Math and Physics/an intensive two-year university level preparation in Math & Physics/advanced post Baccalaureate courses in Math and Physics (UK): *une prépa MP (Maths et Physique)*
a literary and humanities preparatory program: *une khâgne*
to train students (for): *former les étudiants (pour)*

leading to/for the highly competitive entrance exams to the *Grandes écoles*: *pour le concours d'entrée aux* Grandes écoles
the *Grandes ecoles* for scientific/business studies: *les Grandes écoles scientifiques/commerciales*
an engineering school: *une école d'ingénieurs*
a track: *une filière*

📖 Only 7.5% of high school students are admitted to a preparatory program in France.

a high-pressure education system: *un système d'éducation intense*
a highly selective program: *un programme hautement sélectif*
highly competitive/intense: *très compétitif/intense*
a heavy workload: *une lourde charge de travail*
the amount of work: *la quantité de travail*
the work pace: *le rythme de travail*
an oral examination (session): *une colle*
a post-secondary curriculum: *un programme post-bac*
a university-level program: *un programme de niveau licence*
a rigorous program of study/course schedule: *un programme d'études rigoureux*
a stringent testing system: *un système de tests rigoureux*
academic rigor: *la rigueur académique*
advanced math and physics: *maths et physique à un niveau avancé*
an undergraduate program: *un programme de licence*
in record time: *en un temps record*
to join the Grandes ecoles: *être admis dans une Grande école*
to lead to admission (to/into): *conduire à être admis (à/dans)*
to revise (UK)/to review (US): *réviser*
leading to entrance examination (to): *menant au concours d'entrée (à)*
to be awarded admission (to): *être récompensé par une admission (en/à)*
it was/has been a long and arduous road: *la route fut longue et difficile*
only the best and brightest students get admitted (to): *seuls les meilleurs élèves sont admis (à)*
to lay [laid] solid foundations (in): *poser des bases solides (en)*
to give strong foundations (in): *apporter de solides bases (en)*
to acquire a strong background/grounding (in): *acquérir une solide formation (en)*
to provide a thorough grounding (in): *fournir des bases rigoureuses (en)*
to have/to build a solid grounding (in): *posséder/bâtir de solides connaissances (en)*
to assimilate a huge amount of information: *assimiler une grande quantité d'informations*
to deepen one's knowledge: *approfondir ses connaissances*
to enrich one's knowledge: *enricher ses connaissances*
to expand/to extend one's knowledge: *étendre/élargir ses connaissances*
to fortify one's knowledge: *consolider ses connaissances*
to ground one's knowledge (in): *ancrer ses connaissances (dans)*
to round off one's knowledge: *parfaire ses connaissances*
to round out: *parachever, parfaire, compléter*
to round out one's training: *compléter sa formation*
to cap off a program: *conclure un programme*

to ground sb in the basics (of): *enseigner les fondements (de) à qn*
to become proficient (in): *devenir excellent (en)*
to communicate effectively: *communiquer avec efficacité*
to develop a rigorous approach to sciences: *aborder les sciences de façon rigoureuse*
to develop analysis skills/problem solving abilities: *développer des capacités d'analyse/à résoudre les problèmes*
to develop critical thinking: *développer la pensée critique*
to engage in effective problem-solving: *être en mesure de résoudre des problèmes*
to enroll (in a course), to sign up (for a course): *s'inscrire (à un cours)*
to face the challenge (of): *affronter le défi (de)*
to make informed/reasoned decisions: *prendre des décisions justes/raisonnées*
to inform a decision: *éclairer une décision*
to provide a sound training in basic sciences: *offrir une solide formation en sciences fondamentales*
to pursue an undergraduate degree in the sciences/economics: *poursuivre des études de premier cycle en science/en économie*
to earn a degree: *obtenir un diplôme*
to select the top students in science: *sélectionner les meilleurs étudiants en science*
to take up a challenge: *relever un défi*
to train for the selective entrance examinations: *se préparer aux concours d'entrée*
to work under pressure: *travailler sous pression*

☞ **Expressions.** I was admitted to a two-year university level program in advanced mathematics and physics in preparation for the highly selective nationwide entrance exam to the prestigious *Grandes ecoles* for scientific studies: *J'ai été admis dans un programme de niveau licence en maths et en physique, préparant aux concours d'entrée hautement sélectifs menant aux grandes écoles scientifiques* – The prestigious and highly selective Ecole XXX was a blazingly obvious decision considering my background: *La prestigieuse et sélective Ecole XXX s'imposait à l'évidence, étant donnée ma formation scientifique* – Over the two/three years of the preparatory program I consolidated/strengthened/firmed up/fortified my knowledge and sharpened/honed my skills in fundamental math/physics/engineering sciences: *Pendant deux/trois ans j'ai renforcé mes connaissances et aiguisé mes compétences en maths fondamentales/physique/SE*

College/*La fac*

a college: *une fac*
a university: *une université*
a world-class university: *une université de reputation mondiale*
to go to college/school: *aller à la fac*
to be at college: *être en fac*
to graduate from college: *avoir un diplôme universitaire*
a college course: *un cours de licence*
a college track: *une voie universitaire*
to go to medical school: *faire médecine*
law school: *la faculté de droit*

to go to law school: *être étudiant en droit*
to be a student: *être étudiant*
a credit: *un ECTS*
to be accepted into a program: *être accepté dans une formation*
to enrol in a program/to sign up for a program: *s'inscrire à un programme*
to be in the first year of a master's program: *être en première année de master*
to be working towards a BSc: *étudier en vue de décrocher une licence en sciences*
a graduate student: *un étudiant de deuxième cycle (grade de master)*

The Grande ecole/*La Grande école*

to enter a *Grande école*: *entrer dans une Grande école*
to be admitted (to): *être admis (à)*
to be accepted (to): *être accepté (à)*
to gain admission (to)/to succeed in getting admission (to): *réussir le concours d'entrée*
through a highly competitive entrance examination: *par le biais d'un concours d'entrée hautement sélectif*
to take in the best and the brightest students: *recruter les meilleurs élèves*
to choose a school over another: *choisir une école plutôt qu'une autre*
the Ecole Normale Supérieure, Paris ULM Program: *l'ENS Ulm*
(the) École Polytechnique/the Ecole: *l'École polytechnique*

> 🕮 Do not confuse **the École Polytechnique** with a **polytechnic school** or **institute**, which is a technical school offering instruction in many industrial arts and applied sciences. Similarly, the École Polytechnique is more than an engineering school or a university of technology: it is a university for sciences, a public institution of higher education. It is no longer a military academy. Use **the** with École Polytechnique

an institution of higher learning: *un établissement d'enseignement supérieur*
a post-secondary institution: *une institution post-bac*
a top-ranking university for sciences and engineering/a premier institution for sciences/a top ranking university for sciences and engineering: *une université scientifique prestigieuse/de renom, une fac de science et d'ingénierie réputée*
a top-tier school/a top school: *une université de renom*
a top-ranked school: *une université prestigieuse*
a premier public institution: *un établissement public de premier plan*
a renowned science university: *une fac de science réputée*
one of France's top universities for sciences: *une des meilleures facs de science en France*
one of France's leading universities for scientific study: *un des meilleurs établissements en France pour les études scientifiques*
to be ranked among those at the very top schools in the nation: *être classé parmi les toutes meilleures universités dans le pays*
to supply France with top quality civil servants: *fournir à la France des hauts fonctionnaires bien formés*

to work for the state: *travailler pour l'État*
to train the best scientists: *former les meilleurs scientifiques*
to run large firms: *diriger les grandes entreprises*
corporate France: *les entreprises françaises*
a class/a cohort: *une promotion*
a classmate: *un camarade de promotion*
the class of 2022: *la promo 2022*
the incoming class: *la promo entrante*
the outgoing class: *la promo sortante*
the Polytechnique program: *le cycle polytechnicien*
the Polytechnique curriculum: *le programme polytechnicien*
a program/a cursus: *une formation*
an academic schedule: *un programme universitaire*
top academic quality: *un enseignement de premier ordre*
to rank in the top 5%/10%: *être classé parmi les meilleurs*
to rank first (in): *être classé premier (dans)*
a class rank: *un classement dans la promotion*

☞ **Expressions**. I am at present completing my third year: *Je termine actuellement ma troisième année* – I am currently a third-year student: *Je suis actuellement en 3e année* – I am currently in my final year: *Je suis actuellement en dernière année* – I am about to complete my final year: *Je suis sur le point de terminer ma dernière année*

The curriculum/*Le programme*

➔ ***Attention*** *: en anglais et à l'université, les cours sont dispensés par un professeur (***professor***) ; majuscule si devant un nom propre :* Professor Jim Jones. *Ne pas utiliser le mot* **teacher** *qui relève de l'enseignement secondaire.*

a common core of courses/a core curriculum/(a) core course(s): *un tronc commun*
a pluri-disciplinary curriculum/a cross-disciplinary program: *un programme pluridisciplinaire*
a cross-disciplinary approach: *une approche pluridisciplinaire*
a diverse curriculum: *un programme varié*
a broad/wide range of subjects: *un large éventail de sujets*
a wide variety of advanced scientific courses: *un large éventail de cours scientifiques avancés*
to tackle a broad range of subjects: *aborder une large gamme de sujets*
a broadly-based/broad-based curriculum: *un large programme*
the breadth and width of the curriculum: *la variété du programme*
a high-level training: *une formation de haut niveau*
a science-based education: *un enseignement scientifique*
to span a program: *couvrir un programme*
to widen one's way of thinking: *élargir sa façon de penser*
to help sb understand (the mechanisms of): *aider qn à comprendre (les mécanismes de)*

to give an unusual perspective: *présenter une perspective inhabituelle*
to build bridges between courses: *construire des ponts entre les cours*
to add a new point of view: *ajouter un nouveau point de vue*
to initiate sb (to): *initier qn (à)*
to introduce sb (to): *introduire qn (à)*
to offer the keys (to): *offrir les clés (pour)*
the key to success: *la clé de la réussite*
to hold the keys (to one's professional choices): *détenir les clés (de ses choix professionnels)*

☞ **Expressions.** to design a curriculum: *concevoir un programme* – to develop a curriculum: *développer un programme* – to broaden a curriculum: *élargir un programme* – to introduce a subject into a curriculum: *introduire une matière dans un programme* – to be on the curriculum: *être au programme* – areas of the curriculum: *les domaines du programme* – I have taken a variety/diversity of courses: *J'ai suivi plusieurs cours/des cours variés*

Fields of study/*Les domaines d'études*

(mathematical) optimization: *l'optimisation*
a computer simulation/computer model/computational model: *une simulation informatique/numérique*
a deterministic model: *un modèle déterministe*
a differential equation: *une équation différentielle*
a dynamical system: *un système dynamique*
a linear equation: *une équation linéaire*
a mathematical model: *un modèle mathématique*
a neuronal network: *un réseau neuronal*
a statistical model: *un modèle statistique*
a stochastic model: *un modèle stochastique*
applied mathematics: *les mathématiques appliquées*
applied physics: *la physique appliquée*
biochemistry: *la biochimie*
bioengineering: *la bio ingénierie*
biology: *la biologie*
calculus: *le calcul*
chemistry: *la chimie*
classical mechanics: *la mécanique classique*
computer science (CS): *l'informatique*
data science: *la science des données*
analytics (sg. or pl.): *l'analyse de données*
computational finance: *la finance quantitative*
earth sciences: *les sciences de la Terre*
econometrics: *l'économétrie*
economics: *les sciences économiques*
electrical engineering: *le génie électrique*
financial engineering: *l'ingénierie financière*

financial mathematics: *les mathématiques financières*
game theory: *la théorie des jeux*
macro/micro economics: *la macro-/micro-économie*
mathematical modeling/models: *les modèles mathématiques*
statistics: *la statistique*
mathematics/math: *les mathématiques*
nanotechnology: *les nanotechnologies*
operations research (OR)/decision science/management science: *la recherche opérationnelle*
quantum mechanics: *la mécanique quantique*
quantum optics: *l'optique quantique*
quantum physics: *la physique quantique*
quantum statistics: *la statistique quantique*
signal processing: *le traitement du signal*
social sciences: *les sciences sociales*
solid/fluid mechanics: *la mécanique des solides/fluides*
statistical analysis: *l'analyse statistique*
stochastic calculus: *le calcul stochastique*
the Humanities: *les lettres*

➔ ***Attention***

- *Majuscule possible devant les noms de matière mais non obligatoire sauf s'il s'agit d'un titre d'un cours dispensé*
- *Ne pas confondre* **economics** (the science) *et* **economy** (the economy of a country)
- **Math** *ne prend pas de* **s** *en anglais américain. Il en prend un en anglais britannique.*
- *Les noms de matière terminés par un* **s** *(math(s), physics, economics...) sont suivis d'un verbe au* ***singulier***

to take a class/a course (in, on): *suivre un cours (sur)*
to sign up for/to enrol in a course: *s'inscrire à un cours*
to complete a course: *terminer un cours*
a lesson (on): *un cours (sur)*
to pursue a major (in): *faire une spécialisation (en)*
a major/a field of concentration: *une spécialisation*
a double major: *une double spécialisation*
a minor (in): *une matière secondaire (en)*
a theoretical/practical approach: *une approche théorique/pratique*

☞ **Expressions**. This year, my courses are essentially oriented/geared toward...: *Cette année, mes cours sont essentiellement orientés vers...* – I intend to develop my end-of-third-year research internship in this domain: *J'ai l'intention de faire mon stage d'option scientifique de fin d'année dans ce domaine* – Last year's course in applied mathematics gave me insight into modeling real phenomena: *Le cours de math appliquées de l'an passé m'a ouvert des perspectives sur la modélisation des phénomènes réels* – This project also triggered my interest for optics, which made me choose Prof. A's lesson on quantum optics: *Ce projet a suscité mon intérêt pour l'optique, ce qui m'a conduit à choisir le cours d'optique quantique du Prof. A* – I am looking forward to deepening my knowledge in statistical physics next semester through a course on complex systems: *Je suis impatient d'approfondir mes connaissances en physique statistique le semestre prochain en suivant un cours sur les systèmes complexes* – The class will allow me to study the interactions between mathematics and physics, my two main fields of interest: *Le cours me permettra d'étudier les interactions entre math et physique, mes deux domaines d'intérêt*

➔ ***Attention***: to study **at** MIT/Stanford/Caltech: *étudier au MIT/à Stanford/à Caltech*

☞ It was fascinating, not only because it was a new field for me, but because I was able to apply the theoretical tools I had been acquiring to a very practical problem: climate change – Her course on *Industrial Design* taught me to think of all the aspects of a problem before submitting an idea; I acquired a more global vision for facing problems – Wanting to learn about the complexity of international relations influenced by energy needs, I am also following a *Geopolitics and Strategy* course. Next trimester, I will be taking *Economy of the Energy Sector* taught by XX – I have chosen courses in both mechanics and physics, for I believe they hold the technical solutions to the problems we face – I am taking management-oriented courses to be able to mobilize people to move forward on projects that could change the world – I enjoyed *Numerical Analysis and Optimization* because these tools are necessary to solve mechanical problems in complex situations – I enjoyed the cutting edge issues we heard about from numerous researchers, and seeing them model real problems – Then, I will take non-mechanics courses such as…, which I believe will give me an interdisciplinary competence – I also deepened my knowledge with classes in fundamental mathematics, and of course, in computer science. This diversity has given me the ability to approach any scientific question from different angles – My favorite course was the experimental one on the issues of networking in computer science where, again, I enjoyed the elaboration of a program, from its theoretical creation to its practical application – Using my foundations in fluid mechanics, it would be fascinating to work with Professor XX on nanofluids and their nuclear applications – His lectures on *Continuum Mechanics* introduced us to the studies of the behavior of materials and structures – Her course enlarged our vision of the theory, as well as the practice, inviting researchers in each of the class to present and discuss their findings – Her class gave me an understanding of the concepts rather than just piling up calculations – A quantum mechanics class taught by XX immediately grabbed my attention – I would also expect to gain a more practical and professional understanding of the application of these theories – Managing a 200,000k€ budget has given me practical exposure (to)

to specialize (in): *se spécialiser (en)*
a specialization (in): *une spécialisation (en)*
the faculty: *le corps enseignant*
an academic: *un universitaire*
a faculty member: *un membre du corps enseignant*
a faculty advisor: *un professeur responsable*

🕮 In America, students go to **classes**. A **lecture** is a special presentation by a guest speaker, and is open to all the students at a university. A professor lectures to several hundred students. Lectures may be supplemented with regular small group discussions led by teaching assistants (TA). **Classes** are open only to students who have signed up and paid for them.

Academic accomplishments/*La réussite scolaire*

a recipient (of a prize): *le lauréat (d'un prix)*
a science contest: *un concours scientifique*
a science fair: *une exposciences*
an international math competition: *un concours international de maths*
outside the realm of science: *au-delà du domaine scientifique*
beyond the realm of possibilities: *au-delà du possible*
beyond the academic realm: *au-delà du domaine académique*
outside of school: *en dehors des études*
the Olympiads (in math/physics/chemistry): *les olympiades (en math/physique/chimie)*
to be spurred on to excel: *être encouragé à briller*
to obtain a gold/silver/bronze medal: *décrocher une médaille d'or/d'argent/de bronze*

The knowledge gained/*Les connaissances acquises*

a wealth/a trove of knowledge: *un trésor/une mine de connaissances*
a well-rounded candidate: *un candidat bien formé/complet*
know-how (ni): *le savoir-faire*
knowledge (in/on): *des connaissances (dans, en)*
the scientific method: *la démarche scientifique*
to acquire an informed view (on): *se faire une opinion précise (de)*
to acquire the tools: *acquérir les outils*
to walk sb through: *expliquer en détail*
to be conversant (with): *bien s'y connaître (en)*
to be familiar (with): *bien connaître*
to be good (at): *être bon (en)*
to broaden/to widen one's way of thinking: *développer son esprit critique*
to build a vision for the future: *bâtir une vision pour l'avenir*
to build upon solid foundations (in): *bâtir sur de solides fondations (en)*
to strengthen one's foundations (in): *renforcer ses bases (en)*
to consolidate one's understanding (of): *renforcer sa compréhension (de)*
to develop a competency: *développer une compétence*
to develop a deep understanding (of): *acquérir une compréhension poussée (de)*
to draw on a professor's expertise: *tirer profit de l'expertise d'un professeur*
a field of expertise/range of expertise: *un domaine d'expertise*

→ **ADJ + EXPERTISE**. considerable: *considérable* – extensive: *large* – great: *formidable* – appropriate: *qui convient* – relevant: *pertinent* – necessary: *nécéssaire* – specific: *spécifique* – scientific: *scientifique* – professional: *professionnel* – technical: *technique* – technological: *technologique*

→ **VERB + EXPERTISE**. to lack: *manquer de* – to require: *nécessiter* – to acquire: *acquérir* – to develop: *développer* – to gain: *gagner en* – to build on: *accumuler* – to provide: *fournir* – to bring to bear: *mettre en œuvre* – to apply: *appliquer* – to call on: *faire appel à* – to draw on/to rely on: *mobiliser* – to pass on: *transmettre* – to share: *partager*

to gain/to acquire some knowledge: *acquérir des connaissances*
to gain the know how: *acquérir le savoir-faire*
to give a range of powerful tools: *fournir un arsenal d'outils puissants*
to grasp the complexity (of): *saisir la complexité (de)*
to have a smattering (of): *avoir des notions/des rudiments (de)*
to lay solid foundations: *poser de solides bases*
to acquire a targeted foundation (in): *acquérir des bases ciblées (en)*
to lay the groundwork (for): *jeter les bases (pour)*
to provide tools: *fournir les outils*
to take one's studies to the next level: *franchir une étape dans ses études*
to take one's training to the next level: *améliorer sa formation*

☞ **Expressions.** to have a sound knowledge (of): *avoir de bonnes connaissances (en)* – a sound background (in): *une bonne formation (en)* – to provide a sufficient grounding (in): *apporter un bagage suffisant (en)* – to devote one's time (+ ING): *consacrer son temps (à)* – to enhance one's knowledge: *améliorer ses connaissances* – to deepen a subject: *approfondir un sujet* – to study a subject in depth: *étudier un sujet à fond* – to have a thirst for knowledge: *avoir soif de connaissances* – to slake one's thirst: *étancher sa soif* – to apply one's knowledge (to): *appliquer ses connaissances (à)* – I feel that my academic background has prepared me take this next step: *Ma formation m'a préparé à franchir l'étape suivante*

☞ knowledgeable: *savant* – learned: *instruit, savant* – well-read/educated: *cultivé* – skilled/qualified: *qualifié* – competent: *compétent* – well-qualified: *tout à fait qualifié*

to apply one's knowledge: *appliquer ses connaissances*
to adapt one's scientific knowledge: *adapter ses connaissances scientifiques*
to practical purposes: *à des fins pratiques*

Applying abroad/*La candidature à l'étranger*

to apply **to** a university: *postuler à une université*
to apply **for** an MS program: *candidater à un master*
to complete a program: *achever/terminer un programme*
an application: *une candidature*
an application file: *un dossier de candidature*
an applicant: *un candidat*

🕮 A **college** is a postsecondary institution that provides an undergraduate education and, in some cases, master's and doctorate degrees. College, in a separate sense, is a division of a university; for example, College of Business.

a college search: *la recherche d'une faculté*
a college catalog: *un catalogue de cours*
a curriculum: *un programme*
a syllabus/course outline: *un programme (dans un cours)*
to pursue an MSc/MA: *faire un master en sciences/lettres*
an MPhil: *un diplôme d'études approfondies (DEA)*
a graduate program: *un diplôme d'études supérieures (après la licence)*
a college degree: *un diplôme d'enseignement supérieur, un diplôme universitaire*
a double degree: *un double diplôme*
to pursue a graduate degree (in): *faire des études de 2ᵉ cycle (en)*
to be on track to graduate (by): *être bien parti pour décrocher son diplôme (d'ici)*
a transcript: *un relevé de notes*
an attestation: *une attestation certifiée*
a GPA: *une moyenne*
a CGPA: *une moyenne cumulée*
to apply for admission (to): *candidater (à)*
an academic program/a degree program: *un programme d'études*
to go on a campus tour: *visiter un campus*
a world class institution: *un établissement de renommée mondiale*
an opportunity to study: *une chance d'étudier*
a deadline: *une date limite*

📖 **Rolling deadline**: institutions accept applications and admit students at any time during a specific time period until all available spots are filled.

an academic year: *une année universitaire*
a quarter/trimester/term: *un trimestre*
the Spring term: *le trimestre de printemps*
a semester: *un semestre (15-16 semaines)*

📖 The **Ivy League** includes eight schools: Brown University (Providence, R.I.), Columbia University (New York, N.Y.), Cornell University (Ithaca, N.Y.), Dartmouth College (Hanover, N.H.), Harvard University (Cambridge, Mass.), Princeton University (Princeton, N.J.), University of Pennsylvania (Philadelphia, Pa.) and Yale University (New Haven, Conn.). A four-year (undergraduate) degree at one of these elite schools runs a couple hundred grand, give or take – not a crippling cost for upper-class families, but a very crippling cost for everybody else.

Reasons for applying/*Pourquoi candidater*

what makes your program attractive: *ce qui m'attire dans votre programme*
to be in line (with)/in keeping (with): *être dans le droit fil (de)*
to follow on (from)/to be aligned (with) : *s'inscrire dans la continuité (de)*
a logical next step: *l'étape qui s'impose logiquement*

a steppingstone: *un tremplin*
an ideal springboard: *un tremplin idéal*
a launching pad: *une rampe de lancement*
a school of choice: *une école préférée*
the pinnacle of higher education: *le summum de l'enseignement universitaire*
to gain a better grasp (on): *mieux appréhender*
to complement one's education: *compléter sa formation*
to deepen/to broaden one's knowledge (in): *approfondir ses connaissances (en)*
to flesh out one's knowledge: *renforcer ses connaissances*
to strengthen one's knowledge (in): *renforcer ses connaissances (en)*
to round out one's education: *parfaire son éducation*
to establish strong links with the industry: *établir des liens solides avec l'industrie*
to be complementary to one's theoretical education: *être complémentaire de sa formation théorique*
to steer sb toward a specialization: *orienter qn vers une spécialisation*
to steer sb toward a field: *orienter qn vers un domaine*
to join a team of high quality researchers: *rejoindre une équipe de chercheurs hautement qualifiés*

☞ I am applying to Brown University because my investigations have led me to believe that I will find a fecund atmosphere of intellectual interest and diversity in faculty, students and coursework paralleling those I would like to see in myself.

☞ After three years of intensive study in mathematics, physics, and chemistry to prepare for the nationwide competitive exams for the *Grandes écoles*, I began to develop more informed insights into the difficulties involved in bringing about changes in such issues as global warming or the use of hydrogen energy.

☞ I am confident that the broad scientific background I have acquired at the Ecole XXX has prepared me to take this next step.

☞ My classes in economics and biology have provided me with the necessary prerequisites for working on a range of environmental issues at the policy level. – This goal lies behind my current decision to apply for admission to the Technology Policy Program at the Massachusetts Institute of Technology. – My major interest goes to the study of environmental systems, on global and local scales, with the ultimate hope that those studies might help draft meaningful and fruitful policies.

☞ Attending Paris V University provided me with the best experience in my life, in giving me discipline and showing me the stuff which I was made of.

☞ I wanted to do something in the environment and water issues; rather than start as an engineer working for the state I have made up my mind to apply to MIT to round myself off.

☞ to offer an environment conducive to fostering innovative and original ideas

What to expect from coursework or project work/*De l'utilité des cours ou des projets*

a project: *un projet*
a capstone: *un projet de fin d'études*
a touchstone: *une pierre angulaire*
to solve a real-world problem: *résoudre un problème concret*
to help develop ways (of): *contribuer à développer les moyens (de)*
to develop an understanding (of): *aider à comprendre*
to acquire a base understanding (of): *acquérir des bases (en)*
to develop a broad vision (of): *acquérir une large perspective (sur)*
to bring methods (to): *offrir des méthodes (pour)*
to make plain the links (between): *clarifier les liens (entre)*
to provide sb with the ways and means: *fournir à qn les voies et moyens*
to explore the ways and means: *explorer les voies et moyens*
to make a foray into a field: *s'essayer à, faire une incursion dans un domaine*
a deep dive (into)/in-depth examination/analysis/assessment (of)/a comprehensive analysis (of): *une analyse approfondie (de)*
to deep dive (into): *examiner à fond*
to strengthen one's foundations (in): *consolider ses fondamentaux (en)*
to shed light (on): *éclairer*
to teach sb how to: *apprendre à qn à*
to touch upon the complexity (of): *approcher la complexité (de)*
to acquire a global/holistic vision (of): *acquérir une vision globale (de)*
to look forward to following: *être impatient de suivre*
to gain an all-round background (in): *acquérir des connaissances générales (en)*
to ground one's theoretical thinking (in): *approfondir ses connaissances théoriques (en)*
to build on the theoretical foundations/one's knowledge (in): *consolider les fondations théoriques/ses connaissances (en)*
to acquire in-depth knowledge (in/of): *acquérir des connaissances approfondies (en)*
to satiate/to quench one's curiosity (in/of): *satisfaire sa curiosité (en/de)*
to meet one's desire (to): *répondre au désir (de)*
to acquire the fundamentals (in/for): *acquérir les fondamentaux (en/pour)*
to fit perfectly with sb's current interests: *correspondre parfaitement aux intérêts actuels de qn*
the ideal fit to one's project: *ce qui correspond idéalement à son projet / en adéquation avec son projet*
to fit sb for a job/career: *préparer qn à un emploi/une carrière*
to kick start a career: *démarrer une carrière*
to fit in (with): *cadrer (avec)*
the perfect fit: *la solution idéale*
to build bridges (between): *jeter des ponts (entre)*
to widen one's range of skills: *élargir sa palette de compétences*
to upgrade one's skills: *améliorer ses compétences*
to take one's skills to a new level: *élever le niveau de ses compétences*
to give a professional vision: *offrir une vision professionnelle*

II. Thinking through/ *Réfléchir sur soi-même*

Background/*Le milieu*

the family background: *le milieu familial*
a wealthy/well-off background: *un milieu aisé*
an affluent family: *une famille aisée*
an upscale district: *un quartier chic*
well-connected: *d'une famille connue, qui a des relations*
a disadvantaged background: *un milieu défavorisé*
a humble background: *un milieu modeste*
a middle class background: *un milieu bourgeois*
a working class background: *un milieu ouvrier*
non-traditional elements of one's background: *des éléments singuliers dans ses origines*

☞ educational (*académique*), cultural (*culturel*), ethnic (*ethnique*), family (*familial*), religious (*religieux*), social (*social*) + **background**

☞ to come from a privileged background: *être issu de bonne famille* – children from deprived backgrounds: *des enfants issus de milieux défavorisés* – to have a background in science: *avoir une formation scientifique* – to describe/to outline one's background: *décrire son milieu/sa formation*

a low income family: *une famille aux revenus modestes*
a low-income student: *un étudiant aux revenus modestes*
a close-knit family: *une famille unie*
a single-parent family: *une famille monoparentale*
a middle class/working class family: *une famille bourgeoise/ouvrière*
a foster family: *une famille d'adoption*

☞ to belong to a family: *appartenir à une famille* – to be part of a family: *faire partie d'une famille* – to come from a family: *être issu d'une famille* – to run in a family: *être une caractéristique de la famille* – to raise/to bring up a family: *élever une famille* – to support/to feed a family: *nourrir une famille* – within the family: *au sein de la famille* – the elder/the eldest in the family: *l'aîné d'une famille (2/+2)* – to hail (from Morocco): *être originaire (du Maroc)*

☞ **Expressions.** I grew up in circumstances that provide a classic example of the disparity between appearance and reality: *J'ai grandi dans un monde qui est l'exemple même de la disparité qui existe entre la réalité et la fiction* – I was born and raised in Morocco: *Je suis né et j'ai grandi au Maroc* – My family have nurtured in me these qualities: *Ma famille a nourri ces qualités en moi* – My family have passed on values that lay stress on education/sharing/knowledge transmission: *De ma famille j'ai hérité des valeurs qui mettaient l'accent sur l'éducation/le partage/la transmission de connaissances* – one of my key drivers is…: *ce qui me définit, c'est…* – to instil(l) values: *inculquer des valeurs* – to hardwire (into): *inculquer (en)* – deeply entrenched values: *des valeurs solidement enracinées* – My love (for…) is deeply embedded in my personality: *Mon amour (de…) est profondément ancré dans ma personnalité*

origins: *les origines*
to hail (from): *venir (de)*
to fetch up: *se retrouver*
to be born and bred: *naître et grandir*
to be raised (in): *grandir (à/en)*
roots: *les racines*
to go back (to): *remonter (à)*
to breach the middle class: *atteindre la classe moyenne*

Diversity/*La mixité*

social mix: *la diversité sociale*
a diverse student body: *la mixité sociale/ethnique*
the racial makeup: *la composition ethnique*
a mixed race family: *une famille biraciale*
to straddle two national identities: *être à cheval sur deux identités*
to be heir (to): *être l'héritier (de)*
to assemble a diverse student body: *avoir des étudiants de toutes origines*
to tip the balance: *faire pencher la balance*
a cultural tradition: *une tradition culturelle*
a cultural heritage: *un héritage culturel*
a value system: *un système de valeurs*
core values: *des valeurs fondamentales*
to value: *accorder de l'importance (à)*
  a culture that fits sb's values: *une culture qui correspond aux valeurs de qn*
  to attach/to put/to set/to place values (on): *placer ses valeurs (dans)*
  to be a great value (to): *être très précieux (pour)*
  to cherish/to encourage/to foster values (of): *encourager les valeurs (de)*
  to mirror one's values: *être le reflet de ses valeurs*
  to share values (with): *partager des valeurs (avec)*
to come from a cross cultural background: *être issu d'un milieu pluri-culturel*
to struggle to belong (to): *se battre pour appartenir (à)*

to integrate fully: *être pleinement intégré*
to get an edge in the admissions process: *avoir un avantage dans le processus d'admission*
to be underrepresented: *être sous-représenté*
to boost diversity: *encourager la diversité sociale/ethnique*
to motivate (sb): *motiver (qn)*
a motivation (for/behind): *une motivation (pour/à l'origine de)*

✓ extremely/highly/strongly + **motivated**

✓ main, primary (*principal*), underlying (*sous-jacent*), strong (*fort*) + **motivation**

the gender divide: *l'écart entre les sexes*
to tackle gender inequality in STEM: *s'attaquer au problème des inégalités en sciences*
to close the gender divide: *supprimer l'écart entre les sexes*
gender bias: *le sexisme*
the female acceptance rate: *le taux d'admission des jeunes filles*
a female student: *une étudiante*
to be discouraged from studying: *être dissuadé d'étudier*
to gain access to quality education: *avoir accès à une formation de qualité*

🕮 In America men vastly outnumber women majoring in most STEM courses in college and women make up only 28% of the workforce in STEM fields. Closing this gender divide is key to a better future. Solutions to some of our world's most pressing problems could be out there in the minds of girls around the world. (*The Economist*)

to break/to crack the academic glass ceiling: *briser le plafond de verre universitaire*
to crack open the door of research: *entrouvrir la porte de la recherche*
to keep sciences largely the domain of men: *réserver les sciences aux hommes*
to break through a barrier: *franchir une barrière*
a male preserve: *un domaine masculin*
to close the gender gap: *combler l'écart entre les sexes*
to outnumber: *surpasser en nombre*
to be underrepresented: *être en minorité*

☞ A "**gender lightbulb moment**" is a time you became aware of being treated differently because of your gender. For example, a girl not being allowed to play football, or a boy being told he shouldn't play with dolls.

Who am I?/*Qui suis-je ?*

strengths and weaknesses: *les forces et faiblesses*
an extracurricular activity: *une activité extracurriculaire*

outside the trodden academic path: *hors du schéma universitaire classique*
to take a long, hard look at oneself: *s'analyser soigneusement*
to take stock of: *évaluer*
to capitalize on/to take advantage (of): *profiter (de)*
to leverage: *tirer profit de, exploiter*

• **Determination/*La détermination***
to be determined (to + INF): *être déterminé (à)*

✓ absolute, fierce, gritty (*farouche*), dogged (*résolu*), grim (*inflexible*), ruthless (*sans concession*), single-minded (*ferme*), steely (*de fer*), strong (*fort*), clear (*clair*) + **determination** – to intensify/ to strengthen (*renforcer*) + one's **determination/resolve**

☞ **Expressions.** with grim determination: *avec une volonté inflexible* – to be quite/utterly determined: *être tout à fait déterminé* – to be quite/absolutely/resolutely determined: *être absolument/résolument determiné* – I am a competitive person whose primary source of motivation is drawn from/stems from/comes from sport challenges: *J'ai un sens de la compétition dont la source première de motivation provient des défis sportifs*

to make up one's mind (to do sth)/to make a decision (to): *décider (de)*
to have one's mind set (on + ING): *être décidé (à)*
to be full of determination: *être très déterminé*
to show/to reveal determination: *faire preuve de détermination*
to express/to signal determination: *indiquer une détermination*
to lack determination: *manquer de détermination*
to require determination: *nécessiter de la volonté*
to be eager (to + INF): *être prêt (à)*
to be focused: *être concentré*
to shift one's focus (to): *réorienter ses priorités (vers)*
to be disciplined: *être discipliné*
to set one's sights (on): *viser, avoir des vues (sur)*
I believe I have what it takes: *je pense avoir les qualités nécessaires*
resolve: *la détermination*
an unflinching resolve: *une détermination sans faille*
  to resolve to do sth: *se résoudre à faire qch*
  to show resolution: *faire preuve de détermination*
  to strengthen one's resolve: *renforcer sa détermination*
  to make a resolution: *prendre une résolution*

• ***Fields of interest/Les domaines d'intérêt***
an interest (for/in): *un intérêt (pour/dans)*
a domain/an area of interest: *un domaine d'intérêt*
an interest **for** concrete action: *un intérêt* ***pour*** *l'action concrète*

a passing interest: *un intérêt passager*
my research interest: *l'intérêt de ma recherche*
to focus (on): *porter (sur)*
to zero in (on)/to laser focus (on): *se concentrer (sur)*
to lay bare/to unveil/to reveal/to expose: *mettre à nu, exposer*
to be interested (in/by): *être intéressé (par)*
to become interested (in): *s'intéresser (à)*
to be keen (to): *avoir hâte (de)*
to grow keen (on): *s'intéresser de près (à)*
to relish the thought/the prospect/the idea (of): *la pensée/la perspective/l'idée (de) me plaît*

✓ avid (*avide*), burning (*ardent*), close (*cher*), considerable (*considérable*), consuming (*passionnel*), deep (*profond*), intense (*intense*), keen/lively (*vif*), passionate (*passionné*), strong (*fort*), exciting (*passionnant*), stimulating (*stimulant*), thrilling (*captivant*), particular (*particulier*), varied (*varié*), great (*grand*), particular (*particulier*), wide (*large*), scientific (*scientifique*), academic (*universitaire*) + **interest**

✓ **growing interest**: added: *supplémentaire* – budding/nascent: *naissant* – growing/increasing: *croissant* – renewed: *renouvelé*

✓ **general interest**: broad/wide: *large* – serious: *sérieux* – widespread: *répandu* – genuine: *authentique* – abiding: *constant* – lifelong: *de toujours* – passing: *passager* – diverse: *varié* – wide-ranging: *multiple*

to arouse one's interest/to drum up interest/to stir up sb's interest: *susciter l'intérêt*
to catch sb's interest: *attirer l'intérêt de qn*
to develop an interest (in/for): *commencer à s'intéresser (à)*
to evince an interest: *montrer/manifester un intérêt*
to express one's interest: *manifester son intérêt*
to feed one's interest (for): *nourrir son intérêt (pour)*
to generate interest: *créer un intérêt/de l'intérêt*
to have an interest (for): *avoir un intérêt (pour)*
to kindle (one's) interest: *faire naître l'intérêt/aviver l'intérêt (de qn)*
to narrow one's interest (to): *circonscrire son intérêt (à)*
to pursue an interest (for): *cultiver un intérêt (pour)*
to reflect one's interest (in): *refléter son intérêt (dans/pour)*
to revive (one's interest): *renouveler (son intérêt)*
to show one's interest: *montrer son intérêt*
to spark/to touch off one's interest: *déclencher son intérêt*

☞ **Expressions**. to awaken sb's interest: *éveiller l'intérêt de qn* – to whip up/to stimulate interest: *attiser l'intérêt* – to reinforce/to firm up/to strengthen: *renforcer* – to maintain/to sustain an interest (for): *conserver un intérêt (pour)* – **interest can** grow (*croître*), flag (*diminuer*), wane (*faiblir*), lie (in) (*se trouver dans*) – to be of interest (to sb): *présenter un intérêt (pour)* – to hold no interest: *ne présenter aucun intérêt*

✓ **Adverbs**: It is this aspect of work/research that really/greatly/particularly interests me: *C'est cet aspect du travail/de la recherche qui m'intéresse vraiment/beaucoup/particulièrement*

- deeply, especially, extremely, genuinely, greatly, intensely, keenly, more than a little, most, particularly, passionately, seriously, specially, terribly
- truly, fairly, mildly, quite, clearly, obviously, actively
- chiefly, mainly, primarily, always, long
- equally, fairly, mildly, pretty, quite, rather
- inherently, intrinsically, in itself
- scientifically, technologically

to be tempted (by) : *être tenté (par)*
to be encouraged (to) : *être encouragé (à)*
to be aroused (by) : *être stimulé (par)*
to grow (into) : *se transformer (en)*

☞ **Expressions**. out of interest: *par intérêt* – with interest: *avec intérêt* – to add interest: *offrir un intérêt supplémentaire* – the interest of studying such a field lies in…: *l'intérêt d'étudier un tel domaine repose dans…* – it is of paramount interest that (+ sujet + should): *il est primordial que* – to act in the public/common/general interest: *agir dans l'intérêt de tous*

☞ **Expressions**. to turn what is passing interest into passion: *transformer un intérêt passager en passion* – Over the past few years I have developed an interest (for/in): *Au cours des dernières années, je me suis intéressé (à)* – For those who chase their passions relentlessly: *Pour tous ceux qui cultivent leur passion sans répit* – to pursue a passion: *suivre sa passion*

☞ **Expressions**. What I found most interesting in her classes: *Ce que j'ai trouvé des plus intéressant dans ses cours* – What is interesting for me is…: *Ce qui est intéressant pour moi, c'est que* – It is quite interesting for a scientist (to + INF): *Il est très intéressant pour un scientifique (de)* – I would be most interested (in + ING): *Cela m'intéresserait beaucoup (de)* – My interest (in/for) grew when…: *mon intérêt (pour) a cru quand…* – to turn a passing interest into passion: *transformer un intérêt passager en passion* – …would be of great interest to me: *serait d'un grand intérêt à mes yeux* – Throughout this project I developed an unexpected interest for research: *Au cours de ce projet, je me suis découvert un intérêt inattendu pour la recherche* – The interest I place in your department is due to its international reputation: *L'intérêt que je manifeste pour votre département est motivé par sa réputation internationale* – …has spawned growing interest: *…a engendré un intérêt croissant* – I can be described as a passionate person with a keen interest (in): *On peut me décrire comme quelqu'un de passionné, avec un vif intérêt (pour)* – independent of my field of interest: *indépendamment de mon domaine d'intérêt* – My personal interests are in line (with): *Mes intérêts personnels cadrent (avec)* – I cannot help but wonder if these aspects of my personality do not somewhow relate to my interest in…: *Je ne peux m'empêcher de me demander si ces aspects de ma personnalité ne sont pas en quelque sorte liés à mon intérêt pour* – My interest in… is a natural outgrowth of my commitment (to): *Mon intérêt pour… est une exten-*

sion naturelle de mon engagement (dans) – My interest in becoming a researcher extends back to my childhood: *J'ai manifesté de l'intérêt pour le métier de chercheur dès mon enfance*

a passion (for): *une passion (pour)*
a genuine/life-long passion: *une passion authentique/de longue date*
to be passionate (about): *être passionné (par/de)*
to turn into a passion: *devenir une passion*
to confirm sb's passion: *confirmer la passion de qn*
to arouse/to awaken a passion: *faire naître une passion*

• **Curiosity/*La curiosité***
a sense of curiosity: *un sentiment de curiosité*
to be goaded/driven on (by): *être mû (par)*
to be curious (about): *être curieux (de)*
an inquisitive/inquiring mind: *un esprit curieux*
to know how things work: *savoir comment les choses fonctionnent*
to arouse/to awaken one's curiosity: *susciter la curiosité*
to discover the hidden hand (behind): *découvrir le secret qui se cache (derrière)*
to pique one's intellectual curiosity: *soulever la curiosité intellectuelle*
to satisfy one's curiosity: *satisfaire sa curiosité*
to whet sb's curiosity: *attiser la curiosité de qn*

✓ One's curiosity can deepen (*s'approfondir*)/can goad sb on (*pousser qn à*)

✓ great/intense/insatiable/mere (*simple*) + **curiosity**

to be curious (about): *être curieux (de)*
to become/to grow curious (about): *s'intéresser (à)*
to be curious to find out: *être curieux de découvrir*
out of curiosity: *par curiosité*

✓ deeply/intensely/extremely/mildly (*moyennement*)/rather (*plutôt*)/genuinely (*véritablement*)/ naturally (*naturellement*)/somewhat (*quelque peu*) + **curious**

• **Creativity/*La créativité***
to create/creation: *créer/la création*
a spark of creativity: *une étincelle de créativité*
creativeness/creative: *la créativité/créatif*
inventiveness (ni): *l'esprit d'invention*
to invent/an invention/inventive (a): *inventer/l'invention/inventif*
the spirit of invention: *le génie inventif*
an inventor: *un inventeur*

to be the brainchild (of): *être conçu (par)*
an inventor with one's feet firmly planted on the ground: *un inventeur qui a le sens des réalités*
to push into the unknown and the creative: *s'enfoncer dans l'inconnu et le créatif*
to come up with (an idea): *trouver (une idée)*
an out of box concept: *un concept innovant*
to think outside the box: *sortir des schémas établis*
an outside the box approach/perspective: *une approche/perspective originale*
blue sky thinking: *la pensée créatrice*
a disruptive technology: *une technologie révolutionnaire*
a transformative invention: *une invention révolutionnaire*
to harness technology: *maîtriser la technologie*
to shoot for the moon: *tenter de décrocher la lune*
a petri dish for (...) experiments: *un terreau d'expérimentation (pour)*
to contribute original work (to): *contribuer par l'originalité de ses travaux (à)*
to translate into practical change: *concrétiser*
to think creatively: *avoir une réflexion créatrice*
to cook up new ideas: *trouver de nouvelles idées*
to scout for new ideas: *être à la recherche de nouvelles idées*
a hothouse (for new ideas/new talent): *une pépinière (de nouvelles idées/de nouveaux talents)*
to discover/a discovery: *découvrir/une découverte*
to make a discovery: *faire une découverte*
to lead to a discovery: *conduire à une découverte*
to be credited with a discovery: *à qui l'on doit une découverte*
to hit upon/to chance upon: *découvrir (par hasard)*
in a moment of serendipity: *par un heureux hasard*
by serendipity: *par chance*
to tinker/a tinkerer: *bricoler/un bricoleur*

• Leadership/*L'aptitude à diriger*

📖 There is no general agreement about the qualities of a leader. **Field Marshal Montgomery** (1887-1976) thought that a leader "must have infectious optimism, and the determination to persevere in the face of difficulties. He must also radiate confidence, even when he himself is not too certain of the outcome". **Henri Fayol** (1841-1925), an early French writer on management, said that a leader's task is "thinking out a plan and ensuring its success". It is, he added, "one of the keenest satisfactions for an intelligent man to experience". **David Ogilvy** (1911-1999), founder of an advertising agency, Ogilvy & Mather, and himself a leader of some quality, said: "Great leaders almost always exude self-confidence. They are never petty. They are never buck-passers. They pick themselves up after defeat... They do not suffer from the crippling need to be universally loved... The great leaders I have known have been curiously complicated men."

✓ a born/charismatic/effective (*efficace*), great (*formidable*), inspiring (*qui inspire*), inspired (*inspiré*), undisputed (*sans conteste*), strong, powerful + **leader**

to be appointed leader: *être désigné pour diriger*
to choose as leader: *choisir pour diriger*
to become a leader in a field: *devenir une référence dans un domaine*

✓ **Leadership can be** clear (*évident*), effective (*efficace*), firm (*ferme*), outstanding (*remarquable*), strong, dynamic, visionary, personal, collective / joint, poor, weak

to assert personal leadership: *affirmer sa capacité personnelle à diriger*
to assume/to take on, over the leadership: *prendre la direction*
to exercise the leadership: *exercer la direction*
to provide leadership: *apporter la direction*
to show leadership: *montrer que l'on dirige*
the leadership spirit: *l'esprit de dirigeant*
the spirit of entrepreneurship: *un esprit d'entreprise*
entrepreneurial DNA: *l'ADN entrepreneurial*
to aspire to run my own organization: *aspirer à diriger mon entreprise*
to launch a venture: *lancer une entreprise*
leadership skills: *les aptitudes à diriger*
to found one's own start-up/a founder: *fonder sa startup/un fondateur*
leadership qualities: *les qualités pour diriger*
to show one's stripes as a leader: *montrer ses qualités de dirigeant*
under sb's leadership: *sous la direction de qn*
a sense of responsibility: *un sentiment de responsabilité*

☞ **Expressions.** By many measures, this nation leads the world in scientific research, even though its dominance has been slipping of late: *À bien des égards, ce pays est à la tête de la recherche scientifique dans le monde, même si sa suprématie a quelque peu été entamée récemment* – to have a lead in science and technology: *avoir une avance dans le domaine scientifique et technologique* – Your program provides students with the kind of credentials they will need to become leaders in the field: *Votre programme fournit aux étudiants le genre de qualifications dont ils auront besoin pour diriger* – This experience put to test my sense of responsibilities, since I was in charge of the security of all people on board: *Cette expérience a mis à l'épreuve mon sentiment de responsabilité puisque j'étais en charge de la sécurité du personnel à bord*

III. SOP Openers/ *L'accroche*

Interest/*L'intérêt*

my interest (for) was stirred/aroused/raised: *mon intérêt pour… provient de*
to be of great interest (to): *être d'un grand intérêt (pour)*
to capture sb's interest: *attirer l'intérêt de qn*
to develop a keen interest (for): *développer un vif intérêt (pour)*
to firm up sb's interest: *renforcer l'intérêt de qn*
to have one's interest aroused: *provoquer l'intérêt de qn*
to hold sb's interest: *retenir l'intérêt de qn*
to kindle/to spark/to stimulate sb's interest: *stimuler l'intérêt de qn*
to pique sb's interest: *piquer la curiosité de qn*
to rouse/to stir sb's interest: *susciter l'intérêt de qn*
to take an interest (in): *s'intéresser (à)*
my attraction (to): *mon attirance (pour)*
I was drawn to (science): *j'ai été attiré par (la science)*
to set sb up on the path (to): *mettre qn sur la voie (de)*
to set out on a challenging path: *s'engager dans une voie exigeante*
to offer a pluralistic approach (to): *offrir une approche pluraliste (de)*

☞ **Expressions**. That interest for (…) has stayed with me throughout the years: *Cet intérêt pour (…) ne m'a pas quitté tout au long de ces années* – a passion which has guided me in many of my academic choices: *une passion qui a guidé le choix de mes études* – My interest (for) was firmed up while…: *Mon intérêt (pour) fut renforcé alors que…*

Coursework/*Les cours*

a seminar: *un séminaire*

→ **course**: a set of classes or a plan of study on a particular subject, usually leading to an exam or qualification (Cambridge Dictionary). Example: a three-year course in quantum physics/a course in creative writing

a tutorial: *des travaux dirigés (TD)/travaux pratiques (TP), une petite classe*
an elective: *un cours facultatif/optionnel, une option*
course content: *le contenu du cours*
courses on offer: *les cours proposés*
to choose a further course: *choisir un cours supplémentaire*
to complement a course: *compléter un cours*
to take/to follow a class/course (on): *suivre un cours (sur)*
to be thrilled to take a course (on): *être excité à l'idée de suivre un cours (sur)*
an additional course: *un cours supplémentaire*
to teach a course: *enseigner*
to attend a class: *assister à un cours*
to register/to sign up for a class: *s'inscrire à un cours*
to hold a class: *faire cours*
to open the door (of): *ouvrir la porte (de)*
the learning curve: *la courbe d'apprentissage*

✓ an intensive course: *un cours intensif* – a crash course: *un cours de remise à niveau* – an advanced course: *un cours avancé* – a foundation course: *un cours fondamental* – an introductory course: *un cours d'introduction* – a refresher course: *un cours de remise à niveau* – a thought-provoking course: *un cours qui invite à réfléchir* – an honours course (UK): *un cours de licence (US), un cours réservé aux meilleurs étudiants* – a general knowledge course: *un cours de culture générale*

✓ A course can be fulfilling/stimulating: *stimulant* – compelling: *captivant* – rewarding: *gratifiant* – thrilling: *excitant* – exciting: *passionnant* – boring: *ennuyeux* – oriented towards/geared to: *orienté vers* – fascinating: *fascinant* – uplifting: *inspirant, exaltant* – far-reaching: *d'une portée considérable* – intellectually fulfilling: *intellectuellement gratifiant*

☞ **Expressions.** in the course of a class (on) I attended (in + date): *pendant un cours (sur) auquel j'assistai (en + date)* – The class I followed on thermodynamics was to be a game changer in my academic life: *Le cours de thermodynamique allait provoquer un changement radical dans mes études* – I was introduced to the field (of) in a course taught (by): *J'ai découvert le domaine (de) pendant un cours (de)* – Although I am an economics major, what I have learned as an undergraduate can be applied in many ways to data science: *Bien que me spécialisant en économie, ce que j'ai appris en licence peut s'appliquer à bien des points à la science des données* – the courses listed above: *les cours mentionnés supra*

☞ **Expressions.** What I liked about studying economics was the breadth of the subject: *Ce que j'ai bien aimé en économie, c'est l'étendue du sujet* – to get the most from studying a subject: *tirer le maximum de profit de l'étude d'un sujet* – an integral part of a well-rounded liberal arts education: *une partie intégrante d'une formation complète en lettres et sciences humaines* – My undergraduate training in the sciences has provided me with a solid background for advanced work: *Ma formation de premier cycle en science m'a doté d'un solide bagage pour des études plus poussées* – to gain a solid understanding (of): *obtenir une bonne compréhension (de)* – to gain substantial experience (in): *acquérir une solide expérience (dans)*

The past/*Le passé*

looking back over the years: *en examinant le passé*
a scene indelibly etched in my memory: *un souvenir indélébile*

A conference (on…) I attended years ago: *Une conférence (sur…) à laquelle j'ai assisté il y a des années* – It was when Professor Jones introduced… that it all became clear to me: *Quand le professeur Jones a présenté… j'ai soudain compris* – Reading Prof. Jones's book on climate change, it dawned upon me that: *En lisant le livre sur le changement climatique du Professeur Jones, j'ai soudain compris que/il m'est apparu que*

with hindsight/in retrospect: *rétrospectivement*
on second thoughts: *à bien y réfléchir, en y repensant*
looking back: *avec le recul, après coup, a posteriori*

The family/*La famille*

to follow in one's father's footsteps: *suivre la voie tracée par son père*
to run in the family: *être de famille*
to defy one's family's wishes (that I should become an engineer): *aller à l'encontre des vœux de sa famille (de devenir ingénieur)*
the first in the family to graduate (from): *la première dans la famille à être diplômée (de)*
to break with family tradition: *rompre avec la tradition familiale*
to trailblaze/to pave the way: *ouvrir la voie*
a trailblazer/pathbreaker: *un pionnier, un innovateur*
to overcome apprehensions: *surmonter les appréhensions*
to give the lie (to): *contredire*

The final introductory sentence/*La dernière phrase de l'introduction*

Harvard is definitely the place I want to go: *Harvard est à coup sûr l'endroit qu'il me faut*
to be a good fit: *être le bon choix*
to fit in with one's goals: *correspondre à ses objectifs*
to suit one's goals (of): *répondre à ses objectifs (de)*
to be in continuity (with)/in line (with): *être dans le droit fil (de)*
to be a unique opportunity (to): *présenter une occasion unique (de)*
to be the next logical step: *être logiquement l'étape suivante*
to concretize a career goal: *concrétiser ses ambitions professionnelles*
to forge ahead/to forge on (with): *aller de l'avant (dans)*
to soldier on: *persévérer (envers et contre tout), tenir bon*

☞ **Expressions.** a next logical step towards accomplishing my professional goal: *être la suite logique dans la réalisation de mes ambitions professionnelles* – that hopefully will lead me (to): *qui, je l'espère me conduira (à)* – Your program and my scientific interests perfectly align: *Votre programme et mes intérêts scientifiques coïncident parfaitement* – to align with one's academic priorities: *coïncider avec ses priorités universitaires*

IV. Research/ *La recherche*

The doctoral program/*Le programme doctoral*

a PhD/Ph.D. (US)/DPhil (UK): *un doctorat*
a thesis advisor: *un directeur de thèse*

> 🕮 A **thesis** is a written work containing the results of research on a specific topic prepared by a candidate for a bachelor's or master's degree.

a major professor: *un directeur de jury de thèse*
a doctoral degree: *une thèse (le diplôme)*
to confer a doctoral degree: *décerner le titre de docteur*
a dissertation: *une thèse*
to earn a doctorate: *obtenir un doctorat*
to pursue an academic career: *faire une carrière universitaire*
a doctoral program: *un programme de 3e cycle*
to make a lasting/significant contribution (to): *contribuer durablement/de façon significative (à)*
to continue my education through a postdoctoral fellowship: *poursuivre ma carrière par un postdoc*

> 🕮 **Qualifying examination**: an examination given to students who have completed required coursework for a doctoral degree, but who have not yet begun the dissertation or thesis. A qualifying examination may be oral or written, or both, and must be passed for the student to continue.

Research interests/*Les intérêts en recherche*

> → ***Attention***: research is **always singular** in English. Her research **has** proved that...: *Ses recherches ont montré que...*

research (on/in): *de la recherche (en)*
a research team: *une équipe de recherche*
a researcher/a research worker: *un chercheur*

to do/to carry out research (on/into): *faire de la recherche (en)*
a sector/field/domain of research: *un domaine de recherche*
to search out (solutions): *chercher (des solutions)*
to come up with a solution: *trouver une solution*
to delve into the world of research: *plonger dans le monde de la recherche*
to do a deep dive (into): *faire une analyse approfondie (de)*
to take sb in a deep dive into: *amener qn à faire une analyse approfondie de*
cutting-edge research/breakthrough research: *la recherche à la pointe*
on the leading edge (of): *à la pointe (de)*
leading edge research: *la recherche de pointe*
at the forefront: *à l'avant-garde*
the forefront of technological innovation: *l'avant-garde en matière d'innovation technologique*
to foster innovation: *encourager l'innovation*
to drive innovation: *être le moteur de l'innovation*
to find one's way into the mainstream: *être adopté par le grand public*
a wave of innovation: *une vague d'innovations*
a burst of innovation: *des innovations tous azimuts*
technological innovation: *l'innovation technologique*
to harness new technologies: *dompter de nouvelles technologies*
the pace of innovation: *le rythme des innovations*
to take a product/service from idea to market: *développer une idée/un service et (la/le) commercialiser*
a dawn of technological optimism: *une nouvelle ère d'optimisme technologique*
to unleash a new dawn of discovery: *déclencher une ère nouvelle de découvertes*
to lift living standards: *améliorer la qualité de vie*
to be on the cusp of progress: *être à la pointe du progrès*
transformative potential: *le pouvoir de transformer*
to conduct research (on): *mener des recherches (dans)*
to undertake research: *entreprendre des recherches*
a research engineer: *un ingénieur de recherche*

☞ **Expressions.** Her research is based on: *Ses recherches s'appuient sur* – Research yields/produces: *Les recherches débouchent (sur)* – Research has revealed (that): *Les recherches ont montré (que)* – as a budding researcher: *en tant que chercheur en herbe* – the takeaway from her research is that…: *le point fort de sa recherche est que…*

a research project that involves: *un projet de recherche qui implique*
a team-based research project: *un projet scientifique collectif*
a take home project: *un projet à faire à la maison*
a master's research project: *un projet de fin d'études*
to engage in a research project: *se lancer dans/entreprendre un projet de recherche*
to be involved in a project: *être impliqué dans un projet*
to onboard (a project/company): *intégrer (projet/entreprise)*
to complete a project: *terminer un projet*
to take charge of a project: *être responsable d'un projet*
to pool one's efforts: *mettre ses efforts en commun*

to make science progress/to advance science: *faire avancer la science*

✓ **Researchers** study (*étudient*), investigate sth (*enquêtent, font des recherches sur*), discover (*découvrent*), find sth (*trouvent qch*), find out that (*découvrir que*)

my research focuses (on): *mes recherches portent (sur)*
to laser in (on): *porter (sur)*
my research interests lie (in): *les centres d'intérêt de ma recherche se situent (dans)*

✓ **Research can be** ground-breaking (*innovant*), detailed (*détaillé*), in-depth (*approfondi*), extensive (*étendu*), investigative *(d'enquête)*, meticulous/thorough (*méticuleux*), pioneering (*original*), empirical (*empirique*), cutting-edge (*à l'avant-garde*), indefatiguable (*inlassable*)

a research internship: *un stage de recherche*
to secure an internship: *obtenir un stage*

☞ **Expressions.** Her expertise (on) will be crucial in giving my research the required background: *Son expertise (sur) sera déterminante pour donner à ma recherche les fondements nécessaires* – The faculty research matches my academic interests: *Les recherches menées par les professeurs correspondent à mes intérêts théoriques* – The lab research parallels my own: *Les recherches du labo sont à l'image des miennes* – I have looked into her research (on): *J'ai étudié ses travaux de recherche (sur)* – I would like to seek the guidance (of): *Je souhaiterais être supervisé (par)*

to apply what one learned in class: *appliquer les connaissances acquises en classe*
to assist a researcher (on): *aider un chercheur (à)*
to be a testing ground of the theory: *permettre de tester la théorie*
to put a theory to the test: *éprouver une théorie*
to be a litmus test (of): *être un test décisif (de)*
to be exposed to research: *être confronté à la recherche*
to develop research interests: *poursuivre des intérêts de recherche*
to gain experience in the field: *acquérir une expérience dans le domaine*
to get hands-on experience (in): *avoir une expérience concrète (de)*
unparalleled hands-on experience: *une expérience concrète à nulle autre pareille*
to match one's intellectual interests perfectly: *correspondre parfaitement à ses intérêts intellectuels*
to put theory into practice: *appliquer la théorie*
to put knowledge into practice: *appliquer les connaissances*
to shape and nurture sb's intellectual faculties: *façonner et nourrir les facultés intellectuelles (de qn)*

☞ **Expressions.** Research epitomizes what I find most enjoyable and what I would most like to pursue as a profession: *La recherche représente ce que j'aime le plus et ce que je voudrais faire plus tard dans ma vie* – I have been fortunate to have the opportunity to take part in a number of projects over the last few years: *J'ai eu la chance de participer à un certain nombre de projets au* *cours des dernières années* – I value independent research, my undergraduate work attests to this bias: *J'accorde de l'importance à la recherche indépendante, comme en atteste mon travail en fac*

☞ to bend biology to man's will: *soumettre la biologie à la volonté de l'homme* – to display impressive progress: *faire preuve de progrès impressionnants* – Adversity forces societies to advance: *L'adversité contraint les sociétés à aller de l'avant* – to spur further bold steps: *encourager d'autres mesures audacieuses* – to rise to the challenges: *être à la hauteur des défis*

under the guidance/supervision (of): *sous la direction (de)*
unsupervised: *sans supervision*
with minimal/scant supervision: *avec une supervision minime*
with hardly any supervision: *avec un encadrement de pure forme*

The research project/*Le projet de recherche*

to carry out a project: *exécuter un projet*
to conduct a project: *conduire un projet*
to lead/to spearhead a project: *mener/diriger un projet*
to make inroads (into): *faire des progrès (dans)*
to plan out a project: *prévoir un projet*
to pursue a project: *poursuivre un projet*
to see a project through/to complete a project: *terminer un projet*
to undergo a project: *entreprendre un projet*
to work on a team/to be part of a team: *faire partie d'une équipe*
to team up/to join forces (to): *unir ses forces (en vue de)*
to work in teams of three: *travailler par équipes de trois*
how to work with others/in team: *comment travailler en groupe*
to bring people together: *réunir les gens*

- I work **on** a team = I manage/control/influence a team.
- I work **with** a team = I collaborate/cooperate with a team.
- I work **in** a team = I am one of that team.

to analyze/to process/to drill data: *analyser des données*
to sift through data: *trier des données*
a wealth/trove of data: *une mine de données*
an amount of data: *une quantité de données*
to be data-savvy: *être expert en données*
to carry out an experiment: *faire une expérience*
to conduct an experiment: *mener une expérience*
to design experimental methodologies: *concevoir des méthodes expérimentales*
to confront ground-level realities: *se frotter aux réalités du terrain*

to benchmark (against): *comparer (avec)*
experience in the field: *l'expérience sur le terrain*
field-based: *sur le terrain*
to draft a report: *rédiger un rapport*
to draft preliminary conclusions: *rédiger les premières conclusions*
to participate in a project: *participer à un projet*
to work in a project of three: *collaborer à trois à un projet*

✓ **A project can be** exciting (*passionnant*), stimulating (*stimulant)*, rewarding (*enrichissant*), enticing (*attirant*)

Lab work/*Les travaux expérimentaux*

a research lab: *un labo de recherche*
lab work/experimental work (ni): *les travaux expérimentaux*
practical work/lab work (UK)/lab (US)/a practicum [pl. practica, practicums]: *les travaux pratiques (TP)*

☞ A **practicum** is a course (sometimes a single session, but not limited to one) that teaches you how to do something by having you do it. It focuses on observation and involves the supervised practical application of a previously studied theory. A practicum (also called (industrial) work placement, especially in the UK) is common for education and social work majors. In some cases, the practicum may be a part-time student teaching placement that occurs the semester before a student's full-time student teaching placement.

an experiment: *une expérience*
a lab experiment: *une expérience en laboratoire*
a lab test (on): *un test en laboratoire (sur)*
an experimental module: *un module expérimental*
laboratory/lab equipment/apparatus: *le matériel de laboratoire*
to carry out measurements: *faire des mesures*
to conduct experiments: *mener des expériences*
to serve as a lab assistant: *faire office d'assistant de laboratoire*
under laboratory conditions: *selon les conditions de laboratoire*

The research paper/*L'article de recherche*

to write a resarch paper (on): *rédiger un article (sur)*
to submit a paper: *soumettre un article*
an academic/scholarly journal: *une revue savante*
to peer review: *faire évaluer par ses pairs*
peer review: *l'évaluation par ses pairs*

to review/to referee an academic paper: *soumettre à un comité de lecture*
scholarly peer review/refereeing: *la lecture critique par les pairs*
one publication is currently pending: *une publication est actuellement en cours*
to be suitable for publication: *convenir pour un article*

The findings of one's research/*Les résultats de ses recherches*

to present one's findings: *présenter ses résultats*
tried and true/tested results: *des résultats éprouvés*
a breakthrough: *une découverte capitale*
to make a breakthrough: *percer*
to blaze new trails: *tracer de nouveaux chemins*
to break new ground: *faire de nouvelles découvertes*
to give an insight (on/of/into): *donner un aperçu (de)*

✓ **Verbs + insight**. to afford: *permettre* – to give/to offer: *offrir* – to provide sb with: *fournir* – to produce/to yield: *donner* – to gain/to get/to obtain: *obtenir*

☞ **Expressions**. to gain from experience: *apprendre de l'expérience* – to benefit from a more experimental approach: *profiter d'une approche plus expérimentale* – I learnt that, in research the ability of individuals to work as a team is essential: *J'ai appris qu'en recherche, la capacité de chacun à travailler en groupe est essentielle* – Throughout this project I developed an unexpected interest for research: *Pendant le projet, je me suis découvert un intérêt inattendu pour la recherche* – I found out how fundamental it is to get a good control of experimental measurements in the building up of a theory: *Je me suis rendu compte à quel point il est essentiel de bien maîtriser les mesures expérimentales quand on construit une théorie* – The difficulty of this work was making sure everyone was working efficiently, embracing complementary areas on a subject that none of us could master by themselves: *La difficulté était de s'assurer que tout le monde travaillait avec efficacité, en tenant compte des complémentarités de chacun à propos d'un sujet que personne ne pouvait maîtriser seul*

to analyze data: *analyser les données*
to answer a hypothesis: *répondre à une hypothèse*
to complement the theory: *compléter la théorie*
a theory-based course: *un cours théorique*
to confront the theory with reality: *confronter la théorie et la réalité*
an idea that holds weight: *une idée qui a son importance*
to construct a hypothesis: *construire une hypothèse*
to define a research hypothesis: *définir une hypothèse de recherche*
to test a hypothesis: *tester une hypothèse*
to disprove/to prove: *réfuter/prouver*
to establish relationships (between): *établir des relations (entre)*
to experiment the validity of a theory: *tester la validité d'une théorie*

to find out more (about): *en savoir plus (sur)*
to make connections: *faire le lien*
to manipulate variables: *manipuler les variables*
to understand cause and effect: *comprendre les causes et conséquences*
a rule of thumb: *une règle empirique*
to predict phenomena: *prévoir des phénomènes*
to test the conclusions of a study: *tester les conclusions d'une étude*
to do background research: *faire des recherches préliminaires*
to provide an ideal test case (to): *montrer de façon irréfutable*

☞ **Expressions.** to move from an abstract idea to a concrete achievement: *passer d'une idée abstraite à une réussite concrète* – to provide sb with a pragmatic approach to complement my current theoretical studies: *offrir une approche pragmatique pour compléter mes études théoriques actuelles*

The project and the human factor/*Le projet et le facteur humain*

an enriching experience: *une expérience enrichissante*
project management: *la gestion de projet*
a project leader: *un chef de projet*
a team project: *un projet d'équipe/en équipe*
a paired project: *un projet en binôme*
to be in charge (of): *être responsable (de)*
a person in charge: *un responsable*
to manage one's time well: *bien gérer son temps*
to meet deadlines: *respecter les échéances*
to allocate/to distribute tasks: *répartir les taches*
to liaise with the industry: *travailler en relation avec l'industrie*
a fruitful exchange of ideas: *un échange d'idées fructueux*
to rub ideas (with): *échanger des idées (avec)*
to bounce ideas off sb: *partager des idées*
to learn from one another: *apprendre des autres*
to complement each other: *se compléter les uns les autres*
to develop skills: *développer des compétences*

V. Work Experience/ *L'expérience professionnelle*

Working/*Le travail*

✓ **Tough work can be** arduous (*ardu*), hard (*dur*), back-breaking (*éreintant*), demanding (*exigeant*), intensive (*intense*), gruelling (*pénible*), tough (*dur*), rewarding (*gratifiant*), heavy (*lourd*), dirty (*sale*), delicate (*délicat*), humdrum (*routinier*), repetitive (*répétitif*)

✓ **Uplifting work can be** purposeful (*significatif*), fascinating (*fascinant*), valuable (*précieux*), outstanding (*remarquable*), thorough (*approfondi*), ground-breaking (*innovant*), pioneering (*de pionnier*)

group work/teamwork: *le travail en groupe/en équipe*
paired work: *un binôme*
humanitarian work: *le travail humanitaire*

✓ to carry out: *exécuter* – to do (some work)/to put in a lot of work (on/in): *beaucoup travailler (à)* – to get some work done/to take on/to undertake: *se charger de, entreprendre*

✓ to get down to/to set about to: *se mettre à* – to carry on: *continuer* – to complete: *terminer* – to hold up: *retarder* – to schedule: *prévoir, organiser* – to oversee/to supervise: *superviser* – to require: *nécessiter* – to hand in one's work: *rendre son travail* – to involve: *impliquer* – to mean: *signifier*

✓ to keep up the good work: *continuer à faire du bon boulot* – the pressure of work: *la pression du travail* – a work in progress: *un travail en cours* – to be congratulated/to be praised for one's work: *être félicité pour son travail*

✓ **To work** + hard/steadily (*régulièrement*), around the clock (*sans s'arrêter*), full time (*à plein temps*), efficiently (*efficacement*), closely with (*en étroite collaboration avec*), together with (*ensemble avec*), independently (*indépendamment*), away (at) (*sans arrêt*)

☞ **Expressions**. undaunted by the fear of failure/failing: *nullement impressionné par la peur d'échouer* – failure teaches success: *on apprend de ses échecs* – success depends on one's backbone, not one's wishbone: *le succès dépend des efforts, pas des rêves* – the desire to jump in and take the matters into one's own hands: *le désir d'intervenir et de prendre personnellement les choses en main* – to make high demands of oneself: *exiger beaucoup de soi* – to result in disappointment: *finir par être déçu*

☞ **Hooks**. relevant work experience – what settled my vocation was... – my vocation in life was... while doing... – to arrange a work placement with – to set one's heart on – to meet deadlines is a key skill – my choice of degree was confirmed when... – to show a sense of initiative

☞ a plant: *une usine* – a shop: *un atelier* – a workstation: *un poste de travail*

the development of working skills: *le développement de compétences professionnelles*
to apply one's learning/knowledge (to): *appliquer ses connaissances (à)*
a case study: *une étude de cas*
case stories: *des cas concrets*
hands-on/real-world applications in case studies: *des applications concrètes à des études de cas*
to solve a real-world problem: *résoudre un problème concret*
to provide useful experience: *apporter une expérience utile*
to rub shoulders with: *côtoyer*
to share the workers' lives: *partager la vie des ouvriers*
to spur on one's team: *encourager son équipe*
to work on the assembly line: *travailler sur la ligne de production*
to work on the shop floor: *travailler comme ouvrier*
to work with/for a company/a startup: *travailler pour une entreprise/startup*

☞ **Expressions**. to practise one's skills in the workplace: *mettre ses compétences en application* – a chance to test one's career plans: *une occasion de jauger ses objectifs professionnels* – to leverage one's expertise: *se servir de son expertise* – to bring knowledge and expertise: *apporter ses connaissances et son savoir-faire* – to impress a potential employer: *faire bonne impression auprès d'un employeur potentiel* – to contribute to the competitiveness of a company: *contribuer à la compétitivité des entreprises* – to improve one's CV: *améliorer son CV* – to have a competitive edge in the job market: *avoir une longueur d'avance sur le marché du travail* – to learn valuable skills: *apprendre des compétences recherchées* – to add to a sense of fulfillment: *contribuer à l'épanouissement personnel* – to apply one's knowledge and skills in an industrial setting: *appliquer ses connaissances et compétences dans un milieu industriel* – to develop confidence: *développer la confiance* – to prepare for a career: *se préparer à une carrière* – to transition to goals and challenges ahead: *se préparer à des objectifs et défis à venir* – to define future career goals: *définir des objectifs de carrière* – to improve one's employability: *améliorer sa capacité à décrocher un emploi* – to link academic study and theory to real industrial practice: *faire un lien entre les études et la théorie et une véritable pratique industrielle* – to confirm existing career aims: *conforter dans ses choix professionnels* – to apply problem solving in a real work environment: *mettre en œuvre la résolution de problèmes dans un environnement professionnel* – to assess a possible company for future employment: *évaluer une entreprise susceptible de nous intéresser professionnellement* – to learn beyond the classroom: *compléter sa formation*

The gap year/*L'année de césure*

a gap year: *une parenthèse utile*

📖 **Gap years** aren't a recent phenomenon. During the 1700s in England, young British elites went on 'Grand Tours' around Europe to broaden their horizons and gain cultural exposure. In modern times, gap years began as "hippy trails," a post-cold war Britain movement of young people overlanding from Europe to Asia in search of love, freedom, and betterment. Gap years are actually anything but a vacation. They are a period of proactive travel designed to help students explore academic and career pursuits, gain new experiences, interact with other cultures, increase personal growth, and gain deeper insight into achieving their goals. Gap year experiences such as traveling, working, or volunteering abroad require more independence, self-sufficiency, and motivation than the average classroom setting. Students complete gap years with stronger personal and professional skills and get more confident about the direction of their future.

to take a gap year: *faire une année de césure*
a chance to re-focus/to regroup: *une occasion de se remobiliser*
a career plan/career objectives/career aspirations: *un projet professionnel*
a career possibility: *une possibilité de carrière*
to develop career objectives: *construire un projet professionnel*
to map out a plan for one's career goals: *définir son projet professionnel*
to clarify one's career goals: *clarifier son projet professionnel*
a mind-expanding experience: *une expérience enrichissante*
a mind-changing experience: *une expérience qui a changé ma façon de penser*
a positive outlook (on): *un aperçu positif (de)*
a turning point in my life: *un tournant dans ma vie*
time for reflection: *du temps pour réfléchir*
to be better prepared to benefit (from): *être mieux préparé à bénéficier (de)*
to boost one's job prospects: *améliorer ses perspectives d'emploi*
to broaden one's horizons: *élargir ses horizons*
to decide on a professional career path: *décider du choix d'une carrière*
to decide on one's path in life: *décider de sa carrière*
to do an overseas experience: *partir à l'étranger*
to escape the daily grind: *échapper au train-train quotidien*
to experience another culture: *découvrir une autre culture*
to explore a career: *découvrir une carrière*
to gain a new perspective on life: *voir la vie différemment*
to gain experience: *acquérir de l'expérience*
to immerse oneself in a culture: *faire une expérience en immersion*
to learn a great deal of responsibility: *apprendre le sens des responsabilités*
to face up to the reality (of): *se frotter à la réalité (de)*
to open new vistas (on): *offrir de nouvelles perspectives (sur)*
to pursue a passion: *vivre une passion*
to recharge one's batteries: *recharger ses batteries*
to step away from the treadmill: *prendre de la distance/hauteur*

to step out of one's comfort zone: *sortir de sa zone de confort*
to be confronted to another side of life: *voir un autre côté des choses*
to take a break from coursework: *faire une pause dans ses études*
to take a year off: *prendre une année de congé*
to take a step back: *prendre du recul*
to take time off: *souffler*
to widen one's perspective (on): *élargir ses perspectives (sur)*

☞ **Expressions.** to experience an enhanced understanding of global issues, cultural diversity and abstract ideas: *acquérir une meilleure compréhension des problèmes du monde, de la diversité culturelle et des idées abstraites* – to stand out from the crowd: *se distinguer des autres* – to receive a head start in life: *prendre un avantage dans la vie* – skills building: *l'acquisition de compétences* – to explore career pursuits: *explorer des pistes professionnelles* – heightened self-awareness: *une conscience de soi accrue* – to improve one's maturity: *mieux grandir* – to build maturity/independence: *se forger une maturité/indépendance* – to develop the soft skills necessary for effective social interaction: *développer un savoir-être pour échanger utilement avec autrui* – to grow one's independence: *développer son indépendance* – to get to know oneself outside of the school setting: *apprendre à se connaître en dehors du cadre scolaire* – to grow a sense of purpose: *développer une motivation* – a more focused approach to learning: *une meilleure préparation aux études* – to figure out what one wants to do: *réfléchir à ce que l'on veut faire*

Military duty/*Le service militaire*

leadership training: *la formation à la gestion des hommes/au commandement*
to be part of the school's first year curriculum: *faire partie du programme de 1re année*
a period of human and military formation: *une période de formation humaine et militaire*
a rite of passage: *une étape importante*
military education and training: *la formation militaire*
to do one's military service: *faire son service militaire*
to enlist in the military: *s'enrôler*
to join/to go into the Army/Navy: *s'enrôler dans l'armée/la marine*
as a trainee officer/officer cadet: *en tant qu'élève officier*
an officer in charge: *un officier responsable*
to be excused from serving: *être exempté de service militaire*
to serve in the army: *servir dans l'armée*
to serve one's country: *servir son pays*
civil defense/civil defence/civil protection: *la sécurité civile*
civil protection (PROTEC)/civil defence (UK)/civil defense (US): *la protection civile*
a civilian service: *un service civil*
commando training: *un stage commando*

☞ **Expressions.** a highly stressful environment: *un environnement très stressant* – close to the conditions of combat operations: *proche des opérations de combat* - parachute training: *l'entraînement parachutiste* – a joint-combined exercise: *un exercice conjoint* – to participate in a land operation:

participer à une opération terrestre – to protect a sensitive site: *protéger un site sensible* – I received extensive training that was both physically and emotionally intense: *J'ai suivi un entraînement intensif et intense, à la fois physiquement et émotionnellement* – I learned as much about the value and dynamics of teamwork as I did about my own personality and abilities: *J'en ai appris autant sur la valeur et la dynamique de l'effort de groupe que sur ma personnalité et mes capacités*

basic training: *les classes*
a boot camp: *un camp d'entraînement*
to undergo basic training/to do one's basic training: *faire ses classes*
an army training base: *une base d'entraînement de l'armée*
a training exercise: *un exercice d'entraînement*
a training instructor: *un instructeur*
a military/officer academy: *une école militaire*
the French Armed Forces: *l'Armée française*
the land forces: *les forces terrestres*
the Foreign Legion: *la Légion étrangère*
the special forces group: *les forces spéciales*
the Naval infantry: *les fusiliers marins*
to serve on a French vessel: *servir sur un vaisseau français*
the French Navy: *la Marine française*
an officer on the watch (OOW): *un officier de quart*
to ply the seas: *naviguer sur les mers*
to call at a port: *faire escale dans un port*
to be on night watch: *être de quart*
to see the world: *voir le monde*
to be deployed: *être en mission*

📖 **SEAL team**: US Navy forces organized, trained, and equipped to conduct special operations with an emphasis on maritime, coastal, and riverine environments – **Commandos Marine** (units): Special Operation Forces (SOF) of the French Navy. They are nicknamed *Green Berets.*

the French Air Force: *l'Armée de l'air*
Air Transport Squadron of the Air Force: *un escadron de transport de l'Armée de l'air*
to fly aboard: *voler (à bord de)*
a flight: *un vol*
an air base: *une base aérienne*
to be stationed: *être basé*
overseas: *à l'étranger*
10,000 miles away from France: *à 15 000 km de la métropole*
the military: *les militaires*
an enlisted man: *un engagé*
a serviceman: *un engagé (volontaire)*
a recruit: *une recrue*
an NCO (non-commissioned officer): *un sous-officier*

☞ a unit: *une unité* – a squad: *un escadron* – a platoon: *un peloton* – the barracks: *la caserne* – a fire brigade (UK)/department (US): *une brigade de sapeurs-pompiers*

to be in command (of): *commander*
to lead: *conduire, mener*
to drill/to train (a recruit): *entraîner (une recrue)*
the élite mountain infantry of the Army/the mountain corps: *les chasseurs alpins*

☞ climbing: *l'escalade* – a penchant for daring climbs: *un goût pour les ascensions audacieuses* – cross-country skiing: *le ski de fond* – winter/summer mountain leadership: *la direction des opérations en hiver/en été* – mountain guiding skills: *les manœuvres en montagne* – to scale mountains: *gravir des montagnes* – to build an igloo shelter: *construire un igloo* – to survive extreme temperatures: *survivre à des températures extrêmes* – to live in extreme conditions: *vivre dans des conditions extrêmes* – to live in a hostile environment: *vivre dans un environnement hostile*

the police forces/services: *la police/les services de police*
child assistance services: *les services d'aide à l'enfance*
the gendarmerie: *la gendarmerie*
an anti-drug squad: *une brigade des stupéfiants*

☞ to take part in arrests/patrols: *participer à des arrestations/patrouilles* – an investigation: *une enquête* – a drug bust: *un raid contre des trafiquants de drogue*

the firefighters: *les pompiers*
the Paris fire brigade: *la Brigade des sapeurs-pompiers de Paris (BSPP)*

☞ to handle stressful situations: *faire face à des situations stressantes* – to cope with emergencies/to deal with emergency situations: *faire face à des situations d'urgence* – to be in need of assistance: *avoir besoin d'aide* – to save lives: *sauver des vies* – to rescue: *sauver* – a rescue worker: *un sauveteur* – an emergency medical technician: *un ambulancier* – an emergency vehicle/EMS vehicle/a first aid vehicle: *un véhicule de premier secours* – a first aid worker/first aider: *un secouriste* – first aid training: *la formation aux premiers secours* – a nontransporting EMS vehicle/fly-car/response vehicle: *un véhicule radio-médicalisé (VRM)* – to do/to perform CPR (on): *faire la réanimation cardio-pulmonaire/cardio-respiratoire (sur)* – to be trained in CPR: *être formé à la réanimation* – to respond to an emergency: *intervenir sur une urgence* – first-aid techniques: *les gestes de premier secours* – to take care of: *prendre en charge* – a call for service/service call: *une intervention* – a dispatcher: *un régulateur* – regional health authorities: *une agence régionale de santé (ARS)* – an aid station: *un poste de secours* – field conditions: *la réalité sur le terrain* – when a human life is at stake: *quand une vie humaine est en jeu* – to cope with extreme situations: *faire face à des situations d'urgence* – to keep a cool head in any kind of life-threatening situations: *garder son sang-froid dans n'importe quelle situation périlleuse* – to avoid panicking: *éviter de paniquer*

☞ to face the grim/harsh/stark reality (of): *affronter la triste/dure réalité (de)* – the grim reality of everyday life: *la triste réalité de la vie quotidienne* – to face the grim prospect (of): *faire face à la sombre perspective (de)* – to break the grim news to the family: *annoncer la triste nouvelle à la famille* – to confront reality: *faire face à la réalité* – a sobering part of my existence: *une partie de ma vie qui donne à réfléchir* – to grow more mature: *mûrir* – to develop a sense of responsibility: *développer le sens des responsabilités*

a road traffic collision: *un accident de la voie publique*
a life-threatening situation: *une situation critique*
to assist a delivery: *participer à un accouchement*
to prevent suicides: *prévenir les suicides*
a suicide case: *un cas de suicide*
to be in cardiac arrest: *être en arrêt cardiaque*
acute respiratory distress syndrome (ARDS): *le syndrome de détresse respiratoire aiguë (SDRA)*
psychological/mental/emotional pain: *la détresse psychologique*
to give in to stress: *céder à la pression*
to make decisions under pressure: *prendre des décisions sous la pression*
to gain a strong sense of discipline: *acquérir un sens aigu de la discipline*

☞ **Expressions**. the pressure of emergency situations: *la pression provoquée par l'urgence des situations* – situations in which there is little tolerance for error or indecision: *des situations qui ne tolèrent pas l'erreur ou l'indécision* – to work in an unfamiliar environment: *travailler dans un environnement peu familier* – to take part in firefighting operations: *participer à des opérations de lutte contre les incendies* – I was put in charge of the training of a group made up of men who were older and often more experienced and who came from backgrounds and cultures different from mine: *On m'a mis à la tête d'un groupe d'hommes plus âgés et expérimentés venant d'horizons et de cultures différents des miens* – It was a sound introduction to leadership training: *Ce fut une bonne introduction à l'exercice des responsabilités* – It instilled in me a sense of responsibility as well as commitment for a task my education had not foreordained me to accomplish but which I ultimately found to be highly rewarding: *Cela m'a appris le sens des responsabilités et de l'engagement pour une tâche à laquelle mon éducation ne m'avait pas préparée mais qu'en fin de compte j'ai trouvé des plus enrichissantes* – This experience taught me stress control: *Cette expérience m'a appris à maîtriser mon stress* – This determination and a healthy spirit of competition then spilled over into the academic world: *Cette détermination et un bon esprit de compétition ont rejailli sur mes études*

to be in charge of basic training: *être responsable de la formation élémentaire*
a French overseas regiment that provides military and professional training to unemployed and unskilled young people/a special regiment for 18-26-year-old unemployed civilians: *un service militaire adapté (SMA)/un régiment spécial pour les 18-26 ans sans emploi*

☞ to have a drug problem: *se droguer* – to drop out of school: *décrocher* – a dropout: *un décrocheur* – to find one's place in active life: *s'intégrer dans la société active* – to learn one's choice of a profession: *apprendre à choisir sa profession* – to give a smattering sense of responsibility:

inculquer des notions de responsabilité – to put on the right track: *remettre sur de bons rails* – to move forward in the right direction: *aller dans le bon sens* – the path to follow: *le chemin à suivre* – the steps to be taken (to): *les mesures à prendre (pour)*

The work placement/*Le stage*

a work placement (scheme): *un stage (en entreprise)*
an internship: *un stage*
a hands-on/blue collar work placement: *un stage ouvrier*
work experience: *une expérience de la vie active*
a short-term placement program: *un stage court*
a summer job/a vacation job: *un boulot d'été*
hands-on training: *un stage pratique*
a(n) (un)paid training scheme: *un stage rémunéré/non rémunéré*
a work placement agreement: *une convention de stage*
to secure an internship: *obtenir/décrocher un stage*
to do a work placement/an internship/work experience: *effectuer un stage*
a short-term/long-term internship: *un stage court (<3mois)/long (6-12 mois)*
job shadowing: *un stage d'observation*
a final year internship: *un stage de fin d'études*
a block release training course: *une formation en alternance*
a day release vocational training: *un stage en alternance*
work-based learning: *le stage en alternance*
experiential: *fondé sur l'expérience*
a training period: *une période de stage*
a training report: *un rapport de stage*
a training scheme offer: *une offre de stage*
to intern (with): *être stagiaire (chez)*
an intern, a trainee: *un stagiaire*
a training allowance: *une indemnité de stage*
a work placement mentor/tutor/supervisor: *un tuteur de stage*
to be supervised (by): *être encadré (par)*
a foretaste of one's future career: *un avant-goût de sa future carrière*
to gain insight (into): *avoir un aperçu (de)*
to build valuable experience: *acquérir une expérience utile*
to develop/to refine skills: *développer/affûter des compétences*
to gain professional feedback: *avoir le retour de professionnels*
to test-drive a career: *tester son appétence pour une carrière*
to be given a return offer: *proposer de revenir travailler (dans la même société)*

☞ **Expressions**. to provide real-life experience: *fournir une expérience concrète* – to gain skills that can be applied (to): *acquérir des compétences qui peuvent s'appliquer (à)* – to apply one's theoretical background: *appliquer ses connaissances théoriques* – to put theory/theoretical knowledge into action/practice: *passer de la théorie à l'action* – to pinpoint one's strengths/weaknesses:

identifier ses forces/faiblesses – to define the fields one needs to focus on: *définir les domaines sur lesquels se concentrer* – to narrow down one's choices (of): *mieux cerner ses choix (de)* – to become more qualified (to handle): *devenir plus qualifié (pour gérer)* – to explore a career one is interested in: *explorer une profession qui intéresse qn* – to make helpful connections: *établir des relations utiles* – to get one's foot in the door (of): *mettre le pied à l'étrier (de)*

Career goals/*Les objectifs de carrière*

📖 "I want to suggest to you that whether or not you have a job, everyone has a vocation, and that vocation is to live a life that is worth living. The best advice I can give is that which St. Paul gives us in Romans 12, where he says to the likes of you, who all look alike from here, "Be not conformed to this world." Do not join the throng. Don't get lost in the crowd. Don't be a part of the cookie-manufactured college generation, but stake out for yourselves some extraordinary, maybe even eccentric, piece and place of the world, and make it your own." (Rev. Peter J. Gomes, Professor, Harvard University)

to establish a goal: *établir un but*
to pursue a goal: *poursuivre un objectif*
to work towards/to strive for a goal: *travailler à atteindre un but*
to achieve/to attain/to reach a goal: *atteindre un but*
to be committed to one's goals: *tenir à remplir ses objectifs*
not to let anything get in the way: *tout faire pour parvenir à ses fins*

When talking about prospects and talents, be straightforward without bragging, realistic without being unnecessarily self-deprecating, a tough balance to reach.

✓ A **goal can be** ambitious/achievable/unrealistic/elusive (*qui vous échappe*), personal (*personnel*), common (*commun*), strategic (*stratégique*), clear (*évident*)

to carve/to craft one's own path: *tracer sa voie*
to be free to chart one's own course: *être libre de choisir sa voie*
to set a meaningful course for one's own life: *décider d'une orientation professionnelle sérieuse*
to point to a career (in): *suggérer une carrière (dans)*
to sharpen one's career plan: *préciser son plan de carrière*
to change course: *changer d'orientation*
to adopt/to follow/to pursue/to take a course of action: *suivre une voie*
to follow… into a career: *suivre les traces de…*

📖 "The tragedy of life does not lie, young folk, in not reaching your goal. The tragedy lies in having no goal to reach. It is not a calamity to die with dreams unfulfilled, but it is a calamity not to dream. It is not a disaster to not be able to capture your ideals, but it is a disaster to have no ideals to capture. It is not a disgrace to not be able to reach all the stars, but it is a disgrace to have no stars to reach for." (Tavis Smiley, Radio and television talk-show host, Commencement address 2007, Rutgers University).

career prospect: *la perspective de carrière*
job prospect: *la perspective d'un emploi*
employment prospect: *la perspective d'emploi*
short term ≠ long term prospect: *une perspective à court ≠ long terme*
to offer a prospect: *offrir une perspective*
to be excited by a prospect (of): *être excité à l'idée (de)*
in prospect (loc.): *en perspective*
to set/to train one's sights on: *viser, aspirer à atteindre*

→ **POSITIVE PROSPECT**. attractive: *attirant* – exciting: *passionnant* – inviting: *tentant* – bright: *brilliant*

→ **NEGATIVE PROSPECT**. daunting: *décourageant, intimidant* – bleak: *peu encourageant, sinistre* – limited: *limité* – poor: *mince*

→ **VERB + PROSPECT**. to be excited at: *être stimulé à la perspective de* – to relish: *savourer* – to welcome: *accueillir* – to boost: *encourager* – to enhance: *améliorer* – to improve: *améliorer* – to ruin/to wreck: *ruiner* – to damage: *nuire à* – to diminish: *diminuer* – to review: *passer en revue, examiner* – to assess: *jauger* – to examine/to look into: *examiner*

to be attracted (by): *être attiré (par)*
to appeal to (sb): *plaire*
to hold great appeal for sb: *plaire beaucoup à qn*
to be highly attractive: *être très attirant*
to hold a fascination for sb: *exercer une fascination pour qn*
to hold the promise (of): *promettre (de)*
to have a vision: *avoir une vision*
to ignite the imagination: *enflammer l'imagination*
to follow in one's father's tracks: *suivre les traces de son père*
to found/to start one's own business/a company: *fonder/créer son/une entreprise*
to pursue a business venture: *chercher à créer son entreprise*
to chase the tech gold rush: *chercher à faire fortune dans la tech*
to spin iphone apps: *concevoir des applications pour iphone*
to strike out on one's own: *voler de ses propres ailes*
to envision a future: *envisager un avenir*
a career track/path: *une voie professionnelle*
a career choice: *un choix professionnel*
  to build/to carve out a career: *se construire une carrière*
  to embark on a career: *se lancer dans une carrière*
  to embrace/to take up a career: *embrasser une carrière*

to launch a career: *lancer une carrière*
to pursue a career (in): *poursuivre une carrière (en, dans)*
to start a career (in): *commencer une carrière (dans)*
to start out on a career: *démarrer une carrière*
a career in research: *une carrière dans la recherche*
a multifaceted career: *une carrière diverse*
to shape a personal path: *façonner un itinéraire personnel*

☞ **Expressions.** to be best suited to a career in which personal and human considerations are given highest priority: *être plus apte à une carrière dans laquelle les considérations personnelles et humaines prennent le pas sur tout le reste* – to have a professional goal that excites (sb): *avoir un objectif professionnel qui passionne (qn)* – to give purpose to one's life: *donner un sens à son existence* – a purpose-driven life: *une vie qui a un sens* – before starting off with one's career: *avant de se lancer dans une carrière*

to become a civil servant: *devenir fonctionnaire*
to become a researcher: *devenir chercheur*
to devote one's life to research: *consacrer sa vie à la recherche*
to do research: *faire de la recherche*
to embrace an academic life: *choisir une carrière universitaire*
to enter public service: *intégrer la fonction publique*
to go into research: *choisir la recherche*
to launch one's own business: *lancer son affaire*
to pursue an academic track: *poursuivre une carrière universitaire*
to serve the state: *servir l'État*
to work for the state: *travailler pour l'État*
to start one's own company: *créer son entreprise*
to work in the public/private sector: *travailler dans le secteur public/privé*
an academic: *un universitaire*
to become a professor: *devenir professeur*
to combine teaching and research work: *allier enseignement et recherche*

Experience/*L'expérience*

to enjoy an experience: *apprécier une expérience*
from my experience: *pour l'avoir vécu*
in the course of my life: *au cours de mon existence*
in the course of time: *au fil du temps*
a tribute to sb's accomplishments: *témoigner du succès de qn*
to have a sense of accomplishment: *avoir le sentiment d'avoir réussi*
to acquire hands-on/practical experience: *acquérir une expérience pratique*
an eye-opener: *une révélation*
a light-bulb moment: *un déclic*

☞ **light-bulb moment** : from the representation of an illuminated light bulb above a character's head in a cartoon or comic strip, to indicate that they have had an idea.

a moment of sudden inspiration/revelation/recognition: *une révélation*
to have a direct/first-hand experience: *avoir vécu personnellement*
the one and lasting work experience: *l'expérience qui m'a le plus marqué*
to be exposed (to): *être mis au contact (de)*
to gain significant experience: *acquérir une bonne expérience*
to provide first-hand exposure: *confronter directement*
to draw on one's experience: *tirer parti de son expérience*
to learn by/through/from experience: *apprendre sur le terrain*
to capitalize on/to leverage an experience: *tirer profit d'une expérience*
to be hand-picked to participate (in): *être sélectionné pour participer (à)*

☞ **Expressions.** Experience has taught me (that): *L'expérience m'a appris (que)* - This experience has made a deep impression on me: *Cette expérience m'a fortement marqué* – a lasting impression: *une impression durable* – This experience has helped me perceive the world of work from a new angle: *Cette expérience m'a permis de percevoir le monde professionnel sous un angle nouveau* – It has provided me with a renewed glance on my life: *Elle m'a permis de regarder ma vie d'un œil nouveau* – Internships and summer positions during my college education provided valuable exposure to potential careers in these fields: *Les stages et les boulots d'été pendant mes études universitaires m'ont permis de découvrir des possibilités de carrière dans ces domaines* – This experience was remarkable because it afforded me the privilege of making a positive difference in the lives of others: *Cette expérience fut remarquable car elle m'a offert le privilège de compter pour les autres* – My accomplishments also included semifinalist standing in the national math, physics and chemistry olympiads: *Parmi mes succès, une place de demi-finaliste dans les olympiades de physique et de chimie*

→ **Positive experience**: enjoyable: *plaisant* – challenging: *un défi* – exhilarating: *stimulant* – enriching: *enrichissant* – rewarding: *gratifiant* – fruitful: *fécond* – exciting: *passionnant* – unique: *unique* – unforgettable: *inoubliable* – disappointing: *décevant* – extensive: *large* – unrivalled: *sans égal* – valuable: *riche* – varied: *varié*

→ **Difficult experience**: harrowing: *pénible* – painful: *douloureux* – traumatic: *traumatisant* – unnerving: *agaçant* – unsettling: *déstabilisant* – hair-raising: *terrifiant* – humbling: *qui rend humble* – sobering: *qui donne à réfléchir* – salutary: *salutaire*

→ **Past experience**: real-life: *réel* – past: *passé* – childhood: *d'enfance* – early: *précoce* – learning/formative: *formateur*

Opportunity/*L'occasion*

to grasp/to seize/to take up an opportunity (to): *saisir une occasion (pour)*
to jump at an opportunity: *sauter sur une occasion*

to miss out on an opportunity: *manquer/laisser passer une occasion*
to offer/to open up/to provide an opportunity: *offrir/présenter/fournir une occasion*
to pass up an opportunity: *laisser passer une occasion*
to take advantage of/to make the most of an opportunity: *profiter d'une occasion*
the opportunity of a lifetime: *l'occasion de ma vie*

➔ **ADJ + OPPORTUNITY**. considerable/plenty of: *nombreux* – exciting: *passionnant* – favorable: *propice* – golden: *en or* – great/marvellous/tremendous/welcome: *formidable/bienvenu* – historic: *historique* – ideal: *rêvé* – little: *mince* – lost/missed: *manqué* – once-in-a-lifetime: *unique* – rare/unique/unparalleled: *à nul autre pareil* – unprecedented/unrivalled/unmatched: *sans égal* – wasted: *gâché* – wonderful: *merveilleux*

Achievement/*La réussite*

a feeling/a sense of achievement: *un sentiment de réussite*
educational achievement: *la réussite scolaire*
a peak achievement: *le sommet de la réussite*
to achieve a goal: *atteindre un objectif*
an accomplishment: *une réussite*
a crowning achievement: *le couronnement*

➔ **ADJ + ACHIEVEMENT**. considerable/extraordinary/impressive/major/no mean: *et pas des moindres* – significant/notable/outstanding: *remarquable* – remarkable/tremendous: *formidable* – rare/unique/solid/crowning: *suprême* – lasting: *durable* – proudest: *dont je suis le plus fier*

➔ **VERB + ACHIEVEMENT**. to represent/to constitute: *représenter/constituer*

Skills/*Les compétences*

➔ **Skills can be** considerable, consummate (*accompli*), great, remarkable, basic (*de base*), necessary, essential, practical (*pratique*), entrepreneurial (*d'entrepreneur*) – a range/a set of skills/a skillset: *un ensemble de compétences* – a mastery of skills: *une maîtrise des compétences* – a scientist of considerable skill: *un savant au talent considérable/très talentueux* – skilled in the art (of): *maître dans l'art (de)*

a competence/competency: *une compétence, une aptitude*
analytical skills: *des compétences en maths*
communication skills: *des talents de communication*
management/managerial skills: *des talents de gestion*
observational skills: *des qualités d'observation*
organizational skills: *des talents d'organisation*

problem-solving skills: *des capacités à résoudre les problèmes*
a problem-solver: *qui résout les problèmes*
reasoning abilities: *les capacités à raisonner*
time management skills: *la capacité à gérer son temps*
to acquire skills: *acquérir des compétences*
to apply one's skills (to + ING): *appliquer ses compétences (à)*
to be equipped with a solid background (in): *avoir un solide bagage (en)*
to be equipped with the necessary skills (to): *être armé des compétences nécessaires (pour)*
to bring along skills (in): *apporter avec soi des compétences (en)*
to broaden one's skills: *élargir ses compétences*
to build [built] on one's skills: *accroître ses compétences*
to develop/to exercise one's skills: *développer/exercer ses talents*
to improve/to increase/to enhance/to upgrade one's skills: *améliorer ses compétences*
to improve/to strengthen/to consolidate one's skills: *améliorer/renforcer ses compétences*
to learn skills: *apprendre des compétences*
to sharpen one's skills: *affûter ses compétences*
to outperform (sb): *faire mieux que (qn)*

☞ **Expressions**. I came to realize the importance of possessing a wide range of competences which an exclusively theoretical curriculum cannot provide on its own - The small structure of this mission was an ideal framework to help me understand what it takes to create a business

VI. The Personal History Statement (PHS)/*L'expérience personnelle*

Teaching/*L'enseignement*

a tutor: *un tuteur*
an oral examiner: *un colleur*

📖 In America, students may seek **tutors** for extra help in subjects they are having trouble in. Tutors are usually more advanced students or graduate students who do this as a way of supplementing their income. They are not official employees of the college or university. An **instructor** is generally someone that teaches a practical skill (golf instructor/ski instructor/swimming instructor, for example). We also find a history/biology/math instructor, though.

to mentor: *guider, conseiller*
a course assistant/teaching assistant: *un instructeur*
a graduate teaching assistant/part time lecturer: *un chargé de cours*
a teaching fellow: *un chargé de TD*
a seminar supervisor/leader: *un chargé de travaux dirigés*
a practical work supervisor: *un chargé de TP*
a research fellow: *un chargé de recherche*
an undergraduate student: *un élève de licence*
an underprivileged/deprived student: *un élève défavorisé*
a disenchanted student: *un élève désabusé*
disaffected: *insatisfait, hostile, révolté*
disengaged from school: *déscolarisé*
to be clueless/unmoored/rudderless/disconnected: *être paumé/sans repère*
to drift/to be adrift: *dériver/être à la dérive*
to come from a broken home: *être issu d'un foyer désuni*
to have a poor command (of): *mal maîtriser*
shut out of society: *rejeté par la société*
to give/to get a foothold in life: *mettre un pied dans la vie*
to dumb down the value of education: *rabaisser la valeur de l'éducation*
to bring back into the mainstream: *ramener dans le giron*
to put back on the straight and narrow: *remettre sur les rails*

☞ **Expressions.** to lose faith in the school system: *perdre confiance dans le système éducatif* – to come from underprivileged estates/projects: *être issu des cités* – to come from a rough district: *venir d'un quartier difficile* – a school targeted for special aid: *une école située en ZEP* – a priority education zone: *une ZEP*

🕮 "In the treatment of poverty nationally, one fact stands out: there are twice as many white poor as Negro poor in the United States. Therefore I will not dwell on the experiences of poverty that derive from racial discrimination, but will discuss the poverty that affects white and Negro alike." (Martin Luther King)

Music/*La musique*

a musician/a player: *un musicien*
a music lover: *un mélomane*
a music-oriented personality: *tourné vers la musique*
in parallel to my academic studies: *parallèlement à mes études*
to play music/to make music: *faire de la musique*
to be into rock music: *être mordu de rock*
a passion for music: *une passion pour la musique*
to play a musical instrument: *jouer d'un instrument de musique*
to start playing an instrument: *commencer à jouer d'un instrument*
to play the piano: *jouer du piano*
to practice the clarinet: *pratiquer la clarinette*
to take up the trumpet: *se mettre à la trompette*
to sing in the choir: *chanter dans le chœur*
to play in a musical: *jouer dans une comédie musicale*
a music academy/music school: *un conservatoire de musique*
to study piano at the National Academy: *étudier le piano (au conservatoire national)*
to compose/a composer: *composer/un compositeur*
solfeggio/solfa/solmization: *le solfège*
to play in a band: *jouer dans un orchestre*
to join a band: *faire partie d'un orchestre*
to perform/a performance: *jouer, se produire/un concert, un spectacle*

☞ **Expressions.** I also enjoy expressing myself through music: *J'aime aussi m'exprimer à travers la musique* – Although I am not a virtuoso on any instrument, I have played the violin since the sixth grade: *Bien que n'étant pas virtuose, je fais du violon depuis la classe de 3ᵉ* – I write songs on the piano and guitar: *J'écris des chansons pour le piano et la guitare* – Music has been one of the mainstays in my life: *La musique est l'un des piliers dans ma vie*

Volunteering/*Le bénévolat*

volunteer work/volunteer service: *le bénévolat*
to do volunteer work (for): *faire du bénévolat (pour)*
to do charity work: *faire du bénévolat (pour des associations humanitaires)*
to do work for/to work for a charity: *travailler pour une association caritative*
to volunteer (for): *faire du bénévolat en faveur (de)*
to volunteer for service (in): *se porter volontaire (pour)*
a volunteer worker: *un bénévole*
to be a volunteer: *être bénévole*
a charity: *une association caritative*
a church group: *un groupe chrétien*
a homeless assistance operation, team/a reach out operation: *une maraude*
to be a homeless outreach worker: *faire les maraudes*
to provide assistance (to sb)/to go to sb's assistance: *porter secours (à qn)*
to leap to sb's rescue: *voler au secours de qn*
a humanitarian association: *une association humanitaire*
an NGO: *une ONG*
to work for an NGO: *travailler pour une ONG*
civic engagement/civic participation: *l'engagement citoyen/la participation citoyenne*
community service activities: *les activités d'intérêt général*
people in social distress: *les gens en détresse sociale*
subpar living conditions: *des conditions de vie médiocres*
public spiritedness: *le sens civique*
the Red Cross: *la Croix Rouge*
to act out of a sense of civic duty: *agir par esprit civique*
to add one's stone (to): *ajouter sa pierre (à)*
to alleviate human suffering: *soulager la misère humaine*
to be committed (to)/commitment: *être engagé (à)/l'engagement*
to be dedicated/dedication: *être dévoué/le dévouement*
to come forward: *se porter volontaire*
to contribute (to) (+ ING): *contribuer (à)*
to deliver meals: *livrer des repas*
to distribute food/hot drinks/blankets: *distribuer de quoi manger/des boissons chaudes/des couvertures*
to do humanitarian work: *travailler dans l'humanitaire*
to experience homelessness: *connaître la rue*
to give a helping hand: *donner un coup de main*
to give assistance (to): *porter assistance (à)*
to give back to the community: *rendre à la communauté*
to add to a community: *contribuer à une communauté*
to hand out breakfasts: *servir des petits déjeuners*
to help out homeless people/the homeless: *aider les sans-abri*
to help reintegrate into society: *aider à se réinsérer dans la société*
to prepare for re-entry: *se préparer à la réinsertion*
to involve oneself in a wide array (of): *s'impliquer dans un grand nombre (de)*
to join the volunteer staff: *rejoindre l'équipe des volontaires*

to live on the street/to sleep rough: *être à la rue/coucher sous les ponts*
to man a soup kitchen: *servir la soupe populaire*
to organize a food drive: *organiser une collecte alimentaire*
to provide care/medical ambulatory aid: *fournir des soins en ambulatoire*
to sensitize sb to the problems (of): *sensibiliser qn aux problèmes (de)*
to raise sb's awareness of a problem (among the general public): *sensibiliser le public à un problème*
to serve the community: *servir la communauté*
to sign up (for): *s'engager (à)*
to teach civic responsibility: *enseigner la responsabilité civique*
a non-profit (organization): *une association à but non-lucratif*

☞ **Expressions.** I find a rewarding the chance of giving to other people part of your time when everything always went well for you: *C'est enrichissant de consacrer une partie de votre temps pour les autres quand tout vous a toujours réussi* – to help people retain their humanity: *aider les gens à rester digne* – to make a difference in other people's lives: *compter pour autrui*

a girls'/boys' camp: *une colonie pour filles/garçons*
a youth camp: *un camp de jeunes*
a youth group leadership training certificate: *un brevet d'animateur (BAFA)*
a camp counsellor: *un moniteur de colonie de vacances*
a summer camp/holiday camp/sleepaway camp: *une colonie de vacances*
to attend summer camp: *partir en colonie de vacances*
a summer camp director: *un directeur de colonie de vacances*
a camp leader: *un directeur de camp*
a Scout leader/Scout master: *un chef scout*
a troop leader: *un chef de troupe*
to join the boy scouts: *devenir scout*
to organize a summer camp: *organiser un camp d'été*
to plan field trips: *organiser des sorties*
scouting activities: *des activités de scoutisme*
a scouting experience: *une expérience de scoutisme*

Involvement in campus life/*L'implication dans la vie du campus*

the student body: *le corps étudiant*
a student association: *un club d'étudiants*
a society: *un club, une association*
an officer (in an association/club): *un membre (d'une association)*
a chair: *un président*
a vice-chair: *un vice-président*
a junior enterprise: *une junior entreprise (JE)*
a cultural club: *une association culturelle*
a video club: *un cinéclub*

a drama club: *un club théâtre*
a cooking club: *un club cuisine*
a youth center: *un club de jeunes*
to be involved (in): *être impliqué (dans)*
to join a student club/to sign up (for): *s'inscrire (dans)*
a student-founded organization: *une association créée par les étudiants*
to become a member (of): *devenir membre (de)*
to be in charge (of): *être responsable (de)*
a student music festival: *une fête étudiante*
to run a club: *diriger une association*
to organize events: *organiser des événements*
an awareness-raising event: *un événement de sensibilisation*
Orientation week/O-week/Freshers' Week: *la semaine de l'orientation*
an orientation leader: *un responsable de l'orientation*
the Week of Welcome (WOW): *la semaine d'intégration*
to help orient new students: *aider à orienter les nouveaux étudiants*
to welcome new students: *accueillir les nouveaux étudiants*
the student government/council: *le Bureau des élèves (BDE)*
to be president of the student government: *diriger le BDE*
to run for/to stand for: *se présenter*
to serve on student government: *être membre du bureau des élèves*
to be elected student representative: *être élu au BDE*
an Academic Board Council: *un conseil d'établissement*
to serve/to sit on the board of regents/board of trustees: *siéger au CA*
to organize student activities: *organiser la vie étudiante*
to represent student interests/concerns: *défendre les intérêts des étudiants*
to sponsor campus-wide programs: *parrainer des événements sur le campus*
a student representative: *un délégué étudiant*

Public speaking/*L'art oratoire*

a speaking course: *un séminaire sur la parole*
a communications course: *un cours de communication*
communication apprehension: *la peur de communiquer*
a speaking intensive course: *un cours d'éloquence intensif/une formation à la prise de parole*
a reticence course: *un cours pour les timides*
to be crucial to getting a job: *être crucial pour décrocher un emploi*
to be shy: *être timide*
stage fright/nerves: *le trac*
  to have, to experience stage fright/to suffer from stage fright: *avoir le trac*
  to have butterflies in the stomach: *avoir l'estomac noué*
  to overcome one's shyness: *surmonter sa timidité*
to conquer one's stage fright: *vaincre le trac*
anxiety: *la nervosité, l'angoisse*

to ease the anxiety: *calmer l'angoisse*
to get one's ideas across: *transmettre/faire passer ses idées*
class participation: *la participation en cours*
a speech lab: *un laboratoire de la parole*
to be paralyzed in social situations: *être paralysé en société*

Sport/*Le sport*

to play/to do sports: *faire du sport*
to be into sports: *faire du sport (à fond)*
an athlete: *un sportif*
to do sports at the national level: *faire du sport de haut niveau*

✓ You can **do** sport or **play** sports. But **NOT** practise sports – You play a game: *jouer un match* – You are a team player – You belong to a team – You are on/in a team – You join a team – to make the team: *être sélectionné* – to field a team: *aligner une équipe* – to be called up: *être appelé* – to be selected (for): *être sélectionné (pour)*

sportsmanship: *la sportivité*
team spirit: *l'esprit d'équipe*
collective spirit: *l'esprit collectif*
team effort: *le travail d'équipe*
a team/individual sport: *un sport d'équipe/individuel*
a men's/women's team: *une équipe masculine/féminine*
an opponent: *un adversaire*
winter sports: *les sports d'hiver*

➔ Alpine skiing/downhill skiing: *la descente* – crosscountry skiing: *le ski de randonnée* – off-piste skiing/backcountry skiing (US): *le hors-piste* – fencing: *l'escrime* – rowing: *l'aviron* – field and track: *l'athlétisme* – adventure racing/expedition racing: *le raid nature/multisport*

to compete: *concourir*
competitive: *qui a l'esprit de compétition*
to achieve outstanding sports performances: *briller en sport*

➔ to enter/to take part in a competition/a contest: *participer à une compétition* – to win a competition/a contest: *remporter une compétition* – to withdraw from competition: *se retirer de la compétition* – to beat off/to fight off competition: *repousser la concurrence* – to have an undying love of sport: *être fou de sport*

➔ cut-throat (*à couteaux tirés*), fierce (*féroce*), intense/keen (*vif*), severe (*sévère*), stiff (*rude*), strong (*fort*) tough (*dur*), healthy (*sain*) + **competition**

a tournament: *un tournoi*
a match/a game: *un match*
a teammate: *un équipier*
to be fit: *être en forme*
to keep fit: *garder la forme*
an all-round athlete: *un athlète complet*
an athletic personality: *une personnalité athlétique*
to shape one's personality: *façonner la personnalité*
to be keen on sports: *être passionné de sport*
to be sports-crazy: *être fou de sport*
to train hard: *s'entraîner dur*
to be a thrill seeker: *rechercher des sensations*
to clinch a title: *remporter un titre*
to break a record: *battre un record*
to set/to establish a record: *établir un record*
to shatter/to smash a record: *faire voler un record en éclats*
to score/to pull off a victory: *remporter une victoire*
a school of hard knocks: *une école de la vie*
to teach the importance of collective action: *enseigner l'importance de l'action collective*

☞ **Expressions.** to be on the A team: *être dans l'équipe A* – to serve as captain of the varsity team: *servir comme capitaine de l'équipe universitaire* – to distinguish oneself through sports: *se distinguer par le sport* – Sports are a key element in my life: *Les sports, c'est primordial pour moi* – Gymnastics has played a pivotal role in my life: *La gymnastique a joué un rôle central dans ma vie* – to involve oneself in sports with great regularity: *pratiquer un sport très régulièrement* – to mold athletes into officers able to lead troops: *transformer des athlètes en officiers capables de diriger des troupes* – to hold a pivotal position on the pitch: *occuper une position clé sur le terrain* – to acquire a sense of stategy: *acquérir un sens de la stratégie*

→ **Sports qualities.** aptitude (for): *l'aptitude (à)* – skill: *l'adresse* – to be good (at): *être bon (en)* – to excel: *exceller* – accuracy: *la précision* – accurate: *précis* – daring: *audacieux* – boldness: *la témérité* – bold: *téméraire* – fearless: *intrépide* – strength: *la force* – power: *la puissance* – energy/punch: *l'énergie* – zip/pep: *l'enthousiasme* – endurance/stamina: *l'endurance* – vigorous: *vigoureux* – vigor: *la vigueur* – resistance: *la résistance* – resistant: *résistant* – resilience: *le ressort* – resilient: *résistant* – souple: *souple* – lithe: *leste* – courage/the guts: *le courage* – grit: *le cran* – gritty: *qui a du cran* – aggressiveness: *l'agressivité* – coordination: *la coordination* – suppleness: *la souplesse* – gifted: *doué* – balance: *l'équilibre* – to improve: *améliorer* – to perfect: *perfectionner* – matchless/unrivalled: *sans égal*

☞ **Expressions.** I made the French junior Olympic ski team: *J'ai fait partie de l'équipe olympique junior de ski française* – I shifted my focus from skiing to wrestling: *Je suis passé du ski à la lutte* – I hold a black belt: *Je suis ceinture noire*

Traveling/*Les voyages*

hiking/trekking: *la randonnée*

🕮 Travelers to distant places have always done the most in bringing peoples together. Since ancient times, immigrants have helped bridge cultural gaps, foster better understanding and tried bringing their home country and their country of origin closer.

to travel abroad/overseas: *voyager à l'étranger*
to travel extensively (to/in): *voyager beaucoup (dans/à)*
to travel to distant lands: *visiter des pays lointains*
to travel round the world/to travel to the four corners of the world: *voyager dans le monde entier*
a seasoned/well-seasoned traveler: *un voyageur aguerri*
to backpack/a backpacker: *voyager sac au dos/un randonneur*

➔ ***Attention.*** *Ne pas confondre* **travel** *(voyage), indénombrable, avec* **trip** *et* **journey** *(tous deux dénombrables).* **Journey** *désigne un voyage plus ou moins long* (a journey across India), **excursion** *est un voyage de courte durée, pour le plaisir,* **trip** *est un voyage de courte durée pour le plaisir ou pour des raisons professionnelles* (business trip). I've made many interesting trips/journeys – I'm fond of travelling – the journey to Mars

to get an insight (into): *permettre de comprendre*
to learn a culture from the inside: *découvrir une culture de l'intérieur*
to travel off the beaten track: *voyager hors des sentiers battus*
to acquire cross cultural skills: *acquérir des compétences interculturelles*
to live on a cross-cultural campus: *vivre sur un campus cosmopolite*

☞ **Expressions.** to be more broad-minded, receptive to the habits and cultures of others – to follow one's father's postings – I spent three years in Athens, five years in Milan, and two years in Rabat due to my parents' professional pursuits – It has been a sound preparation for the global world in which I am destined to work in my professional life

Lessons gained from experience/*Les leçons tirées de l'expérience*

➔ ***Attention:*** *quand vous parlez de votre expérience personnelle et de ses conséquences actuelles, utilisez le present perfect* (have + ed)

a life experience: *une expérience humaine*
a life-changing/a life-enhancing experience: *une expérience qui a changé ma vie*
a learning experience: *une leçon de vie*
to draw lessons from experience: *tirer des leçons de l'expérience*
to jump at the chance to learn: *sauter sur l'occasion d'apprendre*

to gain an insight (into): *apprendre à découvrir*
in a non-academic environment: *dans un milieu non-universitaire*
to push (back) one's limits/to stretch oneself/to push oneself: *repousser ses limites*
to push the boundaries of science: *repousser les frontières de la science*
to go beyond boundaries: *transcender les frontières*
to put oneself to the test/to challenge oneself: *s'éprouver*
to go out of one's way to challenge oneself: *faire tout son possible pour s'éprouver*
to teach a lesson in fortitude: *donner une leçon de courage*
to test oneself intellectually: *se mettre à l'épreuve intellectuellement*
to surpass oneself/to outdo oneself: *se dépasser*
to perform beyond one's expectations: *dépasser les espérances*
to grow both personally/professionally: *mûrir d'un point de vue personnel/professionnel*
to learn a great deal about oneself: *apprendre beaucoup sur soi*
to navigate the uncharted waters (of): *naviguer dans les eaux inconnues (de)*
has led me to believe that…: *m'a amené à penser que…*
has revealed to me that…: *m'a appris que…*
has opened my eyes on…: *m'a ouvert les yeux sur…*
has strengthened my feeling that…: *m'a conforté dans le sentiment que…*
to lay a course: *naviguer tout droit/en ligne droite*

☞ **Expressions**. In that position, I gained a greater awareness (of): *À ce poste, j'ai acquis une plus grande conscience (de)* – What I discovered was that…: *Ce que j'ai découvert, c'est que…* – This was a great confidence booster to me: *Cela m'a vraiment redonné confiance en moi* – I have also become aware that…: *Je me suis aussi rendu compte que…* – I have learnt from my errors: *J'ai appris de mes erreurs* – This turned out to be one of the best experiences in my life: *Cela s'est révélé être une des meilleures expériences de ma vie* – My experiences have deepened my insight (into): *Mes expériences ont approfondi ma connaissance (de)* – It has given me a critical perspective on my inner life: *Cela m'a apporté une perspective critique sur ma vie intérieure* – The experiences both here as in Britain were inspiring to me: *Mes expériences, ici comme en Grande-Bretagne, m'ont beaucoup appris* – to extol the power of perseverance when confronting adversity: *vanter/louer le pouvoir de la persévérance devant l'adversité*

☞ It was a chance to unravel more about my personality, qualities and weaknesses: *Ce fut une occasion d'en apprendre davantage sur ma personnalité, mes qualités et mes faiblesses* – to thrive on feeling productive: *réussir quand on a le sentiment de produire* – My life to date has taught me lessons that can't be learned in a classroom: *La vie jusqu'à présent m'a enseigné ce que l'on n'apprend pas en classe* – Complementing my Mexican experience was my three-month summer internship with an oncologue: *Outre mon expérience au Mexique, il y a eu mon stage de trois mois pendant l'été chez un oncologiste* – Working (in/for) was a pivotal experience in several ways: *travailler (à/pour) fut une expérience cruciale à maints égards* – First, I gained remarkable insight into the way…: *Tout d'abord ce fut une occasion remarquable d'apprendre/de faire connaissance/de mieux connaître…* – I made a decision that changed the course of my life: *J'ai pris une décision qui a changé le cours de ma vie* – My experience gave me exposure to…: *Mon expérience m'a permis de connaître…* – I have acquired a distinctive sense of intellectual responsibility for helping the less fortunate: *J'ai acquis un sens marqué de la responsabilité intellectuelle en aidant les moins fortunés que moi*

☞ My background in science, decision-making skills, judgment, ability to interpret data and capacity to communicate with others, all of these assets are brought into play as...: *Ma formation scientifique, mes capacités à prendre les décisions, mon jugement, mon aptitude à interpréter les données et à communiquer avec les autres sont autant de qualités qui entrent en jeu alors que...* – I have come away from this experience with a better understanding (of): *Je ressors de cette expérience avec une meilleure compréhension (de)*

➔ ***Attention.*** to help sb (to)/to become aware of/to be sensitized to the problems of/to be acquainted with/to be familiarized with (a problem) – to familiarize sb with: *familiariser qn à (un problème)*

To wrap it up/*Pour conclure*

to be given a chance of admission/to be admitted (to): *avoir une chance d'être admis (à)*
to be granted privilege of admission: *avoir l'honneur d'être admis*
to enhance the reputation of a program: *rehausser la réputation d'un programme*
to uphold the standards of excellence: *maintenir les critères d'excellence*
to be ideally suited (to provide): *être idéal (pour apporter)*
to be ideally prepared (for/to): *être idéal pour préparer (à)*
to prepare for the next chapter of one's life: *préparer le prochain chapitre de sa vie*
to be the next best stage to move closer to my career objectives: *être le meilleur tremplin pour me rapprocher de mes objectifs de carrière*
to be career-ready: *être prêt pour une carrière*
a high standard: *un niveau d'exigence*
to give what one has received back to others: *rendre aux autres ce que l'on a reçu*
to help narrow down one's academic/professional choices: *aider à mieux définir ses choix académiques/professionnels*
to help define a career path: *aider à définir une voie professionnelle*
to emerge as an industry leader: *se distinguer comme dirigeant dans l'industrie*
to gain a competitive edge: *avoir une longueur d'avance*

🕮 Go-to-market strategy (GTM strategy): an action plan that specifies how a company will reach target customers and achieve competitive advantage.

to help play a decisive role: *contribuer à jouer un rôle décisif*
an essential step forward in my training: *une étape essentielle dans ma formation*

➔ Stanford's Master's program is ideally suited to provide me exactly the kind of grounding I am looking for – Given my interests and concerns, I feel Yale is the very best place for me – The facilities and traditions of excellence combined with the caliber of the student body make me confident that I will be stimulated throughout the course of my studies - I feel confident in my ability to succeed there, hoping to have demonstrated a commitment to and some ability in the field of data science – The program will serve as a vital foundation for gaining knowledge in my intended field – to become a professional who can rise to the tasks at hand

VII. La traduction de bulletins/ *Vocabulary for transcripts translation*

a bien progressé ce trimestre	*has made good progress this term*
à condition de travailler plus vite	*if he/she works more quickly/faster/if he applies himself more effectively*
a des difficultés	*has faced some difficulties*
a été capable d'augmenter sa moyenne	*was able/managed to raise his grades*
a été très actif en classe	*brought great energy to the class*
a eu du mal à saisir les notions	*struggled to comprehend the material*
a fait de bons progrès	*has made solid progress/has come a long way*
a fait des progrès remarquables ce trimestre	*has made remarkable/significant progress this term*
a bien redressé la situation ce trimestre	*has put things back on an even keel this term*
à fort potentiel	*with a high potential*
a fourni de très gros efforts	*has demonstrated tremendous effort*
à l'écrit	*in her/his written work/does well in the written papers*
à l'oral	*in oral presentations/oral assessment*
a montré de l'intérêt prononcé (pour)	*has shown marked interest (in/for)*
a montré de l'intuition	*has shown insight*
a participé activement aux débats	*was/has been an active participant in our debates*
à peine moyen	*only just average*
à peu près convenable	*just average/only just adequate/adequate, no more*
a sauvé la mise	*has saved the day*
acceptable	*acceptable/satisfactory/fairly good*
accrochez-vous	*keep on working/good work, keep it up/keep up the good work*
actif et dynamique en classe	*an active, outgoing presence in class*
admis	*admitted/pass*
adresse	*address*
allemand	*German*
anglais	*English*
animer le cours	*to liven up the class*

année scolaire	*school year/academic year (UK)*
appliqué	*diligent, assiduous, hard working*
appréciations des professeurs	*professors' assessment/comments*
appréciations du proviseur	*headmaster's (UK)/principal's (US) comment/evaluation*
assez bien	*fairly good*
assez bien dans l'ensemble	*satisfactory on the whole*
attentif en classe	*who pays close attention to the subject*
attitude exemplaire	*a model/perfect attitude in class*
auréolé de gloire	*in a blaze of glory/covered in glory*
avec mention bien	*with high honors*
avec mention très bien	*with highest honors*
avec succès	*successfully*
ayez confiance	*remain confident/be confident*
ayez confiance en vous	*be self-confident/have self-confidence*
ayez confiance en vos capacités	*be confident in your abilities*
baccalauréat (examens)	*high school finals/diploma (US)/A-levels (in sciences) (UK). This certificate gives university entrance qualification. (It is advisable to mention the subjects taken,* i.e. *math, physics, etc.)*
baisse ce trimestre	*has done less well this term*
bases demeurent insuffisantes	*basics in need of revision*
bavard	*talkative*
beaucoup d'efforts	*has worked hard*
beaucoup de progrès	*has made good/solid/strong progress*
bien	*good/solid/strong*
bien au-dessus de la moyenne	*way above average*
bon début d'année	*good/solid start to the year*
bon élève	*good student*
bon ensemble	*good/strong results on the whole*
bon niveau	*good level*
bon travail	*good work*
bonne fin d'année	*good end-of-year results*
bonne participation	*active class participation*
bonnes connaissances (de/en)	*good knowledge (of)/good skills (in)/good command (of)/sound knowledge (of)/sound understanding (of)*
bons résultats	*solid/strong results*
bosseur/bûcheur/bourreau de travail	*an eager beaver, a swot (péj.)*

capacités d'abstraction	*capacity for abstract thinking/abstraction abilities*
c'est bien	*well done*
c'est mieux	*definite/marked improvement*
c'est bien mieux	*you have made significant progress*
c'est très bien	*very good/excellent*
c'est très encourageant	*it is quite encouraging*
capable d'aborder les problèmes d'un point de vue original	*able to view issues from a fresh perspective*
capable d'initiative	*(cap)able to take initiatives*
capable d'organiser les informations	*able to organize information*
chahuteur	*disruptive/unruly/a troublemaker*
cherche à atteindre la perfection	*strives for perfection*
classe	*class*
classé premier	*ranked first*
classé dans les premiers	*ranked in the top 5%*
classement	*ranking (US)*
classement annuel	*annual rank/ranking*
clé de la réussite	*key to success*
colles	*oral exams/mock assessments/formative assessments/preliminary orals*
compositions	*written exams*
connaissances	*knowledge/skills*
consciencieux	*conscientious/thorough/meticulous*
continucz!	*keep on working hard!/keep up the hard work!/keep up the good work!/ keep it up!*
convenable	*satisfactory*
correct	*satisfactory/acceptable results/fairly good*
correct dans l'ensemble	*acceptable results on the whole*
couronné par	*capped with*
couronné de succès	*successful/crowned with success/capped with success*
créatif	*creative abilities*
dans l'ensemble	*in general/overall/on the whole*
de bonnes idées	*your ideas are good/sound*
de fines capacités d'observation	*shrewd powers of observation*
de temps en temps	*every now and then/from time to time/sometimes*
décevant	*disappointing results*
décision de fin d'année	*end-of-year decision*

décision de fin de trimestre	*end-of-term decision*
démarrage satisfaisant	*satisfactory beginning*
démarrage très satisfaisant	*highly satisfactory beginning*
des capacités	*has shown abilities*
des capacités non exploitées totalement ce trimestre	*has not worked to the best of her/his abilities this term*
des efforts à faire	*could try harder/must work harder*
des idées intéressantes	*interesting/compelling ideas*
des progrès en fin de trimestre	*end-of-term grades (US)/marks (UK) have improved*
des progrès notables	*marked progress*
des progrès spectaculaires	*outstanding progress*
des progrès tout au long de l'année	*steady improvement throughout the year*
des résultats au-dessus du lot	*stellar results*
démarrer l'année en fanfare	*to have a spectacular start of year*
destiné à un brillant avenir	*cut out for a brilliant future/has a brilliant future ahead of her/him*
DEUG	*first part of Bachelor's degree (equivalent to two years of undergraduate studies) (also called associate degree, US)*
deuxième trimestre	*second term/quarter (business)*
devoir	*essay, paper, assignment*
devrait bien réussir	*should do well on the competitive exams*
digne de confiance	*trustworthy*
dissipé	*inattentive*
doit consolider ses bases	*needs to strengthen the fundamentals*
doit persévérer	*must keep on trying/must try even harder/continue the good work* (plus positif)/*must persevere*
donner tout son sens (à)	*to make the full meaning (of) clear*
doté d'un esprit curieux	*endowed with/equipped with/blessed with an inquiring mind*
doté d'une volonté de fer	*endowed with an iron will*
doué pour les maths et les sciences	*with a high aptitude for math and science*
du bon travail dans l'ensemble	*excellent work overall*
du travail	*has worked hard*
du travail cependant	*in spite of hard work*
dynamique	*dynamic (US)/enthusiastic (UK)*
écrit encore irrégulier	*written work of uneven quality/variable standard in/of written work*
éducation physique	*sports/phys. ed. (US)*
efforts à poursuivre	*must continue to work hard*

élève agréable	*a pleasant student*
élève capable	*an able student*
élève consciencieux	*a conscientious student*
élève doué	*a gifted student*
élève intéressé	*a committed student*
élève motivé	*an assertive learner/committed student*
élève sérieux	*a hard-working student*
élève travailleur	*a hard-working student*
élève vif	*a brilliant student/student with a quick mind/bright student*
en bonne voie	*on the right track*
en ce sens	*accordingly/with this in mind*
en légère baisse ce trimestre	*has done (slightly) less well this term*
en moyenne	*in general/on average*
en progrès	*is making good progress*
en tête de classe	*ranked at the top of the class*
en voie d'amélioration	*is progressing/is improving/is doing better*
encore bien juste	*results remain below par/subpar/weak*
encourageant	*encouraging results (in)*
ensemble convenable	*satisfactory work overall*
ensemble tout à fait correct	*quite satisfactory work on the whole*
ensemble très moyen	*very average/much room for improvement/some scope for improvement*
ensemble trop moyen	*fair on the whole*
ensemble un peu juste	*results are a bit below par/somewhat below par*
ensemble un peu trop juste	*overall grades remain shaky*
esprit curieux	*an inquiring mind*
esprit de synthèse	*deductive skills/ability to summarize/ability to see the big picture*
esprit de finesse	*a keen mind/a sharp mind*
esprit vif	*quick-witted/quick on the uptake*
essayez de rester concentré	*try to concentrate more*
essayez de travailler plus régulièrement	*try to work more regularly*
être à la hauteur/acceptable	*to pass muster*
être à la hauteur des attentes	*to live up to expectations*
être au-dessus de la moyenne	*to be above average*
être diplômé	*to graduate (from)*
être une autre chose	*a horse of a different color*

étudiant motivé, impliqué et curieux	*a driven, engaging, and inquisitive student*
excellent résultats	*excellent results*
excellent travail	*excellent work*
excellents résultats toute l'année	*excellent results all year long*
exercice de synthèse	*text summarization test*
faire des progrès	*to make progress*
fait preuve d'une vraie passion	*has shown genuine passion for the subject*
faites attention à	*pay attention to*
forte progression	*has made excellent progress*
franc succès	*resounding success*
français	*French/philosophy*
frappé au coin du bon sens	*to bear the stamp of common sense*
gros progrès	*huge progress*
honorable	*good results*
il faut plus d'investissement	*try to apply a little more energy*
il faut progresser	*can and must do better*
il faut viser plus haut	*try to do even better/set your sights higher*
il ira loin	*he will go far/promising future*
il faudrait un travail approfondi	*in-depth work required*
interrogations	*oral exams*
intuition/intuitif	*intuition/intuitive*
inventif	*inventive*
Italien	*Italian*
j'ai confiance en votre succès final	*I am confident you will be successful in the final exams*
j'attendais mieux	*disappointing results*
j'attends mieux	*you must try harder*
l'ensemble reste insuffisant	*her/his averages are still too low*
l'oral reste encore moyen	*can progress in oral expression/the oral work remains average*
lacunes important	*some major gaps*
lacunes inquiétantes	*you have overlooked serious points*
langues	*(modern) languages*
le succès est au rendez-vous	*it is a great success/success has come knocking*
le travail a porté ses fruits	*hard work has proved beneficial/has paid off*
lent	*slow on the uptake*
les résultats à l'écrit sont fort modestes	*poor/inadequate written work*

lettre de référence	*letter of reference, referee's letter, testimonial*
maintenez votre effort	*keep up the efforts/keep up the hard work*
malgré une petite faiblesse au premier devoir	*despite a slight weakness on the first assignment*
(un) manque de concentration	*(a) lack (of) concentration*
manque de dynamisme	*lack of enthusiasm (UK)*
manque de dynamisme à l'oral	*lack of enthusiasm/of dynamism (US) in oral work*
mathématiques	*mathematics/math*
matières	*courses*
(une) matière	*subject matter/discipline*
matière principale	*major field of study*
médiocre	*(way) below par*
méthodique dans son approche	*thorough in approaching the subject/leaves no stone unturned*
motivation	*motivation*
moyen dans l'ensemble	*average work*
moyenne	*average*
moyenne de la classe	*class average*
multiplier les succès	*to build on success/to go from success to success*
nationalité	*citizenship*
né à	*birthplace*
né le	*birthdate/born on/born*
ne laisse rien au hazard	*leaves nothing to chance*
ne négligez pas l'oral	*work on oral expression*
ne perdez pas confiance en vous	*do not lose confidence/faith in yourself*
négligé	*careless/inattentive/sloppy*
nets progrès	*much improvement this term*
niveau atteint	*level obtained*
niveau insuffisant	*insufficient/inadequate level*
nom	*name*
nom de famille	*last name (US)/family name*
non admis	*not admitted/fail*
non satisfaisant	*unsatisfactory*
notes	*grades (US, used for letters)/marks/percentage (UK)*
on espérait des progrès plus significatifs	*better progress was expected*
oral éliminatoire	*oral work is a prerequisite/need to focus on oral work*
orfèvre en la matière	*expert/leader in the field*

participation en classe	*input into group/in group activities/classroom participation/class participation*
participer à	*to participate in*
parvenir à ses fins	*to get one's own way*
pas de notes ce trimestre	*no marks/grades this term/na (not available)*
passable	*pass/passable/fair results*
passionné par la matière	*passionate about the subject*
persévérance	*perseverance*
persévérant	*persevering*
pétillant	*a sparkling personality*
peu attentif	*inattentive*
peut mieux faire	*can do better/can still improve/there is room for improvement*
philosophie/français	*philosophy*
physique	*physics*
place, rang	*ranking/rank/place (UK)/has come second, third, etc. in the class*
plaisant	*good-humored, enjoyable*
plus de difficultés ce trimestre	*has encountered more difficulties this term*
possède une bonne compréhension du sujet	*has a clear understanding of subject matter*
poursuivez vos efforts	*carry on doing your best/carry on the good work*
premier semestre	*first semester*
présence discrète mais travail efficace	*an unobtrusive presence but cogent work*
prendre le rythme	*to get in the groove*
prendre tout son sens	*to take on its full meaning*
prénom	*first name/forename (UK)*
program	*curriculum, syllabus*
progrès confirmés ce trimestre	*(your) grades/marks have improved this term*
progrès encourageants	*encouraging progress*
progrès sensibles	*noticeable progress*
prometteur	*promising*
proviseur	*headmaster (UK)/principal (US)*
quelques progrès	*some progress*
qui n'a pas peur de prendre des risques	*not risk-adverse/averse*
récolter les bénéfices	*to reap the rewards/benefits (of)*
rentrée	*new school term*
restez vigilant	*beware (negative)/remain combative (positive)*
résultats	*results/performance*

résultats acceptables	*satisfactory results*
résultats convenables	*results are satisfactory*
résultats écrits bien modestes	*written work is average*
résultats en baisse	*has done less well this term*
résultats en dents de scie	*erratic results*
résultats en progrès	*grades/marks are improving*
résultats réguliers tout au long de l'année	*steady results all year long*
résultats encore trop justes	*adequate results/can do better*
résultats encourageants	*encouraging results*
résultats faibles	*weak/poor results*
résultats médiocres	*average results*
résultats restent fragiles	*grades remain under average/(the) marks remain shaky*
résultats trop médiocres	*well below average*
résultats trop moyens	*not good enough*
retourner un problème dans tous les sens	*to look at a problem from all angles*
réussite scolaire	*academic success/educational achievement*
réussite totale	*complete success*
rupiner	*to cram, to swot*
s'accrocher	*to work hard/to be assiduous*
s'exprime bien	*articulate*
sciences de l'ingénieur	*engineering sciences*
sciences industrielles	*industrial design*
se donner beaucoup de mal pour	*to get out of one's way to*
se mettre au diapason	*to get up to speed*
se montrer à la hauteur	*to rise to the occasion*
se terminer en apothéose	*to finish/to go out in a blaze of glory*
sens aigu	*a strong sense of/a talent for*
sens littéraire	*a fine sense of style*
sérieuses lacunes (en)	*serious gaps (in)*
sérieux	*serious work*
solaire	*that radiates a positive energy around her/him, calm and serene, shines on others*
stage	*work placement (UK), internship (US), training period*
stage de formation	*training course*
stage de découverte d'entreprise	*work placement*
stagiaire	*intern*

succès éclatant	*howling/smashing/roaring success*
surmonter des difficultés	*to overcome difficulties*
tenace	*tenacious*
toujours du bon travail	*still doing great/once again good results*
tous les espoirs sont permis	*I have every reason to be hopeful for your success/there is every reason to be hopeful.*
tout à fait satisfaisant	*highly satisfactory work/very satisfactory/most satisfactory work*
traduction	*translation*
traduire	*to translate*
trait de génie	*stroke of genius*
travail correct	*satisfactory work*
travail peut être plus performant	*you can do better*
travail régulier tout au long de l'année	*has produced steady work all along the year/all (the) year round*
travail soutenu	*you have worked hard*
travaux dirigés	*tutorial (small group), seminar*
travaux pratiques	*practical work, a practical*
très bien	*highly satisfactory work*
très bon élève	*very good/talented student*
très bon travail, réfléchi	*very good work, well thought out*
très bon trimestre	*excellent term*
très motivé	*strongly motivated*
très satisfaisant	*highly satisfactory*
trimestre	*term*
troisième trimestre	*third term*
un de ces rares élèves tels qu'on en rencontre qu'une seule fois dans sa carrière	*one of the most exceptional students I have encountered in my 15 years of teaching*
un début bien terne	*a slow beginning*
un dernier devoir encourageant	*good results in the final essay*
un élément essentiel de la classe	*a unique and worthy asset in class*
un élément moteur du cours	*a driving force in the class*
un élément unique dans la classe	*a stand-out student in the class*
un élève brillant	*an outstanding/stellar student*
un intérêt soutenu pour cette matière	*a strong/sustained interest in the subject*
un peu décevant	*results are somewhat disappointing*
un peu juste	*below average*
un peu trop irrégulier	*results are somewhat erratic*

un plaisir de travailler avec lui	*a pleasure to have in class*
une année satisfaisante	*good results for the academic year*
une belle progression	*is progressing/has been progressing well*
une qualité rare et forte chez un élève	*a rare and impressive quality in a student*
vif	*quick on the uptake/a sharp mind/has a mind as sharp as a steel trap/ sharp as a tack*
viser	*to set one's sights on/to train one's sights on*
visez plus haut	*you can do better/set your goals higher/reach for the stars*
vivant	*lively*
vous devez progresser en accentuant les efforts	*you must progress and work harder/a little more effort and progress will come*
vous pouvez améliorer les résultats	*you can do better*
vous pouvez encore progresser	*you can do even better*
vous pouvez progresser	*you can do better/there is margin for improvement*
vraiment très bien	*excellent/outstanding work*

PART V
SAMPLES OF STATEMENTS

I. SOPs

– 1 –

While interning with the Paris Fire Brigade, I was confronted to issues that, at first sight, had not much in common with science. How to geolocate the vehicles and optimize intervention, how to better group together the equipment, how to call into action additional fire engines in case of catastrophes, sports events or terrorist attacks. Collecting and drawing on past data and then building statistics models would provide fire fighters with efficient ways to organize the map, allocate resources and react in record time. Such are the issues concerning the applied side of a field, Statistics and Probability, that I am eager to develop my knowledge in. Currently a third-year student at the École Polytechnique – I gained admission in 2014 – my ambition is to become a data scientist working in the social media tech or health care industry. This has led me to apply to Harvard for its A.M. in Statistics.

In Polytechnique, I decided to follow the Data Science specialization program that includes Machine Learning courses, *Topological Data Analysis*, and the *Art of Regression*. This track has confirmed my curiosity for the statistical theories that question the robustness of the results delivered by the algorithms. My previous curriculum can explain my strong interest for this field: the preparatory program allowed me to deepen my understanding of Linear Algebra, Advanced Calculus, Programming and Algorithm prior to admission to Polytechnique, whose first-year curriculum provided in-depth knowledge in several sciences. In my second year, I broadened my horizons with Biology; as well Applied Mathematics. Probability, Statistics, optimization methods and how to model random events were fascinating topics, for the effectiveness and accuracy of the methods implemented to solve real issues, which I applied in other courses such as *Econometrics*. This latter course presented the fundamental tools for statistical modeling, testing and decision making in economics-related problems, exposing the wide range of applications in statistics. In line with my interest for Computer Science, I attended *Algorithm Design and Analysis*, as well as *Massive Data Processing* that were complementary to my knowledge in statistics and useful for the implementation of the theory.

As an intern during the summer 2016 with ESJ Capital Partners, an edge fund specialized in real estate in Florida, I contributed to improve the investment analysis process of the company. The challenge was to focus on the company's investments in the charter school business. To do so, I had access to a large and actualized database of demographic information such as income, age profile, household expenditures across the 50 states. I then built a predictive analytics tool based on those parameters and taking into account the schools already existing in each area, listed by a search engine I self-programmed, so as to assess investment opportunities. However successful the program was, it raised many theoretical questions: I was confronted to programming and model design challenges which the Harvard program will help me to understand better through courses such as *Generalized Linear Models* and *Multivariate Statistical Analysis* following up on my present *Art of Regression* and *Machine Learning* classes.

I am currently doing a paired research project with Air France (AF), the national airline company. The focus is on revenue enhancement taking into account such constraints as passenger seats, pilots down time, flight schedules and connections, aircraft flying hours, flight crew rotation as well as seasonal offers. The goal of the project is to optimize profits so as to improve the company's drawing power. As part of this project, I am designing models of the company's fleet in order to obtain a better passenger distribution. What is exciting is that we interact with AF's Operations Research Department, an opportunity to pinpoint the statistics problems that we come across and apply the theory.

Within a team project, I worked with Prof Dominique X. developing two smartphone apps, the first about organizing sport tournament, tracking scores live, putting a team together and managing the contest, and, overall promoting sports activities in the university. To do so, I used HTML, Javascript and PHP. I would be eager to use those skills in Prof Pfister's Data Visualization class, deepening the understanding of complex data through visual representation. The second—Cookoo—is a meal-sharing platform, consisting in matching students who cook and those who are looking for company and a meal. Revenue is generated through Lydia, a payment system that we implemented. I am also part of a hand sign recognition project that consists in identifying hand gestures and translating them in words.

Harvard is the right fit to build on and broaden my knowledge while sharpening my reasoning and analytical abilities. Several courses have caught my attention. I am particularly intrigued by problems bearing on missing data: Prof R's class should improve my understanding on that question. Another class is *Generalized Linear Models* lectured by Mark G. whose research on how to rank chess players resonates with my own smartphone project. He added value by aggregating other parameters such as confidence, according to the rating deviation. His methods are also applied to health care, another echo to my stint with the Fire Brigade and my personal ambition. Prof D. has developed fascinating research on statistical inference. Using data drawn from the population with some form of samples, we can make propositions such as assessing population's distribution or properties. I would be eager to attend his class. Finally, Prof K's *Multivariate Statistical Analysis* is an apt follow up to my Machine Learning class that would help expand my knowledge in supervised and unsupervised learning problems and multivariate inference subjects.

The knowledge and skills I have built have prepared me ideally for a career in data science. My ambition is to work in the R&D department of a health care company and, depending on opportunities, leverage my knowledge and launch my own firm, building up on the enriching experience of my second-year team research project.

– 2 –

The on-going project I am carrying out with Veltys is typical of what I enjoy doing: modeling a soccer club's preferences to determine whether the club should invest in its formation center or trade new players on the transfer market. The mix between scientific culture and technical fluency to solve concrete issues is precisely what appeals to me in Berkeley's IEOR program. I want to build and develop disruptive services in the high-tech scene, such as software development, as was the case during my Summer 2016 internship, when I built a value-adding predictive interface. Contributing my technical knowledge and expertise to help companies grow is a way of moving the technology forward: in that regard the Bay Area ecosystem beckons, once I have enhanced my formation at Berkeley. At the Ecole XXX, where I am a third-year student, I am specializing in a master's level program called *Corporate Strategy and Finance*. My ambition is to work for the advisory business, and to do so, I need to expand my skills both in the management and in computational areas, and apply them by working for the firm. That is why I am applying to Berkeley's IEOR Master of Engineering program.

Ecole XXX's theory-fraught content has left ample room for project work, which I seized upon. As a result-driven person, I enjoy enhancing my skills and delivering results. My current work for Veltys is bound to have an impact on the operations of France's Professional Football League, and thus contribute to regulate a market worth hundreds of millions of dollars. The research I am carrying out in sport economics draws on the sifting and processing of mountains of empirical data from which we establish patterns, highlight links through match outcomes, and predict financial impact. The statistical methods in Econometrics and the tools such as linear regression, in Stata, have proved handy to come up with various correlations and inferences and reach relevant conclusions. That project has been conducted within the framework of an *Econometrics* class but relies on some of the concepts learned in a *Microeconomics* course as well, thus making the science kicking and alive.

A year-long project with a bulge-bracket bank consisted in applying machine learning techniques to financial market operations. The goal was to analyze whether machine learning could be a more useful tool in pricing derivatives than Monte Carlo methods, and deliver almost instant results. We modeled the pricing of several classical call options on Python with gradient boosting: the algorithm identified patterns in datasets from the stock market, and returned the price as a function depending on significant parameters of the market. Since the algorithm was slow, our method consisted in running the program at night, when the markets were closed, and profiting from early pricing in the day. As head of the project, I coordinated the action, distributed the tasks, and made sure to move forward in a smooth and constructive way.

In a second-year research project, under the supervision of Dr Alexandre E., I studied numerical approximation with regards to Lagrangian interpolation, an optimization problem that has applications in numerical analysis and computer engineering. We aimed at empirically verifying conjectures and theorems like Rivlin, Erdös and Hesthaven inequalities linking the interpolation error to Lebesgue's constant and the interpolation points chosen. We observed the approximation curves on Scilab, with equidistant nodes, and with the Gauss-Lobatto-Legendre subdivision. The project included bibliographical work as well, looking for information in Hesthaven's research[1]. Even though the project was weighted in favor of the theory, I did enjoy the format, studying in the morning, applying research in the afternoon, looking into the science and trying different problem-solving avenues.

1. J. S. Hesthaven, *From electrostatics to almost optimal nodal sets for polynomial interpolation in a simplex*, Siam J. Numer. Anal. (1998) Society for Industrial and Applied Mathematics. Vol. 35, No. 2, p. 655-676, April 1998

In a second-year project in computer science we used parallel programming (the Message Passing Interface) to analyze the 3D sequence of a protein, which was the object of a competition amongst researchers in biology who had to determine it as accurately as possible, knowing only the genomic sequence. My task was to compare the predictions to the real-life structure, which I had access to, and rank them. I used C++ to read the files, analyze the 3D predictions, and make comparisons. I first ran my algorithm on one processor, then extended the work to other processors through the Message Passing Interface, resulting in much more effective computing. What thrilled me was applying the parallel computing theory to solve autonomously a concrete research problem.

My background rests on robust knowledge. Following the preparatory program, where I attended a Mathematics, Physics and Chemistry track, I went on to expand my knowledge base at Ecole XXX. In the second year, I attended classes in applied mathematics, computer science and economics, domains I have kept looking into in my third year.

The applied mathematics courses were designed to give me practical tools applicable to other fields, like randomness and statistics in *Economics*, or numerical approximation and optimization in *Computer Science*. These courses included exercises or projects using Scilab.

I attended computer science courses in order to acquire programming skills in Java and C++ and therefore be intellectually comfortable when it comes to using computer-related tools. The algorithmic background I got from these courses helped me get a solid command of other programming languages (Python and R) as well.

I got an overall view of economics by attending microeconomics, macroeconomics, international economics and business economics courses in the second year. I am furthering this knowledge in my third year by taking classes in finance, industrial organization and econometrics, in which I often use Stata, like in my third-year project with Veltys.

Berkeley's program offers several courses I would be eager to attend. For example, the class on *Risk Modeling, Simulation and Data Analysis* has caught my attention. Indeed, I am interested in using the mathematical tools I learnt in Applied Mathematics in the past two years to quantify risk and influence decision-making in nowadays' industrial organization. Furthermore, Prof Lee S's research in discrete event simulation is an inspiration to me, and I would be thrilled to learn by his side.

I am also drawn to the *Optimization Analytics* course, taught by Ilan A., whose research in financial engineering matches my interests. I see this course as the perfect opportunity to deepen my knowledge of optimization theory, and apply my computer skills to real-world problem-solving.

The course on *Production Planning and Logistics Model* appeals to me as well, all the more so as Operations Research is at the core of my academic interests: it is typical of my general desire to learn new skills that are applicable to concrete industry and business problems. Furthermore, given all his publications on supply chain management, I would be honored to be one of Prof Phil K's students.

I have also set my mind on Berkeley's Capstone Project, which would be a fantastic opportunity to apply my skills. I would love working with Berkeley's on-campus industrial partners, particularly with high-tech firms such as Samsung and Google.

I expect to work on many projects next year, in contact with researchers who work on topics that inspire me, and this is why Berkeley's program is so enticing. Furthermore, I strongly believe that in such a hi-tech oriented curriculum as the IEOR Master of Engineering's, I will find personal fulfillment as well as exciting work opportunities.

– 3 –

It is from my father that I caught the virus of mechanics, for he has long been a collector of farm tractors built in the early fifties. Watching him work on them, I learned that every single piece with its specific function was necessary to make one working unit. However, I preferred working on a smaller scale, and chose to build gas-powered radio-controlled boats, from body to motor, including the transmission and remote control. At the same time, I took every opportunity that the French system offered me to study physics, leading first to the post-secondary preparatory classes for the competitive exams for the *Grandes Ecoles* and then to the *Ecole XXX.* I chose the Ecole because of the multidisciplinary curriculum which is allowing me to develop a wide perspective of the application of mechanics. The more I study, the more I am attracted to small scale mechanical systems. When Robert T., during a lecture on MEMS, spoke of the use of a lab-on-a-chip to analyze DNA, I was totally thrilled. Here was something, a whole "lab" on a millimetric chip, which corresponds exactly to what I want to do as a profession: create just such small-scale complex systems with multiple components from different fields. I knew then that MEMS was the field I would focus on. This has led me to apply to the M.S. program in MEMS/Nanotechnology at UCLA, with the main objective to pursue a Ph.D.

At the *Ecole*, in addition to specializing in mechanics, I chose to deepen my knowledge in fundamental physics to better understand the behavior of small-scale bodies; but I also chose applied mathematics to be able to deal easily with the equations in mechanics. First and foremost, the *Continuum Mechanics* course given by John L. and the *Fluid Mechanics* course by Henry H. have given me an exciting range of powerful tools. Notions of strain and stress, viscosity and surface tension, along with dimensional analysis, potential flows and matched asymptotic expansion now allow me to deal with simple issues that had previously been over my head, such as the lift of a wing or the move of tidal bore, but also with complex systems. It is very satisfying to be learning the skills used daily by mechanical engineers to design their systems. Then, in the *Quantum and Statistical Physics* course, I came to better understand small scale phenomena such as the semi-conductivity, the superconductivity and the superfluidity of helium. Understanding the behavior of elementary particles and comprehending how electronic components work made learning the many theories appealing and satisfied my desire to come closer to the infinitely small. The *Numerical Analysis and Optimization* course showed me practical ways of resolving numerically the equations used in mechanics. I used both the finite difference method and the finite element method during a simulation project carried out with a teammate on magnetohydrodynamics (MHD). Having been given all the equations of the MHD (which are not solvable in general), we graphed the numerical solutions for several different issues. I thoroughly enjoyed working on a challenging problem at the cutting edge of mechanics, finding solutions numerically, and dealing with mechanical issues from initial data to the results.

Last year I carried out a research project in microfluidics, about the self-shaping of 3D-microobjects using the evaporation of a micro-droplet. The process is simple: droplets were laid down on two-dimensional PDMS shapes. Then the surface tension raised the sides and with the evaporation of the droplets, each form became a 3D-object such as a tetrahedron or a tube. We studied the applications of this process in both pharmaceutics and electronics. In the first, we were able to create an "intelligent" micro-pill with an opening controlled by the pH (thanks to a polymer membrane); in the second, we researched how to create a 3d-pixel with a three layer-membrane like in PLED technology. Using fluid mechanics at a micro-scale for applications in biology and electronics was very satisfying; indeed, it felt like a first step towards being able to create a lab-on-a-chip and MEMS in general. I was also particularly impressed by the balance of forces (gravity against surface tension) which occur at micro-scale, and was even more fascinated by the applications this could lead to in a diversity of areas. It is both a dynamic and creative field. The fascination for micro-fluidic devices led me to take on a project about a micro-dispatcher supervised by Dr. T. The challenge was to generate an exponential concentration profile in a micro-channel: I am now in the process of creating a micro-fluidic network of serpentine channels with flows of different concentrations. This project has strengthened my desire to go deeper into the field of MEMS, and I am eager to develop other more complex micro-devices for biology or electronics. During an electronic project, I developed a wireless device controlling a telescope. Given the objective of wireless control, I had to find the controlling protocol and to create the appropriate electronic device. I was excited by the freedom of action I had and by the possibilities of electronics. Next Spring, I am looking forward to a three-month research internship in Professor Roberto H's Laboratory for Mechanical Engineering at UC Berkeley. I expect to be working on micro-mechatronics, thus combining my interest in mechanics and micro-scale systems.

My desire to establish a career working with microsystems, microfluidics and multidisciplinary applications is now leading me to apply to the MEMS and Nanotechnology M.S./Ph.D. programs in Mechanical and Aerospace Engineering at UCLA. Visiting Professor C.M. Ha's Bio MEMS-laboratory last summer, I was especially fascinated by their work on bio-actuators and micro-devices able to detect molecules. Here is a creative team I would be honored to join. My search also led me to the micro-manufacturing lab of Professor Wei Wang, whose micro-pumps and electrowetting-on-dielectric actuators would allow me to continue to expand my knowledge in the field I touched upon during my micro-dispatcher project. In order to enhance my skills in MEMS behavior and control, Dr. Jin's course in *Microsciences* seems essential to me. In addition, I would very much like to take on a creative project such as the one required by Professor J. Jones in his course on *Micromachining and MEMS*, for I believe it would allow me to voice my creativity by designing an operational product.

Science has always been a passion for me, and so has working in a team. My strongest team experience has been this past year, working in a student association of eight members in charge of the technical functioning of all student events, especially the parties. Because of the demand for sound and lighting systems our association is called upon almost every day. As president, I supervise a 40,000€ budget, along with 200,000€ of equipment. Each member of my team is truly dedicated, and has helped build a great team spirit, even for the smallest tasks, in spite of long hours and often little sleep. We all agree that the high moments, like watching 7,000 people at the gala following our rhythms with great joy, are worth the months of sometimes difficult preparation. The whole team feels that our sharing has enriched our lives and will remain engraved in our memories. During my eight-month leadership training in the police force, working in poor suburbs, I experienced this same deep importance of working together. Every day, our team stepped into dangerous areas where the population threw stones, burned cars, provoked riots. In the midst of action, everyone knew his specific function and realized that his life could depend on the awareness of his colleagues. I will always be committed to improving my listening skills and to building a team atmosphere wherever I work.

My future career will be creating microsystems inside a research group of a firm, developing new ways of applying mechanics to find innovative and efficient solutions, using the extraordinary diversity and freedom of MEMS. I look forward to seeing products being developed from conception, through the maturation process, to commercialization and industrialization. It is the M.S./Ph.D. programs at UCLA in MEMS/Nanotechnology that can give me the necessary tools to become that "father" of microproducts for the future.

– 4 –

The 2002 *Prestige* oil spill – one of a series of ecological accidents – had a personal impact on my life and gave a forceful orientation to my study, strengthening a long-standing interest for the environment and Earth protection. Taking part in the clean-up operations, I grew aware that the environment had become a factor that should no longer be ignored and that man does play a decisive role in shaping or destroying nature. After my undergraduate studies in the preparatory classes and at the Ecole XXX where I was admitted in 2012, my firm desire today is to explore further how man's civil engineering projects can be better integrated into the environment. Berkeley's MSc in Engineering and Project Management will provide me with the tools required for economic and environmental analysis of civil infrastructure systems and help me to become acquainted with the management of projects. Hence my decision to apply.

At XXX, one of the top-ranking universities for science in France, I followed a multidisciplinary curriculum, studying among other courses Mechanics, with Professor S., Economics and Biology. Each course helped me grasp one aspect of environmental engineering: the tools used by an engineer to evaluate the reliability of structural components and systems, the integration of externalities when assessing the cost of a project and the influence of pollutants on organisms. What I found most interesting was to compare the different methods of problem-solving, such as case studies in Economics, scaling laws in Fluid Dynamics and numerical computation in Applied Mathematics and Mechanics. This year, which is my final year, I am majoring in Fluid Dynamics, with Professor B.-B., and Ecoscience (Practices in Theoretical Modelling, Biodiversity, Sustainable Development and Mathematical Models for Ecology).

My lab work reflects the variety of my academic training. My first research project in 2001 was on tokamaks, toroidal structures achieving plasma confinement in order to master nuclear fusion. I worked on the different methods of measurement of plasma temperature and density as well as the various instabilities which disrupt plasma confinement. In 2004, I carried out a year-long scientific team project on the optimisation of the distribution of mobile phone antennas. I was put in charge of the team and was thus responsible for assigning the different tasks and managing the information. We had to assess the direct and indirect costs of the antennas, study electromagnetic wave transmission and use a new type of nature-inspired algorithm: particle swarm optimisation. I discovered that as every group member gets deeper into his/her research, it becomes increasingly vital and challenging to handle the flow of information among the team. This year, I have been leading a project on the environmental impact of the rejection of hot water into rivers by thermal power plants. Through this project, under the supervision of Professor B., I have been dealing with highly technical questions on fluid dynamics, while strengthening my determination to work in industrial ecology. This upcoming spring, I have been selected for an internship by the French giant utility EDF to study the impact of nuclear waste on future generations. All my research work points in one direction: if man is to take into account various environmental constraints, he must possess a holistic knowledge, but also a capacity to absorb the minutiae of one particular field.

I also developed my organisational and communication skills through the preparation of school events. I was part of the 30-member team organising the 2003 job fair, during which students, the corporate world and scientific laboratories get together and exchange ideas. I was in charge of the Scientific Research Forum, and set up a round table dedicated to discussing state-of-the-art research in environmental protection. I am now organising the forum "Equation" on sustainable development with HEC, the leading business school in France. This experience has helped me to understand the need for important firms like the Total oil company or the nuclear power group Areva, to hire all-round engineers with a strong background in science, project management and an emphasis on environmental engineering. In those projects, the communicative skills I had acquired as a teaching assistant in Chemistry for undergraduate students proved eminently useful.

At first, I was attracted by the Master of Science in Environmental Engineering and its emphasis on water quality. Then, I realized that if I wanted to change policies on pollution, I had to work as a project manager, and therefore, I needed to acquire stronger management and financial skills. Thus, I decided to channel my energy into the MSc in Engineering and Project Management because it also suits best my interest in life-cycle economic and risk analysis. Professor H's advice has comforted me in my choice. The knowledge gained in *Civil Systems and the Environment* will be at the heart of my work throughout my career while Professor B's course in *Risk Assessment and Management of Engineered Systems* will offer an interesting human-based approach to anticipating accidents, using the tools developed by Berkeley, the SYRAS and the SMAS. The Consortium on Green Design and Manufacturing is a unique opportunity to complement my training with contacts with the world of industry, and conduct cross-disciplinary research in industrial ecology within Berkeley's laboratories.

Following my graduate studies, I plan to use the tools acquired in the department of Civil and Environmental Engineering to assess the impact of major civil engineering projects on nature. One of my goals is to eventually be put in charge of these projects in an international company, using the knowledge acquired in the MSc in Engineering and Project Management. Besides, I do not rule out the possibility of working for a public agency on the influence of major water policy decisions, thanks to the course in *Planning and Management of Environmental and Water Systems*. Finally, I hope that this experience both in the public and private sector with the broadened view acquired at Berkeley will allow me to work for the UN Environment Programme.

Joining UCB's Civil and Environmental Engineering's department is therefore a chance for me to learn more about the skills needed to manage a project, while strengthening my knowledge in environmental engineering. I am confident that my love of new experiences will provide me with great dynamism and motivation in Berkeley's highly challenging atmosphere. I definitely think that my interdisciplinary academic record and my various experiences in team management on a multicultural campus will contribute to enhancing the reputation of excellence of your department.

– 5 –

In [1], Professor Steven Neil Evans addresses the question of the zeros of a random p-adic polynomial system over Zp and gives an exact computation of their expected number when the polynomial's coefficients have independent, identically distributed standard Qp-Gaussian distributions. The complexity of the setting caught my attention as the system of polynomials was not over a usual field but over the strange and unintuitive field of p-adic numbers and the polynomial entries were set to be in the ring Zp. All these new concepts and strange settings stirred a curiosity for mathematics in general (the way math brings order and theoretical rigor to the seemingly chaotic and random events of nature) and applied math in particular, first nurtured in the preparatory program and later at Ecole XXX where I gained admission in 2016. Currently a third-year student, I am specializing in a master's level program in applied mathematics, with a definite bent for probability theory and statistics. I was thrilled to discover such intricate connections between probability and p-adic numbers. How could probability and statistical theory help us unfold the mysteries of other branches of mathematics? How far can we extend the usual and familiar tools of probability to cover the less common ground of mathematical theory? Those are questions that puzzle me and that have triggered my desire to apply for doctoral studies at the University of California Berkeley for I am convinced it has the key to help me pursue the answers.

I took several advanced courses as an undergraduate ranging from *Galois Theory* to *Quantum Mechanics* but my fascination with randomness led me to focus on probability theory which grew when I worked on an elective course project on MM algorithms and generalized Bradley-Terry models under the supervision of Prof Eric S. Given a dataset on Nascar, the project's objective was to estimate the model parameters by likelihood maximization using a MM algorithm. I was thrilled by the idea of uncovering hidden patterns in data that seemed random at first. I grew even more passionate about the theory of probability when I attended the *Random Events Modelling: Markov chains and Martingales* course.

I later worked on a course project with Prof Emmanuel G. on Hawkes processes and probability estimation in a rare event setting. My objective was to estimate the probability of a tweet-apocalypse and provide an error estimation as well. We chose to model tweets arrival times using a Hawkes process with exponential decay, and by performing a tricky change of measure we were able to use Importance Sampling techniques to estimate the rare event probability. The results were published in the HAL Archives. Exploring different routes and overcoming several difficulties while working on it, this project gave me a first taste on what research was about. Subsequently, I naturally chose to apply for a summer internship in the field of probability and statistics.

As a summer intern at BNP Paribas, I worked on enhancing their liquidity forecasting model which was based on client behavior analysis and stochastics calculus. My supervisor gave me free rein to change what was necessary to make the model more realistic and accurate, thereupon I tested several techniques and tweaked many parameters in my search for a better model. The forecasting I developed was a big success when tested in by BNL a subsidiary of BNP Paribas in Italy.

I am currently working on a research project with Prof G. on Brownian motion in confinement: we are trying to learn more about the probability that a Brownian motion trajectory up to a certain time stays confined in a ball with a given radius. I am also working with Profs G. and Xavier A. on tropical-geometry and log-barrier interior-point methods to analyze a counterexample of strong polynomial complexity presented in their paper [5]. We hope to generalize the results proved in [5] to other types of barriers using tropical geometry tools and max-plus algebra. Enrolled in *Stochastic Models in Finance* and *Monte Carlo Methods for Stochastic Simulation* courses this semester, my interest in probability theory has become even more pronounced.

Discovering new and complicated mathematical concepts has always been an attraction to me. While reading a paper [2] published by Dr. Steven Evans where he addresses the concept of Gaussian Distributions and Brownian motion to locally compact, non-discrete fields using a specific characterization of the Gaussian distribution based on orthogonality. I was fascinated by these new discoveries and, hungry for more, my attention was caught by a paper written in 2017 [3] by Dr. Jim P., Dr. E. where they investigated the span of Brownian motion. Their findings concerning topological properties (on Hausdorff dimension of multidimensional Brownian motion span in particular) of the random span set uncover more of the structure and hidden proprieties of Brownian motion and allow us to better understand its behavior.

Motivated by my desire to get familiar with these new concepts I read another paper [4] in which Dr. Evans extends the concept of U-statistics to local fields. Under the condition that the local field K has characteristic zero and that support of the i.i.d random variables (X_k) on K is compact, Prof. Evans establishes the convergence in distribution of the U-statistics corresponding to the variables X. This result initiates the investigation of the properties of U statistics on other algebraic structures than the reals and shows that some familiar limit theory properties in the real numbers setting can be extended to the local field setting. After getting acquainted with some of the relevant literature I have developed a particular interest for probability theory on algebraic structures, finite and discrete structures.

Several courses offered by the Department of Statistics have caught my attention. The courses I would like to follow include *Probability* taught by Jim P., *Advanced Topics in Probability and Stochastic Processes* taught by Fraydoun R. and *Theoretical Statistics* with William F. These courses will allow me to broaden my knowledge in probability and statistics and deepen my understanding of probability theory. I am confident that my academic background has prepared me well to pursue a PhD in statistics at U.C Berkeley.

My goal in life is to pursue an academic career and conduct research in probability theory, statistics, and mathematics in general. I left my home country, Morocco, spurred on by my hunger for science and the challenges that the rural region I come from could not offer. Moving to Paris and then gaining admission to XXX (at the top of the class) my ambition is to become a researcher in my own right. I am confident that the cross-disciplinary nature of U.C Berkeley's Statistics PhD program will help me achieve my dream should I be granted the privilege of admission.

[1]: The expected number of zeros of a random system of p-adic polynomials. Comm. Probab. 11, 278-290

[2]: Local Fields, Gaussian Measures, And Brownian Motions, Steven N. Evans U.C. Berkeley, CA 94720-3860

[3]: The Spans In Brownian Motion, Steven N. Evans, JIM PITMAN, AND WENPIN TANG

[4]: Local field U-statistics. *Algebraic Methods in Statistics and Probability, Steven N.Evans*

[5]: Log-Barrier Interior Point Methods Are Not Strongly Polynomial Xavier Allamigeon, Pascal Benchimol, Stéphane Gaubert, and Michael Joswig.

– 6 –

Natural-language understanding is one of the most promising AI-hard problems. As of today, most of human knowledge is available in text form, be it in books, newspapers or web pages. If an AGI is ever destined to help advance scientific research, then it will need to process and understand, in some way, centuries of text-form data: "Text is knowledge" as Prof. Christopher Manning phrased it. Yet one of the most daunting challenges of unsupervised machine learning is to take context and prior knowledge into account. Hopefully, "Knowledge is in the text" and that inherent recursion places the problem at the heart of a virtuous circle, which is why I find the topic so exhilarating. Currently a third-year student at the Ecole XXX where I was admitted in 2014, my ambition is to apply the further knowledge I will acquire in AI, NLP and cryptography, and either work for the high-tech industry or possibly embark on the entrepreneurial path. Stanford's MS in Computer Science is therefore the next way station.

My school's program provided me with a generic overview of the problems at stake in today's research work, broadening my knowledge areas while narrowing down my scientific interests. Building on a strong mathematical background – that was early on rewarded in national and international math contests – I rooted my knowledge in math classes, such as *Galois Theory* lectured by David H., and its natural continuation, *Algebraic Number Theory.*

Yet, it was the *Foundations of Computer Science* course that proved a revelation to me. Starting from a math content, the class led me to understand how some of the most complex questions could be related to real-world issues. For example, it is widely believed that in polynomial time, a deterministic sequential machine is not able to solve the same set of decision problems as a non-deterministic machine. But a constructive proof of this assertion's negation would have groundbreaking consequences both negative – it would void many cryptographically secure systems – and positive – it could revolutionize the way we apprehend mathematical research. I therefore opted to gradually shift my focus from math to computer science, deepening my knowledge of the field in Stéphane G.'s *Computational Logic* course, which explains how artificial intelligence can be applied to mathematical reasoning. The fact that Turing machines, recursive functions and lambda-calculus are all equivalent concepts disrupted my way of thinking of computer programs.

My interest in computer science was also fueled by the *Principle of Programming Languages* and the *Algorithm Design and Analysis* courses; both included hands-on experiences that allowed me to conceive and implement algorithms that efficiently solved seemingly difficult problems. I especially enjoyed the instant result and concrete side of applied sciences combined with the elegance of the code written, while benchmarking my implementations of Knuth-Morris-Pratt, Boyer-Moore and Karp-Rabin's algorithms for the string-search problem.

Yet it was thanks to Eric G.'s *Parallel and Distributed Programming* course that I fully embraced the potential of computer programming and the role of computer science in solving complex problems, combining the computational power of many machines to overcome a slow-down in Moore's law. New problems - such as race conditions - appeared with this new asynchronous style of programming. Implementing and running the MapReduce algorithm using the MPI library over a cluster of 96 computers was a compelling example of cloud computing.

At my school, I also seized opportunities to take part in year-long projects allowing me to deepen my understanding of a very specific problem while leveraging my coding skills. Last year's team project was to send off fireworks to write in the sky and was a collaboration between the LadHyX laboratory and a pyrotechnist entrepreneur. As a proof-of-concept, my teammates conceived a miniature model of the cannons using electromagnets that I synchronized using Raspeberry Pis, using techniques I acquired through my *Networking* course. It was an unsuccessful but enriching attempt to bridge the gap between scientific research and the entrepreneurial world, and gave me a foretaste of the pipeline between academics and production.

Another project, supervised by Prof. Thomas C., focused on performing a man-in-the-middle attack on a Wi-Fi router, showing that WPA2 security does not protect from insider attacks. To do so, we rerouted the queries flowing through the network towards our own server, enabling us to add a custom script to every webpage the victim loaded, so that we could capture his passwords and every other form data submitted through HTTP.

An undergraduate research work in number theory gave me a glimpse of what advanced research was like and proved that I was prepared to deliver the kind of energy and thought power it requires. I proved the local version of the Kronecker-Weber theorem, stating that any abelian extension of Q_p must be contained in some cyclotomic extension, a problem that requires a good understanding of p-adic numbers, local fields, advanced number theory, topics not usually analyzed at this stage of studies.

Outside the curriculum, I have put my computer skills to good use. While doing my leadership training, I took responsibility in the process of matching my fellow trainees with available positions in the French Army, by implementing the Kuhn-Munkres algorithm for producing a perfect matching under constraints. The IT society I lead provide technical support to the student community, design software according to the students' needs and help them build up programming skills that are useful both for their academic studies and professional life. This one-year experience with 20 people passionate about helping others has firmed up my sense of community service and enhanced my qualities as a team player.

My coursework has also started bringing answers to the deepest questions that haunt me, in the field of artificial intelligence, and more specifically in Natural Language Processing. The *Massive Data Processing* course has offered some insights of the most advanced tools that can be used in this field and led me to think that applying deep learning techniques, such as the use of recurrent neural networks or recursive neural networks, could pave the way to even more progress in NLP. That is why I look forward to the *Text Mining* course that I will attend next semester. In that respect, I was more than excited to discover that Prof. Manning's class on *NLP with Deep Learning* actually focuses on the very topics I want to go deeper into. The Stanford NLP group has proven to be one of the most productive teams in this specific area, developing and maintaining the Stanford CoreNLP toolkit, among which the part-of-speech tagger widely used in both the academic and industrial NLP community. I would be eager to be part of it.

Another field of interest is cryptography. Acquiring a better understanding of group theory and finite fields through my mathematical classes eventually allowed me to sate my curiosity in how cryptologic systems actually worked. As a matter of fact, machine translation – an area of research in NLP – shares some similarity with the fundamental techniques used in cryptanalysis. Although breaking asymmetric cryptosystems like Textbook-RSA – as I have learned to do in the *Cryptography* course – is of little relevance in NLU, the common philosophy behind these two fields tends to explain why, to a lesser extent, I nurture some interest for that particular branch of computer science. In that respect, Prof. Dan Boneh's *Cryptography* courses are of particular relevance to me.

Stanford's Master of Science program allows students to keep broadening their knowledge of various areas of computer science while also focusing on a specific topic, namely AI. By deepening my knowledge of NLP, I hope to acquire a set of state-of-the-art skills to fully apply my potential to the NLU problem. My desire to push back the boundaries of this science is also enhanced by the will to create a tech company that will make use of the latest advances in the field.

– 7 –

My ambition is to contribute to the topics of non-convex optimization, high-dimensional statistics, random matrix theory and the analysis of network-structured data. These objectives grew out of an early interest in the deep connection between statistical physics, information theory and computation, as my curriculum and research experiences inform. In order to acquire the knowledge necessary to conduct this research, I am applying to the Ph.D. program of the Statistics Department at Stanford University.

My passion for problem solving goes back to the mathematics and physics competitions I took part in during high school. I was among the five students selected to represent France at the 2012 International Physics Olympiads, where I was awarded a silver medal. These experiences convinced me to follow the French preparatory program that led me to the *École Normale Supérieure* program (Paris ENS Ulm) where I was admitted in Mathematics (ranked 10 to the nationwide entrance exam).

During my first year at ENS, I completed both a B.Sc. in pure Mathematics and a B.Sc. in Physics. I took courses in *Algebra, Integration, Probability* and *Statistical Physics*. The *Rigorous Aspects of Statistical Mechanics* and *Non-equilibrium Statistical Physics and Phase Transition* courses offered my first insights into the study of disordered systems and collective behavior. Prof. Bernard D.'s lectures on randomness and the descriptive power of probabilistic ideas were a marked influence on my formation. I subsequently chose the Master of Theoretical Physics at the *International Center of Fundamental Physics* (ENS Paris), where I grounded the study of natural phenomena in mathematical reasoning. Fascinated by the reading of *Information, Physics and Computation* [i], I devoted most of my master courses and my two internships to the study of statistical physics tools and their applications. The subjects included random matrix theory, graphical models, inference, stochastic processes, as well as a physics approach to information theory and optimization. Eager to concentrate on the mathematical foundations of these topics, I signed up for the master-level *Probability Seminar* and *Statistics* course (taught by Stéphane B.) at the ENS Mathematics Department.

By the end of my Master, my interest had narrowed down on the field of statistics. For my fourth and final year at ENS, I therefore interned at Stanford University with Prof. Andrea M. and at MIT with Prof. Guy B.

During a five-month stay at the *Los Alamos National Laboratory* under the supervision of Sc. Misha C., I explored the gauge symmetry of graphical models associated to a skew-rotation of their alphabet, and its application to inference. The most natural gauge fixation leads to the BP approximation as well as its exact correction in terms of a loop series. Even if the project only yielded partial results, it got me acquainted with standard relaxation techniques and heuristics used in computer science and statistics. An application that I developed consisted in using message-passing equations to approximate the marginal probability of a spreading process on a graph and inferring its diffusion parameters, which proved particularly robust with respect to noisy and partial information (early results submitted in [ii]). In a second project with Marc V. (Sc., LANL), I applied loop calculus to correct the Bethe free entropy of LDPC codes above the dynamical phase transition (where metastable states appear and local algorithms fail). I then used it, with combinatorial techniques, to show the concentration to zero of the bit-error probability almost up to the MAP threshold (condensation threshold above which decoding is impossible). This result was presented at Allerton 2015 [iii]. At Stanford, I would enjoy digging further into the applications of message-passing algorithms and replica symmetry breaking with A. M. and Sourav C.

In parallel, I looked into the possibility of using the tractability of two-dimensional models (Temperley-Lieb algebraic structure) in the learning context. This unsuccessful project, in cooperation with Marc V., led nonetheless to the introduction of a new class of estimators for learning general graphical models, the Interaction Screening Estimator, which was later shown [iv] to be sample optimal for bounded-degree Ising models (first algorithm to prove it). This first success sparked my interest for high-dimensional statistics and the information-theoretic implications of priors. I am now working with M. V., Sidhant M. (Sc. LANL) and G. B. on understanding the interplay between incoherence condition, sparsistency and thresholding. A. M.'s research on the trade-off between complexity and correlation decay and Emmanuel C. on restricted isometries are quite appealing on this respect.

My interest for non-convex optimization started from my lectures on replica symmetry breaking phase transition and the idea that spin glass could be used as a surrogate to investigate optimization problems in machine learning (e.g. work by Arous and LeCun). During my stay at Stanford, with A. M. and Ph.D. student Song M., we found out that the bad saddle points (which are the problematic points for optimization) lie close to the global optimum in the case of the low rank SDP relaxation of the max-cut problem (Burer-Monteiro approach). We used this structural information to devise a complexity-bound for the Trust-region method on this non-convex problem.

Two experiences further confirmed my interest in statistics: the 2015 LHC data analysis (Higgs Boson, *CMS experiment*, CERN) and my work on the D-Wave 2X, a quantum annealing computer developed by *D-Wave Systems* (using noise and imperfections to efficiently sample from a binary distribution and calibrating D-Wave using learning algorithms on its output).

Through my internships, I have achieved a high-level of maturity both in mathematics and in research that I now want to leverage further. Stanford's Statistics Department's strong emphasis on theory will allow me to pursue my current research interests in the analysis of message-passing algorithms, high-dimensional data and non-convex problems. In addition to these subjects, I would be very excited to work with A. M. on SDP and community detection related problems. I am equally interested in the theoretical works of Sourav Chatterjee and Amir Dembo on random matrix theory and sparse random graphs and of Lester Mackey on matrix concentration inequalities, with which I got acquainted during my stay at Stanford.

I believe that statistics, as the mathematical foundation of the statistical methodologies used in data analysis and machine learning, will dramatically impact a wide range of disciplines, from artificial intelligence to communication and biology. I am eager to bring my own contribution!

In advance, I thank the admissions committee for reading my letter.

[i] Mezard M, Montanari A. Information, physics, and computation. Oxford University Press; 2009 Jan 22.
[ii] Lokhov AY, Misiakiewicz T. Efficient reconstruction of transmission probabilities in a spreading process from partial observations. arXiv preprint arXiv:1509.06893. 2015. Presented at *Conference on Complex Systems* 2015.
[iii] Vuffray M, and Misiakiewicz T. Concentration to zero bit-error probability for regular LDPC codes on the binary symmetric channel: Proof by loop calculus. *2015 53rd Annual Allerton Conference on Communication, Control, and Computing (Allerton).* IEEE, 2015.
[iv] Vuffray, Marc, et al. Interaction Screening: Efficient and Sample-Optimal Learning of Ising Models. *arXiv preprint arXiv:1605.07252* (2016).

– 8 –

Stanford, through the work of its Applied Cryptography group, has had a key role in the emergence of Fully Homomorphic Encryption [4]. When thinking about the consequences of AI, many people describe a dystopian future in which some companies know about every aspect of everyone's life, but this cryptographic primitive, along with other modern Obfuscation techniques, lets us envision a world where citizens have full control over their data. I intend to dedicate my PhD to the study and design of cryptographic primitives that enable computations on encrypted data, with a focus on computations relevant to one of the fastest-growing areas of computer science: machine learning. I believe that Stanford's program - given the extent of Dan B's work on obfuscation in cryptography and his interest and expertise in machine learning would provide me with the ideal environment to conduct my research.

I discovered modern cryptography during my first internship at a Palo Alto startup, when I was asked to draft a report on Encrypted Search. It encouraged me to work on a research project on Identity-Based Encryption [1] at Ecole XXX. I later followed Ben S's *Advanced Cryptology* course, during which I got to implement Extendable Output Hash Functions, Elliptic Curve Diffie-Hellman, Elliptic Curve Factorization, and Post-Quantum Cryptosystems. I am currently interning with the Crypto Team at Ecole XXX. We have submitted work on Homomorphic Encryption to a Cryptography conference, in which we show how to efficiently compute a weighted sum of several client's encrypted inputs without revealing the individual inputs.

My ambition is to continue working on cryptographic primitives that enable full or controlled privacy during computations, typically those relevant to machine learning. I am particularly interested in designing homomorphic schemes that enable the application or the training of machine learning models, from linear regression to advanced neural networks, on encrypted data. I would like to build schemes for homomorphic encryption with performance far greater than what we can achieve today on machine learning tasks. To that end, I believe it worth investigating a primitive that would combine fully homomorphic encryption and fully key homomorphic encryption [2]: from any ciphertext for plaintext x under public-key pk, one can obtain a ciphertext for plaintext f(x) under public-key (f,f(pk)), for any efficiently computable function f.

A weaker version of this "double homomorphism" is used in our paper, and we have since used another, drawing inspiration from BGN [3], to design a different Homomorphic Encryption scheme, which we've implemented using MIRACL, a C cryptography library. I am currently working on demonstrating its practicality by using it to tackle a standard machine learning benchmark.

This project has highlighted the importance of having robust machine learning knowledge when designing cryptosystems for machine learning applications: we have noticed that principal component analysis could be performed homomorphically on our ciphertexts, which helps speed up evaluation. Many issues also arise when trying to force float-based machine learning models in cryptographic settings. When considering the related setting of training machine learning models on encrypted data, the potential leakage of information about individual instances in the training set from queries to the final model also means machine learning expertise is required if one is to give a meaningful evaluation of the security of a scheme.

To understand robustness and privacy issues associated with machine learning in more detail, and to reach the level of expertise necessary to the design of machine learning models that remain usable and efficient within the framework of encrypted data, I look forward to taking foundational courses such as AI, machine learning and statistical learning theory.

On top of my research experience in top French institutions, I come strong-armed with a solid background in mathematics and computer science theory, acquired through the preparatory program and courses at XXX, and my experience writing code for personal productivity, academic projects, and as a software engineering intern in Silicon Valley, where I have witnessed first-hand the challenges in bringing to life user-friendly projects that do not compromise security and privacy. Once I have completed my studies, Stanford's geographic proximity and strong ties to Silicon Valley's tech giants would prove a great asset in helping me move to the industry to ensure my work translates into better privacy in the real-world.

References

[1] Dan Boneh and Matt Franklin. Identity-based encryption from the weil pairing. In Advances in Cryptology-CRYPTO 2001, pages 213-229. Springer, 2001.
[2] Dan Boneh, Craig Gentry, Sergey Gorbunov, Shai Halevi, Valeria Nikolaenko, Gil Segev, Vinod Vaikuntanathan, and Dhinakaran Vinayagamurthy. Fully key-homomorphic encryption, arithmetic circuit abe and compact garbled circuits. In Annual International Conference on the Theory and Applications of Cryptographic Techniques, pages 533-556. Springer, 2014.
[3] Dan Boneh, Eu-Jin Goh, and Kobbi Nissim. Evaluating 2-dnf formulas on ciphertexts. In TCC, volume 3378, pages 325-341. Springer, 2005.
[4] Craig Gentry *et al.* Fully homomorphic encryption using ideal lattices. In STOC, volume 9, pages 169-178, 2009.

– 9 –

During a summer internship, I was assigned to a branch of the Civil Security Service where we took part in a mock full-scale emergency response drill with several other European fire-fighting and civil protection units. The staged accident involved a train carrying radioactive waste going off the rails near a densely populated area. My responsibility was to coordinate work between numerous units in order to increase the efficiency of the rescue teams and limit the impact of the mishap. That experience greatly sharpened my awareness of the dangers involved in such accidents, the threats of nuclear energy including the hazards posed by nuclear materials. It strongly motivated me to work in the domain of new technologies. I want to acquire the tools and skills sets to assess the risks associated with the spread of technologies new and less new, regulate their deployment, and generally be directly involved in the decision-making process. As a final year undergraduate student at University XXX, I have always been fascinated by science but I am most interested in channeling my scientific background into practical applications. Consequently, I have determined to apply to the TPP, in order to acquire in-depth knowledge of the contemporary economic, business, and ethical issues related to energy and technology.

My undergraduate curriculum consisted of a broad range of courses from biology to computer science and economics. Currently, I am majoring in physics, which I have found to be a most satisfying and challenging area of study that inspires and drives me to master the fundamental principles. Among the several exciting classes I have attended, two stand out: a course on nuclear physics taught by Professor Martin L., and another one on *Quantum Optics* lectured by Alain B. Not only did they provide me with the basics of theory to understand the mechanism of fusion, allowing me to become acquainted with cutting edge research paving the way to clean energy resources but they also offered an opportunity to apply my knowledge to concrete projects. I am conducting experimental work in laser-created plasmas under the supervision of Professor Victor C. The subject of this lab research course is strongly related to Thermonuclear Fusion where I believe the future of energy lies. My second major, in economics, will complete the education acquired through my first-year course and provide me with the advanced technical background to study macroeconomics models. Additionally, it will give me a better grasp of resources management and environmental questions while introducing the economic issues of sustainable development.

Research is an integral part of the program. Last year's team research project was on fluid mechanics. It focused on the hydrodynamic instability study of the Sea Orbiter. This on-going project gathered many research institutes including NASA and aimed at building a revolutionary floating oceanographic science platform that would drift along with the currents, allowing scientists to conduct submarine research without acoustic nuisance as well as providing astronauts with a training facility simulating weightlessness. It was an exceptional case study on an experimental subject as we built a model craft to verify our theoretical results, developing thereby my ability to take initiatives. As we were working in a seven-student team, it was an excellent approach to strengthening my micromanagement and team-working skills. Furthermore, I recently signed up for a seminar held between the University XXX and HEC Business School focusing on how to start a high-tech company. My team and I are to carry out a project on an intuitive digital frame for the elderly to download family picture from the Internet over a phone line. The challenge, both technological and social, is to design a tool simple enough for senior citizens to adopt it. It is bound to be an original, positive technological contribution, and therefore a most enriching entrepreneurial experience for me.

Straddling two cultures, I have developed a keen awareness of cultural differences between Europe and Asia. I was brought up in a multigenerational and multicultural household. My mother was born in Vietnam, my father in Cambodia and both have roots going back to China. They fled the killing fields to settle in France in 1975 and start a new life. Receiving both a Chinese education and a French instruction at school, I developed an acute sense of responsibility towards both the community I belong to and the country where I was born. I am an extremely attentive people-person. My personal culture has drawn much from my parents' wisdom and pragmatism. While instilling with me fundamental values such as honesty, humility and determination, they motivated me to study Chinese language and culture. I owe it to my parents to continue as they have taught me, and to make the most of my academic opportunities.

After extensive research, I have identified the Technology Policy Program as the only one that can fully provide me with the key competences in leadership and decision-making that I must acquire in order to proceed with my career. In that respect, not only will the *Law, Technology, and Public Policy* course introduce me to a new domain of study but they will also provide me the tools to shape policy. While giving my education a managerial twist, the variety of your program will help me gather knowledge in several areas, from economics, business, and social science to public policy. It is important to have a multidisciplinary background to tackle environmental issues in order to fully understand their causes and impact. The TPP program has acquired a solid experience of thirty years in the education of leaders, which will serve me in the professional career I expect to carve out for myself. While travelling in Asia, I've grown acutely aware of the major technology issues at stake. For example, I have seen the havoc wrought by air pollution on the country's environment while it is facing rapid economic and demographic growth. The courses will enable me to reflect upon vital issues, bringing me forward-looking perspectives. The MIT offers an opportunity to combine another degree. I would like to study nuclear science and engineering. I am particularly interested in the question of the energy efficiency. The energy supply is a major issue: at stakes, the pertaining problems of not only provide enough power for all but also preserve the environment. I've also grown fond of leading projects and your program is in line with my aspirations. In addition, MIT's international campus and multicultural environment will offer me a one-off chance to share ideas with people from various horizons.

Living in Europe while remaining closely connected to Chinese culture, I know that I can play a significant role in bridging the Eurasian gap, and, in that respect, studying at an American University would be a major milestone on my way to an international career. A career which I envision working for an NGO or a public agency dedicated to environmental problems, including energy. Having strong skills in science and languages (I speak fluent Chinese) coupled with a clear-headed vision of making our environment a better place to live are what I can bring to MIT. I am confident that the TPP will offer the tools that I still need to achieve my goals.

– 10 –

What is the primary structure of life? How does life become motion? How does life organize itself? What complexity! What stimulating wonderments for a physicist like me! Biology, by the mystery it opens, the concreteness it brings and the laws of physics it respects, has galvanized the attention of the physics expert I am blooming into. I have always been interested in physics, but its connection with biology is something I have discovered recently. It is at the interface of these two domains, biology and physics, that I see myself working in the future. This is the reason I am applying to the doctoral program in Applied Physics in the School of Engineering and Applied Sciences at Harvard University.

For my undergraduate studies, I chose the foremost French program in physics and math during which I undertook my first research project on the brightness of materials. The first goal was to find and perfect models of surface materials which would explain how these surfaces interact with light. The theoretical part was fascinating, but it was a two-month laboratory internship with the ELDIM corporation, working on the EZLite machine, side by side with professional scientists that made me think I might want to do research for a career. It was creative and challenging looking for theoretical models and applying them to real issues.

I then chose the Paris-Saclay University for its multidisciplinary and high-quality education and for its outstanding research environment. Thus, I have been able to develop my pluri-scientific culture and my interest in research. Last year, I took part in a seven-month team research project in association with the LePrince Ringuet Laboratory. Our aim was to build algorithms capable of exploiting raw data from a calorimeter for the future International Linear Collider (ILC). We used experimental and theoretical data (from a calorimeter prototype at the Hamburg Desy and GEANT4 simulation software) that are generated by the particle passing through the calorimeter. From this raw data, we distinguished the different events responsible for the loss of energy, analyzed them and calculated the actual energy deposit. I enjoyed doing this project, for both the scientific and organizational challenges. I learned a lot, but also became aware that I prefer to work on more concrete research which has applications in everyday life. Having an overview of an entire project and its impact on our society is what thrills me.

Also last year, I discovered experimental physics thanks to Olivier K.'s course taught in the SPEC (*condensed matter physics*) laboratory at the CEA (France's Alternative Energies and Atomic Energy Commission). My partner and I studied atomic junctions in gold and niobium samples at different temperatures thanks to a break-junction system. We built a metallic bridge suspended over a few millimeters. Pulling its edges apart, we measured the evolution of the resistance of the system in relation to the imposed bending of the sample. I knew the Ohm law was not faithful on small scales, but it was exciting to observe this quantum phenomenon firsthand. Seeing the limits of classical theory in such an ordinary phenomenon as conductivity made me aware of the importance of applications in breaking new ground in the future. Seeing how profound the implications of experimental physics can be, I felt my passion for this field growing strong.

My interest in physics gained fresh impetus when I discovered advanced biology through the course in *Molecular Physiology and Pathophysiology of the Cell* taught by Yves G. and Jean-Louis M. This course unveiled for me an unsuspected reality. I was gripped by the study of such basic functions as respiration at a cellular and molecular level. I was not aware of all the dangers breathing implies for the organism and I was struck by the complexity of the defences the cell implements to protect itself from what makes us live: oxygen. This simple discovery opened my mind to the variety of actions and antagonisms our body manages each second. Becoming aware of that reality, I also saw the role physics can play in helping us expand our understanding of life processes, both at their basic level (that of a single molecule or cell) and on a statistical scale. Being a physicist, these possibilities stimulate my imagination and I can see myself working in teams discovering new links between these two fields.

I am currently in my final undergraduate year and have decided to specialize in Physics. With courses in *Physical Biology, Quantum Optics, Soft Matter Physics, Quantum Physics of Condensed Matter*, I am expecting to find the bridges between these physical fields and biology. The introductory course devoted to the physics of biological objects, collections and processes, and *Physics of Polymers and Biological Membranes* are providing me with the introduction I have been longing for to biophysics, the field I plan to work in. The courses in *Soft Surface, Electrons in Solid Physics and Statistical Theory of Fields: from Polymers to Phase Transitions* are supplying me with a mastery in soft and condensed matter, a basis for my future approach to biological objects. I am also studying *Quantum Optics* and lasers. Light has transfigured physics throughout the twentieth century, and been the source of numerous advances. It is now opening new frontiers by enabling investigation within very short times and distances. The laser, the greatest invention of the twentieth century, is a powerful tool for investigating biological processes and I am enjoying discovering both the theory and the practical uses. My current project is creating a femtosecond cavity, analyzing its characteristics, then using it to observe other phenomena, such as the generation of coherent XUV light.

The projects I have undertaken have, periodically, appeased my ardent desire to understand and showed me how rewarding and meaningful research is. I feel confirmed in my choice of working towards a doctorate. I would like to acquire expertise in a very specific field, which will transform my vision of the future. With that competence, I would like to innovate, to offer something new, both concretely and in the more immaterial domain of comprehending the world. I need to do fundamental research to face the deep unknown, but at the same time I like working on concrete issues. I can see myself doing academic research and working as a consultant on technical issues to help businesses or governments find new solutions thanks to my investigations.

This vision is what has led me to Biophysics in the Applied Physics Graduate Program. I would like to apply my knowledge to an unanswered issue. Three labs truly appeal to me: these are the Prentiss lab (on single molecule investigation, from DNA to binding systems), the Cluzel lab (on sources of behavioral variability of a cell) and the Weitz lab (on mechanics of cells and biological networks). I would be happy doing research in any of these fields, for they all use physics and mathematics to understand the complexity of living systems. I also yearn to study more advanced and more specific physical and biophysical concepts, drawing on my strong multidisciplinary background. I would definitely take the course *Molecular Mechanism of Gene Control* as it would provide me with biological insight to issues that fascinate me. As strong as I may be in physics, I need more biological mastery to have a thorough grasp of biophysics and to discover new questions in the field. I would also study *Optical Imaging in Biological Science* to learn the available research techniques and to become part of the process of their continuous improvement. This instrumental aspect attracts me because it is often there that error or discovery arise. For all these reasons, your program is perfect for me: not only does it meet my expectations of a graduate program, but I feel it will challenge my views, helping me to become the scientist I yearn to be, finding breakthroughs that will improve society.

– 11 –

What does the Robot-Soccer World Championship of October 2004 in Korea have to do with my interest in electrical engineering? Watching these robots interact with their complex and changing environment as well as with each other, I could not help being amazed at how they could recognize and adapt to their surroundings, and at the same time how easily and unexpectedly they were outwitted. This led me to take all the computer science classes available to me during the second year pluri-scientific program at University XXX, and to choose the field of robotics for a simulation project on a team of war robots. Programming their strategies to destroy enemies using their leader's radar information was challenging and fun and allowed me to acquire skills in parallel programming and communication network strategies. This project confirmed my interest for robot guiding, and made me realize I wanted to apply my skills to more concrete projects in electrical engineering, rather than just simulation.

Last year also allowed me to acquire an acute capacity for problem-solving in several domains ranging from mechanics, economics, biology, pure math and quantum physics to architecture. Thinking about specializing in robotics, I took courses in computer science (object orientated programming, graphs, languages) and in applied math (mathematical models for practical problems, probabilities), all of which I enjoyed. In addition to these classes was a year-long team research project, which I chose in electronics to sharpen my programming skills. We designed the Engine Control Unit (ECU) of our school's prototype for the Shell Eco-Marathon, an automobile race in which we had to use the least fuel per kilometer, grappling with all the unexpected results and practical problems that are sidestepped in a simulation. Being project-leader for the algorithm of the ECU led me into the world of FPGA programming, learning on the job with advice from engineers from our two sponsors, Thales (information systems for Aeronautics, Space and Defence) and Peugeot (car manufacturer). I enjoyed the coordination meetings involving all the different teams which designed various auto parts and the planning of our own industrial project.

Project coordination was not new to me at that time. During a gap year, I worked for seven months as a science consultant and personal assistant for several teachers in Paris' disadvantaged northern suburbs. Whether it was planning class sessions, leading science information meetings for teachers or searching for teaching materials to start a district Science Knowledge Center, I threw all my energy into creating a positive vision of hands-on science among students and teachers alike, starting cooperative projects like the Biology Garden or the Hot Air Balloon. I loved seeing my ideas come to life through hard work, obstinacy, persuasion and cooperation. Back in school, wanting to renew this rewarding experience, I joined the student association BEST (Board of European Students of Technology) and was vice-president for the organization of a ten-day scientific symposium for students from 16 different countries. Overcoming fundraising difficulties, administrative negotiations and accommodation trouble, our team put together an amazing program that I am proud of and not likely to forget. Through the process, my perseverance and enthusiasm survived, and I learned how to carry on with a project until its goal is reached.

Working on the chip in the ECU project, I found low-level programming useful for understanding the way a processor functions, but wanting to try upper-level types of programming led me to a second project. Still intrigued by robotics, I went back to my first love with an experimental lab class on autonomous mobile robots in which we were free to program a three-wheeled machine for a mission of our choice. My partner and I equipped our robot with a video-camera and programmed it to follow walls, detect electric plugs and stop in front of them, so it could later plug itself in and manage its energy by itself. Working on control systems, motion planning and image processing was fascinating. Trying to make "our baby" understand and interpret its unpredictable world helped me realize that, in the wide range of skills involved in robotics, image processing was my favorite topic.

It is this mixture of math and algorithms which allowed me to create a bridge from the real world to a model of reality, giving our robot its independence. These few months spent in the lab proved to be some of the most exciting moments of my scientific life.

Thus, this year, I am specializing not in computer science as I had planned, but in optimization, communications and signals, which includes classes in *Signal Processing*, but also *Control Systems, Operations Research, Constraint Programming, Communication Networks and Parallel Programming*, all of which will have direct applications in autonomous robot design. I am continuing my experimentation with image processing with a first-semester project on turbo decoding of salt-and-pepper noise. With our signal processing professor, Olivier R., we are attempting to detect the bits of an image that were flipped in a noisy channel using a soft-in/soft-out iterative decoder. At each iteration, we reconstruct the image and process it to detect noisy pixels using a fuzzy algorithm. We then use the additional information for the next iteration of the decoder. I am enjoying finding ways to apply the new concepts I am learning to my current research project, and am already thinking about the next one. Second semester, I would like to focus on object recognition, using learning algorithms which I have not yet studied, but which already intrigue me. This will give me some of the cutting-edge tools I am looking forward to using in the future.

Next Spring, I hope to do my five-month research internship at the National Center for Scientific Research (CNRS) in the Systems Analysis and Architecture Lab (LAAS) in Toulouse, working on a two-armed manipulator robot. Working in a team to coordinate the movements of the robot using data from two cameras, one on each arm, to perform everyday or industrial manipulation tasks will be my first professional experience. A second possibility is to work in the Vehicle-Infrastructure-Driver Interactions Lab (LIVIC) at the *École des Ponts et Chaussées* (Paris), in computer vision for 3D analysis of road situations. In either of these internships, I expect to be able to use much of the theory I have been learning at the Ecole and to discover the computer vision techniques needed in cognitive robotics. After my masters, I would like to work for a few years in this particular field, perhaps in Japan. Then, I believe I will have enough experience to make an enlightened choice for my Ph.D. subject, in image processing or perhaps in a different area related to artificial intelligence.

With these goals in mind, I now need to deepen and diversify my professional tools. The master's program in Electrical Engineering at Stanford offers just the right environment to allow me to expand my theoretical training and apply it to numerous possibilities of innovative projects. The classes on *Digital Video Processing* and *Speech Signals Processing* would allow me to build on my current foundation in sound and image processing, and the latter would be useful in human-robot interactions. While building my skills in the E.E. Department, it would also be exciting to study artificial intelligence in the Computer Science Department, something I have not been able to do at school. Classes like *Computer Vision* with Sebastian T. and *Machine Learning* with Andrew Ng would be perfect to add depth and thoroughness to my internship experience. Of course, I would be truly thrilled to help in many of the labs, my first choices being the Stanford AI Lab and the Stanford Center for Image Systems Engineering, where I could use probabilistic models for vision issues like object recognition. There I know I would be both learning and contributing.

I look forward to the technical challenges that await me if I am accepted at Stanford and am more than ready to meet them, enjoy them and achieve expertise in the field of my future career. Throwing all my skills and energy into the project at hand comes naturally to me. This is what I have done at my school, what I would like to do at Stanford, and what I will do in the future, which I believe will lead to breaking new ground for scientific progress.

– 12 –

During my second year as an undergraduate, I carried out an experimental project on the delays of cement setting, the understanding of which is crucial for oil extraction. In the Huttinger laboratories near Paris, I characterized the evolving rheology of the cement paste, measuring different physical variables, principally viscosity and propagation velocity of ultrasonic waves, and observed the effect of the various parameters which act in petroleum applications, chiefly pressure and temperature. This was definitely the triggering experience that instilled into me the will to deepen my theoretical knowledge and technical competence in the field of mechanics, and more precisely in fluid mechanics. Indeed, I am highly attracted by its twofold description, both experimental and computational; as well as its situation at the crossroads of many sciences, namely physics, mathematics, chemistry and even biology; not to mention its wide range of industrial applications and research perspectives. To develop the necessary skills to pursue in this specialty, I am determined to follow the Master of Science in Mechanical Engineering program offered at the Massachusetts Institute of Technology.

All along my life I have shown scientific curiosity, eager to understand the reasons why, and the ways by which, the world functions as it does. That is what motivated me, upon my high-school graduation with honors, to apply for and be accepted to an intellectually challenging university program, renowned to provide its students with in-depth groundings in various sciences. Seizing this opportunity, I have broadened my knowledge in physics, applied mathematics and economics, and fed my keen interest for mechanics and fluid mechanics at the same time, by attending Professors H.'s and R.'s classes. These academic pillars have played a fundamental role in building up my desire to pursue in this field, by confirming my initial perception of it and delivering me the tools to understand it more deeply. I have therefore naturally chosen to specialize in fluid dynamics this year, giving answer to this desire and nourishing it, by following classes that I find fascinating.

My education has not only given me strong scientific knowledge, along with a rigorous mind, but it has also trained me for research work, mainly thanks to two projects in which I took part, in the course of my studies. The first one was a year-long team project in applied mathematics, during which we elaborated a road traffic simulation based on the cellular automata model, completed by a thorough analysis and interpretation of the results. It was enriching on different levels, being an authentic exercise in teamwork, long-term planning, and autonomous work, as minimal assistance was offered from professors. The second project, in image processing and for which the most intense work was surely delivered, consisted of an ambitious reconstruction of the whole iris recognition technique. For three months, it associated experimental work with theoretical understanding, under the guidance of Professor L. Thanks to this experience, I gained a genuine taste for research, as I acknowledged how gratifying it is to deeply understand an issue and propose new methods of resolution. Finally, I have undertaken an exciting project within my specialty this year, on the aerodynamic study of bird wing airfoils, and the role played by feathers on turbulence control.

I believe that carrying out research, beyond acquiring solid academic groundings, is an important step before becoming a research engineer, as is my intention. This profession is definitely the one which most closely matches my expectations of intellectual challenge, and contribution to society, a commitment illustrated by my volunteer work in an association, during which I supervised mentally disabled children. Engineering is another way of giving back to society, and I look forward to a career as a research scientist in a multi-national oil company. Not only does this sector offer dynamic research ventures in the field of fluid mechanics, and allow interaction with other sciences, but it also corresponds to the international, multilingual environment I'm looking for, and which I have experienced since my early childhood by living in such countries as the United Arab Emirates, Egypt, Gabon, the United States and Canada. Seeking such diversity, I chose to train in Madrid, Spain, last summer, within a team of different backgrounds, in the IT firm Portos-Gonzales. I also plan to do a five-month internship abroad this upcoming spring, in the Research and Development department of an oil company, based in the United Kingdom.

In order to attain the level of preparation required for my future work, I wish to complete the Master of Science in Mechanical Engineering program offered at MIT. The courses offered in the department would certainly enable me to deepen my knowledge in Fluid Dynamics, and supplement it with study of complementary subjects such as Heat and Mass Transfer or Thermodynamics. Moreover, the leading research activities taking place in the Dimitris Microfluids Mechanics Laboratory specifically appeal to me, as I would greatly enjoy working on particle-laden flows, instabilities and nonlinear rheology, which match my interest in petroleum applications and my long-term goals. The promising technology involved in Professor M's research on artificial silk has remarkably drawn my attention, and I would be thrilled to be part of that generation of innovative engineers whose work opens up new perspectives of useful applications. Finally, I am attracted by the flexibility of your program, which allows following some classes in other departments as well. I am indeed looking forward to improve my understanding of complex fluids, or interface science, in the Department of Chemical Engineering, these topics being an in-depth complement to the mechanical engineering approach to fluid mechanics.

It is therefore throughout these different aspects that I do believe a Master of Science in Mechanical Engineering at the Massachusetts Institute of Technology is definitely the most appropriate program to fulfill my professional and personal ambitions. I hope that through my motivation, hard work and human skills, I will contribute to the Institute's mission for the advancement of Science and be a helpful, energetic asset to my professors and peers. I would be most honored to be granted the chance to join this ever-challenging and intellectually rich environment.

– 13 –

My first step into science was through ancient Latin and Greek, two subjects I adored in junior high school. Both languages allowed me to develop a logical vision, which would later progress with the study of mathematics; but Greek also showed me a subtle relationship between what is said and what is implied, which I would again find when studying physics and chemistry. This love for language, philosophy and science deepened with the years, but at the age of sixteen, I was encouraged to participate in a chemistry competition beyond my age group. I actually made it to the national level and in two months I learned more chemistry than I would have learned in three years of academic courses, which explains my third prize in the nationals one year later. By that time, I had no desire to abandon chemistry, a passion which guided me in many of my academic choices. As a chemistry student, I am used to seeing several answers to a problem, for there are numerous ways to synthesize a product; yet, my work also consists in making a choice. This is a challenge I enjoy and one of the reasons I would like a career which requires not only scientific feasibility, but also the use of strategy. It is also the reason I am applying to the Technology and Policy Program at MIT.

Having strengthened my theoretical base in mathematics, physics and chemistry during my early undergraduate years I chose to diversify further by adding economics, biology and the humanities. In the class entitled *Corporate Stakeholders: An Introduction*, Professor John G. stated: "Engineers think that when a product is good it will be easy to sell: not true." This comment, and the entire course, spoke right to my desire to be more than a scientist, for I would like to have a multifaceted career which uses scientific competence but also requires knowledge of markets and people.

I have always enjoyed working in a team, for working with other people allows me to develop open-mindedness and communication. During my second year, I worked with five fellow students on a six-month research project. Our subject was on the evolution of proteins in silico which allowed us to combine biology, mathematics, computer science, chemistry and physics in search of a model for evolution. Motivating and organizing friends who are specialists in diverse fields was an experience which required me, as head of the project, to develop diplomatic tactics to keep people on the same track and build a global vision. A second experience, as the captain of the university's rugby team, taught me, again, how hard it is to gather everyone's participation to reach a common goal, and how satisfying it is when your team works together. The four-month process of organizing a trip to Italy for seventy rugby players was one of the most challenging management experiences I have had, and also one of the most enjoyable. I learned to delegate and trust my judgement of people.

This year I am majoring in chemistry and economics. I am especially enjoying the seminar about sustainable development. It has shown me the difficulty of creating development strategies which take into account more than economic benefits. Caring about the environment or respecting human rights are universally accepted as important, but in reality, concrete action is, economically, far from simple. This is the kind of issue I would like to work on during my professional career and this is why I will be doing a four-month research internship next spring with Saipem, Inc where I will be involved in the construction of a 1,600km pipeline in Russia (Sakhalin Islands). This large-scale project will give me the opportunity to face practical problems beyond my theoretical education. Understanding the geopolitical situation and managing workers in difficult conditions are experiences I am eager to acquire.

By nature, I like to concentrate on work which produces concrete results. This leads me towards a career in industry where responsible strategies of technology implementation are important. When I read the strategic program plan, "Leaders who are Engineers," written by Daniel Hastings, I realized that TPP offers exactly the training I am looking for. At the moment I am studying the consequences of the Rio de Janeiro Earth Summit, and I am wary of political incentives, such as the Kyoto protocol, where there is no international institution with the power to ensure its application. I now realize that technology needs the proper laws to be positively effective for society. The political, social and legal aspects of technology are elements I expect to use in my future career, which is why I am attracted to the Technology and Law program led by Dr. Carl A. My personal background mixing chemistry and economics makes me feel more sensitive about subjects which link sustainability, trade and environment, and thus, it would be a great asset for me to do research on any subject of that kind.

As I need to develop my theoretical and practical knowledge of work organization, the course taught by Dr. Bill C.G., *Organizational Processes*, would be perfect. My experience as head of a team deepened my desire to improve my understanding of human relationships. The paradox of human behavior, both unpredictable and rational, fascinates me. This interest for human demeanor especially within the frame of a work environment leads me to want to work with Dr C.B. in his research on large-scale systems change or labor-management relations. I can see myself as a future manager of the optimization of a company supply chain, and would thus need to study human relationships to open the communication lines before proposing any technical solutions.

My skills in technology and my inclination for social sciences are too strongly linked to separate them from each other. I believe that my place is at the crossroads of these two entities. My discussions with Ron De G. (TPP'04) confirmed that although my scientific training has been thorough and diverse and my management experience varied, I still have many gaps which I believe would be filled by MIT's TPP program.

– 14 –

I was first introduced to Financial Mathematics when my father, a professor of Finance at the University of H. (Tokyo) took me to the Louis Bachelier Conference at the College de France back in 2000. I ended up attending several conferences among which one given by Marc Yor on stochastic processes new developments, which opened my eyes to a domain of research which, although not entirely foreign to me, was at that time a promising and exciting field for the budding mathematician that I was then. I was only 17 and about to take my French A-levels (which I subsequently passed with very high honors). It was therefore natural for me to choose the arduous path that would lead to a scientific university; after two years of intensive studies in the preparatory classes, I was admitted to the Ecole XXX in 2006, anxious to explore further those mathematics topics, still unchartered and yet so appealing. Even though I have specialized in math, applied math and computer science, I do have my feet firmly in the ground; the school does provide a fundamentally theoretical training in those different subject matters, yet without the opening onto the real world that I am looking for. Your program therefore offers a splendid opportunity to enhance the theoretical knowledge I have acquired with concrete and applied research and seems the next logical step to further my professional ambition. Hence, my decision to apply to Princeton for the Master of Engineering in the Operation Research and Financial Engineering Department.

Mathematics has always been the backbone of my studies and my concerns. During my second year at the Ecole XXX, I took several courses thereof especially a course in *Applied Mathematics* taught by Pascal P. and a course of *Differential Equations*. It provided me with the basic knowledge on theoretical and numerical solving of partial differential equations needed in financial mathematics. I also attended a course in *Statistics* about testing and estimation. I studied other subject matters – as the school program is built around a core curriculum of scientific subjects – among which an Economics course taught by Pierre P. This year, which is my final year, I am majoring in applied mathematics with a strong specialization in financial mathematics. I am attending Jul L's course on *Stochastic Calculus* and one on time series and random processes analysis. At the moment, I am conducting a research work on the pricing of Asian options with implementation and comparison of Forward Shooting Grid, Hull and White as well as Monte Carlo with variance reduction methods.

This upcoming semester, I will be studying a second major in economics selecting courses akin to financial markets (such as economics and game theory).

I have done experimental work as well. First, I did a research work about Gaussian quadrature rules and orthogonal polynomials, which are very useful in the numerical integration theory. At school, I studied the membrane vibration evolution using finite elements taught in applied mathematics courses. Besides, I led a one-year long term team research project in mechanics centered on the study of the movement of the Pilat dune (Europe's highest sand dune) and in particular the influence of pine trees in avalanche triggering. After preliminary observations in-situ, we conducted simulations with the help of a discrete model and then tested our numerical results in laboratory. As the person in charge, I realized that any model need be tested through the constant comings and goings between theory and practice. In the course of this project, I learnt to deal with different personalities, which is also an important parameter to take into account in the financial industry.

Although gifted with a mathematician's mind, I am fully aware that pragmatism has a role to play in the work of an engineer and scientist. My second internship in Tokyo in August 2004 strengthened this feeling and confirmed my liking for assuming responsibilities. I was employed in the software department and wrote java programs and video contents for the Ricoh firm. Through my work and the contacts that I established with programmers, I was made aware of the need to establish sound coordination and relations based on trust. Time to listen to others is instrumental in the capacity to act as I also realized through my campus activities. I am fully involved in a French and Japanese association whose mission is to set up links between students of top-ranking universities in France and Japan. In September 2007, we played host to a group of Japanese exchange students visiting Paris. I was responsible for fund-raising and logistics. This upcoming summer, I will be doing a four-month internship with an investment bank in London, which will provide me with a first-hand experience of the realities of the financial market. I will be working as an assistant to a trader on commodities pricing and will thus be given the chance to observe how a trader makes use of theoretical models. Such an experience will come in handy to prepare for the master in finance you offer.

Studying at the Operations Research Financial Engineering Department will definitely be a good introduction to the new challenges that financial markets have to face in hedging and pricing derivatives precisely because you are at the leading edge of applied research in those fields. I am highly interested in the *Stochastic Modelling* course because it perfectly fits in with what I am looking for in my studies which is adapting models to take real market behavior into account. I read Ehran Cinlar's book on *Introduction to Stochastic Processes* which helped me to understand the basis in financial mathematics. Above all, your program offers a wide array of subjects that leave the door open to several professional paths. I will have a better grasp of the possibilities on offer when time comes to select a career. Being of French and Japanese descent, my goal is not to remain closeted in one or two countries only. I do envision myself working between Tokyo and New York or London, first in a bank where I could hone my skills as a researcher helping devise original models and, later on, take charge of a project that might be applied across different continents. After a few years building up on my experience and broadening my knowledge in option pricing, I would certainly expect to assume a desk's chief responsibility. However, I do not rule out the possibility of working for a private company.

I believe I have a solid scientific background to apply to your master program. I have done various scientific research and my life experiences could prove valuable in the multicultural environment of Princeton University. The ORFE Department is but the first step toward fulfilling my dream which, given the reputation of your school, is bound to enhance my professional prospect, should I be granted the honor of working with and for you.

– 15 –

How to explain that the price of EUR/USD, when observed at high frequency, does not follow the dynamics of a geometric Brownian motion? That was one of the questions that kept puzzling me – back in the summer 2010 – while interning on *Societe Generale*'s Foreign Exchange Trading Team. My mission was to model liquidity risk and its seasonality with time series models (ARMA and GARCH), in order to develop a new market making system. That initial question led to many others such as what is the "true" dynamics of price in the high frequency framework or how to estimate volatility. Through extensive reading, *viz.* Zhang, Mykland and Aït-Sahalia's seminal work, I went on learning more about this phenomenon – called "microstructure" – moving ever further into uncharted, yet tantalizing territory. While the knowledge I gained first in China, then in the French academic system program did instill many valuable concepts, I am eager to make the transition from applying those concepts, from examples and laws, to finding ways towards the expression of new concepts that are in me to create. Princeton's Ph.D. Program in ORFE is the perfect environment for this transition.

I chose to focus on probability and statistics. Professor Marc H.'s second-year *Statistical Methods* course, in which I was introduced to parametrical estimation and statistical tests, opened up whole new vistas on how statistics can be applied to several industries, especially finance. I took a marked interest in Professor Jean D's *Stochastic Calculus in Finance* course, as I was able to extract succinct ideas from complex calculus. A case in point is the analysis of the proofs of the Black-Scholes formula: Itô's lemma and martingale representation each yields to different ways of proving the formula. The former uses partial differential equations whereas the latter is based on stochastic processes. The Feynman-Kac formula unifies those two points of view, which at first sight are difficult to reconcile.

Carrying out advanced research does not only require knowledge in a specific field, but also a solid scientific culture. The course taught by François A. expanded my knowledge to include mathematical analysis and numerical solutions of PDEs as well as constrained minimization. This class led to a project in which I modelled and simulated fluid flow and its microstructure. In computer science, I carried out a Java-based programming project, whose goal was to design coding and decoding algorithms that reduce the number of errors in data transmission. I adapted the method of branch and bound to this project, which led to building a significantly faster algorithm for code optimization.

Further experiences have whetted my appetite for research. In my second year, I did a year-long team project with five schoolmates under the supervision of professionals from *Societe Generale*. The goal was to build a financial coverage for real estate property. Our approach was to replicate a real estate index and then optimize the composition of the replicating portfolio by simulated annealing and genetic algorithms. As group leader, my tasks included team management, conceiving models and implementing the algorithms. Our work, whose solution produced excellent results in back testing, was praised by *Societe Generale* for its rigor, originality and thoroughness.

Pursuing my initial interest in statistics applied to stochastic processes, I did another research project this year about *High Frequency Correlation, Lead-lag Estimation and Market Impact* supervised by Professor Mathieu R. Asynchronous observation and microstructure noise are two main concerns while computing statistics with high frequency data, rendering traditional estimators of realized volatility and correlation totally obsolete. In this context, I investigated the Epps Effect, microstructure modelling as well as consistent correlation and volatility estimators. Multiple applications in finance were taken into consideration such as estimating the lead-lag parameter or reducing market impact during the liquidation of a portfolio. These applications rest on Hayashi and Yoshida's correlation estimator and are typical of the interactions which help develop the science. Learning from others and then making one's own contribution in return is exactly how I envision research. This Spring, to round out my expertise, I have been selected for a five-month internship with BNP Paribas' High Frequency Trading Team in London, during which I will go on studying microstructure modeling, devise statistical arbitrage strategies and improve market making system.

Princeton's Ph.D. program in ORFE is the best fit to continue investigating problems, for example on microstructure modeling or volatility and covariation estimation. I have read with a keen interest Professors YACINE AÏT-SAHALIA's and JIANQING FAN's research and I would enjoy working under their guidance. I was also excited reading their papers on jump detecting and hope to pursue further in that direction. Doing advanced research in financial econometrics and broadening my understanding of other financial mathematics domains are two of my goals while carrying out doctoral work. After graduation, my ambition is to undertake research in academia and, in turn, pass on the knowledge I have gained – an experience which, incidentally, I drew on as a volunteer teacher for underprivileged children and as an oral examiner in the preparatory program.

I have always nurtured a strong passion for mathematics, as evidenced by the prizes I won in nationwide competitions in China and two silver medals in the International Mathematics Competition for University students. Moving from China to France has demanded resilience and the capacity to adjust to fast-paced environments. The time is now ripe to take the science one step further: not only nourishing myself through the application of Cartesian principles – such as rigorous reasoning – but contributing to advancing knowledge through the bold concepts of self-reliance expounded by Thoreau and Emerson. In other words, moving beyond mere mastery of received knowledge and into the realm of creativity.

– 16 –

In a conference he gave at the *Collège de France* in 2007, Pierre-Louis Lions raised the problem of *Mean Field Games*: this new research topic involves studying the limit of Nash equilibriums for N-player games when N tends to infinity, being modeled by *HJB equations*. The theory has wide applications in the financial markets, such as the formation of volatility. But to be able to fully grasp their impact, such problems require in-depth study at an advanced level which only a doctoral program can assess fully. This is one of the reasons that has led me to apply to Princeton's ORFE program for a Ph.D. in Financial Engineering.

Mathematics has been a long-standing passion. In my high school years, I took part in the National Mathematics Contest and won second prize, which encouraged me to pursue a career in Mathematics. Even though I had been admitted to Fudan University, I seized the opportunity to go to France through a French-Chinese program under the aegis of the ministries for Higher Education. Thus, I enrolled in the rigorous *preparatory program* in which students are trained at the advanced level in math and physics. I was admitted to the Ecole XXX, one of the top universities for sciences.

In the first two years, several courses laid the solid foundations in pure and applied mathematics. In the *Dynamical Systems* course, I studied the theories of ordinary differential equations, such as the Ergodic Theory. *Distribution Theory* provided me with tools to study partial differential equations. *Markov Chains* led me to discover how to construct stochastic algorithms for solving deterministic issues. Problems such as Google's PageRank are direct applications of this course.

Parallel to my coursework at Ecole XXX, I enrolled in a program at Paris VI University (UMPC) to expand my knowledge and was awarded a Bachelor's degree in Applied Mathematics in June 2011. The *Numerical Analysis* course was challenging as I discovered diverse methods for numerical implementation. *Convex Optimization* offered a unique chance to solve real problems by linear programming.

This year, I'm following the Master's program with a double concentration: *Stochastic Calculus and Financial Mathematics* (taught by Marc D.) and *Introduction to Non-Parametric Estimation and Statistical Learning.* In the former course, I focus on the Black-Scholes theory from the martingale approach, reading some works by K. Ito and R. C Merton and thus getting insights into how the domain has developed. In the latter course, I have delved into the nonparametric estimation problems such as optimality of estimators and adaptive methods. In addition, I have also read papers relevant to topics, such as high-dimensional statistics.

Research has been past and parcel of my curriculum. Three projects stand out. Last year, I worked on a team research project on fundamental mathematics. The subject was about how to find roots of a polynomial in the complex plane, which had been studied by Professor McMullen in the 80's. After some bibliographical work on holomorphic dynamics, it was made clear that there was no generally convergent algorithm to find roots of a polynomial of degree more than 4 in the complex plane. Taking the problem from theory to practice, we implemented several algorithms by applying Newton's method to resolution. Another research project was about how to simulate airflow in man's lung. After analyzing the function of different parts of man's lung, I simulated the respiratory system by a coupled system of Stokes and Navier-Stokes equations. I suggested an improved method of simulation which had a more precise accordance to experiments. This year, I have worked on lookback options under the supervision of Professor Timothy F., I studied lookback options in general models in which we cannot calculate the price explicitly. I resorted to numerical methods to obtain an approximate solution to the associated stochastic partial differential equation. Then, I focused on recent research on a stochastic control approach to no-arbitrage bounds given marginals. Instead of adopting the Skorohod-Embedding-Problem approach, we came up with a dual formulation which converts the super-hedging problem into a continuous martingale optimal transportation problem. I have implemented several programs to solve numerically the optimization problem.

The ORFE program attracts me for several reasons linked to the state-of-the-art research in financial mathematics and statistics. I have been intrigued by the topic of stochastic games. Following Professor Ronnie Sircar's *Exploration and Exhaustibility in Dynamic Cournot Games*, which analyses the stochastic effect of resource exploration in *Cournot models*, I grew convinced that such problems are crucial in finance and worth exploring as well. *Stochastic control* is another choice subject. Back to China in 2008, I attended a conference given by Professor Shige P. on FBSDE and its applications to optimal stopping problems. Such a matter, studied by Professor René Carmona, could be a possible domain of research to me. I am also interested in pricing and hedging in incomplete markets. In complete markets, this problem is solved with respect to the unique equivalent martingale measure. However, a contingent claim entails risks which cannot be hedged completely. Therefore, strategies should be devised to reduce risks to the minimum. In *Convex Hedging in Incomplete Markets*, Professor Birgit R. addresses risk preference problems with respect to risk measures, initiated by Follmer and Leukert. And Professor Patrick C. gave specific examples of such risk measures in *Risk Measures on Orlicz Hearts*. These are examples of problems that I am keen on investigating.

Upon completion of the PhD program my ambition is to go into research and a teaching career. I believe the ORFE program can help achieve my goals. I have developed strong reasoning skills as well as problem-solving abilities. In addition, I have made the most of the tools gained in my studies to investigate problems of my own. I expect the ORFE program to provide further opportunities to work at the cutting edge and bridge the gap towards achieving my professional goals.

– 17 –

The marked influence financial institutions exercise on our economy was made self-evident during an internship carried out with Morgan Stanley last year. Even on industrial markets such as Energy and Commodities, financial intermediaries are prevailing. On the one hand, they bring financial innovation, for instance by extracting additional value from power plants through the monetizing a "hidden optionality". On the other hand, I observed numerous situations where their increased bent for risk was jeopardizing the stability of those markets, preventing the latter to give the relevant price signals. I reached the conclusion that only a credible and balanced regulation could enable those still young markets to work efficiently. I have resolved to explore further the question of optimal regulation in financial markets, with a view to determining how it can contribute to value creation and social welfare. Given the complexity of the issues, the doctoral program in economics of Harvard University is the best step in that direction.

I believe my academic background has provided the appropriate training for a Ph.D. After two years in the preparatory program during which I focused on mathematics and physics, I chose to enter the Ecole XXX in order to follow its broad-ranging science curriculum and make the sensible choice of a career. My subsequent decision to major in applied mathematics and economics allowed me to construct a solid foundation in mathematical theories useful to an economist. This included statistics, econometrics, and stochastic models. It helped me to acquire a solid grasp of the theoretical issues raised through my economics coursework, including Microeconomics and Macroeconomics, economics of uncertainty and international economics. Upon graduation in 2006, ranking 2nd out of 400 students, I was admitted to the *Corps des Mines*, a government program which trains France's top civil servants for industry and research, and which consists of two years of work experience followed by one year of academic courses with a focus on economic policy.

One professional experience has shaped my outlook more than the others. For my first *Corps des Mines* internship, I chose to join the PSA-Citroën car making factory located in Aulnay, a rough suburb of Paris. As deputy line manager, I learned the art of compromise, building upon skills developed as student representative for the board of regents, namely a keen sense of responsibility and public interest. A tough six-week strike proved a valuable introduction to the reality of the world of work and industrial relations. Both parties were so adamantly entrenched in positions they considered legitimate that dialogue often bordered on the impossible. I realized at what point sociopolitical issues can easily fuel the flames of ideological conflict, and I am deeply convinced that economics plays a key role in society by bringing in the objectivity of scientific research.

Research experiences have complemented my academic studies, and showed me that first-hand research is the critical part of economics. The most defining experience, an internship with the IMF, was concerned with the design of public expenditure management systems in developing countries, with a view to deterring corruption. I realized then what powerful and relevant tools contract theory and game theory are in order to tackle issues in economic policy. Previously, I had carried out various lab work and team-based research projects. Lab work in physics helped me develop intellectual rigor, teaching me to observe before modeling, and finally to test experimentally – lessons which are applicable in economics.

My research ambition is to participate in the reflection upon the regulation of the financial system, starting from a microeconomic approach. Given the key role played by information, a necessary step consists in thoroughly parsing the contracts that link the actors of the financial markets, in order to analyze the various situations of moral hazard and determine what the true incentives of each actor are. Studying under the guidance of such pioneers of contract theory as Dr. Philippe A. and Dr. Oliver H. would be a unique chance to work towards the understanding of apparently irrational dynamics, the very ones that threaten the stability of the system. In *Why Are There So Many Banking Crises?*, Prof. Xavier F. and Prof. Jean-Charles R. demonstrate that capital markets cannot be complete, and that market discipline only works with a credible regulator. I would be keen on studying with Dr. Arthur S. how these findings can be translated to other markets where financial intermediaries prevail. In addition to the question of optimal regulation, I would be eager to study the contribution of financial markets to social welfare. To what extent, for example, do recent financial crises cast new light on the work carried out by Dr. Jeremy G. and Dr. Boyan J. in *Financial Development, Growth and the Distribution of Income?* The interchange between disciplines encouraged in Harvard's Department of Economics would be an exceptional opportunity to broaden my perspectives from different angles.

After completing a Ph.D., I intend to pursue a career as an economist, either in academia or in a public institution. The best way to stay at the forefront of research is to teach, for which I have a special liking as I discovered while TAeing in the undergraduate program. Serving as an economic advisor for the political sphere is an interest too, as I believe that decisions of economic policy can hardly be taken without an academic expertise. The Harvard faculty is a case in point, advising policy-makers across the borders. I am also interested in working for an independent agency such as the Energy Regulation Commission or the Financial Markets Authority, where the know-how acquired on complex regulatory issues could bring in significant value added.

If given the opportunity and honor to be admitted, I would look forward to bringing to Harvard my strong reasoning skills, my intellectual rigor, in addition to my boundless curiosity and my team-oriented temperament. I would do my utmost to contribute to the excellence of the program.

– 18 –

Fostering innovation and technologies in order "*to move toward more sustainable patterns of consumption and production*" as mandated by the UN Goal 9 in "The 2030 Agenda for Sustainable Development", adopted by the United Nations, might remain a pipe dream for many companies, especially SMEs which sometimes face insuperable barriers when faced with the necessity to innovate. Currently in my third year at XXX, where I rank in the top 8% of the cohort, I am building my technical skills and business knowledge to take on the sustainable development challenges of technological innovation as prescribed by UNO through science and entrepreneurship coursework. In the long run, my ambition is to hold managerial positions in companies offering creative solutions in order to comply with the UN 2030 agenda. Eager to fill the gaps in my formation and benefit from a more practical education, I am applying to Stanford for the Management Science and Engineering Master's program.

Science has been a lodestar throughout my academic pursuits. After laying a solid knowledge base in the preparatory program, I strengthened my training in mathematics, physics and computer science at XXX by taking stimulating and multidisciplinary classes. However, one subject particularly piqued my interest: mechanics. My second year was an opportunity to explore this discipline in-depth through various courses, including *Continuum Mechanics*. This course, which offered a first-hand approach to the study of materials in three dimensions, was complemented in my third year with the *Material Behavior* course. I combined my taste for mechanics with my interest for the environment, through the *Atmosphere and Ocean Dynamics* course with **Jean D**. This course focused on the major meteorological dynamics as well as the impact of global warming on weather patterns. In parallel, *Business Economics* shed light on strategy and economics, two pillars on which science and technology are to rest to have maximum impact. Willing to combine mechanics and business, I am currently specializing in a master's program in *Technological Innovation* that is a mix between business and mechanical engineering courses.

Conducting research-based work has been a litmus test of my theoretical knowledge. In my second year, I did a research project in mechanics supervised by **Céline D**. The goal was to improve the sports performance of the French archery team in view of the 2024 Olympic Games. Accuracy during this high-level event is a key factor of success, therefore we dedicated ourselves to studying the boundary layer around the arrow. We made several studies at different Reynolds numbers: in a hydraulic channel with an arrow printed with a 3D printer, in a wind tunnel and in live shooting.

Willing to get familiarized with the business world, I took up a position on the HSBC France M&A team, under the supervision of **Maria T.**, drafting pitches for prospects and following through with the delivery of a sell-side deal. It was an opportunity to acquire technical skills in accounting as well as some financial culture. This internship firmed up my bent for business and strategy in addition to my fondness for science.

Being part of the Junior-Enterprise revealed and bolstered my taste for the strategy of organizations. I implemented the communication strategy, using social networks to communicate to companies, organizing events raising funds, while keeping the school staff abreast of our actions through supporting documentation. This effective strategy was rewarded with the "Best communication strategy" prize awarded by the National Confederation of Junior-Enterprises. As project manager, I oversaw groups of students during missions and followed up on their relations with clients. The association meant a strong time commitment in order to allow students to discover the business world's best practices and to apply their academic knowledge in the best way possible.

The M.S. in Management Science and Engineering offers courses that fit in with my current interests and academic expectations, both from a quantitative and qualitative viewpoint. The concentration *Technology and Engineering Management* is a perfect match for my interest in innovation in the technical sector. Kathleen E.'s paper *Superior strategy in entrepreneurial settings: thinking, doing and the logic of opportunities* raised my awareness of the environment in which executives establish superior strategies by developing simple rules and improvising in real time. I would like to learn more through *Strategy in Technology-based Companies* taught by Prof E, which would be a one-off opportunity to deepen my third-year course *Introduction to Strategy and Marketing,* taught by **Philippe G.**, applied to technology through case studies. I also wish to follow *Fundamentals of Data Science* by Ramesh M. to familiarize myself with data analysis, a key tool in companies' decision-making process. His work on the influence of a course planning tool on student behavior highlights the many applications of data analysis and the surprising results it can lead to. Eager to expand my knowledge of legal issues, I would also be interested in discovering how it applies in the context of start-ups through *Patent Law and Strategy for Innovators and Entrepreneurs* with Julia L. Finally, *Stochastic Modelling* lectured by Marcus F. would be an opportunity to keep exploring statistics and probabilities and learn how to frame time-dependent random problems.

Experience outside the curriculum has shaped my character and steeled my resolve. I chose to do my leadership training in the *Gendarmerie Nationale.* I did field work and carried out awareness campaigns in middle and high schools to message about harassment, and the dangers of online bullying. This experience was also an opportunity to hold my own as a young female officer cadet in a field largely dominated by men. My fresh perspective on different situations, my innovative ideas and my relentless curiosity earned the respect of the non-commissioned officers.

The Stanford program, along with my professional experience, would be a perfect enabler to contribute in a meaningful way as an engineer. Isabelle KOCHER, former CEO of ENGIE, has been an inspirational figure, working in an energy market in transition, revamping the company strategy and focusing on low-carbon energy production. By accelerating the electrification of Africa, she positioned ENGIE as a leader on the continent in order to meet the Goal 7 of "The 2030 Agenda for Sustainable Development": universal electrification. My ambition is to take a leaf out of her book, and Stanford in this regard will be a key step forward in concretizing my career goals.

II. PHS Samples

– 1 –

The *École Polytechnique* has provided me with life enhancing experiences beyond the academic realm which have turned me into a mature and sensible person. Thus, I developed leadership skills during the eight months I spent in the French Commando forces for the first year. I was assigned a platoon of thirty young recruits whom I had to train and drill, while at the same time I taught them the fundamentals of mathematics and physics. Some of them came from broken homes or disadvantaged backgrounds, had barely gone to school and therefore had a poor command of the French language, which made it difficult to understand them and be understood by them. I took upon myself to start language remedial classes during which we worked not only on communication skills and expression but also on the notions that have contributed to reinforcing the fabric of society, such as solidarity, compassion, courtesy, self-respect and respect for others. I must say that I drew considerable pleasure and satisfaction to see my young recruits turn into men capable of abiding by the rules of society. The Army gave them a second chance and I was proud to see that they made the most of it. For me, it was personal achievement which was praised by my hierarchy.

Working in multicultural environments is something that I had been familiar with, given the numerous stays I have made outside France. For example, I spent three years in Athens, five years in Milan, and two years in Tunisia due to my parents' professional pursuits. Those experiences have led me to be more broad-minded, receptive to the habits and cultures of others and in a way, it has been a sound preparation for the global world in which I am destined to work in my professional life.

For personal and family reasons (I have an autistic kid brother), I have been involved in volunteer associations, helping handicapped children. I have seen how difficult but also how essential it is for disabled people to be integrated into society and have them share activities with the others. Looking after my brother has taught me to be acutely aware of other people's needs, to be humble in my own achievements and, above all, that selflessness and solidarity are perhaps the only ways and means to make a world better for all those who aren't as privileged or gifted as I have been.

I believe I have a good sense of organization. It is something I became more familiar with, when I set up, planned and managed 4-day week end so as to develop the spirit of community among the French and international students of the new class last year. I also volunteer for a local association tutoring disadvantaged kids from troubled districts who want to get ahead in life but lack the proper family environment to study.

My taste for team work and collective effort probably finds its roots in the many sports I have practiced. Having played rugby for eight years, I am particularly aware of the importance of each member in a team. This sport carries values I share and have developed during other experiences, for example when I volunteered as a maintenance worker in Redwood National Park last summer, taking care of the hikers' trails, making sure that the environment be properly respected by each for the benefit of all. It was hard work, but all the more rewarding as I also discovered that it cuts across cultural and linguistic barriers. United in a common goal and serving a same purpose, we in the team worked all the better. It was for me an unforgettable and enriching moment in holidays during which I felt useful.

I see my studies as a way of sharing the same values that have inspired in my personal life. Aware that doing graduate work is a once in a lifetime opportunity, I am determined to make the most of it, not only on the academic and intellectual level but also the personal and human one. In a world that is becoming ever more technology-oriented I want to make sure that man should not be the slave of techniques that he can't control but the enlightened master of a destiny he will help to build for the better. UC Berkeley, with its open-mindedness and its cross-cultural campus, holds a special attraction to me. It is bound to be a new step forward in my training that will contribute not only to complete my education but also and especially turn me into an all-round scientist, fully aware of today's and tomorrow's challenges.

– 2 –

All of my life I have had the chance to have supporting parents that encouraged me to pursue in the fields I am strongly interested in. That is why I went through three years of preparatory program that helped me understand thoroughly the foundations of mathematics, physics and computer science. I am fully aware of the chance I have to be surrounded by relatives helping me to get through obstacles, supporting me and giving me incentives to perform in a privileged context. In return, after those three hard-working years, I felt I had to contribute to the happiness of others.

As a student at *Polytechnique*, I carried out a seven-month leadership training within the Paris Fire Brigade where I served on a first aid and emergency vehicle as chief of the rescue team. For several months, as cadet officer, I rotated between night and day shifts, on various missions (car crashes, domestic accidents and suicide as well as cardiac arrests cases). It was physically and psychologically intense, and required self-control and a cool head when delivering the right orders to be efficient and quick when lives were at stake. I was also in charge of training the new firefighters teaching them first aid but also Mathematics to help them move up through the ranks. They taught me as well, by the experience I had with them, how to take meaningful decisions, to communicate with the team, to listen to their advice, which finally improved the efficiency of the team during rescue interventions.

I chose to serve in that unit to leave my comfort zone, to be confronted to another side of life and help people in need, especially the homeless, elderly and isolated people but also clueless teenagers threatening to take their own lives. All in all, it was one of the best experiences that taught me much about myself while helping others.

Parallel to my stint with the firefighters, I also volunteered to teach high school students outside my duty hours, and in a way pass on the knowledge that I had been given, as well as the skills I had acquired while preparing the entrance exams. The example of my mother teaching me math was certainly inspirational in my desire to do the same for others.

Back on campus and seeking responsibilities and a way to contribute to the student community, I decided to be the representative of the 30-odd sports team I practiced and played with and more generally shared communal activities with. At the crossroads between the students and the school management I was confronted to all sorts of issues, psychological, physical, emotional, involving students with sometimes delicate personal situations. I would always leave my door open and they knew that they could count on me for support and to help them navigate through their difficulties. If I did not always provide the solutions myself – I would often turn to the military hierarchy or the school health center – yet it was a learning experience that taught me that a listening ear, empathy, compassion and selflessness are universal virtues, be it in your profession or in life. On the bright side, my goal was also to gather those students together, by organizing dinners, trips, events that reinforced the team's cohesion and spirit of solidarity.

I was also the treasurer of the school's Basketball association (I have been playing basketball for over ten years and I picked up the sport at university). In charge of managing a 4k€ budget, I allocated the funds to organize basketball events. Maintaining a balance between activities that usually gathered 500 students was sometimes a difficult but always a telling example in prioritizing your duties to the group.

I also decided to get involved in an association with a deeper impact on campus life: X-Entreprises which organizes the annual career fair that musters more than 200 hundred companies in IT, consulting, banking, insurance, and high-tech. The 600k€ turnover is hereafter distributed to all the campus associations. I was the manager of the consulting sector representing three members and, whose purpose was to persuade over 30 consulting companies to participate in this event and guide them through the registration process. I gained a lot from that experience by taking a first step into the professional world, communicating with human resources offices, leading a team to reach a target.

However straight my academic and family life may have been, I have never chosen to watch it idly going by. Far from it. Life has been a treasure trove of opportunities that have inspired me to always strive and become a better person. In that regard, dedicating part of my time to others has been the most enriching aspect, shaping my personality that aspires to inspire and looks forward to lending a helping hand, thus making the community stronger.

– 3 –

My personality and worldviews might be better explained in the light of a foot handicap I was born with. I was afflicted with shorter Achilles tendons, which has had a direct impact on the way I stand, walk and run. Even though I was operated on countless times, I still stand up on the outside part on my feet only, which results in a singular gait and, quite often, sends painful shock reaction whenever I move my legs.

Though not always inconvenient on a daily basis (I try to swat away the thought), this disability has been a physical challenge when I want to run, as I cannot go as fast as I would like to, which has significantly hampered my sport performances. This is an obstacle I had to overcome when I entered my university, which has a sports admission test. Despite this handicap, and being a persistent person, I have always striven to play sports: I played tennis as a child, picked up basketball in my middle and high school years, and rugby when I entered Polytechnique, where I am competing in the intercollegiate championships, and working hard to overcome this disability by compensating in developing physical and technical qualities.

This challenge has nourished me with a strong sense of empathy towards physically challenged people. I know what it feels like to be singled out for a disability. My commitment to the national pilgrimage in Lourdes as a stretcher-bearer served this purpose: furthermore, this experience helped me take a relative long view on my feet problem, especially when I helped seriously disabled people. It therefore strengthened my will to face and accept life as it is, be a doer, and not a whiner.

My school operates under the aegis of the Ministry of Defense (it used to train the future officers and engineers of the French Armed Forces). My first year included one month of military training followed by a six-month formation and internship in a specific branch of the French army. In the army, the common good of the team is larger than an individual's suffering, and I learnt to never feel sorry for myself. Even though I wanted to join the ground forces for those six months, since I had enjoyed the first month of training a lot, I was denied permission to do so, since I could not put up with standing in the same position for too long. I therefore elicited to join the French Police Forces instead, and turned an initial frustration into an enriching experience. I also seized on the opportunity to serve my country by helping the Paris firefighters in developing fire control techniques, as part of my internship in the Fire Department of the Paris Police Headquarters Central Laboratory.

Indeed, I love my country and its traditions, and besides my military status, I promote French culture thanks to my engagement in the oenology club. My passion for wine has been transmitted through my family that comes from Burgundy. My forebears settled in the region in the 17th century and started their wine business. I regularly return to St Martin sous Montegu, a little wine village, and enjoy the unique sight of the rolling vineyard hills and the long conversations during which, today, my grandparents reminisce about the wine harvesting times of yore. Their story is their legacy. It is my duty to preserve and transmit it in turn. Because wine is one of France's riches, I have sought to share its secrets by joining the oenology association, hosting blind tasting events and dinner parties, where we match food and wine, and to which we invite students, including international students, a way of introducing them to France's culture from the inside.

I have also served the student community by involving myself in the logistics team of the organization of the PIMUN 2016, a yearly event hosted in Paris where students from all over the world are invited to debate in debates similar to those taking place in the United Nations. My next project is the organization of the 2014 class' Farewell weekend, which will happen shortly before students leave the campus. It is for us the last opportunity to spend some time together, reminisce, and look towards a bright future. More personally, it will be the crowning achievement of my investment for the student body.

I look forward to sharing my love of French culture with American and international students in California, and contribute my sense of service to both Berkeley's student life and serious projects next year.

– 4 –

I have long been intrigued by the concept of 'difficulties faced by women in science'. It is true that my choice of the École Polytechnique and then Electrical Engineering and Computer Science put me in a gender minority. With most of my friends being men, I sometimes feel like a citizen from 'Girl-land' with a permanent resident status in 'Boy-land', used to speaking the local language and following the local traditions, fitting in naturally without my difference being an issue. In my future career field, I intend to make sure, as usual, that I stand out for my character and my competence, not my gender.

During my first-year leadership training for the Ecole, I worked for seven months as a science consultant and personal assistant for several teachers in Paris' disadvantaged northern suburbs. Whether it was planning class sessions, leading science information meetings for teachers or searching for teaching materials to start a district Science Knowledge Center, I threw all my energy into creating a positive vision of hands-on science among students and teachers alike, starting cooperative projects like the Biology Garden or the Hot Air Balloon. I loved seeing my ideas come to life through hard work, obstinacy, persuasion and cooperation. Back in school, wanting to renew this rewarding experience, I joined the student association BEST (Board of European Students of Technology) and was vice-president for the organization of a ten-day scientific symposium for students from 16 different countries. Overcoming fundraising difficulties, administrative negotiations and accommodation trouble, our team put together an amazing program that I am proud of and not likely to forget. Through the process, my perseverance and enthusiasm survived, and I learned how to carry on with a project until its goal is reached.

Having lived seven months in California at a very young age, I grew up in France, learning to read and speaking to friends indifferently in French or English at the International School in Grenoble. In high school I devoured literature, from Virginia Woolf and Arthur Miller to Victor Hugo and Louis-Ferdinand Céline. Living naturally between the two cultures, I didn't realize how lucky I was until it ended. I decided to follow my elder brother into the local French school for 10th grade. As the school year moved on, I started to develop a strange feeling that all the students were too normal, all coming from the same neighborhood and speaking the same language. Only then, restricted to a single culture, did I understand the scope of my enjoyment of different people and languages. The following year I gladly chose to return to my old school, where I cultivated international friendships with full awareness.

My most intense international experience remains my two-month internship in a Costa Rican coffee cooperative, living, eating, working and celebrating memorable birthdays with local shopkeepers and farmers. It took me a several days to understand the local dialect, but the people in town were welcoming and curious, and we spent long hours comparing and enjoying cultural differences. These moments remain in my mind as unforgettable, and have encouraged me to look for my graduate program in a new country, where I will be able to live not days or months, but several years, to become comfortable with the culture myself.

As I am preparing to leave the country I was born in, I understand clearly how much I owe to my upbringing. The influence of my engineering parents and my early start with English were given to me. However, it has been my choice to become fluent in three languages and enter the best engineering schools available. Today, I believe that the greatest limitations one can experience are self-limitations. My decision for Berkeley follows naturally in my traditions of choosing the highest quality education possible and enjoying every international environment I can find.

Dans la même collection

Centre Poly-media

Achevé d'imprimer en octobre 2022 sur les presses
du Centre Poly-Média de l'École polytechnique.
Dépôt légal : 4e trimestre 2022
ISBN 2-7302-1698-2 • ISSN 2104-9963 • *Imprimé en France*